# THE OFFICIAL PRICE GUIDE TO POCKET KNIVES

BY
JAMES F. PARKER
AND
J. BRUCE VOYLES

EDITOR
THOMAS E. HUDGEONS III

FIRST EDITION
THE HOUSE OF COLLECTIBLES, INC., ORLANDO, FLORIDA 32809

**IMPORTANT NOTICE.** The format of **THE OFFICIAL PRICE GUIDE SERIES**, published by **THE HOUSE OF COLLECTIBLES, INC.**, is based on the following proprietary features: **ALL FACTS AND PRICES ARE COMPILED THRU A COMPUTERIZED PROCESS** which relies on a nationwide sampling of information obtained from noteworthy collectibles experts, auction houses and specialized dealers. **DETAILED "INDEXED" FORMAT** enables quick retrival of information for positive identification. **ENCAPSULATED HISTORIES** preceed each category to acquaint the collector with the specific traits that are peculiar to that area of collecting. **VALUABLE COLLECTING INFORMATION** is provided for both the novice as well as the seasoned collector: How to begin a collection; How to buy, sell, and trade; Care and storage techniques; Tips on restoration; Grading guidelines; Lists of periodicals, clubs, museums, auction houses, dealers, etc. **AN AVERAGE PRICE RANGE** takes geographic location and condition into consideration when reporting collector value. **A SPECIAL 3rd PRICE COLUMN** enables the collector to compare the current market values with the last's years average selling price . . . indicating which items have increased in value. **INVENTORY CHECKLISTS SYSTEM** is provided for cataloging a collection. **EACH TITLE IS ANNUALLY UP-DATED** to provide the most accurate information available in the rapidly changing collectors marketplace.

All of the information, including valuations, in this book has been compiled from the most reliable sources, and every effort has been made to eliminate errors and questionable data. Nevertheless the possibility of error, in a work of such immense scope, always exists. The publisher will not be held responsible for losses which may occur, in the purchase, sale, or other transaction of items, because of information contained herein. Readers who feel they have discovered errors are invited to WRITE and inform us, so they may be corrected in subsequent editions. Those seeking further information on the topics covered in this book, are advised to refer to the complete line of Official Price Guides published by The House of Collectibles.

© MCMLXXXIII The House of Collectibles, Inc.

All rights reserved. No part of this book may be reproduced or utilized in any form or by any means, electronic or mechanical, including photocopying, recording, or by any information storage and retrieval system, without permission in writing from the publisher.

Published by: The House of Collectibles, Inc.
Orlando Central Park
1900 Premier Row
Orlando, FL 32809
Phone: (305) 857-9095

Printed in the United States of America

Library of Congress Catalog Card Number: 82-84635

ISBN: 0-87637-372-4

# TABLE OF CONTENTS

| | |
|---|---|
| Introduction | 1 |
| History of Pocket Knives | 2 |
| Blade Patterns | 5 |
| Pocket Knife Styles | 6 |
| Knife Nomenclature | 8 |
| Grading The Condition | 8 |
| Counterfeit Pocket Knives | 12 |
| Handmade Pocket Knives | 14 |
| How To Buy And Sell Pocket Knives | 15 |
| How To Store, Clean And Repair | 23 |
| Knife Organizations | 29 |
| How To Use This Book | 31 |
| Sharpening Guide | 32 |
| **Case** | 33 |
|     Older Case | 42 |
|     Case Tested | 58 |
|     Case XX's | 82 |
|     Case XX U.S.A. | 98 |
|     Case XX U.S.A. (10 Dot) | 105 |
|     Case XX U.S.A. (9 Dot) | 110 |
|     Case XX U.S.A. (8 Dot) | 114 |
|     Case XX U.S.A. (7 Dot) | 117 |
|     Case XX U.S.A. (6 Dot) | 121 |
|     Case XX U.S.A. (5 Dot) | 125 |
|     Case XX U.S.A. (4 Dot) | 128 |
|     Case XX U.S.A. (3 Dot) | 131 |
|     Case XX U.S.A. (2 Dot) | 134 |
|     Case XX U.S.A. (10 & 9 Dot) Lightning "S" | 137 |
|     Case XX U.S.A. (8 Dot) Lightning "S" | 140 |
| Ka-Bar | 143 |
| Keen Kutter | 168 |
| Parker | 171 |
| Remington | 203 |
| Schrade | 218 |
| Shapleigh | 221 |
| Winchester | 224 |

## BECOME AN "OFFICIAL" CONTRIBUTOR TO THE WORLD'S LEADING PRICE GUIDES

Are you an experienced collector with access to information not covered in this guide? Do you possess knowledge, data, or ideas that should be included?

If so, The House of Collectibles invites you to **GET INVOLVED**.

The House of Collectibles continuously seeks to improve, expand, and update the material in the **OFFICIAL PRICE GUIDE SERIES**. The assistance and cooperation of numerous collectors, auction houses and dealers has added immeasurably to the success of the books in this series. If you think you qualify as a contributor, our editors would like to offer your expertise to the readers of the **OFFICIAL PRICE GUIDE SERIES.**

As the publishers of the most popular and authoritative Price Guides, The House of Collectibles can provide a far-reaching audience for your collecting accomplishments. *Help the hobby grow* by letting others benefit from the knowledge that you have discovered while building your collection.

If your contribution appears in the next edition, you'll become an **"OFFICIAL"** member of the world's largest hobby-publishing team. Your name will appear on the acknowledgement page, *plus you will receive a free complimentary copy.* Send a full outline of the type of material you wish to contribute. Please include your phone number. Write to: **THE HOUSE OF COLLECTIBLES, INC.,** Editorial Department, 1900 Premier Row, Orlando, Florida, 32809.

# INTRODUCTION

Pocket knife collecting, at one time a relatively small hobby confined mostly to the southern and southwestern U.S., is now "big league" in every sense of the word. Knife shows, held in all parts of the country, draw larger and larger attendance. More dealers are selling pocket knives than ever before, and far more hobbyists are buying them. Prices have been rising faster than on many other types of collector's items, because of the increased competition and the very real scarcity of many specimens. For the investor, the person seeking a hobby that's truly different and exciting, the swapper, the lover of fine craftsmanship and artistry — the pocket knife hobby is hard to beat.

For more than half a decade, the "Bible" of pocket knife collecting has been — and continues to be — *THE OFFICIAL PRICE GUIDE TO COLLECTOR KNIVES,* by James F. Parker and J. Bruce Voyles, published by The House of Collectibles ($9.95, available at better bookshops or directly from the publishers, 1900 Premier Row, Orlando, Fla. 32809 — add $1.50 for shipping and handling). This pocket version of the OFFICIAL GUIDE fills a need long felt in the hobby, and has been planned both to serve those who DO and DO NOT own the full-size edition.

Readers of *THE OFFICIAL PRICE GUIDE TO COLLECTOR KNIVES* anxiously await the publication of each new annual edition, for the latest pricing information. Naturally, values are constantly changing, as in any active hobby. If a knife rises from $75 to $125 from one edition to the next, this leap did not occur overnight but was a gradual process spread over (usually) the whole year. As the pocket version of the OFFICIAL GUIDE will be issued approximately six months BEFORE the next edition of our full-size guide, it will provide a *pricing update* on many of the knives. It will show the collector exactly what is happening in the market RIGHT NOW, without having to wait an entire year for fresh information.

But this is far from the only purpose of the pocket version. At a popular price of $2.50, it will introduce many beginners and would-be collectors to the fascinating world of pocket knives: those who might be wondering, "Are pocket knives the hobby for me?" It will provide a basic working knowledge of the hobby,

## 2 / HISTORY OF POCKET KNIVES

fully as authoritative as the standard OFFICIAL GUIDE at $9.95. Further, this reduced version is SPECIALLY DESIGNED as a take-along book — a handy, easy-to-pocket volume that will be ready for instant reference at any knife show, antiques shop, swap meet, or anywhere that you might have the opportunity to buy or trade for a collector knife.

Thus it can be used in conjunction with the standard-size OFFICIAL GUIDE, or by itself.

To readers just discovering the hobby of pocket knife collecting, we extend a cordial welcome. We think you'll enjoy yourself — and you might even make some cash profit along the way!

# HISTORY OF POCKET KNIVES

Knives themselves are of course of ancient origins, and have been made of various materials down through the years. Forerunners of knives were known in all prehistoric cultures, since a cutting tool was essential for survival. Before man had the knowledge or equipment to forge metal, his knives were crafted from whatever materials Mother Nature placed at hand. Stone knives were created by laborious smoothing down the sides of one stone with another. Flint knives, much more efficient, could be made more quickly by shipping small pieces until a sharp cutting edge was formed. Primitive peoples also made knives from many different kinds of wood, by sanding the wood into sharp edges with a rough stone.

The earliest metal knives, also of prehistoric origin, were made of bronze in what anthropologists refer to as the Bronze Age. Since then, knife making has been continuous for thousands of years and has spread all over the globe.

Of course there have been many advances and improvements. Since the European "middle ages" (c. 476-1500 A.D.), knife blades have mostly been made of steel, since the metals used in earlier knives — bronze, copper, brass, iron — soon corroded. Along with improvements in materials came the desire for better styling, more decoration, lighter weight, finer balance, and other features. Knife making became a flourishing trade, and many types were produced to meet the needs of rich, poor, and middle income customers.

The POCKET KNIFE had its ancestors among the sheath and scabbard knives of early times — transportable knives that could be carried on the person. Most knives were not carried as weapons in the days of (say) Henry VIII's England, but as handy utensils. Hosts did not place knives on the dinner table, so if you didn't have one of your own, you picked up the meat and gnawed at it. There was a real and pressing need for knives that could be carried around with a minimum of fuss. Changing fashions in dress also played a role, in setting the stage for the coming of pocket knives. No, it was NOT the development of pants pockets, but rather the style for wearing long swords, which came into vogue in the 1600's. It was not too practical to use a 3-foot sword to carve one's roast beef, so TWO knives had to be carried instead of one. Then, more than ever, size and handiness became a factor, as the second knife was to be used strictly at the table or for other domestic purposes.

It is not known precisely when the first folding knife was made. Long standing tradition states that its manufacturer was one Jacques De Liege (Jack of Liege, a city in Belgium), and the time was somewhere in the 17th century. This was supposedly how the "jack" knife got its name.

Folding knives proved popular, and to a large extent their popularity was boosted by one special type of folding knife — the pen knife. Writing was done in olden times with quill pens, made from goose quills and carved into a nib at the tip. The nibs frequently clogged with ink or became mushy, so it was necessary to pare them quite often — unless one was wealthy enough to just discard the pen and start a new one. Pen knives made especially for the purpose had their debut in the late 1600's. They were first made at Sheffield, England, the British headquarters of fine cutlery. Small size was a selling point for penknives, as the task of pen paring did not require a long blade. In fact it could be accomplished with a blade only an inch long, but the handle needed to be longer for secure gripping. Many of the early penknives were decoratively finished and are museum pieces. By the mid 1700's, penknives and jack knives were being

## 4 / HISTORY OF POCKET KNIVES

sold all over the European continent, and in America as well through the import of foreign specimens.

From that time until the mid 1800's, many cutlery makers produced folding knives as a sideline to their regular merchandise. Although they were considered novelty items, everyone wanted them, including the upper stratas of society. For those who could afford the best, specimens with delicate carving and painting were produced; some were with the best grades of enamel, others featured sterling silver or carved and inlaid pearl or ivory. These were termed "fruit knives." Then when the Industrial Age began around 1840, ushered in by the steam engine, factory production of knives began on a large scale. Folding knives were among the standard output of knife factories in all parts of the U.S. by the 1890's though some concentrated much more on this type of knife than others.

Also in the 1800's, knife manufacturers discovered another excellent path to added profits: the advertising knife. These knives carried messages and/or logos of business firms, mostly retailers, as well as places of amusement. They were made on a contract basis, by which the purchaser received a substantial discount (in exchange for agreeing to buy a large quantity). Mostly the firms whose slogans appear on these knives gave them away as premiums. Then there was a similar species, also originating in the 1800's: the souvenir knife, carrying the name of a tourist attraction. Of course, all are collector's items, and some are quite scarce — and many reproductions have been made recently too.

Before the 19th century had ended, manufacturers had found numerous ways to promote the appeal and sale of pocket knives. One of these was to incorporate other gadgets into the knife, in addition to the basic blade. A knife could have two or three different kinds of blades, or a corkscrew for extracting the cork on beverage bottles. When soft-drink manufacturers switched to capped bottles, this gave knife makers something else to supply: a cap opener. Of course while this was going on, many single-blade knives without accessories were still being brought out on the market. Establishment of the Scouting movement in the early 1900's was another boon to the pocket knife industry, as each Scout had to have at least one pocket knife.

By 1910 the pocket knife makers were making strong use of advertising. Their ads were appearing in all the youth-oriented magazines as well as magazines on hunting and fishing. Some requested readers to write for catalogues; others sold their knifes directly from the ads and most just let the reader know the knife was available at their hardware store. Then, too, pocket knives were used as premiums in various promotions. Youngsters were given a pocket knife if they succeeded in soliciting a certain number of new subscriptions for a magazine or newspaper, bought a new pair of boots, or if they sold a given quantity of greeting cards or other items. At the same time, salesmen were sent out to canvass with pocket knives. Usually they traveled through rural areas, where a pocket knife would be of greater use than in a city or town. Mostly they called upon shopkeepers for the purpose of obtaining quantity orders, since sales of individual knives to the public were not too profitable. Their traveling rolls contained samples of various types of blade and handle styles offered by their employer.

## BLADE PATTERNS

Most manufacturers produced similar patterns, and it is almost impossible to determine the maker of a knife without a logo stamped somewhere on the knife. Most logos are stamped on the tang of the master blade.

Not illustrated is a long pull. A long pull is a nail mark that runs from the swage to the tang.

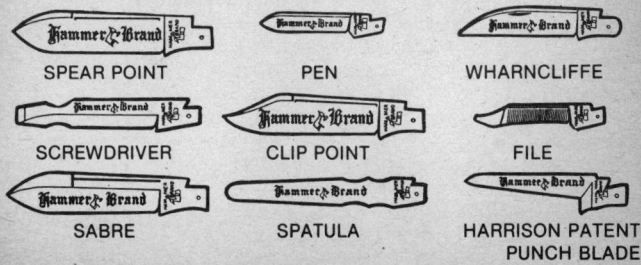

SPEAR POINT     PEN     WHARNCLIFFE

SCREWDRIVER     CLIP POINT     FILE

SABRE     SPATULA     HARRISON PATENT PUNCH BLADE

## 6 / POCKET KNIFE STYLES

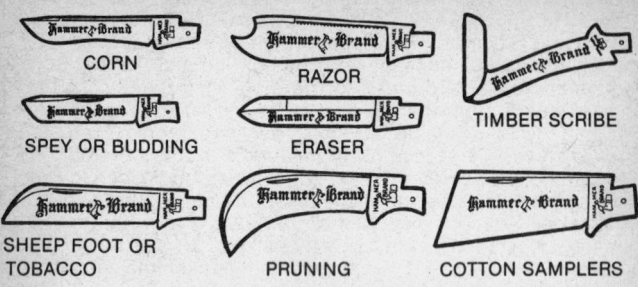

- CORN
- RAZOR
- TIMBER SCRIBE
- SPEY OR BUDDING
- ERASER
- SHEEP FOOT OR TOBACCO
- PRUNING
- COTTON SAMPLERS

## POCKET KNIFE STYLES

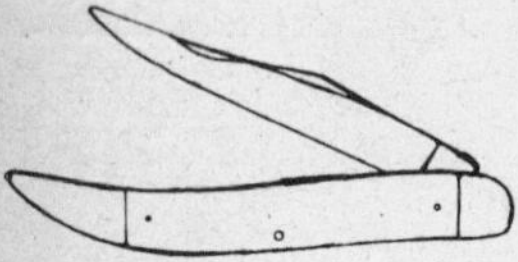

- TEXAS TOOTHPICK
- DADDY BARLOW 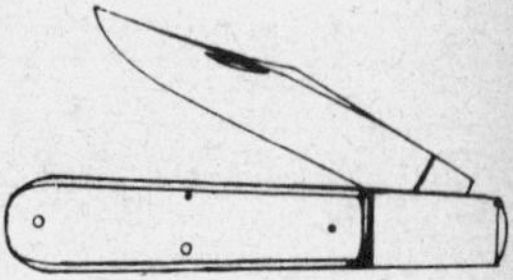
- HAWKBILL 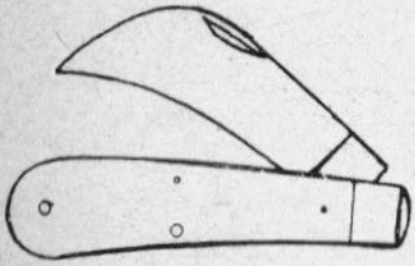
- MAIZE 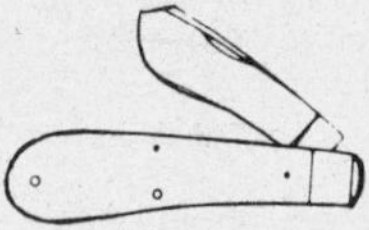
- SWELL END JACK 
- DOGLEG JACK 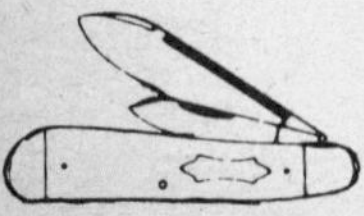
- SCOUT 
- EQUAL END JACK

## POCKET KNIFE STYLES / 7

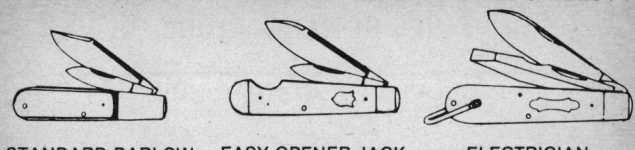

STANDARD BARLOW     EASY OPENER JACK     ELECTRICIAN

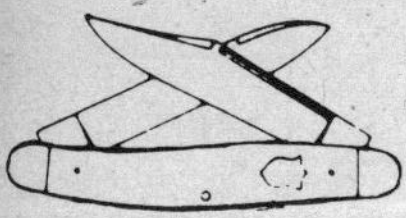

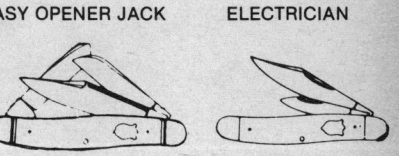

MOOSE     PREMIUM STOCK     SERPENTINE JACK

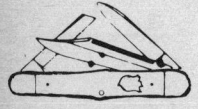 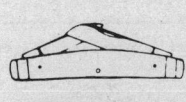 

SWELL CENTER     CONGRESS PEN     MUSKRAT

SENATOR PEN     LOBSTER PEN     SLEEVEBOARD PEN

CATTLE

# 8 / KNIFE NOMENCLATURE
# KNIFE NOMENCLATURE

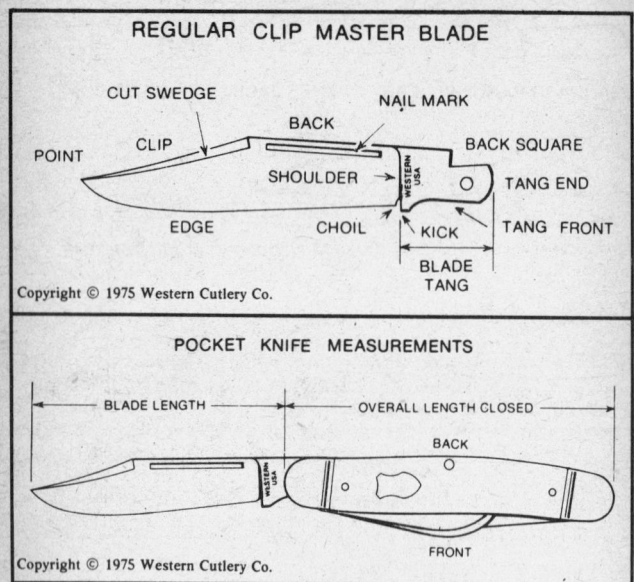

Copyright © 1975 Western Cutlery Co.

Copyright © 1975 Western Cutlery Co.

# GRADING THE CONDITION

As with most collector's items, the condition of a knife plays an important role in arriving at its market value. Collectors and dealers are willing to pay higher prices for knives in well-preserved condition, than for specimens showing evidence of use, damage or deterioration. Two specimens of the same identical knife may be worth vastly different sums, just because of the condition factor. It's worthwhile to learn about condition and

## GRADING THE CONDITION / 9

the effect it has on values BEFORE you do any buying. Many beginners congratulate themselves on getting "bargains" at 20% or 30% lower than the established market values, only to discover later that their knives are worth a small fraction of that value because of inferior condition. Even if you as a collector are not disturbed by defects or wear in the condition of a knife, you will certainly not want to pay a "mint" price for a knife that shows evidence of use or damage.

As far as collecting status is concerned, the mint specimens are of course at the head of the list. Mint is the most desirable for ANY knife, and mint condition is ALWAYS worth a premium. This does not mean that specimens in a lower grade are not "collectable." Traditionally, collectors sought out the mint specimens and bypassed just about everything that could not be classified as mint. Now that prices have gone up for mint knives — and the number of mint knives on the market had DECREASED, there is increased interest in used specimens. Knives that would have been rejected several years ago for being non-mint are now going into collections. There is nothing wrong with buying used knives, so long as the condition is not TOO bad, and the price charged by the seller is fair. There should always be a substantial discount from the mint price, for any knife which cannot be rated as mint. A difference of just 10% or 20% is not fair. You should never pay 80% or 90% of the mint value for a used knife, regardless of whether the knife is new or old, scarce or common. In most cases a fair market price for a used knife is one-half the mint value. This is for a specimen which merely shows signs of use, such as resharpening, but is not damaged or defaced and has no missing parts. When a knife is damaged or defective, the value is considerably less, in some cases only 10% that of a mint specimen or even lower.

Naturally the older knives are more difficult to find in mint condition, which holds true of "collectibles" in general. This is not a case of deterioration with age but results purely from circumstances. If a great deal of knife collectors had been active in the 19th century, specimens of 19th century knives in mint condition would be plentiful on today's market. They would have been carefully stored by the original owners and by successive generations, and without receiving any actual use their original

## 10 / GRADING THE CONDITION

factory condition would now be preserved. However, this was not the case. Hardly anyone was collecting knives in the 19th century or even in the early part of the 20th century. Guns, antiques and other valuables were kept as heirlooms — knives were thrown away. Those who DID collect went about the hobby in a much cruder fashion than the modern knife hobbyists. They were interested merely in owning the knife and took no pains to keep it in mint condition. This of course is understandable as there was no collector's market at that time, and nobody could sell a mint specimen for a premium price — so why bother? And of course the vast majority of knife buyers in the 19th and early 20th centuries were not collectors in any way, shape or form. They bought the now-collectable knives for actual use. The prices back then were a small fraction of the sums these knives now command as collector's items, so the buyers did not have any substantial investment in them. They were used in hunting, camping, and for many other purposes — just as the manufacturers advised them to be in their catalogues and advertising literature. And then just as now, most knives carried for use ended up lost. One modern company estimates their knives will be carried less than two years before they are lost. Very few individuals wanted to buy a knife for show or display, regardless of how attractive the case or blade might be. Considering the frugality of our ancestors, this would certainly have been considered a waste of money. Why own something if you cannot get any use out of it? There was just no collecting spirit at work back then, and this is why a very minimal proportion of the fine early knives are discovered in mint preservation. With the later knives, the story is quite different. As the knife collecting hobby grew in the post-World War II years, more and more of the better-grade knives were bought by collectors rather than for actual use. The collectors put them away, and thus the percentage of mint factory-fresh newer specimens circulating today is considerably high. As you reach the 1970's the percentage grows higher and higher, since by then many more fine pocketknives are being bought from the retail market by hobbyists and knife dealers.

The different gradings of a knife vary with the individual but most collectors and dealers use the guidelines of the National

## GRADING THE CONDITION / 11

Knife Collectors Association, which describes the conditions as follows:

**MINT**—A factory fresh knife, absolutely original as it came from the manufacturer, not carried or sharpened, a perfect knife.

**NEAR MINT**—A new knife that has seen some time, shows some slight carry or shop wear, blades snap perfectly, handles show no cracks.

**EXCELLENT—SHOW NO MORE THAN** 10% blade wear, handles are sound, no cracks, blades snap good.

**VERY GOOD**—About 25% blade wear, slight cracks in handles, may have one lazy blade. Stamping clearly visible to the naked eye, no blades changed or repaired.

**FAIR**—50% blade wear, blades lazy, cracks and chips in handles, handles replaced with same type, blades repaired, stampings faint, but readable with a glass.

**POOR**—Blades very worn, handles bad or missing, blades have been replaced with the same type, reading of the stamp is almost impossible even with a glass, good mostly only for parts.

To be a good knife collector you must get into the practice of examining each specimen carefully before buying or trading for it. There is a natural temptation to buy on sight, if you've been searching for a certain knife and finally locate one at a show. This can be dangerous! Examination of the condition must include all components of the knife and its decoration. The collector must be careful not to overlook any faults, but at the same time he should realize that certain faults are less serious than others, and do not affect the value nearly as much. A simple stress crack in the handle of a knife, which will be found on many knives that are otherwise in mint or near-mint condition, is not the same thing as a broken handle, but it is very hard to see if you rush. It does not normally reduce the value by more than 10%, and should not be cause for rejection of a high-quality, scarce knife that one needs for his collection — so long as the price is right.

Many old knives are grimy or greasy when discovered. This applies especially to those found at garage sales, flea markets, in pawn shops and other secondary sources away from the main channels of the knife market. When a knife reaches the floor of a show, it will be already cleaned up. Do not imagine that these bright gleaming specimens at the shows were found in just that condition, especially when the age is 50, 70, or 100 years. Most of them needed a good cleaning and received it. It is not an undertaking for the amateur, but a professional knife repairer can work wonders in cleaning any kind of specimen, but untrained or careless cleaning can ruin the value of an old knife.

# COUNTERFEIT POCKET KNIVES

The counterfeit knife is the topic of a great many knife collectors, and in the course of the conversation they do a lot of swearing about it, but precious little is told to beginning collectors about how to detect them. It seems that the knowledge of what to look for in a counterfeit should be a secret, told only after the beginner has the trust of the old sage collector and is deserving. While interviewing collectors and dealers for this article most expressed concern that an article on how to detect counterfeits could easily be an article on how to counterfeit, and then they would clam up. All the while, beginners were buying counterfeits, discovering it, and quitting knife collecting. If the information below tells how to counterfeit but still stops some beginning collector from dropping out of the hobby, it will be worth it.

Fortunately, most counterfeiters don't have the equipment or parts necessary to make a foolproof counterfeit, and there are certain things to look for in detecting a counterfeit.

The most important thing is to know your knife. There are few Case Canoe collectors who would not look extra close at a 62131 XX with bone handles, or a Rough Black collector who would buy a Rough Black 6111 ½ Lockback. This familiarity with a knife will sometimes ring a bell in your head when one "just doesn't look right"

I have noticed that most counterfeits are around the $50.00 price range. Cheaper priced knives are not worth the effort, and more expensive knives usually mean the buyer wants return privileges and will have the knife inspected by several knowledgeable collectors.

Case stags are popular among many collectors, and are popular among counterfeiters as well. The thing to look for first is to be sure that a Case stag has a 5 as the first pattern number digit. If it is a 5, then look for signs of etching and buffing. The 5 denotes genuine stag handles, and was discontinued in 1970, but some bone handled knives, with a 6 as the first pattern number digit, are counterfeited by buffing off the 6 and engraving the 5 with a jeweler's engraver. Look to see if the number 5 is stamped the same size and spaced the same as the other numbers. The dots on knives made in 1970 should be evenly spaced and have 10 of them. (Some knives were made by Case in collector's sets in 1973 and some of these had 8 and 9 dots under the logo. The collector should be familiar with which ones were so stamped. The information is in most Case collector's guides.)

Some counterfeits glue the shield on the stag. The genuine article has two rivets attaching the shield and are visible inside the knife where they attach to the liner.

On any knife, look for sign of work, be suspicious of one almost new blade or handle and the rest of the knife well-worn. Look for hammer marks on the inside of the knife. Few battered knives leave the factory in a hammered up condition.

Check the thickness of the tang as compared with the backspring to see if the old logo has been buffed off completely and be careful of light stamped knives. Compare the stamping of a known good knife.

Use a match or toothpick and try to scratch the black from around the logo. If the black comes out easily and it is shiny underneath, beware, because blades are stamped before they are heat treated and the black is hard to come off on a good knife.

On a Case knife the main backspring rivets are spun. A Case knife without spin rivets was probably tampered with.

Brass rivets are usually used with brass liners, as are nickel silver rivets used with nickel silver liners.

One time rusty blades that have been buffed will be dull and have a slick edge, while a good genuine knife will be sharp.

A major thing is to *TAKE YOUR TIME* and look over the knife carefully, later will usually be too late.

## HANDMADE POCKET KNIVES

Some of the nicest knives around are coming from the one man workshops of custom makers. The knives from these craftsmen are just like a fine painting or sculpture. They are works of art, a form of metal sculpture, with adornments such as engraving, etched blades, ivory scrimshawed handles, and much more. As any knife that is collected today, they are going up in price, and when you buy one there are two ways you can go.

The first is to buy from a relatively unknown knifemaker who produces a superior knife but has not had the publicity and achieved the fame of some of the better known makers. If his knives are truly superior, they will soon become the object of many collectors, and he will soon raise his prices as demand increases, thereby increasing your investment. Too, some collectors look only for the early cruder work of custom makers. The bad point is if he loses interest and drops his quality, you will not gain on your investment.

The second way is to buy the knives only from well-known makers. This has the advantage of a ready market when you decide to sell, and probably increasing your investment. However, the drawback is that many of the makers are years behind in orders, and when you buy their knives it will require a more substantial investment than that of an unknown maker.

We recommend that you never buy a knife of shoddy workmanship or a handmade knife with no name stamped on it. True, there are some famous maker's knives floating around in the market with no name stamped on them, but it takes an experienced hand to identify them.

When you buy a custom folder, some of the things to look for are as follows:

*Fit:* The handles fit flush and tight with the bolsters or are they filled with epoxy to take up the space?

*Nailmark:* Is the nailmark as good as that of most factory knives? This is where most custom makers blow it.

*Bolsters:* If the liners and bolster are the same material, can you tell where the bolster and liner join? If you can, beware.

*Pivot Rivet:* Can you tell where it is? On a good knife it should not be visible.

**Lock:** Does the knife lock and unlock easily?
**Evenness:** Does the backspring come back level with the liners in both the open and closed position?
**Polish:** Is the polish good or are waves visible? Is the inside polished?
**Grind Lines:** Are both sides of the blade ground even?

This is a starting guideline for the buyer of a custom folder. The best advice was given to us by Wayne Goddard, a knifemaker of the first rank from Oregon. He said, "I can tell you what to look for a hundred times, but the only way to really tell is to go to a well-known maker who makes top quality knives, look his folders over and then go look at the one you are considering buying. There is where the difference will show." Following are some custom knives from the files of the Blade magazine, used with permission.

# HOW TO BUY AND SELL POCKET KNIVES

Collectible pocket knives are available from a wide variety of sources. Most of the sources for buying can also be used for selling and swapping. The art of swapping comes into play a great deal in this hobby for most collectors, more so than in most hobbies. Knife collecting has a heritage deeply rooted in swapping and trading. Long before there were knife books, clubs, shows or professional dealers, those who admired finely made knives made most of their acquisitions by swapping. In fact knife swapping was developed into an art, by its top practitioners. Using nothing more than duplicate or unwanted knives from their own collections, plus big doses of personal persuasiveness, they built outstanding arrays of knives. Many of these folks would have considered it an evil to actually BUY a knife — that would have taken the fun out of it, not to mention the feeling of conquest. Of course, times have changed since then. But you will still find plenty of opportunities to do some good old-fashioned knife swapping, so be ready! But today the shows have almost given way entirely to buying or selling. When swapping, most of the dealers will "trade up." That is, they will take a more valuable, better condition knife and in turn give a lesser knife, a little money, and swap in that manner. Even in this day and age, a keen collector still ends up with profits on most of his swaps. He might not go around doubling his money, which is on the verge of impossibility, but he comes away with very satisfactory gains of 10%, 20% or slightly more. The success ratios of the old-time swappers cannot be matched in the 1980's, simply because most knife owners are attuned to current market values. They do not let rarities slip through their fingers. The way to make a profitable swap is not to fool anybody, but:

1. Find someone who's been searching and searching for the knife you want to swap.

2. Offer to trade it for one that has a slightly higher book value (assuming your specimen — and his specimen — are in the same condition). You won't need too much flair for salesman to accomplish this. Anyone who really wants your knife SHOULD be more willing to trade for it, than buy it. Chances are, the knife you're getting was acquired a few years ago (or more), at a price well under its current market value. Thus the collector who swaps with you is really saving money, compared to what his expense would be in BUYING the knife. If he has any kind of head on his shoulders, he will realize this. He will also realize that his knife would fetch considerably less than its current book value, if sold to a dealer for cash. If he could get only 65-75% of its value in selling to a dealer, he is obviously smarter to swap it for 80-90% of its value.

Obviously the major channel of supply in this hobby is the professional dealers, who sell through shops and by mail-order, as well as touring the show circuit. They exhibit at the knife shows, and many of them likewise exhibit at gun shows and flea markets. Some of them are exhibiting at a different show almost every weekend of the year and log tens of thousands of miles in travel annually. There are sure to be shows in your area where knife dealers are exhibiting, even if you do not live near a dealer's shop. You can also buy by mail, from the pricelists or personal "quotations" offered by these dealers.

How do the fulltime pro dealers operate? Just like any other businessmen who buy and sell collector's items for a livelihood. There is no dark cloud of mystery overhanging their operations. They buy from the public and from knife makers, and they sell to the public. Some hobbyists (mostly beginners who don't really know the score) think the dealers charge too much for their knives, or pay too little when they buy. Well, let's put ourselves in the dealer's place for a minute. For one thing the dealer is offering a pretty unique service to his customers. He is doing something for them that very few of them could accomplish on their own. He is sifting through the entire knife market, using connections far more extensive than a collector would have, to accumulate a good stock of knives for his customers. He is using his expertise to reject fakes and doctored specimens so they will not reach the hands of his clients. In a sense he is a kind of protection shield for his customers. He does the detective work and the appraising, and anyone can take advantage of the fruits of his labor — by paying the market price (or thereabouts) for his knives. He offers convenience and in a way he DOES save you money, since you would probably spend a fortune in gas or long-distance phone calls tracking down the knives he has in stock. The dealers do not have any secret sources of supply. They buy in the marketplace just as collectors do, but the fact that they also buy FROM collectors gives them a wide range of potential acquisitions. The dealers are constantly having knives and whole collections of them offered to them for sale. No private collector could put himself in this kind of situation, without doing a great deal of advertising and setting himself up as a dealer and buying large collections of knives they didn't collect and breaking them up singly. Which would mean adding to his expense!

Do dealers pay too little when they buy? A dealer cannot pay the full market price of a knife or even a sum approaching full market value. Everything the dealer buys is destined for resale, so there must be a clear margin of profit involved. It is not just a question of selling for more than he paid. A collector can be satisfied selling for more than he paid, even if it's just 10%. Dealers have to pay for advertising, shipping, travel and various other overhead. If they don't sell for at least 25% more than they paid, they won't even break even. And, of course, the dealer is ALWAYS taking some kind of risk when he buys, since there is not guarantee WHEN the knife will be sold, or what the market value will be at that time. He may have to reduce the selling price in order to make a sale.

## 18 / HOW TO BUY AND SELL KNIVES

Without any doubt, you can build a collection faster by doing business with the professional dealers, than in any other way. Chances are you will also have a higher quality collection that way, as the odds on acquiring reworked or other "bad" knives are much less. In buying from antiques shops, pawn shops, flea markets and local people, you will need to have a pretty high level of personal expertise, to protect yourself. Of course it is entirely possible to acquire this expertise, through the use of this book and by handling and inspecting many knives before you do any heavy buying. But even with buying from dealers some of the knives you may want will be difficult to fine. Rare knives are just that — RARE.

When you do business with the professional dealers, don't just rely on reading their pricelists or ads. Lists and ads are fine, but the dealers sell many knives which never get listed. They come in and go out too fast! If you're seeking any special knives, make up a list of them and forward it to the dealer. Chances are he has a few already in stock and can offer them directly from his stock. On the ones he cannot supply at the moment, he will file your "want list" for future reference. When those particular knives cross his path, he will notify you. This gives you the opportunity to buy them before they reach his list, and before they go along with him on his show rounds. Be sure you make a prompt decision in these situations; it is impossible for the dealers to hold any knives for more than a week at most. If you become a valued customer of any dealer, you will find that he goes out of his way to get the best possible specimens for you at the best prices. This is like having a fulltime agent working in your behalf.

The flea markets and knife shows are among the best "secondary sources" for picking up collectible knives. Many good knives pass through flea markets — so do loads of near-worthless ones that aren't worth a hobbyist's second glance. Obviously you need to know your knives and their values before you can buy wisely at flea markets. You can't count on the sellers to supply you with any information. Even those who are perfectly honest and would like to help usually know little or nothing about their knives. This is to your advantage if they're pricing a $50 knife at $10. But quite often the reverse happens.

Most flea market exhibitors have at least a vague notion that SOME knives are valuable. If they have a box of miscellaneous knives to sell, they're scared to death of pricing them too low. So, in guessing at a value, they often guess much too high. They will put a general price of (say) $75 each on all their knives, which may consist of ten worth under $50 and perhaps one worth $100. So you need to be able to recognize that one underpriced knife. Just because something is being sold at a flea market, this is no assurance that its price is below the fair market value. A beginner will go around buying up every knife he sees at a market, then discover later that he could have saved money buying the very same ones from a top dealer.

Many knives at flea markets have come out of attics, garages and basements. They're likely to show varying degrees of grime on the handle, which makes them a lot less visually appealing than knives exhibited at knife shows. However, ordinary dirt and grime can be cleaned off, so this should not be a reason to reject any knife if it's otherwise a good buy. Instead of looking at the grime, examine the specimen for structural defects such as cracks as well as missing parts, and also for authenticity (whether the handle is the right one for that knife, and other details as discussed in the article on counterfeits).

Prices at flea markets are usually negotiable. If the price of a knife is not marked on it, don't appear TOO interested when you inquire about it. Play it casual — you might even try wearing old clothes, so the seller will assume you aren't the type to carry bundles of cash. When a price is named, you can be pretty sure it isn't a "take it or leave it" price. Most likely it's the price the seller HOPES he can get. But nearly everybody who exhibits at flea markets wants to make sales rather than pack their things up and try again next week. Try for a better price — you can't lose anything! But be diplomatic and polite about it. Don't stress bad features of the knife, as a reason for a discount. Don't say the knife isn't really worth that much. Just tell the seller how much it would be worth to YOU. Who knows? Maybe you're a dealer buying for resale. Maybe you couldn't care less about collector value — you want the knife to slice pizzas with. You'll find in most such situations, the price will come down. It may end up going down by 50%, and even at that point the seller is probably doing very nicely. Chances are, the knife was bought by one of his relatives or ancestors and tossed in a trunk 20 years ago. He has absolutely no investment in it, nor any use for it.

Be thorough and investigative at flea markets. Don't let appearances fool you. Only on rare occasions will you come upon a neat table arrayed with knives, as you would at a knife show. Most of the sellers at flea markets are offering a mixed bag of merchandise, so you may need to hunt through it to find their knives. They could be in a barrel on the ground or behind the table. They might even be in a closed box, since some exhibitors are not well versed in the science of displaying merchandise to its best advantage. Whenever you see a box with miscellaneous things piled in it, there could be a knife at the bottom! Even just one decent find makes the searching worthwhile. And that is precisely what you should do — search, not ask. By asking, you're apt to be charged a higher price.

At the knife shows it's an entirely different state of affairs. This does not mean you cannot find bargains. There are bargains and "buys" at every knife show. Many of them are passed by, simply because there's so much to occupy your attention. If an exhibitor does not have his selling prices marked on his knives, you might bypass them just because you ASSUME that every one is priced at the full market level. This is not necessarily the case. An exhibitor might have duplicates from his collection that he would willingly sell below their full value, or perhaps he is not aware of the value of some of his knives. Not all the exhibitors are fulltime dealers — and even the fulltime dealers can occasionally make mistakes! For one thing an exhibitor might not have correctly identified his knife. In that event his selling price could be much higher or much lower than the prevailing value. Of course at a knife show, most of the visitors are well informed and any kind of colossal bargain is not apt to last long. This is why you should try to attend on the opening day, and preferably right after the doors open. Additionally, the floor will not be too crowded at that point and you can get close to all the tables without blocking the aisles. The best procedure is to take a tour of all the exhibitors' tables upon entering the show, rather than spending much time at any one table. Experienced show-goers can "make the rounds" quickly, even at a large show. Even though it is impossible to do anything more than glance from table to table that quickly, you will get a good idea of what everybody is selling. And you may, even with fast glances, spot some "buys." If you see something fabulous on this tour-around, stop and buy it. Don't count on coming back later. By then, several hundred other collectors will have walked by the table. If the buy is THAT good, others are going to notice it, too. Stop and buy it, but don't engage in more conversation than is necessary. Then continue on your tour! Later, when you've gotten the "feel" of the show, you can tour all the tables again, this time at a more leisurely pace. Count on spending at least two to four hours at the show, to check out each exhibitor's offerings in depth. Don't forget that what you see on the tables is only a PORTION of the knives available. Each exhibitor has others in his carrying bags, ready to be shown to you on request. The exhibit space at shows is so limited that most dealers can only display a selection of their knives.

You can sell or swap knives at the show, if you want to. Of course you can rent a table of your own, as many collectors do, if you have many knives available for swapping and selling. Otherwise just bring them along when you visit the show. The cost of renting exhibit space varies from one show to another, so you will need to make specific inquiries. Also, it is usually necessary to book your table well in advance, as some shows sell out their tables three or four months before showtime. At the last minute there will be space available only if someone cancels out. To cut down on the expense of space rental, and to beef up your exhibition of knives, you could go into partnership with another local hobbyist and rent the table jointly. Of course you will then need to keep track of the proceeds due to each of you. The only problem is doing this arises when a customer wants to buy one of your knives and one of your partner's — and wants to get a discount. You may be willing to offer a discount, and your partner isn't! But generally speaking it does help to have a partner with you at shows, especially for security reasons. Each can watch the table while the other is away.

When exhibiting at a show, be sure all your knives have been correctly identified and evaluated. Clean them up if necessary and oil them if this has not been done within the past few weeks — you want them to look their best. You can improve their visual appeal and salability by displaying them on a black velvet cloth, or other dark material. Do not place them directly on the table-top without using a backing material. Of course the best way to display knives at a show is in a glass-top traveling case. These have hinged lids and a lock, and greatly reduce the danger of theft. They also make your display more impressive as they suggest that your knives are quite valuable and worth keeping under lock and key! But of course they are an additional expense, and if you don't plan to be a regular exhibitor at knife shows they may not be worthwhile for you. You can order these from mail order dealers listed in this book.

You can charge full market prices if you're exhibiting at a show, as this is what many of the other exhibitors will be doing. On the other hand, you may be more interested in doing a large volume of business, than in obtaining the full market price for each knife. It's up to you. The smartest approach is usually to start out with prices fairly close the the book range, when the show opens. You're certain to make some sales that way, and if business slows down midway through the show you can always come down a bit on your prices. Don't panic. Don't slice the prices sharply when the show has just two more hours to run. There is no earthly reason why you should give your knives away, just for the sake of making sales. At some shows the buying pace is heavier than at others. If you attend a number of shows as an an exhibit, you will hit some where things are dull — they aren't that way just for you, but for most of the exhibitors. Take your unsold knives home, and try again the next time around. If everybody else is doing business except you, maybe the quality of your knives does not measure up to those of other exhibitors or the presentation is poor. Sometimes this is the fault of floor location. Certain floor locations have more traffic passing by them than others.

If you want to sell your knives by mail, there are several ways this can be done. You can sell to one of the specialist dealers, or you can run advertisements and sell to collectors. The advantage of selling to dealers is that you can usually make quicker sales that way. The advantage in selling to collectors is that you may be able to obtain a higher price. There is no perfect way to sell!

In selling to dealers through the mail, your approach will probably be governed by the number of knives you have for sale. Some collectors firmly believe that a phone call to the dealer is the best method — they feel that a letter or listing is apt to go unnoticed. If you have a number of knives to sell it is wise to make up a list, stating the manufacturer, style, pattern number, and all other relevant information just as you find on a dealer's pricelist. Also be sure to indicate the physical condition of each knife. You may or may not want to indicate a selling price. Generally speaking a list showing prices is more effective. When a list does not carry prices, it means more work for the dealer as he has to calculate his buying offers — and at the same time he may be wasting his effort, if the seller is intent on getting full market prices. You should be aware, before approaching any dealer, that the maximum price you can expect to get for any knife is about 75% of the book value, and for many knives you will have to be satisfied with somewhat less. Armed with this knowledge, there should be no problem in figuring up the prices for your knives. You can show individual prices, and then (if the collection is a large one) a "lot price," representing a discount if the entire collection is purchased. Let the dealer know whether you are offering the knives exclusively to him, or to other dealers as well. This can be done by inserting the words "subject to prior sale" on your list, if other dealers are receiving the same list.

# HOW TO STORE, CLEAN AND REPAIR

Attention to *condition* does not end when the purchase of a knife is made. Condition enters into the price, and the condition of a knife (regardless of price) may be the determining factor in whether you want it for your collection. But just as the condition of a knife may have changed from "factory mint" to some lesser grade, before reaching your hands, it is entirely possible for the condition to change AFTER the knife is safely housed in your collection. Deterioration in condition is not just something that

## 24 / HOW TO STORE, CLEAN AND REPAIR

former owners allowed to happen, as the result of not realizing a knife's value. Collectors, too, are sometimes responsible for deterioration in condition, not of course by placing the knife to actual use but by improperly cleaning or storing it.

The problem here of course is that collectors, even in this very enlightened day and age, are not universally educated on the hazards to which a fine knife can fall prey. There are still some lingering fragments of the old pre-collector philosophy about knives: they're sturdy, they're rugged, they're made to last for generations. Of course they are. Manufacturers were justly proud of the fact that their knives could absorb hard everyday use and keep coming back for more. A knife won't melt if it gets wet. But staying intact and being serviceable for use is quite a different matter than remaining in the best grades of collector condition. Collector knives call for special attention in handling and storage that would be unnecessary under normal circumstances. The materials from which each specimen is made must be taken into account, and the hobbyist needs to have some working knowledge of the reactions of those materials to different methods of storage and cleaning. In short, knives are definitely not fragile in the accepted sense, but to keep them in the best possible collector condition they must be treated as though they were.

The question here is a twofold one, as the collector will want to put his valued knives into the best possible condition when he acquires them, then keep them that way. By doing this he may increase the market value of some of his knives, though of course a used knife can never be returned to mint state condition. At worst the careful collector will maintain his knives in the condition in which they were acquired.

In considering cleaning and storage, it is essential to know the types of damage and deterioration to which knives are prone; that is, what CAN hurt them, what CANNOT hurt them, how to REPAIR OR REMOVE IT, and (once the knife is in your possession) how to GUARD AGAINST IT. The following is a brief summary of the more common condition problems encountered with pocket knives:

**Rust.** Rust is of course the universal enemy of all metallic objects, except those made of aluminum or other rustproof elements. Rust is simply another name for corrosion. Copper corrodes the fastest of all metals, but the others (with the exception of gold) are subject to corrosion to one degree or another depending on storage conditions. Knives should be examined for rust spots before making a purchase. Minor rust is not a serious defect in itself, and of course it will be encountered pretty frequently on the older knives, which have not received very careful attention from their early owners. The formation of rust is encouraged mainly by dampness. Moisture activates certain elements within the metal, which break through to the surface and form a mold or fungus. Thus, rust is sometimes referred to as "metal mold." The extent to which rust forms (and the speed of its development) is governed by the degree of exposure to moisture. If something comes into contact with water, rust will form rapidly. If submerged in water for a period of time, rust will not only develop quickly but will cover all the metallic elements of the object. Even after the entire surface has been coated with rust, the process does not end — if circumstances are unchanged. More and more of the metal turns to rust, until eventually only a crust of corrosion remains; there is no more metal. The object has been transformed into a rust cast of itself, though the "cast" is far from an exact duplicate of the object: it is bulkier and misshapen, since the rust development is not even on the whole surface.

Though contact with water is the most conducive situation for rust, it can also occur without actual water contact. Water is carried in the atmosphere through humidity. The humidity percentage is the amount of water content in the air at any given time, which can range from 0% to 100%. So long as the reading is above 0% — which it always is, even indoors — the air has some moisture and rust is invited. Knive collectors who believe that rust cannot attack their specimens; because their rooms are humidity-controlled, are mistaken.

Rust can also be encouraged if a metallic item comes into contact with a corruptive substance. Even something as harmless looking as ordinary paper is potentially corruptive. Paper is made with water (in the pulping process), so it has a moisture content. While the paper itself does not rust, since it has no metallic ingredients, it can cause rust to other objects. Therefore a knife should not be wrapped in paper for any great length

## 26 / HOW TO STORE, CLEAN AND REPAIR

of time. This would be entirely safe, however, if the wrapping is applied merely for mailing or taking a knife home from a show.

There are many degrees of rust. The odds of success in removing it will depend on the extent of rust and the depth to which it has eaten into the surface metal. In serious cases of rusting, the original appearance of the metal cannot be restored. The rust has replaced portions of the metal, and when the rust is removed it leaves hills and valleys where the metal has been disturbed. In very bad cases, the object may crack in two or crumble into powder upon attempting to remove the rust. Rust cleanup should be done by a professional knife repairer.

The only effective safeguard against rust is to keep moisture from reaching metallic portions of the knife. This can be accomplished by coating the knife with a suitable dressing which acts as a protective shield, but does not detract from the visual appeal or cause any deterioration of its own. Traditionally, vaseline (petroleum jelly) was used for this purpose, not just with knives but other metal collector's items. It is actually one of the least satisfactory preparations for this use. Vaseline has air pockets and does not do a thorough job of sealing. Moisture will collect beneath the vaseline, with the result that rusting is actually promoted by its use, rather than prevented. Rusting on vaseline-coating objects is in the form of "freckles" or tiny reddish spots which collect in clusters.

A thinner, more liquified oil is better, such as machine oil or gunsmith's oil. It will spread evenly and not develop air pockets. However, in time it will dry out, so you cannot put the knife away for years and forget about it. Each specimen in your collection must receive a periodic re-oiling. Nor is it possible to reduce the need for re-oiling by applying a very heavy coating of oil, as it will still dry out. In fact, the heavier you apply the oil, the gummier and messier it will become, and the more problems you will encounter in applying a fresh coating in the future. Generally speaking, knives should be re-oiled every month. By repeating the process every month you can use a thin coating of oil and never reach the point of messiness. The entire knife should be oiled, not just the metallic components. When re-oiling is done, you need not totally remove the old coating of oil, but the knife should be rubbed with a clean cloth to remove the outer layer of oil. This is important as the oil will have attracted some airborne pollutants in the meantime. You will notice that the rag gets fairly black in the course of this operation! These of course cling mainly to the upper layer, which serves as an outer defense for the lower layer of oil and ultimately of course for the metal. Of course you will handle the knife carefully in oiling, not only out of respect for it but for the safety of your fingers.

There are no knife materials which would be damaged by oil, so you need not hesitate to dress the entire knife. If it does not do any good to the other materials, it will at least do no harm. At the least it will create a good gloss appearance which of course enhances the appearance of such materials as ivory and pearl.

**Scratches.** Minor scratches, while they disqualify a knife from "mint" ranking, are not usually a cause to reject a knife for purchase if the price is fair. This may of course depend on the rarity and the opportunity to buy a mint specimen. While scratches cannot actually be removed in most cases, they will not appear as noticeable when the knife has been properly cleaned and oiled.

**Cracks.** Handle cracks are a common problem with knives, one of the basic causes of knives (especially older ones) dropping into one of the lower condition categories. They occur as the result of accident, such as a heavy object falling on the knife, or improper use of the knife, as in prying with the blade. To many of the early owners (non-collectors, of course), their knives were truly all-purpose tools. They whipped them out whenever occasion called for a tool of some kind, anything from a hammer to screwdriver. So of course they took a beating, and cracks developed — which did not bother the original owners at all, especially as they had paid perhaps $1.25 for a knife which would now be worth $150 or $200 in mint condition. The severity of the crack is the determining factor when judging such a knife's value. Normally a serious collector would not want a knife with a cracked handle, unless the specimen is exceptionally rare and the seller has adjusted his price to a reasonable level. Cracks cannot of course be removed, but their appearance can usually be improved. This is done by filling them in with a substance which will blend with the handle material, then polishing the handle. Though the crack may still be noticeable, it will seem to be nothing more than a hairline crack. Of course it is unfair to

## 28 / HOW TO STORE, CLEAN AND REPAIR

offer such a specimen for sale, without informing the prospective buyer that the condition is not quite what it seems to be.

**Dirt.** This all-purpose heading includes every type of grease, grime, soil, etc., which works its way on or into the knife. It is of course the most common "defect" in old knives, but it cannot be considered an actual defect since removal is nearly always within the realm of possibility. It is really nothing more than a blot against the specimen's physical appearance. With a little experience you will be able to recognize simple dirt on collector knives and distinguish it from more serious problems such as rust. Of course there is the disturbing possibility that dirt, if extensive and thick, might be hiding another sort of defect such as a crack or missing component.

Most dirt found on used knives got there as the result of repeated handling. The knife was handled over and over again with hands that were not too clean, and gradually the dirt became embedded to one degree or another. The extent of dirt and the difficulty of cleaning the knife can be two different things. The dirtiest knives are not always the toughest ones to clean. This all depends on the type of handle, since dirt can work its way into some kinds of handles much better than others. If the handle is a smooth non-porous substance such as metal, it may be extremely dirty but the dirt is merely resting on the surface and can be removed with no trouble at all. On the other hand if the handle is ivory and features high-relief carving with intricate detailing, you have a real challenge in cleaning. The same is true of knives in which the handle decoration is supplied by means of incised or engraved lines. Before you start cleaning these, however, be sure to determine whether the decoration was intended to be "blind" or inked. It was a common practice for incised linework to be inked in, since plain scratched lines on a substance like ivory do not show up very well. After the decoration had been completed, the maker would rub ink (usually black) on the surface, allowing it to soak fully into the incised lines. The excess was the rubbed away. This is the opposite of a "blind" decoration, in which the incised linework is left "as is." Hence if you find black matter imbedded in the lines of decoration, it may well have been placed there by the manufacturer. If it appears uneven and blotchy in places, this is undoubtedly the result of dirt and grime clinging to the original ink. It is possible to remove the dirt without disturbing the ink, which of course is the goal when cleaning such specimens. This is done by using a cleaning agent which will not attack the ink, and by rubbing the surface with a cloth rather than using a brush or any other type of implement. As a cloth will simply sweep across the surface, it cannot remove anything imbedded in the incised linework.

A good polishing paste should be used in cleaning. Anything stronger is not recommended and certainly the commercial cleansers sold in grocery stores are not for use by the knife hobbyist. This may remove the dirt but they contain corrosive agents which will do your knife more harm than good.

# KNIFE ORGANIZATIONS

The one organization we recommend as a "must-join" if you are really interested in knives is the American Blade Collectors. It is run by the authors of this book, James F. Parker and J. Bruce Voyles.

For a cost of only $14.99 per year each ABC member gets a membership card, subscriptions to EDGES and THE BLADE MAGAZINE, free admission to the ABC convention and show, discounted table rates at that show, free appraisals on their collections (within ABC guidelines), right to use ABC authenticity-guarantee forms, and an option on an annual club knife.

The objective of the organization is the advancement of knife collecting in all of its many forms. Naturally some of the ways the ABC does this is through its two publications, EDGES and THE BLADE MAGAZINE.

THE BLADE MAGAZINE is the oldest knife publication still publishing. Established in 1973 as "American Blade Magazine", it has always been in the forefront of the knife industry publication. The American Blade was purchased in 1981 by Parker and Voyles, and the American Blade Collectors is an offshoot of that magazine. The magazine is a color glossy paper publication that runs 80-100 pages each issue, published bi-monthly.

## 30 / KNIFE ORGANIZATIONS

EDGES is a 24 page tabloid newspaper on the knife industry, and it is published four times each year with news stories and inquiring articles about the goings-on inside the business.

The ABC also sponsors THE BLADE SHOW, which is a convention of ABC members and also one of the leading knife shows in the country, featuring a combined show of custom makers, antique pocketknife collectors, razors, collections on display, new knife dealers, and a special booth section where the manufacturers show their wares.

The traditional location is in Cincinnati, Ohio, the first weekend in June.

Since the ABC is an organization for knife collectors, it heeded the cries of its members who complained about the high cost of collectible knives. Thus was born the annual ABC member's knife. Made in a limited edition, the knife is determined each year by a ballot of the ABC life members. The first knife was issued in 1982 at a cost to members of $30.00. Today it brings $60 on the open market, but of course most members kept their knives for their own collections.

At the annual convention beginning in 1983 THE BLADE MAGAZINE will sponsor the induction and maintenance of the "CUTLERY HALL OF FAME", honoring leaders in the knife industry. As Bruce Voyles said, "The business has come a long way, and it is time that someone recognized the leaders in a fitting way. We decided to do it."

The bedrock of the ABC is the life members. They get all membership privileges, plus the additional benefits of voting their preference on the annual club knife, and a special limited edition "life membership" knife, serial numbered with their membership number. All knives are numbered with their membership number if they so desire. In the past ABC shows, life members have also been the guests at free breakfast and dinner banquets. Cost in 1983 for life membership including at 20 year subscription to The Blade Magazine was $200.00 (subject to change without notice).

If you are interested in the American Blade Collectors you can contact them at P.O. Box 22007, Chattanooga, TN 37422 or call 615-894-0339. They would be happy to enroll you on a Mastercard, Visa, or even bill you for the first year's dues. You'll be glad you did!

## HOW TO USE THIS BOOK / 31

Other knife organizations and publications include

Knife World, P.O. Box 3395, Knoxville, TN 37917
The National Knife Association, Chattanooga, TN

# HOW TO USE THIS BOOK

All listings in this book are grouped by manufacturer, and the manufacturers are listed alphabetically. All the knives are listed by their pattern number, except for those of the Parker and Commemorative sections. Parker knives have a name rather than a pattern number, and therefore are listed by their official company name.

The arrangement with Case knives, as you will note, is by the "dot" system. Since 1970, the Case company has used dots on its tang marking, to show (in code) the year of manufacture. Collecting "by dot number" has become the popular approach among Case hobbyists, so the system adopted in this book should provide maximum convenience.

Condition counts greatly in the market value of a collector knife. To better assist the buyer, seller and trader, we have provided prices for two distinct categories of condition: MINT and VERY GOOD. A Mint knife is in the original condition, just as it was manufactured, without any signs of use (and that includes sharpening!). A Very Good specimen shows obvious signs of use but is not defective; the value of a defective knife is much lower than for "Very Good." A knife in Very Good condition has about 25% blade wear, slight cracks in the handle, and possibly one "lazy" blade. The blades are original and have not been repaired (nor are they in need of repair). Stamping is not so worn that it cannot be seen with the naked eye.

## PRICE TREND INDICATOR

A third price column has been provided in the listings section of this book, showing the average value of each item *one year before the current listings were compiled.* This exclusive feature measures market performances and should be of special usefulness to investors as well as dealers and collectors.

## SHARPENING GUIDE

A knife should be kept sufficiently sharp to do the work for which it is intended. When possible, always cut in direction away from body. When this can't be done, keep body, particularly hand and fingers, in the clear. Avoid jerking motions, sudden strains or other movements causing a loss of balance.

**HOW TO SHARPEN** — Hold back of blade up from stone at angle of 10 to 15 degrees as shown in illustration above. Stroke cutting edge against stone in direciton of arrows from heel to point of blade (as though to cut a thin slice of stone), alternating first on one side of blade and then the other. Use a good quality stone such as **CASE'S 6" Oil Stone.** A fine light oil should be applied to the stone since this will produce the sharpest possible edge if smooth even strokes are used. To obtain an extremely keen edge, finish sharpening on **CASE'S Arkansas Stone.**

The stone should be wiped clean of excess oil after each use. This waste oil will carry away with it the fine steel grindings which, if not removed, would soon clog the pores of the stone.

**DO NOT** use a coarse emery wheel or grindstone. Futhermore, improper use of steel disc sharpeners or electric sharpeners may damage even the finest knife blade.

**DO NOT** lay the blade flat on the sharpening stone. It will thin and scar the sides of the blade, and will produce a paper-thin edge which will not stand up in use or remain sharp.

**DO NOT** lay the blade at too steep an angle as the edge will be too blunt for maximum cutting efficiency.

# CASE

## PATTERN NUMBERS

The pattern number system of W. R. Case & Sons allows the collector to tell if a knife has the proper handle, number of blades, and if the proper handles and blades are on the proper pattern knife. However, these pattern numbers can only help on Case knives made after 1949, when the pattern numbers started appearing on each knife.

The pattern number is usually four digits. The first digit is a code for the type of handle material, the second digit is the number of blades, and the last two digits are the factory pattern numbers and "O" between the second and third digits represents a variation of an existing pattern.

When asking for a knife by a pattern number, most collectors learn them by groups of two. Example: They say, on asking to seE a stag trapper (5254), "I would like to see a fifty-two, fifty-four." They do not say, "I would like to see a five-two-five-four."

## THE FIRST DIGIT

The handle material numbers and letters are listed below. An "*" will be used to show a handle material found only on Case Tested XX knives (1920-50):

| | |
|---|---|
| | P-Pakkawood |
| **1**—Walnut | M-Metal |
| **2**—Black Composition | S-Silver |
| **3**—Yellow Composition | R-Red Striped Celluloid* (candy striped) |
| **4**—White Composition | B-Imitation Onyx |
| **5**—Genuine Stag | G-Green and Red Metal flake under clear celluloid |
| **6**—Bone Stag | (this is called Christmas Tree handles)* |
| **7**—* | W-Wire* |

## 34 / CASE

**8—Genuine Mother of Pearl**

**H**-Mottled Brown and Cream Composition*

**HA**-A bathing beauty under clear celluloid*

**9—Imitation Pearl**     **GS**-Gold Stone (Gold Metal Flake)

* The 7 denoted imitation tortise shell in Tested XX days, but when Case introduced its Sharkstooth they originally planned to use Curly Maple and use a 7 to denote it. A few blades were stamped 7, but then the company decided to use Pakkawood dyed black instead, then instead of a 7 a P was used, but the blades stamped 7 were put into the Pakkawood handled knives and will sometimes be found in a Sharkstooth.

Following is an explanation of each handle material, its origin, and current usage.

*Walnut*-has been used on Case knives since 1920.

*Black Composition*-was used since before 1940 and has a smooth glossy texture. It is made by a chemical process.

*Yellow Composition*-has two variations, one being a white line around the outer edge and is sometimes referred to as having a white liner. The handle with a white liner has a deep glossy yellow, and is usually found only on XX or older knives. The other variation is yellow without a white liner and can be found on knives today. At present there is no price difference between the two variations.

*White Composition*-is the same as black composition, only a different color. At present, there are no regular production knives handled in White composition. It was discontinued around 1974.

*Genuine and Second Cut Stag*-was made from the remaining antler after cutting for Genuine stag. It was jigged, and also used. It will be found on knives stamped both 5 and 6, and this type handle has been used only on patterns 5254, 6254, 5375, 6375, 6488, and 5488.

The red and white candy striped, Christmas tree, metal flake, and other Tested material are in most cases a celluloid based material.

Genuine Stag comes from antlers of Indian deer and has been used since the first days of Case. It was temporarily discontinued in 1971, but the company still puts stag handles on its Kodiak Sheath knife and they have twice issued collector's sets of stag handled knives, once in 1973 and once in 1976, and started limited production use again in 1977.

**Genuine Mother of Pearl**-comes from the shell of an Oyster, not a pearl itself. The industrialization of Japan, where most pearl comes from, caused many of the men pearl divers to go to work in the factories. The women cannot dive to the depth that the men could, and the larger pieces of mother of pearl are deep. Consequently, Case has had to cut back on its pearl handled knives. The first cutback came in 1967, and their 1968 catalog listed no pearl handled knives at all, but in 1970 they brought back the 8261, 8279½, 82053 SC SS, and the 8364 SC SS. Case again discontinued all pearl handled knives in 1975 (except 82079½).

**Imitation Pearl**-There are several variations of imitation pearl, the most well-known being cracked ice, which has a flaky look.

## THE FOLLOWING HANDLE MATERIALS ARE DENOTED BY A (6)

**Appaloosa**-is a smooth brown bone not jigged. Case first used this material in 1979.

**Bone Stag**-importation is stopped from time to time due to outbreaks of Hoof and Mouth disease in South America where most of the bone comes from. The material comes from a cow's shin bone, and at one-time, almost every knife manufacturer used bone to handle its knives. Today, in the U.S. only Case handles its knives in bone stag, but it is becoming harder to get. Although the company uses bone as it is available, shortages sometimes force the company to use Delrin, a plastic imitation of bone stag. It would be safe to predict that in a few years bone stag will be discontinued.

**Delrin**-is a chemical process made handle material first used in 1967. It looks much like genuine bone. The way to distinguish between bone and Delrin handles is to look closely at the handles under a strong magnifying glass. With a glass it is possible to see tiny blood channels and pores in genuine bone stag, while Delrin will have no pores. Too, there is usually a bit of discoloration on the edges of bone handles. Since 1974, the shield of a genuine bone stag handled knife will have a circle around the CASE on the shield, while a Delrin or laminated wood handle will not have a circle. Prior to 1974, all shields had the circle around the CASE.

*Green Bone*-is bone stag with a deep green or brownish green tint. It is quite common on Tested knives, and is found on the older XX knives. It was used between 1940 and 1955. It is fast becoming one of the most collectible hand materials.

*High Art*-is a handle material similar to the handle made famous by Canton Cutlery Company. It features a photo under a transparent plastic cover. It is found on the extremely old Case knives and a 1980 commemorative, the HA199½.

*Red Bone*-in its true form is found only on XX or Tested knives. It was probably caused by a certain dye Case was using at the time. A true redbone should have the front handle the same tint as the back handle. Knives that have been displayed on dealer's boards in the sun sometimes fade to a red color, but this is usually a dull finish and will not match the back handle. This isn't a true redbone. Many USA's and Dot knives have beautiful red handles that would be redbone if they were a XX. They bring from $3 to $5 more than the price of regular bone in the same pattern.

*Rough Black*-was used as a substitute for bone stag during and following World War II. It has a rubber-like base and is called Plastag by W. R. Case & Sons. The design has no set pattern of jigging as most handles do.

*Smooth Rose*-is a red bone handle that is not jigged. Case introduced it on their knives in 1979.

## THE SECOND DIGIT

The second digit of the Case pattern numbers tells the number of blades. W. R. Case & Sons made a few patterns with five blades in the Tested XX and Bradford days, but since that time has only made 1, 2, 3, and 4 bladed knives.

## THE REMAINING DIGITS IN THE CASE PATTERN NUMBERS

The remaining digits of a Case pattern number denote the factory pattern number. An "O" denoted a variation from an existing pattern. For example, 06247 is a variation of the 6347, only it has two blades.

On a few knives, the handle material and blade numbers are omitted, leaving only the factory pattern number. Example: 6225½ will be stamped 25½.

## BLADE ABBREVIATIONS

After many pattern numbers there are abbreviations for the various blades or a description of the knife. They are:

**DR-** Drilled through bolster for lanyard
**EO-** Easy Open
**F-** File blade
**I-** Iron liners
**L-** Blade locks open
**½-** Clip master blade
**P-** Punch blade
**PEN-** Pen blade
**R-** Bail in handle
**RAZ-** One arm man blade or razor blade
**SAB-** Saber ground master blade
**SH-** Sheepfoot blade
**SHAD OR S-** No bolsters (shadow)
**SICS OR SC-** Scissors
**SP-** Spray blade
**SS-** Stainless steel blades and springs
**SSP-** Stainless steel blade and springs, polished edge or blade
**T-** Tip bolsters
**¾-** Saber ground like a dagger

**NOTE-** *These abbreviations are sometimes abbreviated further. For example H will sometimes denote SH and E will sometimes denote PEN.*

## STAMPINGS ON CASE KNIVES

W. R. Case & Sons have used a variety of stampings, some of which are illustrated below with the dates they were used. The Case XX stamping was used from 1940-65 with pattern numbers added to the reverse side of the tang in 1949, and in 1965 the company began stamping their knives "Case XX U. S. A." At the time there were rumors that the Case XX was made in Germany. Case did have some file blades made in Germany and the blades were stamped on them, but these were the only ones. In 1970 the logo was again changed, this time to Case XX U. S. A. with 10 dots under the logo. Each year after that, a dot is removed. A 1975 knife will have five dots and a 1979 knife will have one dot, and in 1980 the stamping will be changed again. At each of these logo changes there were large numbers of collectors that bought store displays of the old logo knives. Some can still be found at knife shows, etc., intact as they were bought, but individual knives that have been on those boards usually fade on one side and do not bring as much as knives of the same stamping that were not on a board.

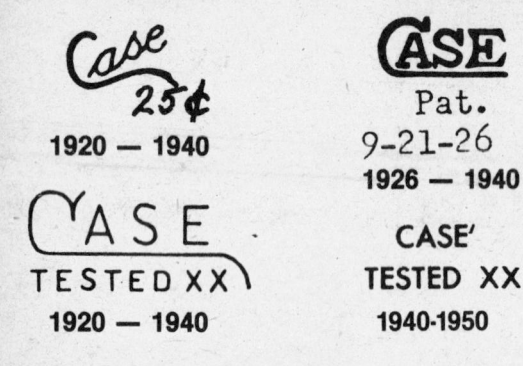

*Case*
25¢
**1920 — 1940**

**CASE**
Pat.
9-21-26
**1926 — 1940**

**CASE**
TESTED XX
**1920 — 1940**

CASE'
TESTED XX
**1940-1950**

CASE / 39

| | |
|---|---|
| CASE XX<br>STAINLESS<br><br>1940 — 1965 | CASE XX<br>METAL STAMPINGS<br>L.T.D.<br>1942 — 1945 |
| CASE XX<br><br>1940 — 1965 | CASE'S<br>TESTED XX<br>1940 — 1950 |
| **CASE**<br>XX<br>1920 — 1940 | CASE<br>XX<br>1940-1965 |
| **CASE**<br>TESTED XX<br>1920 — 1940 | CASE XX<br>U.S.A.<br>1965 — 1970 |

CASE XX
STAINLESS
U.S.A.
1965 — 1970

CASE XX
STAINLESS
U.S.A.
••••••••••
1970

CASE XX
U.S.A.
••••••••••
1970

## CASE SHIELDS

Exact dates of use for the various shields on Case Pocket knives are unknown. Exhaustive research has provided approximate dates for the specimens shown below.

Shield #CS3 was predominantly used from about 1942 to 1974. Case designed shield #CS2 to be used on all pocket knives handled in Derlin and Laminated Wood, because some beginning collectors were having some difficulty in identifying Bone Stag from the handle material mentioned above, especially Derlin. The difference between the two shields is the circle immediately surrounding the word CASE has been deleted.

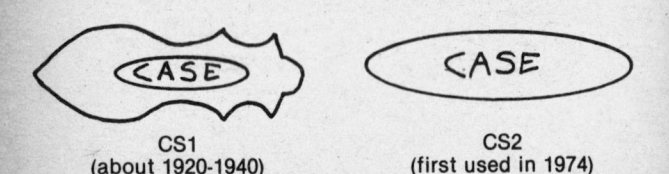

CS1
(about 1920-1940)

CS2
(first used in 1974)

CASE / 41

*CS3
(first used about 1935)

CS7
(about 1910-1940)

CS4
(about 1903-1940)

CS8
(about 1920-1940)

CS5
(about 1900-1940)

CS9
(about 1935-1941)

CS6
(about 1903-1920)

CS9A
(about 1905-1950)

CS9B
(about 1910-1930)

## 42 / OLDER CASE
## CASE CLUB KNIVES

In the past 3-4 years Case has made several Club Knives for various Knife Clubs around the country. These are usually limited production of 50 to 500 pieces that has a special Electroetch or photo etch on one of their standard patterns. Due to the fact that the price of these knives vary so much from locality to locality and due to the fact that there are so many, we have decided not to try to list all of them in a collectors guide such as this.

We will add that usually W. R. Case Company charges $5.00 to $10.00 extra per knife for this custom etching or a different color handle so the knives would be considered more valuable than the standard pattern.

We do strive to list all knives in this guide that has been produced for a national audience.

A number of 6207SPSSP, 6254 and 6254SSP with a variety of dots contain serrated spey blades. This will add $4 to $10 value to the knife.

## OLDER CASE KNIVES

Older Case knives are so termed to include any Case marked knife prior to 1920. This includes several stampings including Case Brothers and W. R. Case stampings — even though they were two different companies at the time. Many of their patterns are so similar that there is nearly no price difference between the two stampings.

Prices in this section are for mint condition. You will probably find less than a dozen mint ones in a lifetime, however the used ones can be found, but the prices should not be confused as prices for a used knife. Used knives are worth much less.

There are too much variety to actually list and illustrate each of these knives, especially when the small quantity encountered by the coutelist.

Knives marked "Case Brothers, Springville, N.Y." will bring 50% higher than these prices. Knives marked "Case Brothers, Little Valley, N.Y." will bring about 25% higher.

## OLDER CASE / 43

| PATTERN NO. | MINT | VG |
|---|---|---|
| ☐ 6100 | 550.00 | 275.00 |
| ☐ P200 | 400.00 | 200.00 |
| ☐ 5200 | 450.00 | 225.00 |
| ☐ 6200 | 550.00 | 275.00 |
| ☐ 9200 | 450.00 | 225.00 |
| ☐ 2201 | 85.00 | 43.00 |
| ☐ 3201 | 85.00 | 43.00 |
| ☐ 3201 R | 85.00 | 43.00 |
| ☐ 6201 | 110.00 | 55.00 |
| ☐ 62001 | 110.00 | 55.00 |
| ☐ 8201 | 130.00 | 65.00 |
| ☐ 82001 | 130.00 | 65.00 |
| ☐ 9201 | 85.00 | 43.00 |
| ☐ 9201 R | 85.00 | 43.00 |
| ☐ P202 | 135.00 | 66.00 |
| ☐ R202 | 135.00 | 66.00 |
| ☐ 1202 D&B | 400.00 | 200.00 |
| ☐ 5202 RAZ | 325.00 | 165.00 |
| ☐ 5202½ | 225.00 | 112.00 |
| ☐ 6202 | 250.00 | 125.00 |
| ☐ 6202 I | 250.00 | 125.00 |
| ☐ 6202 S | 250.00 | 125.00 |
| ☐ 6202½ | 200.00 | 100.00 |
| ☐ 6202½ | 200.00 | 100.00 |
| ☐ B3102 | 125.00 | 62.00 |
| ☐ 63102 | 175.00 | 88.00 |
| ☐ 83102 | 190.00 | 95.00 |
| ☐ 6103 B&G | 100.00 | 50.00 |
| ☐ 6203 | 100.00 | 50.00 |
| ☐ 2104 | 100.00 | 50.00 |
| ☐ 6104 BUD | 190.00 | 95.00 |
| ☐ M204 | 80.00 | 40.00 |
| ☐ 6204½ | 190.00 | 95.00 |
| ☐ 5205 | 300.00 | 150.00 |
| ☐ 5205 RAZ | 300.00 | 150.00 |
| ☐ 5205½ | 300.00 | 150.00 |
| ☐ 6205 | 300.00 | 150.00 |
| ☐ 6205 RAZ | 300.00 | 150.00 |
| ☐ 6205½ | 250.00 | 125.00 |
| ☐ 6106 | 150.00 | 75.00 |
| ☐ 6106 25¢ KNIFE | 200.00 | 100.00 |
| ☐ 5206½ | 150.00 | 75.00 |
| ☐ 6206 | 150.00 | 75.00 |

## 44 / OLDER CASE

| PATTERN NO. | MINT | VG |
|---|---|---|
| ☐ 6206½ | 150.00 | 75.00 |
| ☐ 62006½ | 150.00 | 75.00 |
| ☐ 7206 | 150.00 | 75.00 |
| ☐ 62006½ | 125.00 | 63.00 |
| ☐ 8206 | 200.00 | 100.00 |
| ☐ 3207 | 190.00 | 95.00 |
| ☐ 5207 | 275.00 | 137.00 |
| ☐ 6207 | 275.00 | 137.00 |
| ☐ 8407 | 400.00 | 200.00 |
| ☐ 5208 | 175.00 | 88.00 |
| ☐ 6208 | 150.00 | 75.00 |
| ☐ 3308 | 200.00 | 100.00 |
| ☐ 5308 | 250.00 | 125.00 |
| ☐ 6308 | 225.00 | 113.00 |
| ☐ 8308 | 300.00 | 150.00 |
| ☐ 6209 | 150.00 | 75.00 |
| ☐ 62009 | 150.00 | 75.00 |
| ☐ 62009 RAZ | 225.00 | 113.00 |
| ☐ 62009 SH | 150.00 | 75.00 |
| ☐ 62009 SP | 150.00 | 75.00 |
| ☐ 62009½ | 150.00 | 75.00 |
| ☐ B-3109 W Christmas Tree | 400.00 | 200.00 |
| ☐ 63109 | 350.00 | 175.00 |
| ☐ 83109 | 425.00 | 213.00 |
| ☐ 3210½ | 150.00 | 75.00 |
| ☐ 5210½ | 175.00 | 88.00 |
| ☐ 6210 | 165.00 | 83.00 |
| ☐ 6210 S | 180.00 | 90.00 |
| ☐ 62010 | 165.00 | 83.00 |
| ☐ 6210½ | 165.00 | 83.00 |
| ☐ B1011 | 85.00 | 43.00 |
| ☐ R111½ | 450.00 | 48.00 |
| ☐ 11011 | 95.00 | 48.00 |
| ☐ 3111½ | 400.00 | 200.00 |
| ☐ 6111½ | 500.00 | 250.00 |
| ☐ 6111½ L | 600.00 | 300.00 |
| ☐ 61011 | 95.00 | 48.00 |
| ☐ 6211 | 500.00 | 250.00 |
| ☐ 6211½ | 500.00 | 250.00 |
| ☐ 1212L | 100.00 | 50.00 |
| ☐ 62012 | 95.00 | 48.00 |
| ☐ 61013 | 100.00 | 50.00 |
| ☐ 6213 | 250.00 | 125.00 |

## OLDER CASE / 45

| PATTERN NO. | MINT | VG |
|---|---|---|
| ☐ 6213 | 300.00 | 175.00 |
| ☐ 5214½ | 150.00 | 75.00 |
| ☐ 6214 | 125.00 | 63.00 |
| ☐ 6214½ | 125.00 | 63.00 |
| ☐ P215 | 115.00 | 58.00 |
| ☐ 6215 | 115.00 | 58.00 |
| ☐ 8215 | 150.00 | 75.00 |
| ☐ 6116 | 100.00 | 50.00 |
| ☐ 6116½ | 100.00 | 50.00 |
| ☐ 61016½ | 100.00 | 50.00 |
| ☐ 22016 | 95.00 | 48.00 |
| ☐ 22016½ | 95.00 | 48.00 |
| ☐ 6216 | 115.00 | 58.00 |
| ☐ 6216 I | 115.00 | 58.00 |
| ☐ 6216 S | 115.00 | 58.00 |
| ☐ 6216 EO | 150.00 | 75.00 |
| ☐ 62016 | 110.00 | 55.00 |
| ☐ 62016½ | 115.00 | 58.00 |
| ☐ 62016 S | 115.00 | 58.00 |
| ☐ 6216½ | 115.00 | 58.00 |
| ☐ 6216½ I | 115.00 | 58.00 |
| ☐ 62116 | 80.00 | 40.00 |
| ☐ 2217 | 175.00 | 88.00 |
| ☐ 6217 | 200.00 | 100.00 |
| ☐ B318 SH SP | 175.00 | 88.00 |
| ☐ 3318 SH SP | 150.00 | 75.00 |
| ☐ 3318 SH PEN | 150.00 | 75.00 |
| ☐ 5318 SH SP | 200.00 | 100.00 |
| ☐ 6318 SH SP | 200.00 | 100.00 |
| ☐ 6318 SH P | 200.00 | 100.00 |
| ☐ 6318 SH PEN | 200.00 | 100.00 |
| ☐ 8318 SH SP | 250.00 | 126.00 |
| ☐ 5318 SH SP | 200.00 | 100.00 |
| ☐ 9318 SP PEN | 175.00 | 88.00 |
| ☐ 6219 | 200.00 | 100.00 |
| ☐ 62019 | 210.00 | 105.00 |
| ☐ Y220 | 175.00 | 88.00 |
| ☐ 3220 | 175.00 | 88.00 |
| ☐ 5220 | 250.00 | 126.00 |
| ☐ 6220 | 200.00 | 100.00 |
| ☐ 62020 | 150.00 | 75.00 |
| ☐ 62020 S | 150.00 | 75.00 |
| ☐ 62020½ | 150.00 | 75.00 |

## 46 / OLDER CASE

| PATTERN NO. | MINT | VG |
|---|---|---|
| ☐ 8220 | 350.00 | 175.00 |
| ☐ 9220 | 175.00 | 88.00 |
| ☐ B221 | 150.00 | 75.00 |
| ☐ OB221 | 175.00 | 88.00 |
| ☐ 6221 | 150.00 | 75.00 |
| ☐ 06221 | 130.00 | 65.00 |
| ☐ 06221½ | 130.00 | 65.00 |
| ☐ 08221 | 200.00 | 100.00 |
| ☐ 6321 | 175.00 | 88.00 |
| ☐ G222 | 140.00 | 120.00 |
| ☐ 6222 | 140.00 | 120.00 |
| ☐ 8222 | 110.00 | 55.00 |
| ☐ P223 | 125.00 | 63.00 |
| ☐ 6223 | 125.00 | 63.00 |
| ☐ 9223 | 125.00 | 63.00 |
| ☐ 3124 | 80.00 | 40.00 |
| ☐ 3124½ | 80.00 | 40.00 |
| ☐ 6124 | 80.00 | 40.00 |
| ☐ 6124½ | 80.00 | 40.00 |
| ☐ B224 | 125.00 | 63.00 |
| ☐ 3224 | 90.00 | 45.00 |
| ☐ 63224½ | 90.00 | 45.00 |
| ☐ 5224 | 150.00 | 75.00 |
| ☐ 52024 | 150.00 | 75.00 |
| ☐ 5224½ | 150.00 | 75.00 |
| ☐ 52024½ | 150.00 | 75.00 |
| ☐ 6224 | 85.00 | 43.00 |
| ☐ 62024 | 110.00 | 55.00 |
| ☐ 62024 RAZ | 125.00 | 63.00 |
| ☐ 62024 SH | 125.00 | 63.00 |
| ☐ 62024½ | 125.00 | 55.00 |
| ☐ 8224 | 200.00 | 100.00 |
| ☐ 32025½ | 150.00 | 75.00 |
| ☐ 5225½ | 225.00 | 113.00 |
| ☐ 6225 | 200.00 | 100.00 |
| ☐ 6225½ | 200.00 | 100.00 |
| ☐ 62025½ | 175.00 | 88.00 |
| ☐ 8225 | 300.00 | 150.00 |
| ☐ B226 | 150.00 | 75.00 |
| ☐ 6226 | 150.00 | 75.00 |
| ☐ 62026 | 100.00 | 50.00 |
| ☐ 6226½ | 135.00 | 68.00 |
| ☐ 82026 | 125.00 | 63.00 |

## OLDER CASE / 47

| PATTERN NO. | MINT | VG |
|---|---|---|
| ☐ 62027 | 100.00 | 50.00 |
| ☐ 62027½ | 100.00 | 50.00 |
| ☐ 82027 | 150.00 | 75.00 |
| ☐ 92027 | 90.00 | 45.00 |
| ☐ 92027½ | 90.00 | 45.00 |
| ☐ P228 EO | 175.00 | 88.00 |
| ☐ 2228 | 150.00 | 75.00 |
| ☐ 2228 EO | 160.00 | 80.00 |
| ☐ 2228 P | 150.00 | 75.00 |
| ☐ 6228 | 175.00 | 88.00 |
| ☐ 6228 EO | 225.00 | 113.00 |
| ☐ 6228 P | 150.00 | 75.00 |
| ☐ 62028 | 150.00 | 75.00 |
| ☐ 82028 | 225.00 | 113.00 |
| ☐ 6229½ | 110.00 | 55.00 |
| ☐ 9229½ | 110.00 | 55.00 |
| ☐ P0230 | 115.00 | 58.00 |
| ☐ 02230 | 100.00 | 50.00 |
| ☐ 02230½ | 100.00 | 50.00 |
| ☐ 05230½ | 190.00 | 95.00 |
| ☐ 06230 | 175.00 | 88.00 |
| ☐ 06230½ | 175.00 | 88.00 |
| ☐ 09230 | 150.00 | 75.00 |
| ☐ 09230½ | 150.00 | 75.00 |
| ☐ 6230 SH | 175.00 | 88.00 |
| ☐ 1131 SH | 80.00 | 40.00 |
| ☐ 2231 | 125.00 | 63.00 |
| ☐ 22031 | 125.00 | 63.00 |
| ☐ 2231 | 125.00 | 63.00 |
| ☐ 2231½ SAB | 125.00 | 63.00 |
| ☐ 22031½ | 125.00 | 63.00 |
| ☐ 52031 | 190.00 | 95.00 |
| ☐ 52031½ | 190.00 | 95.00 |
| ☐ 52131 | 450.00 | 225.00 |
| ☐ 6231 | 150.00 | 75.00 |
| ☐ 62031 | 150.00 | 75.00 |
| ☐ 6231½ | 150.00 | 75.00 |
| ☐ 62031½ | 150.00 | 75.00 |
| ☐ 53131 | 1000.00 | 500.00 |
| ☐ 53131 PUNCH | 1000.00 | 500.00 |
| ☐ G232 | 200.00 | 100.00 |
| ☐ 3232 | 125.00 | 63.00 |
| ☐ 6232 | 150.00 | 75.00 |

## 48 / OLDER CASE

| PATTERN NO. | MINT | VG |
|---|---|---|
| ☐ 5332 | 175.00 | 88.00 |
| ☐ 6332 | 175.00 | 88.00 |
| ☐ 3233 | 90.00 | 45.00 |
| ☐ 6233 | 125.00 | 63.00 |
| ☐ 62033 | 125.00 | 63.00 |
| ☐ 8233 | 150.00 | 75.00 |
| ☐ 9233 | 90.00 | 45.00 |
| ☐ 6333 | 140.00 | 120.00 |
| ☐ 9333 | 90.00 | 45.00 |
| ☐ 5234 | 300.00 | 150.00 |
| ☐ G2035 | 200.00 | 100.00 |
| ☐ 5235½ | 110.00 | 55.00 |
| ☐ 5235½ | 175.00 | 88.00 |
| ☐ 6235 | 110.00 | 55.00 |
| ☐ 6235 EO | 140.00 | 70.00 |
| ☐ 62035 | 120.00 | 60.00 |
| ☐ 6235½ | 110.00 | 55.00 |
| ☐ 62035½ | 120.00 | 60.00 |
| ☐ 2237 | 165.00 | 83.00 |
| ☐ 2237½ | 165.00 | 83.00 |
| ☐ 6237 | 185.00 | 93.00 |
| ☐ 6237½ | 185.00 | 93.00 |
| ☐ 5238 | 150.00 | 75.00 |
| ☐ 5438 | 250.00 | 125.00 |
| ☐ 8438 | 300.00 | 150.00 |
| ☐ 1139 | 150.00 | 75.00 |
| ☐ B239 | 225.00 | 113.00 |
| ☐ G2039 | 250.00 | 125.00 |
| ☐ 6239 | 160.00 | 75.00 |
| ☐ B339 | 250.00 | 125.00 |
| ☐ G3039 | 250.00 | 125.00 |
| ☐ 6339 | 275.00 | 138.00 |
| ☐ 63039 | 225.00 | 113.00 |
| ☐ 6539 | 2000.00 | 1000.00 |
| ☐ 11040 | 95.00 | 48.00 |
| ☐ 3240 SP | 350.00 | 175.00 |
| ☐ 6240 | 450.00 | 225.00 |
| ☐ 6240 SP | 450.00 | 225.00 |
| ☐ 6241 | 95.00 | 48.00 |
| ☐ G242 | 120.00 | 60.00 |
| ☐ 52042 | 125.00 | 63.00 |
| ☐ 6242 | 125.00 | 63.00 |
| ☐ 62042 | 80.00 | 40.00 |

*OLDER CASE / 49*

| PATTERN NO. | MINT | VG |
|---|---|---|
| ☐ 82042 | 120.00 | 60.00 |
| ☐ 92042 | 80.00 | 40.00 |
| ☐ 63042 | 150.00 | 75.00 |
| ☐ 83042 | 225.00 | 113.00 |
| ☐ 6143 | 175.00 | 88.00 |
| ☐ 5343 | 200.00 | 100.00 |
| ☐ B224 | 140.00 | 120.00 |
| ☐ 3244 | 120.00 | 60.00 |
| ☐ 5224 | 150.00 | 75.00 |
| ☐ 05244 | 150.00 | 75.00 |
| ☐ 6224 | 125.00 | 63.00 |
| ☐ 06244 | 90.00 | 45.00 |
| ☐ 62044 | 95.00 | 48.00 |
| ☐ 62044 FILE | 95.00 | 48.00 |
| ☐ 8244 | 150.00 | 75.00 |
| ☐ 82044 | 150.00 | 75.00 |
| ☐ 72044 FILE | 150.00 | 75.00 |
| ☐ 08244 | 125.00 | 63.00 |
| ☐ 9244 | 100.00 | 50.00 |
| ☐ B334 SH SP | 135.00 | 68.00 |
| ☐ 3344 SH SP | 115.00 | 58.00 |
| ☐ 5344 SH SP | 225.00 | 113.00 |
| ☐ 6344 SH SP | 150.00 | 75.00 |
| ☐ 6344 SH PEN | 150.00 | 75.00 |
| ☐ 8344 | 250.00 | 125.00 |
| ☐ 9344 SH PEN | 110.00 | 55.00 |
| ☐ 02245 | 95.00 | 48.00 |
| ☐ 02245 ½ | 95.00 | 48.00 |
| ☐ 04245 B&G | 180.00 | 90.00 |
| ☐ 05245 | 200.00 | 100.00 |
| ☐ 05245 ½ | 200.00 | 100.00 |
| ☐ 06245 | 160.00 | 80.00 |
| ☐ 06245 ½ | 160.00 | 80.00 |
| ☐ 2345 ½ | 125.00 | 63.00 |
| ☐ 5345 | 210.00 | 105.00 |
| ☐ 5345 P | 210.00 | 105.00 |
| ☐ 5345 ½ | 210.00 | 105.00 |
| ☐ 6345 | 190.00 | 95.00 |
| ☐ 6345 P | 190.00 | 95.00 |
| ☐ 6345 ½ | 190.00 | 95.00 |
| ☐ 6345 ½ P | 190.00 | 95.00 |
| ☐ 6345 ½ SH | 190.00 | 95.00 |
| ☐ B445 R | 115.00 | 58.00 |

## 50 / OLDER CASE

| PATTERN NO. | MINT | VG |
|---|---|---|
| ☐ 6445 R | 150.00 | 75.00 |
| ☐ 640045 R | 75.00 | 38.00 |
| ☐ G2046 | 140.00 | 70.00 |
| ☐ 3246 | 135.00 | 68.00 |
| ☐ 6246 | 140.00 | 70.00 |
| ☐ 62046 | 120.00 | 60.00 |
| ☐ B346 P | 130.00 | 65.00 |
| ☐ G3046 | 110.00 | 55.00 |
| ☐ 6346 | 130.00 | 65.00 |
| ☐ 63046 | 110.00 | 55.00 |
| ☐ 04247 SP | 110.00 | 55.00 |
| ☐ 5247 J | 500.00 | 250.00 |
| ☐ 05247 SP | 150.00 | 75.00 |
| ☐ 6247 J | 450.00 | 225.00 |
| ☐ 06247 | 110.00 | 55.00 |
| ☐ 06247 PEN | 100.00 | 50.00 |
| ☐ 06247 SP | 100.00 | 50.00 |
| ☐ B3047 | 225.00 | 113.00 |
| ☐ P347 SH SP | 225.00 | 113.00 |
| ☐ 3347 SH SP | 175.00 | 88.00 |
| ☐ 3347 SP PEN | 175.00 | 88.00 |
| ☐ 43047 | 190.00 | 95.00 |
| ☐ 5347 SH PEN | 250.00 | 125.00 |
| ☐ 53047 | 250.00 | 125.00 |
| ☐ 6347 SH PEN | 200.00 | 100.00 |
| ☐ 6347 SH P | 200.00 | 100.00 |
| ☐ 6347 P PEN | 200.00 | 100.00 |
| ☐ 6347 PJ | 400.00 | 200.00 |
| ☐ 6347 SH SP | 200.00 | 100.00 |
| ☐ 63047 | 200.00 | 100.00 |
| ☐ 630047 | 200.00 | 100.00 |
| ☐ 630047 P | 200.00 | 100.00 |
| ☐ 8347 SH SP | 300.00 | 150.00 |
| ☐ 83047 | 325.00 | 163.00 |
| ☐ 9347 SH SP | 200.00 | 100.00 |
| ☐ 9347 PJ | 400.00 | 200.00 |
| ☐ 93047 | 210.00 | 105.00 |
| ☐ 5447 SH SP | 300.00 | 150.00 |
| ☐ 5447 SP P | 300.00 | 150.00 |
| ☐ 64047 P | 300.00 | 150.00 |
| ☐ 94047 P | 300.00 | 150.00 |
| ☐ B1048 | 175.00 | 88.00 |
| ☐ G1048 | 175.00 | 88.00 |

## OLDER CASE / 51

| PATTERN NO. | MINT | VG |
|---|---|---|
| ☐ R1048 | 190.00 | 95.00 |
| ☐ 61048 | 110.00 | 55.00 |
| ☐ B2048 | 200.00 | 100.00 |
| ☐ B2048 SP | 200.00 | 100.00 |
| ☐ G2048 | 200.00 | 100.00 |
| ☐ G2048 S | 200.00 | 100.00 |
| ☐ R2048 | 215.00 | 108.00 |
| ☐ R2048 S | 200.00 | 100.00 |
| ☐ 62048 | 150.00 | 75.00 |
| ☐ 62048 SP | 125.00 | 63.00 |
| ☐ R1049 L | 250.00 | 125.00 |
| ☐ 61049 | 175.00 | 88.00 |
| ☐ 61049 L | 250.00 | 125.00 |
| ☐ B249 | 150.00 | 75.00 |
| ☐ R2049 | 200.00 | 100.00 |
| ☐ 6249 | 200.00 | 100.00 |
| ☐ 62049 | 200.00 | 100.00 |
| ☐ B10050 | 600.00 | 300.00 |
| ☐ CB1050 SAB | 600.00 | 300.00 |
| ☐ C31050 SAB | 500.00 | 250.00 |
| ☐ 310050 | 500.00 | 250.00 |
| ☐ C51050 SAB | 800.00 | 400.00 |
| ☐ 610050 | 600.00 | 300.00 |
| ☐ 61050 | 700.00 | 350.00 |
| ☐ C61050 | 700.00 | 350.00 |
| ☐ C61050 SAB | 700.00 | 350.00 |
| ☐ C61050 L | 1500.00 | 750.00 |
| ☐ C91050 SAB | 600.00 | 300.00 |
| ☐ 6250 | 450.00 | 225.00 |
| ☐ 8250 | 600.00 | 300.00 |
| ☐ B1051 | 200.00 | 100.00 |
| ☐ G1051 | 200.00 | 100.00 |
| ☐ R1051 | 200.00 | 100.00 |
| ☐ R1051 L | 300.00 | 150.00 |
| ☐ 6151 | 500.00 | 250.00 |
| ☐ 6151 L | 550.00 | 275.00 |
| ☐ 61051 | 225.00 | 113.00 |
| ☐ 61051 L | 300.00 | 150.00 |
| ☐ 81051 | 325.00 | 163.00 |
| ☐ 9151 | 500.00 | 250.00 |
| ☐ 6251 | 500.00 | 250.00 |
| ☐ P2052 | 100.00 | 50.00 |
| ☐ 3252 | 240.00 | 120.00 |

## 52 / OLDER CASE

| PATTERN NO. | MINT | VG |
|---|---|---|
| ☐ 32052 | 100.00 | 50.00 |
| ☐ 52052 | 140.00 | 120.00 |
| ☐ 6252 | 250.00 | 125.00 |
| ☐ 62052 | 125.00 | 63.00 |
| ☐ 63052 | 275.00 | 138.00 |
| ☐ 3452 | 280.00 | 140.00 |
| ☐ 54052 | 300.00 | 150.00 |
| ☐ 6452 | 285.00 | 143.00 |
| ☐ 64052 | 250.00 | 125.00 |
| ☐ HA253 | 135.00 | 68.00 |
| ☐ 5253 | 125.00 | 63.00 |
| ☐ 6253 | 115.00 | 58.00 |
| ☐ 62053 | 80.00 | 40.00 |
| ☐ 8253 | 150.00 | 75.00 |
| ☐ 82053 | 100.00 | 50.00 |
| ☐ 82053 SR | 100.00 | 50.00 |
| ☐ 9253 | 80.00 | 40.00 |
| ☐ 6353 | 150.00 | 75.00 |
| ☐ 6353 P | 150.00 | 75.00 |
| ☐ P254 | 1000.00 | 500.00 |
| ☐ 3254 | 1000.00 | 500.00 |
| ☐ 5254 | 1500.00 | 750.00 |
| ☐ 6254 | 1200.00 | 600.00 |
| ☐ 8254 | 2000.00 | 1000.00 |
| ☐ 9254 | 1000.00 | 500.00 |
| ☐ 22055 | 90.00 | 45.00 |
| ☐ 32055 | 100.00 | 50.00 |
| ☐ 62055 | 130.00 | 65.00 |
| ☐ 82055 | 190.00 | 95.00 |
| ☐ 92055 | 125.00 | 63.00 |
| ☐ 64055 P | 425.00 | 225.00 |
| ☐ 62056 | 110.00 | 55.00 |
| ☐ 82056 | 150.00 | 75.00 |
| ☐ 63056 | 175.00 | 88.00 |
| ☐ 83056 | 225.00 | 113.00 |
| ☐ 4257 | 80.00 | 40.00 |
| ☐ 42057 | 75.00 | 38.00 |
| ☐ 8257 | 125.00 | 63.00 |
| ☐ 92057 | 75.00 | 38.00 |
| ☐ 32058 | 75.00 | 38.00 |
| ☐ 6258 | 100.00 | 50.00 |
| ☐ 8258 | 130.00 | 65.00 |
| ☐ 92058 | 90.00 | 45.00 |

## OLDER CASE / 53

| PATTERN NO. | MINT | VG |
|---|---|---|
| ☐ 8358 | 150.00 | 75.00 |
| ☐ P259 | 100.00 | 50.00 |
| ☐ 62059 | 75.00 | 38.00 |
| ☐ 62059 SP | 80.00 | 40.00 |
| ☐ 8259 | 125.00 | 63.00 |
| ☐ 5260 | 250.00 | 125.00 |
| ☐ 8260 | 250.00 | 125.00 |
| ☐ 8360 SCI | 200.00 | 100.00 |
| ☐ 5460 | 300.00 | 150.00 |
| ☐ 8460 | 350.00 | 175.00 |
| ☐ 5161 L | 800.00 | 400.00 |
| ☐ 6161 L | 800.00 | 400.00 |
| ☐ 82062 K | 150.00 | 75.00 |
| ☐ 83062 K | 200.00 | 100.00 |
| ☐ 84062 K | 275.00 | 138.00 |
| ☐ 94062 | 200.00 | 100.00 |
| ☐ B2063 | 150.00 | 75.00 |
| ☐ P263 | 115.00 | 58.00 |
| ☐ 05263 | 110.00 | 55.00 |
| ☐ 62063 | 85.00 | 43.00 |
| ☐ 06263 | 85.00 | 43.00 |
| ☐ 61063½ | 85.00 | 43.00 |
| ☐ 82063 | 100.00 | 50.00 |
| ☐ 08263 | 120.00 | 60.00 |
| ☐ 82063½ | 120.00 | 60.00 |
| ☐ 92063½ | 90.00 | 45.00 |
| ☐ B3063 | 110.00 | 55.00 |
| ☐ 63063 | 120.00 | 60.00 |
| ☐ 83063 | 150.00 | 75.00 |
| ☐ 6264 | 100.00 | 50.00 |
| ☐ 6264 FILE | 100.00 | 50.00 |
| ☐ 62064 | 100.00 | 50.00 |
| ☐ 8264 T | 130.00 | 65.00 |
| ☐ 8264 T FILE | 130.00 | 65.00 |
| ☐ 82064 | 110.00 | 55.00 |
| ☐ 9264 T FILE | 110.00 | 55.00 |
| ☐ B165 | 450.00 | 225.00 |
| ☐ 3165 SAB* | 325.00 | 163.00 |
| ☐ 5165 SAB* | 500.00 | 250.00 |
| ☐ 6165 SAB* | 450.00 | 225.00 |
| ☐ 8165 | 1200.00 | 600.00 |
| ☐ 9165 SAB | 350.00 | 175.00 |
| ☐ G265 | 350.00 | 175.00 |

## 54 / OLDER CASE

| PATTERN NO. | MINT | VG |
|---|---|---|
| ☐ 3265 SAB | 300.00 | 150.00 |
| ☐ 5265 SAB* | 500.00 | 250.00 |
| ☐ 6265 SAB | 450.00 | 225.00 |
| ☐ 8265 | 1200.00 | 600.00 |
| ☐ 9265 SAB | 400.00 | 200.00 |
| ☐ 6366 | 150.00 | 75.00 |
| ☐ 6366 PEN | 150.00 | 75.00 |
| ☐ 8366 PEN | 225.00 | 113.00 |
| ☐ 62067 | 80.00 | 40.00 |
| ☐ 06267 | 90.00 | 45.00 |
| ☐ 82067 | 120.00 | 60.00 |
| ☐ 08267 | 120.00 | 60.00 |
| ☐ B3067 | 140.00 | 70.00 |
| ☐ 6367 | 175.00 | 88.00 |
| ☐ 63067 | 150.00 | 75.00 |
| ☐ 8367 | 200.00 | 100.00 |
| ☐ 83067 | 200.00 | 100.00 |
| ☐ 9367 | 130.00 | 65.00 |
| ☐ 6268 | 100.00 | 50.00 |
| ☐ 8268 | 150.00 | 75.00 |
| ☐ 6368 | 200.00 | 100.00 |
| ☐ 8368 | 280.00 | 140.00 |
| ☐ G2069 | 110.00 | 55.00 |
| ☐ 6269 | 95.00 | 48.00 |
| ☐ 8269 | 130.00 | 65.00 |
| ☐ 9269 | 100.00 | 50.00 |
| ☐ 6369 | 175.00 | 88.00 |
| ☐ 8369 | 300.00 | 150.00 |
| ☐ 6370 FILE | 275.00 | 138.00 |
| ☐ 8370 FILE | 300.00 | 150.00 |
| ☐ 6470 FILE | 250.00 | 125.00 |
| ☐ 5171 L | 1000.00 | 500.00 |
| ☐ 8271 | 190.00 | 95.00 |
| ☐ 8371 | 375.00 | 188.00 |
| ☐ 6172 | 1000.00 | 500.00 |
| ☐ 22074½ P | 200.00 | 100.00 |
| ☐ 62074½ | 225.00 | 113.00 |
| ☐ 62074½ | 225.00 | 113.00 |
| ☐ B3074 | 275.00 | 138.00 |
| ☐ B3074½ | 275.00 | 138.00 |
| ☐ B3074½ P | 275.00 | 138.00 |
| ☐ 5374 | 300.00 | 150.00 |
| ☐ 63074 | 250.00 | 125.00 |

*OLDER CASE / 55*

| PATTERN NO. | MINT | VG |
| --- | --- | --- |
| ☐ 63074½ | 250.00 | 125.00 |
| ☐ 63074½ P | 250.00 | 125.00 |
| ☐ 83074 | 300.00 | 150.00 |
| ☐ 5275 SP | 300.00 | 150.00 |
| ☐ 6275 SP | 275.00 | 138.00 |
| ☐ 06275½ | 300.00 | 150.00 |
| ☐ G375 | 300.00 | 150.00 |
| ☐ 5375 | 350.00 | 175.00 |
| ☐ 6375 | 325.00 | 163.00 |
| ☐ 6276½ | 140.00 | 70.00 |
| ☐ 06276 | 190.00 | 95.00 |
| ☐ 06276½ | 190.00 | 95.00 |
| ☐ 2376½ | 350.00 | 175.00 |
| ☐ 5376½ | 400.00 | 200.00 |
| ☐ 6376 | 350.00 | 175.00 |
| ☐ 6376½ | 350.00 | 175.00 |
| ☐ 4277 | 130.00 | 65.00 |
| ☐ 8277 | 175.00 | 88.00 |
| ☐ 6278 T | 160.00 | 80.00 |
| ☐ GM279 | 75.00 | 38.00 |
| ☐ M279 R | 75.00 | 38.00 |
| ☐ 3279 | 75.00 | 38.00 |
| ☐ 3279 R | 75.00 | 38.00 |
| ☐ 5279 | 115.00 | 58.00 |
| ☐ 6279 | 75.00 | 38.00 |
| ☐ 62079 | 100.00 | 50.00 |
| ☐ 62079½ | 100.00 | 50.00 |
| ☐ 8279 | 110.00 | 55.00 |
| ☐ 8279 SHAD | 110.00 | 55.00 |
| ☐ 82079 | 125.00 | 63.00 |
| ☐ 82079½ | 125.00 | 63.00 |
| ☐ 92079½ | 110.00 | 55.00 |
| ☐ B3079 | 275.00 | 138.00 |
| ☐ 63079 | 275.00 | 138.00 |
| ☐ 63079½ FILE | 250.00 | 125.00 |
| ☐ 83079 | 275.00 | 138.00 |
| ☐ P280 | 140.00 | 70.00 |
| ☐ 6280 | 140.00 | 70.00 |
| ☐ G281 | 125.00 | 63.00 |
| ☐ 6281 | 120.00 | 60.00 |
| ☐ 9281 | 115.00 | 58.00 |
| ☐ 83081 | 150.00 | 75.00 |
| ☐ 64081 | 300.00 | 150.00 |

## 56 / OLDER CASE

| PATTERN NO. | MINT | VG |
|---|---|---|
| ☐ 84081 | 350.00 | 175.00 |
| ☐ 6282 | 110.00 | 55.00 |
| ☐ 8282 | 130.00 | 65.00 |
| ☐ P383 | 325.00 | 163.00 |
| ☐ 2383 | 250.00 | 125.00 |
| ☐ 5383 | 400.00 | 200.00 |
| ☐ 6383 | 350.00 | 175.00 |
| ☐ 6383 SAB | 450.00 | 225.00 |
| ☐ 63083 | 185.00 | 93.00 |
| ☐ 8383 | 500.00 | 250.00 |
| ☐ 83083 | 200.00 | 100.00 |
| ☐ 9383 | 200.00 | 100.00 |
| ☐ 3185 | 150.00 | 75.00 |
| ☐ 6185 | 150.00 | 75.00 |
| ☐ B285 | 225.00 | 113.00 |
| ☐ G285 | 250.00 | 125.00 |
| ☐ R185 | 175.00 | 88.00 |
| ☐ 3285 | 200.00 | 100.00 |
| ☐ 6285 | 300.00 | 150.00 |
| ☐ G2086 | 250.00 | 125.00 |
| ☐ 52086 | 300.00 | 150.00 |
| ☐ 62086 | 275.00 | 175.00 |
| ☐ 82086 | 350.00 | 175.00 |
| ☐ 5287 | 400.00 | 200.00 |
| ☐ 5387 | 600.00 | 300.00 |
| ☐ 6288 | 250.00 | 125.00 |
| ☐ 6388 | 300.00 | 150.00 |
| ☐ 83088 | 185.00 | 93.00 |
| ☐ 5488 | 400.00 | 200.00 |
| ☐ 6488 | 400.00 | 200.00 |
| ☐ 83089 | 175.00 | 88.00 |
| ☐ M2090 R | 75.00 | 38.00 |
| ☐ 83090 SCI | 175.00 | 88.00 |
| ☐ B490 R | 100.00 | 50.00 |
| ☐ 6490 R | 100.00 | 50.00 |
| ☐ 640090 R | 90.00 | 45.00 |
| ☐ GM3091 | 125.00 | 63.00 |
| ☐ GM3091 R | 125.00 | 63.00 |
| ☐ 5391 | 1500.00 | 750.00 |
| ☐ 83091 | 180.00 | 90.00 |
| ☐ 3292 | 150.00 | 75.00 |
| ☐ 5292 | 185.00 | 93.00 |
| ☐ 6292 | 150.00 | 75.00 |

## OLDER CASE / 57

| PATTERN NO. | MINT | VG |
|---|---|---|
| ☐ 33092 | 150.00 | 75.00 |
| ☐ 5392 | 250.00 | 125.00 |
| ☐ 6392 | 200.00 | 100.00 |
| ☐ 6392 P | 200.00 | 100.00 |
| ☐ 630092 | 175.00 | 88.00 |
| ☐ 63092 IP | 225.00 | 113.00 |
| ☐ 6592 | 1500.00 | 750.00 |
| ☐ B1093 | 200.00 | 100.00 |
| ☐ G1093 | 225.00 | 113.00 |
| ☐ R1093 | 225.00 | 113.00 |
| ☐ 61093 | 250.00 | 125.00 |
| ☐ 32093 F | 80.00 | 40.00 |
| ☐ 6293 | 110.00 | 55.00 |
| ☐ 62093 F | 100.00 | 50.00 |
| ☐ B393 | 225.00 | 113.00 |
| ☐ H393 | 200.00 | 100.00 |
| ☐ 4393 | 225.00 | 113.00 |
| ☐ 5393 | 225.00 | 113.00 |
| ☐ 6393 | 200.00 | 100.00 |
| ☐ 6393 S | 200.00 | 100.00 |
| ☐ 6393 PEN | 175.00 | 88.00 |
| ☐ 9393 | 240.00 | 120.00 |
| ☐ 93093 | 120.00 | 60.00 |
| ☐ 05294 | 350.00 | 175.00 |
| ☐ 6294 | 400.00 | 200.00 |
| ☐ 6294 J | 600.00 | 300.00 |
| ☐ 5394 | 1500.00 | 750.00 |
| ☐ 6394 | 1200.00 | 600.00 |
| ☐ B1095 | 200.00 | 100.00 |
| ☐ G1095 | 200.00 | 100.00 |
| ☐ HA1095 | 250.00 | 125.00 |
| ☐ R1095 | 200.00 | 100.00 |
| ☐ 31095 | 200.00 | 100.00 |
| ☐ 61095 | 225.00 | 113.00 |
| ☐ B2095 F | 90.00 | 45.00 |
| ☐ 32095 F | 90.00 | 45.00 |
| ☐ B296 | 150.00 | 75.00 |
| ☐ 6296 | 150.00 | 75.00 |
| ☐ B396 | 200.00 | 100.00 |
| ☐ 6396 | 225.00 | 113.00 |
| ☐ B1097 LEG KNIFE | 300.00 | 150.00 |
| ☐ G1097* | 350.00 | 175.00 |
| ☐ GS1097* | 400.00 | 200.00 |

## 58 / CASE TESTED

| PATTERN NO. | MINT | VG |
|---|---|---|
| ☐ R1097* | 300.00 | 150.00 |
| ☐ P297** | 250.00 | 125.00 |
| ☐ R297** | 250.00 | 125.00 |
| ☐ 3297** | 200.00 | 100.00 |
| ☐ 8297** | 400.00 | 200.00 |
| ☐ 61098 | 200.00 | 100.00 |
| ☐ 32098 F | 125.00 | 63.00 |
| ☐ 62098 F | 110.00 | 55.00 |
| ☐ 6199 | 125.00 | 63.00 |
| ☐ GM2099 R | 85.00 | 42.00 |
| ☐ 3299 | 125.00 | 63.00 |
| ☐ 3299½ | 125.00 | 63.00 |
| ☐ 5299½ | 300.00 | 150.00 |
| ☐ 6299 | 250.00 | 125.00 |
| ☐ 6299½ | 250.00 | 125.00 |
| ☐ 82099 R | 150.00 | 75.00 |
| ☐ 31100 | 375.00 | 188.00 |
| ☐ 61100 | 400.00 | 200.00 |
| ☐ 62100 | 450.00 | 225.00 |
| ☐ 82101 R | 150.00 | 75.00 |
| ☐ 92101 R | 90.00 | 45.00 |
| ☐ M3102 R | 75.00 | 38.00 |
| ☐ 83102 R | 150.00 | 75.00 |
| ☐ 63109 K | 300.00 | 150.00 |
| ☐ 31113 | 250.00 | 125.00 |
| ☐ 61113 | 300.00 | 150.00 |
| ☐ 32113 | 300.00 | 150.00 |
| ☐ 62113 | 350.00 | 175.00 |
| ☐ MAIZE -1 | 95.00 | 48.00 |
| ☐ MAIZE -2 | 95.00 | 48.00 |
| ☐ MUSKRAT | 450.00 | 225.00 |
| ☐ FLYFISHERMAN | 150.00 | 75.00 |
| ☐ 1502 SCOUT | 100.00 | 50.00 |
| ☐ 1503 JUNIOR SCOUT | 80.00 | 40.00 |

## CASE TESTED

| | MINT | VG |
|---|---|---|
| ☐ B100 | 125.00 | 63.00 |
| ☐ G100 | 110.00 | 55.00 |
| ☐ M100 | 90.00 | 45.00 |
| ☐ P100 | 110.00 | 55.00 |

## CASE TESTED / 59

| PATTERN NO. | MINT | VG |
|---|---|---|
| ☐ 3100 | 225.00 | 113.00 |
| ☐ 31100 | 225.00 | 113.00 |
| ☐ 6100 | 600.00 | 300.00 |
| ☐ 61100 | 600.00 | 300.00 |
| ☐ 6200 | 400.00 | 200.00 |
| ☐ 62100 | 600.00 | 300.00 |
| ☐ 9200 | 225.00 | 113.00 |
| ☐ 92100 | 300.00 | 150.00 |
| ☐ 22001 R. | 50.00 | 25.00 |
| ☐ 3201 | 50.00 | 25.00 |
| ☐ 3201 R. | 55.00 | 28.00 |
| ☐ 6201 | 85.00 | 43.00 |
| ☐ 62001 | 85.00 | 43.00 |
| ☐ 82001 | 85.00 | 43.00 |
| ☐ 82001 R. | 110.00 | 55.00 |
| ☐ 82101 R. | 130.00 | 65.00 |
| ☐ 9201 | 50.00 | 25.00 |
| ☐ 9201 R. | 55.00 | 28.00 |
| ☐ 92101 R. | 55.00 | 28.00 |
| ☐ 1202 D&B | 325.00 | 163.00 |
| ☐ 2202½ | 85.00 | 43.00 |
| ☐ 5202 RAZ | 250.00 | 125.00 |
| ☐ 5202½ | 200.00 | 100.00 |
| ☐ 6202 | 125.00 | 63.00 |
| ☐ 6202½ | 75.00 | 38.00 |
| ☐ M3102 | 75.00 | 38.00 |
| ☐ M3102 R | 75.00 | 38.00 |
| ☐ 83102 | 125.00 | 63.00 |
| ☐ 4103 B&G | 90.00 | 45.00 |
| ☐ 6103 B&G | 150.00 | 75.00 |
| ☐ 82103 | 100.00 | 50.00 |
| ☐ 82103 R. | 100.00 | 50.00 |
| ☐ 6104 BUD | 175.00 | 88.00 |
| ☐ M204 | 90.00 | 45.00 |
| ☐ 5205 | 325.00 | 163.00 |
| ☐ 5205 RAZ | 325.00 | 163.00 |
| ☐ 5202½ | 300.00 | 150.00 |
| ☐ 6205 | 300.00 | 150.00 |
| ☐ 6205 RAZ | 325.00 | 163.00 |
| ☐ 6205½ | 300.00 | 150.00 |
| ☐ 6106 | 150.00 | 75.00 |
| ☐ 5206½ | 150.00 | 75.00 |
| ☐ 6206½ | 150.00 | 75.00 |

## 60 / CASE TESTED

**6205**

| PATTERN NO. | MINT | VG |
|---|---|---|
| ☐ 6200 1/2 | 125.00 | 63.00 |
| ☐ 3207 | 150.00 | 75.00 |

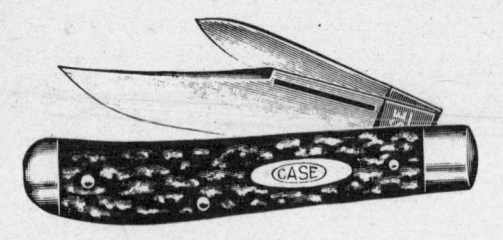

**6207**

| | | |
|---|---|---|
| ☐ 5207 | 300.00 | 150.00 |
| ☐ 6207 | 300.00 | 150.00 |
| ☐ 5208 | 150.00 | 75.00 |
| ☐ 6208 | 100.00 | 50.00 |
| ☐ 2308 | 175.00 | 88.00 |

*CASE TESTED / 61*

| PATTERN NO. | MINT | VG |
|---|---|---|
| ☐ 3308 | 175.00 | 88.00 |
| ☐ 5308 | 300.00 | 150.00 |
| ☐ 6308 | 250.00 | 125.00 |
| ☐ 8308 | 400.00 | 200.00 |

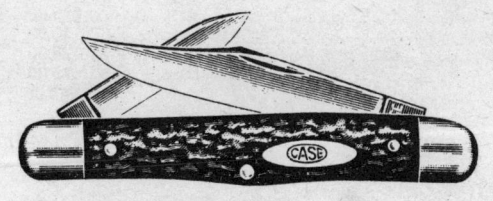

**6208**

| | | |
|---|---|---|
| ☐ 2109 B | 200.00 | 100.00 |
| ☐ 6209 | 150.00 | 75.00 |
| ☐ 62009 | 150.00 | 75.00 |
| ☐ 62009 RAZ | 200.00 | 100.00 |
| ☐ 62009 SH | 150.00 | 75.00 |

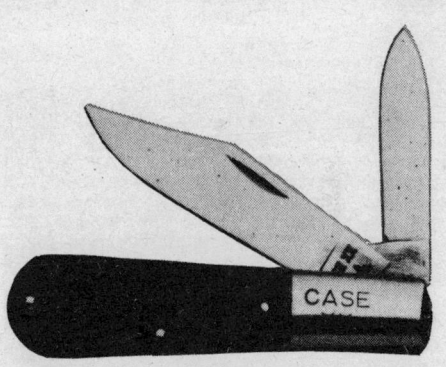

**62009 Sh**

## 62 / CASE TESTED

| PATTERN NO. | MINT | VG |
|---|---|---|
| ☐ 62009 SP | 150.00 | 75.00 |
| ☐ 62009½ | 150.00 | 75.00 |
| ☐ M110 CC | 100.00 | 50.00 |
| ☐ 91210½ | 200.00 | 100.00 |
| ☐ H2210 | 200.00 | 100.00 |
| ☐ T2210 | 225.00 | 113.00 |
| ☐ 3210½ | 140.00 | 70.00 |
| ☐ 5210½ | 175.00 | 88.00 |
| ☐ 6210½ | 175.00 | 88.00 |
| ☐ 62210 | 200.00 | 100.00 |

62210

| | | |
|---|---|---|
| ☐ 92210 | 200.00 | 100.00 |
| ☐ 11011 | 60.00 | 30.00 |
| ☐ H1211½ | 400.00 | 200.00 |
| ☐ 3111½ | 325.00 | 163.00 |
| ☐ 31211½ | 325.00 | 163.00 |
| ☐ 6111½ | 425.00 | 213.00 |
| ☐ 6111½ L | 425.00 | 213.00 |
| ☐ 61011 | 80.00 | 40.00 |
| ☐ 6211 | 475.00 | 238.00 |
| ☐ 6211½ | 475.00 | 238.00 |
| ☐ R1212½ | 300.00 | 150.00 |
| ☐ 31212½ | 175.00 | 88.00 |
| ☐ 2212 L | 200.00 | 100.00 |
| ☐ 31113 | 200.00 | 100.00 |
| ☐ 61013 | 90.00 | 45.00 |
| ☐ 61113 | 200.00 | 100.00 |
| ☐ 61213½ | 450.00 | 225.00 |
| ☐ 6213 | 300.00 | 150.00 |
| ☐ 62113 | 350.00 | 175.00 |

CASE TESTED / 63

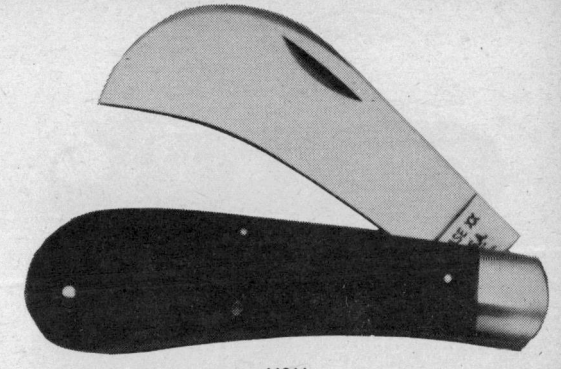

**11011**

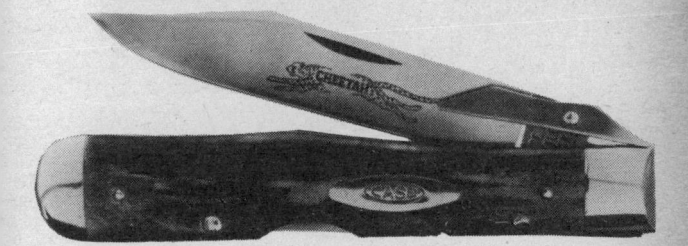

**5111½**

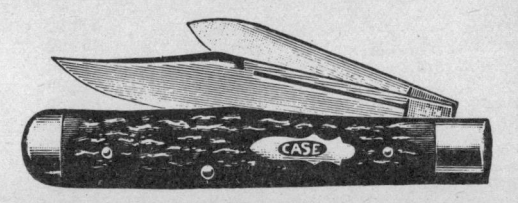

**6211**

## 64 / CASE TESTED

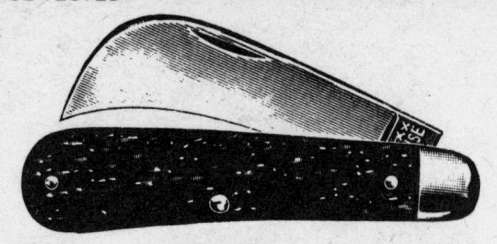

**61013**

**61213½**

| PATTERN NO. | MINT | VG |
|---|---|---|
| ☐ 61214½ | 400.00 | 200.00 |
| ☐ 5214½ | 150.00 | 75.00 |
| ☐ 6214 | 140.00 | 70.00 |
| ☐ 6214½ | 140.00 | 70.00 |
| ☐ 51215½ F | 600.00 | 300.00 |
| ☐ 51215½ G | 600.00 | 300.00 |
| ☐ 61215½ | 550.00 | 275.00 |
| ☐ W1216 | 60.00 | 30.00 |
| ☐ W1216 K | 60.00 | 30.00 |

CASE TESTED / 65

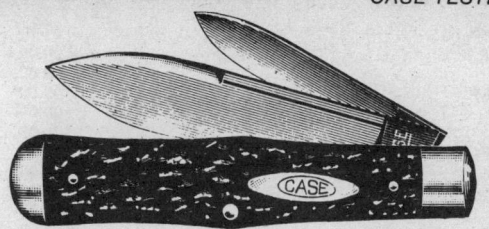

6213

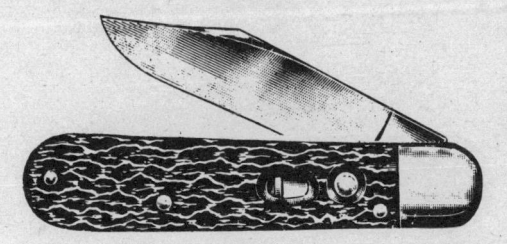

6121４½

6214

## 66 / CASE TESTED

| PATTERN NO. | MINT | VG |
|---|---|---|
| ☐ W1216 P | 60.00 | 30.00 |
| ☐ 6116 | 100.00 | 50.00 |
| ☐ 6116 SP | 100.00 | 50.00 |
| ☐ 6116½ | 100.00 | 50.00 |
| ☐ 6216 | 120.00 | 60.00 |
| ☐ 6216 EO | 175.00 | 88.00 |
| ☐ 6216½ | 120.00 | 60.00 |
| ☐ 2217 | 140.00 | 70.00 |
| ☐ 6217 | 200.00 | 100.00 |
| ☐ M1218 K | 180.00 | 90.00 |
| ☐ 3318 SH SP | 90.00 | 45.00 |
| ☐ 3318 SH PEN | 90.00 | 45.00 |
| ☐ 5318 SH SP | 190.00 | 80.00 |

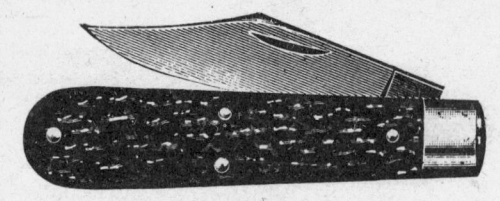

6116½

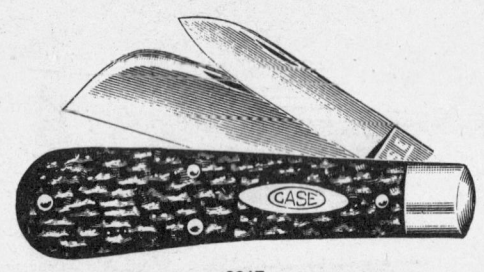

6217

| | | |
|---|---|---|
| ☐ 6318 SH SP | 150.00 | 75.00 |
| ☐ 6318 SH PEN | 150.00 | 75.00 |
| ☐ 6318 SH P | 150.00 | 75.00 |

CASE TESTED / 67

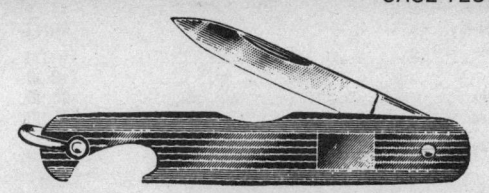

M1218K

| PATTERN NO. | MINT | VG |
| --- | --- | --- |
| ☐ 6318 SH P | 150.00 | 75.00 |
| ☐ 6318 SH PEN | 150.00 | 75.00 |
| ☐ 8318 SH SP | 225.00 | 113.00 |
| ☐ 9318 SH SP | 130.00 | 65.00 |
| ☐ 9318 SP PEN | 130.00 | 65.00 |
| ☐ 9318 SH PEN | 130.00 | 65.00 |
| ☐ 6219 | 175.00 | 88.00 |
| ☐ 62019 | 175.00 | 88.00 |

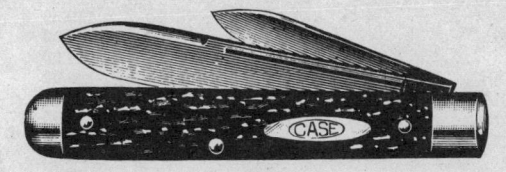

62019

| | | |
| --- | --- | --- |
| ☐ 2220 | 125.00 | 63.00 |
| ☐ 3220 | 125.00 | 63.00 |
| ☐ 5220 | 175.00 | 88.00 |
| ☐ 6220 | 175.00 | 88.00 |
| ☐ 8220 | 350.00 | 175.00 |
| ☐ 9220 | 125.00 | 63.00 |
| ☐ O2221½ | 130.00 | 65.00 |
| ☐ 06221½ | 190.00 | 80.00 |
| ☐ 6222 | 110.00 | 55.00 |
| ☐ 6223 | 125.00 | 63.00 |
| ☐ 9223 | 125.00 | 63.00 |
| ☐ 3124 | 70.00 | 35.00 |
| ☐ 3124½ | 70.00 | 35.00 |

## 68 / CASE TESTED

| PATTERN NO. | MINT | VG |
|---|---|---|
| ☐ 6124 | 110.00 | 55.00 |
| ☐ 6124½ | 110.00 | 55.00 |
| ☐ 2224 SH | 100.00 | 50.00 |
| ☐ 2224 RAZ | 125.00 | 63.00 |

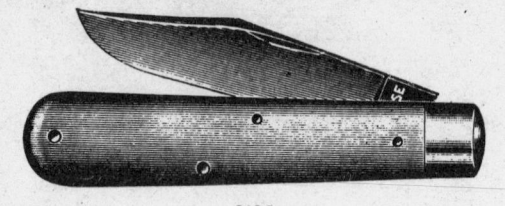

3124

| | | |
|---|---|---|
| ☐ 3224 | 70.00 | 35.00 |
| ☐ 3224½ | 70.00 | 35.00 |
| ☐ 5224½ | 150.00 | 75.00 |
| ☐ 52024 | 150.00 | 75.00 |
| ☐ 52024½ | 150.00 | 75.00 |
| ☐ 62024 | 120.00 | 60.00 |
| ☐ 62024 SH | 120.00 | 60.00 |
| ☐ 62024 RAZ | 150.00 | 75.00 |
| ☐ 62024½ | 100.00 | 50.00 |
| ☐ 32025½ | 150.00 | 75.00 |
| ☐ 5225½ | 200.00 | 100.00 |
| ☐ 02025½ | 175.00 | 88.00 |
| ☐ 62025½ | 175.00 | 88.00 |
| ☐ 6226½ | 170.00 | 85.00 |
| ☐ 62027 | 110.00 | 55.00 |
| ☐ 62027½ | 110.00 | 55.00 |
| ☐ 92027 | 70.00 | 35.00 |
| ☐ 92027½ | 70.00 | 35.00 |
| ☐ M228½ | 110.00 | 55.00 |
| ☐ 2228 | 110.00 | 55.00 |
| ☐ 2228 EO | 130.00 | 65.00 |
| ☐ 2228 P | 150.00 | 75.00 |
| ☐ 22028 | 100.00 | 50.00 |
| ☐ 6228 | 125.00 | 63.00 |
| ☐ 6228 EO | 135.00 | 68.00 |
| ☐ 6228 P | 125.00 | 63.00 |

CASE TESTED / 69

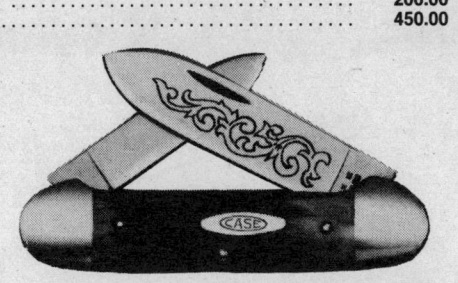

| PATTERN NO. | MINT | VG |
|---|---|---|
| ☐ 62028 | 175.00 | 88.00 |
| ☐ 62028½ | 150.00 | 75.00 |
| ☐ 6229½ | 110.00 | 55.00 |
| ☐ 7129½ | 175.00 | 88.00 |
| ☐ 9229½ | 130.00 | 65.00 |
| ☐ 02230 | 75.00 | 38.00 |
| ☐ 02230½ | 75.00 | 38.00 |
| ☐ 05230½ | 200.00 | 100.00 |
| ☐ 6230 | 150.00 | 75.00 |
| ☐ 06230½ | 160.00 | 80.00 |
| ☐ 06230 SH | 160.00 | 80.00 |
| ☐ 06230 SP | 160.00 | 80.00 |
| ☐ 06230½ | 150.00 | 75.00 |
| ☐ 09230 | 120.00 | 60.00 |
| ☐ 09230½ | 120.00 | 60.00 |
| ☐ 1131 SH | 65.00 | 33.00 |
| ☐ 11031 SH | 60.00 | 30.00 |
| ☐ 11031 SH cc. | 70.00 | 35.00 |
| ☐ 12031 L | 70.00 | 35.00 |
| ☐ 22031 | 70.00 | 35.00 |
| ☐ 2231½ | 80.00 | 40.00 |
| ☐ 2231½ SAB | 80.00 | 40.00 |
| ☐ 22031½ | 80.00 | 40.00 |
| ☐ 52031 | 200.00 | 100.00 |
| ☐ 52031½ | 200.00 | 100.00 |
| ☐ 52131 | 450.00 | 225.00 |

52131

| | | |
|---|---|---|
| ☐ 6231 | 170.00 | 85.00 |
| ☐ 62031 | 150.00 | 75.00 |
| ☐ 6231½ | 150.00 | 75.00 |

## 70 / CASE TESTED

| PATTERN NO. | MINT | VG |
|---|---|---|
| ☐ 62031½ | 150.00 | 75.00 |
| ☐ 53131 | 900.00 | 450.00 |
| ☐ 3232 | 75.00 | 38.00 |
| ☐ 6232 | 140.00 | 70.00 |
| ☐ 5332 | 200.00 | 100.00 |
| ☐ 6332 | 200.00 | 100.00 |
| ☐ 3233 | 80.00 | 40.00 |
| ☐ 6233 | 140.00 | 70.00 |

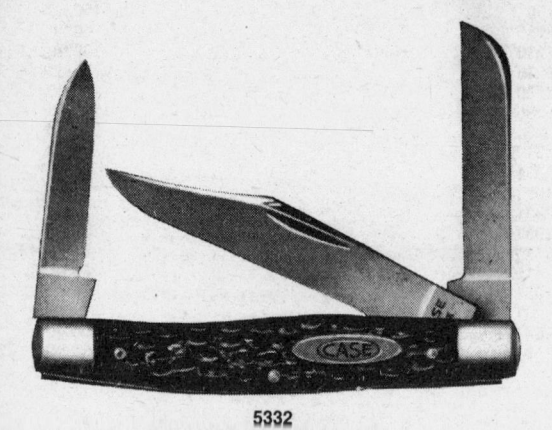

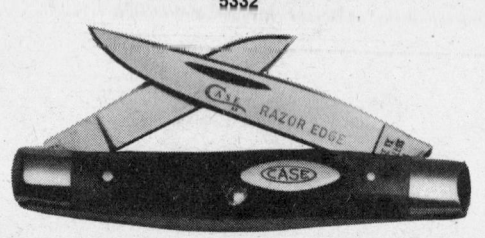

5332

3233

*CASE TESTED / 71*

| PATTERN NO. | MINT | VG |
|---|---|---|
| ☐ 8233 | 170.00 | 88.00 |
| ☐ 9233 | 85.00 | 43.00 |
| ☐ 6333 | 150.00 | 75.00 |
| ☐ 9333 | 90.00 | 45.00 |
| ☐ 5234 | 325.00 | 163.00 |
| ☐ 3235½ | 90.00 | 45.00 |
| ☐ 5235½ | 150.00 | 75.00 |
| ☐ 6235 | 110.00 | 55.00 |
| ☐ 6235 EO | 150.00 | 75.00 |
| ☐ 6235 SH | 125.00 | 63.00 |
| ☐ 6235½ | 100.00 | 50.00 |
| ☐ 6235½ P | 150.00 | 75.00 |
| ☐ 62035½ | 85.00 | 43.00 |
| ☐ 2136 | 85.00 | 43.00 |
| ☐ 6237 | 200.00 | 100.00 |
| ☐ 6237½ | 200.00 | 100.00 |
| ☐ 1139 | 140.00 | 70.00 |
| ☐ 3240 SP | 350.00 | 175.00 |
| ☐ 6240 | 500.00 | 250.00 |
| ☐ 6240 SP | 400.00 | 200.00 |
| ☐ 52042 | 125.00 | 63.00 |
| ☐ 62042 | 100.00 | 50.00 |
| ☐ 82042 | 120.00 | 60.00 |
| ☐ 92042 | 65.00 | 33.00 |
| ☐ 6143 | 175.00 | 88.00 |
| ☐ 3244 | 80.00 | 40.00 |
| ☐ 5224 | 125.00 | 63.00 |
| ☐ 05244 | 110.00 | 55.00 |
| ☐ 6224 | 90.00 | 45.00 |
| ☐ 06244 | 80.00 | 40.00 |
| ☐ 62044 F | 90.00 | 45.00 |
| ☐ 8244 | 150.00 | 75.00 |
| ☐ 82044 | 130.00 | 65.00 |
| ☐ 82044 F | 130.00 | 65.00 |
| ☐ 9244 | 80.00 | 40.00 |
| ☐ B334 SH SP | 200.00 | 100.00 |
| ☐ 3344 SH SP | 90.00 | 45.00 |
| ☐ 3344 SH PEN | 90.00 | 45.00 |
| ☐ 3344 SH P | 90.00 | 45.00 |
| ☐ 3344 SP P | 90.00 | 45.00 |
| ☐ 5344 SH SP | 135.00 | 68.00 |
| ☐ 5344 SP PEN | 135.00 | 68.00 |
| ☐ 6344 SH SP | 200.00 | 100.00 |

# 72 / CASE TESTED

**5344 Sh Sp**

| PATTERN NO. | MINT | VG |
|---|---|---|
| ☐ 6344 SH PEN | 120.00 | 60.00 |
| ☐ 6344 SH P | 120.00 | 60.00 |
| ☐ 6344 SP P | 120.00 | 60.00 |
| ☐ 6344 SP PEN | 120.00 | 60.00 |
| ☐ 9344 SH PEN | 120.00 | 60.00 |
| ☐ 02245 | 85.00 | 43.00 |
| ☐ 02245½ | 85.00 | 43.00 |
| ☐ 04245 B&G | 100.00 | 50.00 |
| ☐ 05245½ | 200.00 | 100.00 |
| ☐ 6245½ | 120.00 | 60.00 |
| ☐ 06245 | 220.00 | 110.00 |
| ☐ 06245½ | 250.00 | 125.00 |
| ☐ 2345½ P | 130.00 | 65.00 |
| ☐ 2345½ SH PEN | 110.00 | 55.00 |
| ☐ 6345 | 250.00 | 125.00 |
| ☐ 6345 P | 275.00 | 138.00 |
| ☐ 6345½ | 250.00 | 125.00 |
| ☐ 6345½ P | 275.00 | 138.00 |
| ☐ 6345½ SH | 250.00 | 125.00 |
| ☐ B445 R | 150.00 | 75.00 |
| ☐ 6445 R | 150.00 | 75.00 |
| ☐ 640045 R | 70.00 | 35.00 |
| ☐ 3246 R | 110.00 | 55.00 |
| ☐ 6246 R | 110.00 | 55.00 |
| ☐ 04247 SP | 120.00 | 60.00 |

CASE TESTED / 73

| PATTERN NO. | MINT | VG |
|---|---|---|
| ☐ 5247 J | 500.00 | 250.00 |
| ☐ 05247 SP | 175.00 | 88.00 |
| ☐ 6247 J | 400.00 | 200.00 |
| ☐ 06247 SP | 150.00 | 75.00 |
| ☐ 06247 PEN | 150.00 | 75.00 |
| ☐ M347 SP P | 150.00 | 75.00 |

6445 R

| | | |
|---|---|---|
| ☐ 3347 SH SP | 125.00 | 63.00 |
| ☐ 3347 SP PEN | 125.00 | 63.00 |
| ☐ 3347 SP P | 125.00 | 63.00 |
| ☐ 43047 | 150.00 | 75.00 |
| ☐ 5347 SH SP | 230.00 | 115.00 |
| ☐ 5347 SH PEN | 230.00 | 115.00 |
| ☐ 53047 | 250.00 | 125.00 |
| ☐ 6347 PJ | 300.00 | 150.00 |
| ☐ 6347 SH SP | 225.00 | 113.00 |
| ☐ 6347 SH PEN | 225.00 | 113.00 |
| ☐ 6347 SH P | 225.00 | 113.00 |
| ☐ 6347 SP P | 225.00 | 113.00 |
| ☐ 6347 P PEN | 225.00 | 113.00 |
| ☐ 6347 SP PEN | 225.00 | 113.00 |
| ☐ 63047 | 200.00 | 100.00 |
| ☐ 630047 | 175.00 | 88.00 |
| ☐ 630047 P | 175.00 | 88.00 |
| ☐ 630047 SP PEN | 175.00 | 88.00 |
| ☐ 9347 PJ | 250.00 | 125.00 |
| ☐ 93047 | 150.00 | 75.00 |
| ☐ 64047 P | 275.00 | 138.00 |

# 74 / CASE TESTED

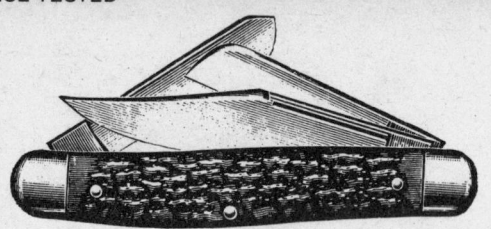

**630047 Sp Pen**

| PATTERN NO. | MINT | VG |
|---|---|---|
| ☐ 94047 P | 200.00 | 100.00 |
| ☐ B1048 | 175.00 | 88.00 |
| ☐ GS1048 | 175.00 | 88.00 |
| ☐ R1048 | 175.00 | 88.00 |
| ☐ 61048 | 120.00 | 60.00 |
| ☐ B2048 | 250.00 | 125.00 |
| ☐ B2048 SP | 250.00 | 125.00 |
| ☐ GS2048 | 250.00 | 125.00 |
| ☐ R2048 | 250.00 | 125.00 |
| ☐ 62048 | 145.00 | 73.00 |
| ☐ 62048 SP | 145.00 | 73.00 |
| ☐ 61049 | 150.00 | 75.00 |
| ☐ 6249 | 225.00 | 113.00 |
| ☐ C31050 SAB | 400.00 | 200.00 |
| ☐ C51050 SAB | 1000.00 | 500.00 |
| ☐ C61050 L | 1750.00 | 875.00 |
| ☐ C61050 SAB | 450.00 | 225.00 |
| ☐ C91050 SAB | 400.00 | 200.00 |
| ☐ CB1050 | 500.00 | 250.00 |
| ☐ CB1050 R | 500.00 | 250.00 |
| ☐ CB1050 SAB | 550.00 | 275.00 |
| ☐ CH1050 | 500.00 | 250.00 |
| ☐ PBB1050 | 275.00 | 138.00 |
| ☐ PB31050 F | 275.00 | 138.00 |
| ☐ 310050 | 300.00 | 150.00 |
| ☐ 61050 | 400.00 | 200.00 |
| ☐ 610050 | 350.00 | 175.00 |
| ☐ 6250 | 450.00 | 225.00 |
| ☐ B1051 | 200.00 | 100.00 |
| ☐ GS1051 | 200.00 | 100.00 |

CASE TESTED / 75

6250

| PATTERN NO. | MINT | VG |
|---|---|---|
| ☐ 6151 | 500.00 | 250.00 |
| ☐ 6151 L | 550.00 | 275.00 |
| ☐ 61051 | 200.00 | 100.00 |
| ☐ 8151 L | 1000.00 | 500.00 |
| ☐ 9151 | 500.00 | 250.00 |
| ☐ 6251 | 600.00 | 300.00 |
| ☐ 9251 | 500.00 | 250.00 |
| ☐ 3252 | 250.00 | 125.00 |
| ☐ 52052 | 150.00 | 75.00 |
| ☐ 6252 | 300.00 | 150.00 |
| ☐ 62052 | 125.00 | 63.00 |
| ☐ 63052 | 350.00 | 175.00 |
| ☐ 3452 | 225.00 | 113.00 |
| ☐ 54052 | 300.00 | 150.00 |
| ☐ 6452 | 300.00 | 150.00 |
| ☐ 64052 | 300.00 | 150.00 |
| ☐ 5253 | 130.00 | 65.00 |
| ☐ 6253 | 110.00 | 55.00 |
| ☐ 62053 | 90.00 | 45.00 |
| ☐ 82053 SR | 90.00 | 45.00 |
| ☐ 9253 | 90.00 | 45.00 |
| ☐ 3254 | 700.00 | 350.00 |

## 76 / CASE TESTED

| PATTERN NO. | MINT | VG |
|---|---|---|
| ☐ 5254 | 1400.00 | 700.00 |
| ☐ 6254 | 1100.00 | 550.00 |
| ☐ 9254 | 1100.00 | 550.00 |
| ☐ 22055 | 95.00 | 48.00 |
| ☐ 32055 | 95.00 | 48.00 |
| ☐ 62055 | 150.00 | 75.00 |
| ☐ 92055 | 95.00 | 48.00 |
| ☐ 64055 P | 550.00 | 275.00 |
| ☐ 4257 | 80.00 | 40.00 |
| ☐ 42057 | 80.00 | 40.00 |
| ☐ 92057 | 80.00 | 40.00 |
| ☐ 32058 | 80.00 | 40.00 |
| ☐ 92058 | 80.00 | 40.00 |
| ☐ 62059 SP | 110.00 | 55.00 |
| ☐ 62059 SP | 110.00 | 55.00 |
| ☐ 62059½ | 110.00 | 55.00 |
| ☐ 5260 | 250.00 | 125.00 |
| ☐ 8360 SCI | 175.00 | 88.00 |
| ☐ 5460 | 350.00 | 175.00 |
| ☐ 5161 L | 700.00 | 350.00 |
| ☐ 6161 L | 700.00 | 350.00 |
| ☐ 6261 | 95.00 | 48.00 |
| ☐ 6261 F | 95.00 | 48.00 |
| ☐ 8261 | 110.00 | 55.00 |
| ☐ 8261 F | 110.00 | 55.00 |
| ☐ 9261 | 65.00 | 33.00 |
| ☐ 9261 F | 65.00 | 33.00 |
| ☐ 2361 F | 150.00 | 75.00 |
| ☐ 84062 K | 350.00 | 175.00 |
| ☐ 94062 | 250.00 | 125.00 |
| ☐ 05263 | 150.00 | 75.00 |
| ☐ 06263 | 80.00 | 40.00 |
| ☐ 62063½ | 80.00 | 40.00 |
| ☐ 08263 | 140.00 | 70.00 |
| ☐ 82063 | 140.00 | 70.00 |
| ☐ 82063 SHAD | 120.00 | 60.00 |
| ☐ 82063½ | 120.00 | 60.00 |
| ☐ 92063½ | 80.00 | 40.00 |
| ☐ 6264 T | 110.00 | 55.00 |
| ☐ 6264 TF | 110.00 | 55.00 |
| ☐ 8264 T | 130.00 | 65.00 |
| ☐ 8264 TF | 130.00 | 65.00 |
| ☐ 9264 TF | 80.00 | 40.00 |

## CASE TESTED / 77

| PATTERN NO. | MINT | VG |
|---|---|---|
| ☐ 5364 T | 200.00 | 100.00 |
| ☐ 8364 T | 175.00 | 88.00 |
| ☐ 8364 SCI | 175.00 | 88.00 |
| ☐ B165 | 600.00 | 300.00 |
| ☐ GS165 | 600.00 | 300.00 |
| ☐ 3165 SAB | 250.00 | 125.00 |
| ☐ 5165 SAB | 450.00 | 225.00 |
| ☐ 6165 SAB | 400.00 | 200.00 |
| ☐ 9165 SAB | 300.00 | 150.00 |
| ☐ 3265 SAB | 275.00 | 138.00 |
| ☐ 5265 SAB | 375.00 | 188.00 |
| ☐ 6265 SAB | 400.00 | 200.00 |
| ☐ 8265 SAB | 400.00 | 200.00 |
| ☐ 9265 SAB | 300.00 | 150.00 |
| ☐ 6465 | 2000.00 | 1000.00 |
| ☐ 6366 | 100.00 | 50.00 |
| ☐ 6366 PEN | 100.00 | 50.00 |
| ☐ 8366 PEN | 250.00 | 125.00 |
| ☐ 06267 | 150.00 | 75.00 |
| ☐ 6367 | 200.00 | 100.00 |
| ☐ 8367 | 200.00 | 100.00 |
| ☐ 9367 | 125.00 | 63.00 |
| ☐ 6268 | 135.00 | 68.00 |
| ☐ 6269 | 100.00 | 50.00 |
| ☐ 8269 | 120.00 | 60.00 |
| ☐ 9269 | 80.00 | 40.00 |
| ☐ 6270 F | 325.00 | 163.00 |
| ☐ 6370 | 325.00 | 163.00 |
| ☐ 8370 F | 400.00 | 200.00 |
| ☐ 6470 | 325.00 | 163.00 |
| ☐ 6470 F | 325.00 | 163.00 |
| ☐ 5171 L | 1000.00 | 500.00 |
| ☐ 6171 L | 1000.00 | 500.00 |
| ☐ 8271 | 200.00 | 100.00 |
| ☐ 8371 F | 200.00 | 100.00 |
| ☐ B172 | 800.00 | 400.00 |
| ☐ H172 | 800.00 | 400.00 |
| ☐ 5172 | 1500.00 | 750.00 |
| ☐ 5172 (ZIPPER) | 1500.00 | 750.00 |
| ☐ 6172 | 1250.00 | 625.00 |
| ☐ 6172 (ZIPPER) | 2000.00 | 1000.00 |
| ☐ 22074½ P | 150.00 | 75.00 |
| ☐ 62074½ P | 200.00 | 100.00 |

## 78 / CASE TESTED

| PATTERN NO. | MINT | VG |
|---|---|---|
| ☐ 5275 SP | 325.00 | 163.00 |
| ☐ 6275 SP | 325.00 | 163.00 |
| ☐ 5375 | 400.00 | 200.00 |
| ☐ 6375 | 400.00 | 200.00 |
| ☐ 6276½ | 225.00 | 113.00 |
| ☐ 2376½ | 200.00 | 100.00 |

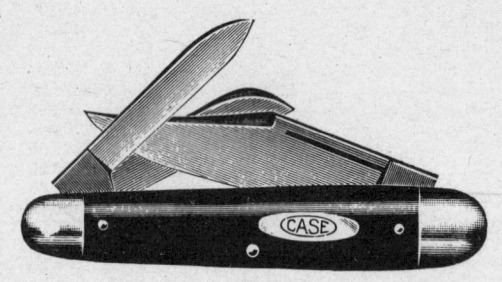

**2376½**

| | | |
|---|---|---|
| ☐ 5376½ | 450.00 | 225.00 |
| ☐ 6376½ | 450.00 | 225.00 |
| ☐ B279 | 125.00 | 63.00 |
| ☐ M279 | 60.00 | 30.00 |
| ☐ GM279 | 60.00 | 30.00 |
| ☐ M279 R | 60.00 | 30.00 |
| ☐ R279 | 110.00 | 55.00 |
| ☐ 2279 | 65.00 | 33.00 |
| ☐ 3279 | 65.00 | 33.00 |
| ☐ 3279 R | 65.00 | 33.00 |
| ☐ 5279 | 140.00 | 70.00 |
| ☐ 6279 | 120.00 | 60.00 |
| ☐ 62079 | 150.00 | 75.00 |
| ☐ 62079½ | 150.00 | 75.00 |
| ☐ 8279 | 140.00 | 70.00 |
| ☐ 8279 SHAD | 140.00 | 70.00 |
| ☐ 82079 | 150.00 | 75.00 |
| ☐ 82079½ | 140.00 | 70.00 |
| ☐ 92079½ | 90.00 | 45.00 |
| ☐ 63079½ F | 300.00 | 150.00 |

## CASE TESTED / 79

| PATTERN NO. | MINT | VG |
|---|---:|---:|
| ☐ 6281 | 110.00 | 55.00 |
| ☐ 9281 | 110.00 | 55.00 |
| ☐ 83081 | 150.00 | 75.00 |
| ☐ B282 | 350.00 | 175.00 |
| ☐ 6282 | 300.00 | 150.00 |
| ☐ 8282 | 350.00 | 175.00 |
| ☐ 2383 | 175.00 | 88.00 |
| ☐ 5383 | 325.00 | 163.00 |
| ☐ 6383 | 400.00 | 200.00 |
| ☐ 6383 SAB | 500.00 | 250.00 |
| ☐ 8383 | 500.00 | 250.00 |
| ☐ 83083 | 150.00 | 75.00 |
| ☐ 9383 | 300.00 | 150.00 |
| ☐ B185 | 170.00 | 85.00 |
| ☐ 3185 | 110.00 | 55.00 |
| ☐ 6185 | 140.00 | 70.00 |
| ☐ B285 | 350.00 | 175.00 |
| ☐ 3285 | 200.00 | 100.00 |
| ☐ 6285 | 300.00 | 150.00 |
| ☐ 7285 | 350.00 | 175.00 |
| ☐ 52086 | 300.00 | 150.00 |
| ☐ 62086 | 300.00 | 150.00 |
| ☐ 82086 | 350.00 | 175.00 |
| ☐ 22087 | 75.00 | 38.00 |
| ☐ 42087 | 70.00 | 35.00 |
| ☐ 5287 | 125.00 | 63.00 |
| ☐ 62087 | 85.00 | 43.00 |
| ☐ 23087 SH PEN | 80.00 | 40.00 |
| ☐ 43087 SH SP | 80.00 | 40.00 |
| ☐ 5387 | 550.00 | 275.00 |
| ☐ 63087 SP PEN | 110.00 | 55.00 |
| ☐ 6288 | 400.00 | 200.00 |
| ☐ 83088 | 175.00 | 88.00 |
| ☐ 5488 | 450.00 | 225.00 |
| ☐ 6488 | 450.00 | 225.00 |
| ☐ 83089 SCI | 175.00 | 88.00 |
| ☐ 83090 SR | 175.00 | 88.00 |
| ☐ 640090 R | 110.00 | 55.00 |
| ☐ GM3091 R | 110.00 | 55.00 |
| ☐ 5391 | 1800.00 | 900.00 |
| ☐ 83091 | 175.00 | 88.00 |
| ☐ 3292 | 130.00 | 65.00 |
| ☐ 6292 | 160.00 | 80.00 |

## 80 / CASE TESTED

| PATTERN NO. | MINT | VG |
|---|---|---|
| ☐ 33092 | 150.00 | 75.00 |
| ☐ 5392 | 250.00 | 125.00 |
| ☐ 6392 | 300.00 | 350.00 |
| ☐ 6392 P | 300.00 | 150.00 |
| ☐ 630092 | 250.00 | 125.00 |
| ☐ 630092 P | 250.00 | 125.00 |
| ☐ 6592 | 1600.00 | 800.00 |
| ☐ B1093 | 300.00 | 150.00 |
| ☐ GS1093 | 300.00 | 150.00 |
| ☐ H1093 | 300.00 | 150.00 |
| ☐ P1093 | 225.00 | 113.00 |
| ☐ R1093 | 250.00 | 125.00 |
| ☐ RNM1093 | 225.00 | 113.00 |
| ☐ 61093 | 250.00 | 125.00 |
| ☐ 32093 F | 100.00 | 50.00 |
| ☐ 62093 F | 165.00 | 83.00 |
| ☐ 5393 | 300.00 | 150.00 |
| ☐ 6393 | 300.00 | 150.00 |
| ☐ 6393 PEN | 300.00 | 150.00 |
| ☐ 9393 | 200.00 | 100.00 |
| ☐ 93093 | 110.00 | 55.00 |
| ☐ 6294 | .00 | .00 |
| ☐ 6294 J | 600.00 | 300.00 |
| ☐ 5394 | 1400.00 | 700.00 |
| ☐ 6394½ | 1500.00 | 750.00 |
| ☐ B1095 | 250.00 | 125.00 |
| ☐ HA1095 | 250.00 | 125.00 |
| ☐ 31095 | 175.00 | 88.00 |
| ☐ B2095 F | 130.00 | 65.00 |
| ☐ 32095 F | 90.00 | 45.00 |
| ☐ 6296 X | 350.00 | 175.00 |
| ☐ B1097 | 300.00 | 150.00 |
| ☐ GS1097 | 300.00 | 150.00 |
| ☐ R1097 | 180.00 | 90.00 |
| ☐ RM1097 | 180.00 | 90.00 |
| ☐ 31097 | 150.00 | 75.00 |
| ☐ R297 | 250.00 | 125.00 |
| ☐ 3297 | 150.00 | 75.00 |
| ☐ 8297 | 350.00 | 175.00 |
| ☐ B1098 | 300.00 | 150.00 |
| ☐ 61098 | 250.00 | 125.00 |
| ☐ B2098 F | 150.00 | 75.00 |
| ☐ 32098 F | 80.00 | 40.00 |

## CASE TESTED / 81

| PATTERN NO. | MINT | VG |
|---|---|---|
| ☐ 62098 F | 190.00 | 95.00 |
| ☐ GM2099 R | 110.00 | 55.00 |
| ☐ 3299½ | 120.00 | 60.00 |
| ☐ 5299½ | 300.00 | 150.00 |
| ☐ 6299 | 250.00 | 125.00 |
| ☐ 6299 SH OP R | 250.00 | 125.00 |

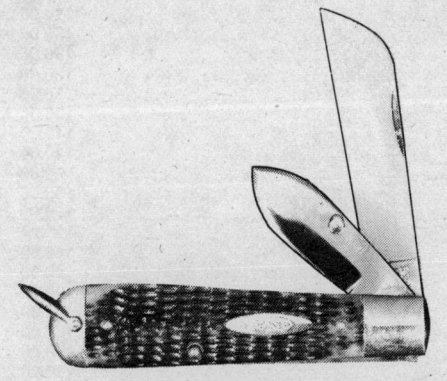

**6299 Sh Op R**

| | | |
|---|---|---|
| ☐ 6299½ | 300.00 | 150.00 |
| ☐ 82099 R | 150.00 | 75.00 |
| ☐ MAIZE -1 | 90.00 | 45.00 |
| ☐ MAIZE -2 | 90.00 | 45.00 |
| ☐ MUSKRAT | 500.00 | 250.00 |
| ☐ FLYFISHERMAN | 175.00 | 88.00 |
| ☐ P200 | 550.00 | 300.00 |
| ☐ 5200 | 600.00 | 300.00 |
| ☐ 6200 | 600.00 | 450.00 |
| ☐ 9200 | 500.00 | 450.00 |
| ☐ P202 | 140.00 | 135.00 |
| ☐ R202 | 140.00 | 135.00 |
| ☐ 63102 | 190.00 | 175.00 |
| ☐ 83102 | 210.00 | 190.00 |
| ☐ 6203 | 150.00 | 65.00 |

## 82 / CASE XX'S

| PATTERN NO. | MINT | VG |
|---|---|---|
| ☐ 2104 | 120.00 | 100.00 |
| ☐ 8407 | 500.00 | 400.00 |
| ☐ 62010 | 180.00 | 165.00 |
| ☐ B1011 | 90.00 | 85.00 |
| ☐ R111½ | 450.00 | 400.00 |
| ☐ 11011 | 95.00 | 95.00 |
| ☐ 6111½ L | 400.00 | 300.00 |
| ☐ 1212 L | 110.00 | 100.00 |
| ☐ 62012 | 130.00 | 95.00 |
| ☐ P215 | 130.00 | 115.00 |
| ☐ 6215 | 130.00 | 115.00 |
| ☐ 8215 | 170.00 | 150.00 |
| ☐ 61016½ | 95.00 | 80.00 |
| ☐ 22016 | 110.00 | 95.00 |
| ☐ 22016½ | 110.00 | 95.00 |
| ☐ 62016 | 90.00 | 80.00 |
| ☐ 62016½ | 130.00 | 115.00 |
| ☐ 62016 S | 130.00 | 115.00 |
| ☐ 6216½ I | 130.00 | 115.00 |
| ☐ 62116 | 140.00 | 80.00 |
| ☐ 62020 | 90.00 | 75.00 |
| ☐ 62020 S | 90.00 | 75.00 |
| ☐ 62020½ | 90.00 | 75.00 |
| ☐ B221 | 160.00 | 150.00 |
| ☐ OB221 | 160.00 | 150.00 |
| ☐ 6221 | 160.00 | 150.00 |
| ☐ 06221½ | 120.00 | 105.00 |
| ☐ 08221 | 175.00 | 160.00 |
| ☐ 6321 | 175.00 | 175.00 |
| ☐ G222 | 100.00 | 90.00 |
| ☐ 8222 | 120.00 | 110.00 |
| ☐ P223 | 140.00 | 125.00 |
| ☐ B224 | 100.00 | 90.00 |

## CASE XX'S

### ONE BLADE
(*XX Frame; **Etched Lengthwise On Blade; "Test XX Stainless")

| | MINT | VG |
|---|---|---|
| ☐ M100 NICKEL PLATED HANDLE | 90.00 | 45.00 |
| ☐ M100 GOLD PLATED HANDLE | 135.00 | 67.50 |
| ☐ M101 | 100.00 | 50.00 |
| ☐ 4100 SS "MELON TESTER" | 45.00 | 22.50 |
| ☐ 6104B "BUDDING KNIFE" | 175.00 | 87.50 |

## CASE XX'S / 83

| PATTERN NO. | MINT | VG |
|---|---|---|
| ☐ 2109B *"BUDDING KNIFE"* | 90.00 | 45.00 |
| ☐ M110 *"SPAYING KNIFE"* | 110.00 | 55.00 |
| ☐ 11011 *"HAWK BILL"* | 30.00 | 15.00 |
| ☐ 61011 *"HAWK BILL"* LAMINATED WOOD HANDLE | 30.00 | 15.00 |
| ☐ 61011 *"HAWK BILL"* BONE STAG HANDLE | 50.00 | 25.00 |
| ☐ 6111½ L *"LOCK BACK"* | 75.00 | 37.70 |
| ☐ 1116 SP *"BUDDING KNIFE"* | 45.00 | 22.50 |
| ☐ 31024½ | 42.00 | 12.50 |
| ☐ 61024½ | 27.00 | 13.50 |
| ☐ 11031 SH | 40.00 | 20.00 |
| ☐ 2136 *"BUDDING KNIFE"* | 140.00 | 70.00 |
| ☐ 1139 *"BANANA KNIFE"* | 150.00 | 75.00 |
| ☐ 6143 *"DADDY BARLOW"* SLICK BACK HANDLE | 110.00 | 55.00 |
| ☐ 31048 | 27.00 | 13.50 |
| ☐ 31048 SP | 40.00 | 20.00 |
| ☐ 31048 SH R *"FLORIST'S KNIFE"* | 65.00 | 32.50 |

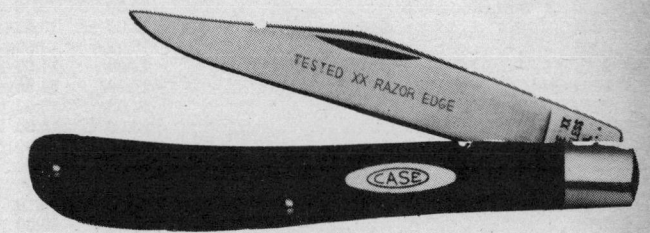

**61048 SS**

| | | |
|---|---|---|
| ☐ 61048 | 27.00 | 13.50 |
| ☐ 61048 SP | 35.00 | 17.50 |
| ☐ C61050 SAB *"BIG COKE BOTTLE"* LAMINATED WOOD HANDLE | 110.00 | 55.00 |
| ☐ C61050 SAB *"BIG COKE BOTTLE"* BONE STAG HANDLE | 150.00 | 75.00 |
| ☐ 5165 SAB *"FOLDING HUNTER"* BOLSTER DRILL FOR LANYARD | 140.00 | 70.00 |
| ☐ 5165 SAB *"FOLDING HUNTER"* BOLSTER NOT DRILLED FOR LANYARD | 130.00 | 65.00 |
| ☐ 5165 *"FOLDING HUNTER"* BLADE FLAT GROUND | 275.00 | 137.50 |

# 84 / CASE XX'S

| PATTERN NO. | MINT | VG |
|---|---|---|
| ☐ 5165 SAB SECOND CUT STAG | 500.00 | 250.00 |
| ☐ 6165 "FOLDING HUNTER" BLADE FLAT GROUND | 250.00 | 125.00 |
| ☐ 6165 SAB "FOLDING HUNTER" LAMINATED WOOD HANDLE | 110.00 | 55.00 |
| ☐ 6165 SAB BONE STAG HANDLE | 130.00 | 65.00 |
| ☐ 6165 SAB ROGERS BONE | 500.00 | 250.00 |
| ☐ 5172 "BULLDOG" | 210.00 | 105.00 |
| ☐ 3185 "DOCTORS KNIFE" | 65.00 | 32.50 |
| ☐ 6185 "DOCTORS KNIFE" | 55.00 | 32.50 |
| ☐ 31093 "TEXAS TOOTHPICK" | 90.00 | 45.00 |
| ☐ 61093 "TEXAS TOOTHPICK" | 75.00 | 37.50 |
| ☐ 1199 SH R SS "GRAFTING KNIFE" | 27.00 | 13.50 |

## TWO BLADE

| | | |
|---|---|---|
| ☐ MUSKRAT | 55.00 | 27.50 |
| ☐ 4200 SS "MELON TESTER" | 150.00 | 75.00 |
| ☐ 3201 | 27.00 | 13.50 |
| ☐ 6201 | 35.00 | 13.50 |
| ☐ 9201 IMITATION PEARL HANDLE | 22.00 | 11.00 |
| ☐ 9201 CRACKED ICE HANDLE | 27.00 | 13.50 |
| ☐ 9201 R IMITATION PEARL HANDLE | 30.00 | 15.00 |
| ☐ 9201 R CRACKED ICE HANDLE | 33.00 | 15.00 |
| ☐ S2 REGULAR PULL | 100.00 | 50.00 |
| ☐ S2 LONG PULL | 125.00 | 62.50 |
| ☐ 2202½ | 110.00 | 55.00 |
| ☐ 6202½ | 27.00 | 13.50 |
| ☐ 6205 | 100.00 | 50.00 |
| ☐ 6205 "RAZ OR ONE ARM MAN" | 80.00 | 40.00 |
| ☐ 2207 | 200.00 | 100.00 |
| ☐ 6207 | 45.00 | 22.50 |
| ☐ 6207 ROGERS BONE | 120.00 | 60.00 |
| ☐ 6208 "HALF WHITTLER" | 27.00 | 13.50 |
| ☐ 62009 "BARLOW" | 35.00 | 17.50 |
| ☐ 62009 "BARLOW" "RAZ OR ONE ARM MAN" REGULAR PULL | 50.00 | 25.00 |
| ☐ 62009 "BARLOW" "RAZ OR ONE ARM MAN" LONG PULL | 55.00 | 27.50 |
| ☐ 62009 SH "BARLOW" BLACK COMPOSITION HANDLE | 125.00 | 62.50 |
| ☐ 62009½ "BARLOW" | 30.00 | 15.00 |

*CASE XX'S / 85*

| PATTERN NO. | MINT | VG |
|---|---|---|
| ☐ 62009½ "BARLOW" BLACK COMPOSITION HANDLE | 100.00 | 50.00 |
| ☐ 6214 | 30.00 | 15.00 |
| ☐ 6214½ | 28.00 | 14.00 |
| ☐ 6216 | 42.00 | 21.00 |
| ☐ 6216½ | 30.00 | 15.00 |
| ☐ 2217 "HALF HAWK BILL" | 225.00 | 112.50 |
| ☐ 6217 "HALF HAWK BILL" | 45.00 | 22.50 |
| ☐ 2220 "PEANUT" | 40.00 | 20.00 |
| ☐ 3220 "PEANUT" | 40.00 | 20.00 |
| ☐ 5220 "PEANUT" | 50.00 | 25.00 |
| ☐ 6220 "PEANUT" | 45.00 | 22.50 |
| ☐ 9220 IMITATION PEARL HANDLE "PEANUT" | 90.00 | 45.00 |
| ☐ 9220 CRACKED ICE HANDLE "PEANUT" | 90.00 | 45.00 |
| ☐ 2224 SP | 135.00 | 67.50 |
| ☐ 2224 SH | 140.00 | 70.00 |
| ☐ 2224 "RAZOR ONE ARM MAN" | 150.00 | 75.00 |
| ☐ 220024 SP "LITTLE JOHN CARVER" | 800.00 | 400.00 |
| ☐ 04247 SP | 100.00 | 50.00 |
| ☐ 05247 SP | 125.00 | 62.50 |
| ☐ 06247 PEN | 30.00 | 15.00 |
| ☐ 32048 SP | 32.00 | 16.00 |
| ☐ 62048 SP | 32.00 | 16.00 |
| ☐ 6249 "COPPERHEAD OR VIETNAM" | 50.00 | 25.00 |
| ☐ 6250 "SUNFISH" LAMINATED WOOD HANDLE | 110.00 | 55.00 |
| ☐ 6250 "SUNFISH" BONE STAG HANDLE | 150.00 | 75.00 |
| ☐ 62024 | 60.00 | 30.00 |
| ☐ 62024½ | 28.00 | 14.00 |
| ☐ 6225 "COKE BOTTLE" "RAZOR ONE ARM MAN" | 175.00 | 87.50 |
| ☐ 6225½ "COKE BOTTLE" | 40.00 | 20.00 |
| ☐ 6227 | 27.00 | 13.50 |
| ☐ 62027½ | 45.00 | 22.50 |
| ☐ 92027½ CRACKED ICE HANDLE | 90.00 | 45.00 |
| ☐ 22028 | 100.00 | 50.00 |
| ☐ 62028½ | 90.00 | 45.00 |
| ☐ 2229½ | 50.00 | 25.00 |
| ☐ 6229½ | 45.00 | 22.50 |
| ☐ 12031 L R "ELECTRICIAN'S KNIFE" | 25.00 | 12.50 |
| ☐ 2231½ LONG PULL STANDARD | 65.00 | 32.50 |
| ☐ 2231½ SAB LONG PULL STANDARD | 35.00 | 17.50 |
| ☐ 22031½ LONG PULL STANDARD | 65.00 | 32.50 |
| ☐ 4231½ LONG PULL STANDARD | 200.00 | 100.00 |

# 86 / CASE XX'S

**6227**

| PATTERN NO. | MINT | VG |
|---|---|---|
| ☐ 6231 REGULAR PULL | 45.00 | 22.50 |
| ☐ 6231½ LONG PULL STANDARD | 35.00 | 17.50 |
| ☐ 62031 REGULAR PULL | 55.00 | 27.50 |
| ☐ 62031½ LONG PULL STANDARD | 50.00 | 25.00 |
| ☐ 5232 | 60.00 | 30.00 |
| ☐ 6232 | 32.00 | 16.00 |
| ☐ 5233 | 45.00 | 22.50 |
| ☐ 6233 | 27.00 | 13.50 |
| ☐ 8233 | 50.00 | 25.00 |
| ☐ 9233 IMITATION PEARL HANDLE REGULAR PULL | 22.00 | 11.00 |
| ☐ 9233 IMITATION PEARL HANDLE LONG PULL | 65.00 | 32.50 |
| ☐ 9233 CRACKED ICE HANDLE REGULAR PULL | 27.00 | 13.50 |
| ☐ 9233 CRACKED ICE HANDLE LONG PULL | 90.00 | 45.00 |
| ☐ 9233 SHAD | 150.00 | 75.00 |
| ☐ 6235 | 35.00 | 17.50 |
| ☐ 6235 EO | 150.00 | 75.00 |
| ☐ 6235½ | 27.00 | 13.50 |
| ☐ 6235 P | 150.00 | 75.00 |
| ☐ 620035 BLACK PLASTIC HANDLE | 23.00 | 11.50 |
| ☐ 620035 LONG PULL BLACK PLASTIC HANDLE | 25.00 | 12.50 |
| ☐ 620035 EO BLACK PLASTIC HANDLE | 110.00 | 55.00 |
| ☐ 620035½ BLACK PLASTIC HANDLE | 23.00 | 11.50 |
| ☐ 620035½ LONG PULL BLACK PLASTIC HANDLE | 25.00 | 12.50 |
| ☐ 62042 | 25.00 | 12.50 |

*CASE XX'S / 87*

| PATTERN NO. | MINT | VG |
|---|---|---|
| ☐ 6202 R | 27.00 | 13.50 |
| ☐ 92042 CRACKED ICE HANDLE | 25.00 | 12.50 |
| ☐ 92042 R IMITATION PEARL HANDLE | 27.00 | 13.50 |
| ☐ 92042 R CRACKED ICE HANDLE | 32.00 | 16.00 |
| ☐ 06244 | 25.00 | 12.50 |
| ☐ 6244 | 25.00 | 12.50 |
| ☐ 2245 SH SP "GRAFTING KNIFE" | 100.00 | 50.00 |
| ☐ 3246 R "RIGGER'S KNIFE" | 140.00 | 70.00 |
| ☐ 6246 R SS "RIGGER'S KNIFE" | 75.00 | 37.50 |
| ☐ 62053 SS | 40.00 | 2.00 |
| ☐ 82053 S R SS | 65.00 | 32.50 |
| ☐ 82053 SR | 50.00 | 25.00 |
| ☐ 82053 SR SS | 40.00 | 20.00 |
| ☐ 9253 | 90.00 | 45.00 |
| ☐ 3254 "TRAPPER" | 100.00 | 50.00 |
| ☐ 3254 "TRAPPER" FIRST MODEL-TESTED FRAME | 175.00 | 87.50 |
| ☐ 3254 "TRAPPER" FIRST MODEL-FLAT YELLOW | 200.00 | 100.00 |
| ☐ 3254 "TRAPPER" MUSKRAT BLADE | 125.00 | 62.50 |
| ☐ 5254 "TRAPPER" | 175.00 | 87.50 |
| ☐ 5254 FIRST MODEL-TESTED FRAME | 225.00 | 112.50 |
| ☐ 5254 FIRST MODEL RED STAG | 500.00 | 250.00 |
| ☐ 5254 MUSKRAT | 200.00 | 100.00 |
| ☐ 6254 "TRAPPER" | 95.00 | 47.50 |
| ☐ 6254 "TRAPPER" FIRST MODEL-TESTED FRAME | 175.00 | 87.50 |
| ☐ 6254 "TRAPPER" MUSKRAT BLADE | 125.00 | 62.50 |
| ☐ 6254 "TRAPPER" SECOND CUT STAG (RARE) | 650.00 | 325.00 |
| ☐ 6254 ROGERS BONE (RARE) | 1200.00 | 600.00 |
| ☐ 22055 REGULAR PULL | 40.00 | 20.00 |
| ☐ 22055 LONG PULL | 90.00 | 45.00 |
| ☐ 62055 REGULAR PULL | 35.00 | 17.50 |
| ☐ 62055 LONG PULL | 100.00 | 50.00 |
| ☐ 92055 | 175.00 | 87.50 |
| ☐ 92055 LP | 85.00 | 42.50 |
| ☐ 4257 "OFFICE KNIFE" WRITING ON HANDLE | 85.00 | 42.50 |
| ☐ 4257 "OFFICE KNIFE" WITHOUT WRITING ON HANDLE | 40.00 | 20.00 |
| ☐ 42057 "OFFICE KNIFE" WRITING ON HANDLE | 85.00 | 42.50 |
| ☐ 42057 "OFFICE KNIFE" WITHOUT WRITING ON HANDLE | 40.00 | 20.00 |
| ☐ 5260 | 190.00 | 95.00 |
| ☐ 8261 | 40.00 | 20.00 |

## 88 / CASE XX'S

| PATTERN NO. | MINT | VG |
|---|---|---|
| ☐ 9261 IMITATION PEARL HANDLE | 27.00 | 13.50 |
| ☐ 9261 CRACKED ICE HANDLE | 30.00 | 15.00 |
| ☐ 05263 | 90.00 | 45.00 |
| ☐ 05263 SS | 45.00 | 22.50 |
| ☐ 06263 | 75.00 | 37.50 |
| ☐ 06263 SS | 30.00 | 15.00 |
| ☐ 06263 F SS | 35.00 | 17.50 |
| ☐ 62063 | 50.00 | 25.00 |
| ☐ 62063 SS | 40.00 | 20.00 |
| ☐ 62063½ SS | 40.00 | 20.00 |
| ☐ 82063 SHAD SS | 65.00 | 32.50 |
| ☐ 82063 SHAD | 75.00 | 37.50 |
| ☐ 92063½ | 75.00 | 37.50 |
| ☐ 5265 "FOLDING HUNTER" MASTER BLADE FLAT GROUND | 250.00 | 125.00 |
| ☐ 5265 SAB "FOLDING HUNTER" | 135.00 | 67.50 |
| ☐ 5265 SAB DR "FOLDING HUNTER" DRILLED FOR LANYARD | 140.00 | 70.00 |
| ☐ 5265 SAB "FOLDING HUNTER" SECOND CUT STAG | 500.00 | 250.00 |
| ☐ MARINER'S KNIFE SET | 65.00 | 32.50 |
| ☐ 6265 SAB "FOLDING HUNTER" BONE HANDLE MASTER BLADE FLAT GROUND | 225.00 | 112.50 |
| ☐ 6265 SAB "FOLDING HUNTER" LAMINATED WOOD HANDLE | 100.00 | 50.00 |
| ☐ 6265 SAB "FOLDING HUNTER" BONE STAG HANDLE | 125.00 | 62.50 |
| ☐ 6265 SAB ROGERS BONE | 500.00 | 250.00 |
| ☐ 06267 LONG PULL | 60.00 | 30.00 |
| ☐ 6269 | 30.00 | 15.00 |
| ☐ 6271 SS | 45.00 | 22.50 |
| ☐ 6271 F SS | 60.00 | 30.00 |
| ☐ 8271 LONG PULL | 175.00 | 87.50 |
| ☐ 8271 REGULAR PULL | 150.00 | 75.00 |
| ☐ 8271 SS LONG PULL | 175.00 | 87.50 |
| ☐ 8271 F REGULAR PULL | 150.00 | 75.00 |
| ☐ 6275 SP "MOOSE" | 55.00 | 27.50 |
| ☐ 2279 SS SHAD | 75.00 | 37.50 |
| ☐ 5279 | 85.00 | 42.50 |
| ☐ 5279 SS | 40.00 | 20.00 |
| ☐ 6279 | 30.00 | 15.00 |
| ☐ 6279 F SS | 35.00 | 17.50 |
| ☐ 6279 SS | 30.00 | 15.00 |

*CASE XX'S / 89*

| PATTERN NO. | MINT | VG |
|---|---|---|
| ☐ 8279 | 80.00 | 40.00 |
| ☐ 8279 SS | 65.00 | 32.50 |
| ☐ 9279 | 80.00 | 40.00 |
| ☐ 9279 SHAD SS | 30.00 | 15.00 |
| ☐ 62079½ *"SLEEVE BOARD"* | 80.00 | 40.00 |
| ☐ 82079½ SS *"SLEEVE BOARD"* | 45.00 | 22.50 |
| ☐ 82079½ *"SLEEVE BOARD"* | 50.00 | 25.00 |
| ☐ 92079½ *"SLEEVE BOARD"* | 90.00 | 45.00 |
| ☐ **M279 SS** *"PHYSICIAN'S KNIFE"* | 25.00 | 12.50 |
| ☐ **M279 F SS** *"PHYSICIAN'S KNIFE"* | 25.00 | 12.50 |
| ☐ 22087 | 25.00 | 12.50 |
| ☐ 52087 | 65.00 | 32.50 |
| ☐ 62087 | 25.00 | 12.50 |
| ☐ 6292 *"TEXAS JACK"* | 35.00 | 17.50 |
| ☐ 6294 *REGULAR PULL* | 125.00 | 62.50 |
| ☐ 6294 *LONG PULL* | 175.00 | 87.50 |
| ☐ 32095 F SS *"FISHERMANS KNIFE"* | 30.00 | 15.00 |
| ☐ 6296X SS *"CITRUS KNIFE"* | 95.00 | 47.50 |
| ☐ 3299½ | 60.00 | 30.00 |
| ☐ 3299½ *"A" BLADE* | 65.00 | 32.50 |
| ☐ 5299½ | 110.00 | 55.00 |
| ☐ 5299½ *"A" BLADE* | 125.00 | 62.50 |
| ☐ 62109X *"SMALL COPPERHEAD"* | 30.00 | 15.00 |
| ☐ 52131 *"CANOE" REGULAR PULL* | 120.00 | 60.00 |
| ☐ 52131 *"CANOE" LONG PULL* | 350.00 | 175.00 |
| ☐ 62131 *"CANOE"* | 200.00 | 100.00 |

## THREE BLADE

| | | |
|---|---|---|
| ☐ 6308 *"WHITTLER"* | 40.00 | 20.00 |
| ☐ 3318 SH SP | 32.00 | 16.00 |
| ☐ 3318 SH PEN | 32.00 | 16.00 |
| ☐ 4318 SP P | 160.00 | 80.00 |
| ☐ 4318 SH SP | 50.00 | 25.00 |
| ☐ 4318 SH SP *MASTER BLADE CALIFORNIA CLIP* | 50.00 | 25.00 |
| ☐ 6318 SP P | 35.00 | 17.50 |
| ☐ 6318 SH SP | 35.00 | 17.50 |
| ☐ 6318 SH SP *(XX TO U.S.A.)* | 65.00 | 32.50 |
| ☐ 6318 SH PEN | 32.00 | 16.00 |
| ☐ 6327 SH SP | 32.00 | 16.00 |
| ☐ 9327 SH SP | 30.00 | 15.00 |
| ☐ 9327 SH SP *CRACKED ICE HANDLE* | 60.00 | 30.00 |
| ☐ 13031 L R *"ELECTRICIANS KNIFE"* | 45.00 | 22.50 |

## 90 / CASE XX'S

| PATTERN NO. | MINT | VG |
|---|---|---|
| ☐ **5332** REGULAR PULL | 95.00 | 47.50 |
| ☐ **5332** LONG PULL | 150.00 | 75.00 |
| ☐ **6332** | 40.00 | 20.00 |
| ☐ **6333** | 30.00 | 15.00 |
| ☐ **9333** IMITATION PEARL HANDLE REGULAR PULL | 30.00 | 15.00 |
| ☐ **9333** IMITATION PEARL HANDLE LONG PULL | 65.00 | 32.50 |
| ☐ **9333** CRACKED ICE HANDLE REGULAR PULL | 30.00 | 15.00 |
| ☐ **9333** CRACKED ICE HANDLE LONG PULL | 75.00 | 37.50 |
| ☐ **6344 SH SP** | 32.00 | 16.00 |
| ☐ **6344 SH PEN** | 32.00 | 16.00 |
| ☐ **33044 SH SP** "BIRDSEYE" | 75.00 | 37.50 |
| ☐ **2345½ SH** | 75.00 | 37.50 |
| ☐ **2345 P** LONG PULL STANDARD | 125.00 | 62.50 |
| ☐ **6345½ SH** | 110.00 | 55.00 |
| ☐ **M346** STAMPED METAL STAMPINGS LTD. | 75.00 | 37.50 |
| ☐ **M346** STAMPED CASE XX MADE FOR U.S.A. NAVY WWII | 65.00 | 32.50 |
| ☐ **3347 SH SP** REGULAR PULL | 32.00 | 16.00 |
| ☐ **3347 SP PU** YELLOW L.P. | 125.00 | 62.50 |
| ☐ **3347 SH SP** LONG PULL | 100.00 | 50.00 |
| ☐ **5347 SH SP** REGULAR PULL | 90.00 | 45.00 |
| ☐ **5347 SH SP** LONG PULL | 140.00 | 70.00 |
| ☐ **5347 SH SP SS** | 100.00 | 50.00 |
| ☐ **53047** | 100.00 | 50.00 |
| ☐ **6347 SH SP** | 40.00 | 20.00 |
| ☐ **6347 SH SP SS** | 80.00 | 40.00 |
| ☐ **6347 SH PEN** | 45.00 | 22.50 |
| ☐ **6347 SP PEN** | 45.00 | 22.50 |
| ☐ **6347 SH P** | 60.00 | 30.00 |
| ☐ **6347 SP P** | 45.00 | 22.50 |
| ☐ **63047** | 45.00 | 22.50 |
| ☐ **93047** | 200.00 | 100.00 |
| ☐ **23055 P** | 350.00 | 175.00 |
| ☐ **8364 T SS** | 90.00 | 45.00 |
| ☐ **8364 SCIS SS** | 90.00 | 45.00 |
| ☐ **5375** REGULAR PULL | 125.00 | 62.50 |
| ☐ **5375** LONG PULL | 225.00 | 112.50 |
| ☐ **5375** SECOND CUT STAG HANDLE REGULAR PULL | 600.00 | 300.00 |
| ☐ **5375** SECOND CUT STAG HANDLE LONG PULL | 650.00 | 325.00 |
| ☐ **6375** REGULAR PULL | 65.00 | 32.50 |
| ☐ **6375** LONG PULL | 125.00 | 62.50 |

*CASE XX'S / 91*

| PATTERN NO. | MINT | VG |
|---|---|---|
| ☐ 6380 "WHITTLER" | 80.00 | 40.00 |
| ☐ 6380 ROGERS BONE | 225.00 | 112.50 |
| ☐ 2383 "WHITTLER" | 80.00 | 40.00 |
| ☐ 2383 SAB "WHITTLER" MASTER BLADE SABER GROUND | 250.00 | 125.00 |
| ☐ 5383 "WHITTLER" | 110.00 | 55.00 |
| ☐ 6383 "WHITTLER" | 55.00 | 27.50 |
| ☐ 6383 SAB "WHITTLER" MASTER BLADE SABER GROUND | 250.00 | 125.00 |
| ☐ 9383 "WHITTLER" | 225.00 | 112.50 |
| ☐ 9383 SAB "WHITTLER" MASTER BLADE SABER GROUND | 275.00 | 137.50 |
| ☐ 23087 SH PEN | 25.00 | 12.50 |
| ☐ 53087 SH PEN | 80.00 | 40.00 |
| ☐ 63087 SP PEN | 30.00 | 15.00 |
| ☐ 83088 SS | 125.00 | 62.50 |
| ☐ 83089 SC F SS | 125.00 | 62.50 |
| ☐ 83090 SC R SS | 150.00 | 75.00 |
| ☐ 5391 "WHITTLER" RED STAG | 1500.00 | 750.00 |
| ☐ 33092 "BIRDSEYE" WITH SHIELD | 65.00 | 32.50 |
| ☐ 33092 "BIRDSEYE" WITHOUT SHIELD | 55.00 | 27.50 |
| ☐ 5392 | 110.00 | 55.00 |
| ☐ 6392 | 45.00 | 22.50 |
| ☐ 6394½ LONG PULL | 600.00 | 300.00 |
| ☐ M3102 R SS | 27.00 | 135.00 |
| ☐ 83102 SS | 125.00 | 62.50 |
| ☐ T3105 SS "TOLEDO SCALE" (NEW) | 75.00 | 37.50 |
| ☐ T3105 SS "TOLEDO SCALE" (OLD) | 175.00 | 87.50 |

## FOUR BLADE

| | MINT | VG |
|---|---|---|
| ☐ CASE'S SS "FLY FISHERMAN" | 100.00 | 50.00 |
| ☐ CASE'S SS "FLY FISHERMAN" (XX TO U.S.A.) | 110.00 | 55.00 |
| ☐ 6445 R "SCOUTS KNIFE" BLACK COMPOSITION HANDLE | 50.00 | 25.00 |
| ☐ 6445 R "SCOUTS KNIFE" BONE STAG HANDLE | 45.00 | 22.50 |
| ☐ 640045 R "SCOUTS KNIFE" BLACK PLASTIC HANDLE | 25.00 | 12.50 |
| ☐ 640045 R "SCOUTS KNIFE" BROWN PLASTIC HANDLE | 25.00 | 12.50 |
| ☐ 64047 P | 45.00 | 22.50 |
| ☐ 64055 P | 500.00 | 250.00 |
| ☐ 54052 | 100.00 | 50.00 |

## 92 / CASE XX'S

| PATTERN NO. | MINT | VG |
|---|---|---|
| ☐ 54052 *(XX TO U.S.A.)* | 120.00 | 60.00 |
| ☐ 64052 | 60.00 | 30.00 |
| ☐ 64052 *(XX TO U.S.A.)* | 90.00 | 45.00 |
| ☐ 5488 *REGULAR PULL* | 125.00 | 62.50 |
| ☐ 5488 *REGULAR PULL (XX TO U.S.A.)* | 175.00 | 87.50 |
| ☐ 5488 *LONG PULL* | 300.00 | 150.00 |
| ☐ 5488 *SECOND CUT STAG HANDLE* | 400.00 | 200.00 |
| ☐ 5488 *SECOND CUT STAG HANDLE (XX TO U.S.A.)* | 400.00 | 200.00 |
| ☐ 6488 *REGULAR PULL* | 80.00 | 40.00 |
| ☐ 6488 *LONG PULL* | 150.00 | 75.00 |
| ☐ 6488 *(XX TO U.S.A.)* | 100.00 | 50.00 |
| ☐ 6488 *SECOND CUT STAG HANDLE* | 300.00 | 150.00 |

## CASE XX "PLASTAG" OR ROUGH BLACK
### ONE BLADE

*(\*XX Frame; \*\*Etched Lengthwise On Blade; "Test XX Stainless")*

| | | |
|---|---|---|
| ☐ 6165 SAB *"FOLDING HUNTER"* | 175.00 | 87.50 |
| ☐ 6165 *"FOLDING HUNTER" FLAT GROUND BLADE* | 200.00 | 100.00 |

### TWO BLADE

| | | |
|---|---|---|
| ☐ MUSKRAT | 200.00 | 100.00 |
| ☐ 6202½ | 40.00 | 20.00 |
| ☐ 6206½ | 85.00 | 42.50 |
| ☐ 6207 | 70.00 | 35.00 |
| ☐ 6208 *"HALF WHITTLER"* | 45.00 | 22.50 |
| ☐ 62009½ *"BARLOW"* | 90.00 | 45.00 |
| ☐ 6214 *WITH SHIELD* | 45.00 | 22.50 |
| ☐ 6214 *WITHOUT SHIELD* | 40.00 | 20.00 |
| ☐ 6214½ | 40.00 | 20.00 |
| ☐ 6220 *"PEANUT"* | 90.00 | 45.00 |
| ☐ 6225½ *"COKE BOTTLE"* | 75.00 | 37.50 |
| ☐ 62028½ | 90.00 | 45.00 |
| ☐ 6231 | 50.00 | 25.00 |
| ☐ 6231½ *LONG PULL STANDARD* | 45.00 | 22.50 |
| ☐ 62031 *REGULAR PULL* | 60.00 | 30.00 |
| ☐ 62031 *LONG PULL* | 70.00 | 35.00 |
| ☐ 62031½ *LONG PULL* | 70.00 | 35.00 |
| ☐ 6232 | 50.00 | 25.00 |

*CASE XX'S / 93*

| PATTERN NO. | MINT | VG |
|---|---|---|
| ☐ 6233 *REGULAR PULL* | 60.00 | 30.00 |
| ☐ 6233 *LONG PULL* | 80.00 | 40.00 |
| ☐ 6235 | 35.00 | 17.50 |
| ☐ 6235 EO | 60.00 | 30.00 |
| ☐ 6235½ | 30.00 | 15.00 |
| ☐ 62042 | 30.00 | 15.00 |
| ☐ 06247 PEN | 70.00 | 35.00 |
| ☐ 62052 | 60.00 | 30.00 |
| ☐ 62055 *REGULAR PULL* | 65.00 | 32.50 |
| ☐ 62055 *LONG PULL* | 85.00 | 42.50 |
| ☐ 6265 SAB *"FOLDING HUNTER"* | 150.00 | 75.00 |
| ☐ 6265 *FLAT GROUND BLADE* | 175.00 | 87.50 |
| ☐ 6275 SP *"MOOSE" LONG PULL* | 140.00 | 70.00 |
| ☐ 6279 | 50.00 | 25.00 |
| ☐ 6279 SS | 35.00 | 17.50 |
| ☐ 6279 F SS | 35.00 | 17.50 |
| ☐ 62087 | 75.00 | 37.50 |
| ☐ 6292 *"TEXAS JACK"* | 85.00 | 42.50 |
| ☐ 6299 | 85.00 | 42.50 |
| ☐ 62109 X *"SMALL COPPERHEAD"* | 65.00 | 32.50 |

## THREE BLADE

| | | |
|---|---|---|
| ☐ 6308 *"WHITTLER"* | 120.00 | 60.00 |
| ☐ 6318 SP P | 70.00 | 35.00 |
| ☐ 6318 SH SP | 70.00 | 35.00 |
| ☐ 6318 SH PEN | 70.00 | 35.00 |
| ☐ 6332 | 100.00 | 50.00 |
| ☐ 6333 *REGULAR PULL* | 65.00 | 32.50 |
| ☐ 6333 *LONG PULL* | 80.00 | 40.00 |
| ☐ 6345½ SH | 110.00 | 55.00 |
| ☐ 6347 SP PEN | 85.00 | 42.50 |
| ☐ 6347 SH SP *REGULAR PULL* | 85.00 | 42.50 |
| ☐ 6347 SH SP *LONG PULL* | 85.00 | 42.50 |
| ☐ 6347 SH P | 85.00 | 42.50 |
| ☐ 63047 | 85.00 | 42.50 |
| ☐ 6375 *LONG PULL* | 160.00 | 80.00 |
| ☐ 6383 *"WHITTLER"* | 180.00 | 90.00 |
| ☐ 6383 SAB *"WHITTLER"* | 250.00 | 125.00 |
| ☐ 63087 SP PEN | 50.00 | 25.00 |
| ☐ 6392 *REGULAR PULL* | 90.00 | 45.00 |

94 / CASE XX'S

## FOUR BLADE

| PATTERN NO. | MINT | VG |
|---|---|---|
| ☐ 64045 | 45.00 | 22.50 |
| ☐ 64047 P | 130.00 | 65.00 |
| ☐ 6488 LONG PULL | 225.00 | 112.50 |

## CASE XX RED BONE

### ONE BLADE

(*XX Frame; **Etched Lengthwise On Blade; "Test XX Stainless")

| | | |
|---|---|---|
| ☐ 61011 "HAWK BILL" | 50.00 | 25.00 |
| ☐ 6143 "DADDY BARLOW" | 60.00 | 30.00 |
| ☐ 61048 | 45.00 | 22.50 |
| ☐ C61050 SAB "BIG COKE BOTTLE" | 175.00 | 87.50 |
| ☐ 6165 SAB "FOLDING HUNTER" | 175.00 | 87.50 |
| ☐ 6185 "DOCTORS KNIFE" | 75.00 | 37.50 |
| ☐ 61093 "TEXAS TOOTHPICK" | 100.00 | 50.00 |

### TWO BLADE

| | | |
|---|---|---|
| ☐ MUSKRAT | 100.00 | 50.00 |
| ☐ 6205 SPEAR BLADE | 100.00 | 50.00 |
| ☐ 6205 "RAZOR ONE ARM MAN" | 100.00 | 50.00 |
| ☐ 6207 | 65.00 | 32.50 |
| ☐ 6208 "HALF WHITTLER" | 45.00 | 22.50 |
| ☐ 62009 "BARLOW" | 50.00 | 25.00 |
| ☐ 62009½ "BARLOW" | 45.00 | 22.50 |
| ☐ 6214 | 45.00 | 22.50 |
| ☐ 6217 | 75.00 | 37.50 |
| ☐ 6220 "PEANUT" | 75.00 | 37.50 |
| ☐ 6225½ "COKE BOTTLE" | 70.00 | 35.00 |
| ☐ 6231 MASTER BLADE SPEAR POINT | 70.00 | 35.00 |
| ☐ 6231½ | 60.00 | 30.00 |
| ☐ 62031 MASTER BLADE SPEAR POINT | 70.00 | 35.00 |
| ☐ 62031½ | 70.00 | 35.00 |
| ☐ 6232 | 60.00 | 30.00 |
| ☐ 6233 | 45.00 | 22.50 |
| ☐ 62042 | 35.00 | 17.50 |
| ☐ 6244 | 40.00 | 20.00 |
| ☐ 62048 SP | 40.00 | 20.00 |
| ☐ 6249 "COPPERHEAD OR VIETNAM" | 80.00 | 40.00 |
| ☐ 6250 "SUNFISH" | 250.00 | 125.00 |

CASE XX'S / 95

| PATTERN NO. | MINT | VG |
|---|---|---|
| 6254 "TRAPPER" | 200.00 | 100.00 |
| 06263 SS | 30.00 | 15.00 |
| 62063½ SS | 40.00 | 20.00 |
| 6265 SAB "FOLDING HUNTER" | 150.00 | 75.00 |
| 62063 SS | 45.00 | 22.50 |
| 6269 | 45.00 | 22.50 |
| 6275 SP "MOOSE" REGULAR PULL | 125.00 | 62.50 |
| 6275 SP "MOOSE" LONG PULL | 200.00 | 100.00 |
| 6279 SS | 30.00 | 15.00 |
| 62087 | 35.00 | 17.50 |
| 6292 "TEXAS JACK" | 75.00 | 37.50 |
| 6294 REGULAR PULL | 200.00 | 100.00 |
| 6294 LONG PULL | 275.00 | 137.50 |
| 62109 X "SMALL COPPERHEAD" | 50.00 | 25.00 |

## THREE BLADE

| | | |
|---|---|---|
| 6308 "WHITTLER" | 90.00 | 45.00 |
| 6318 SP P | 50.00 | 25.00 |
| 6318 SH SP | 50.00 | 25.00 |
| 6318 SH PEN | 50.00 | 25.00 |
| 6327 | 35.00 | 17.50 |
| 6332 | 70.00 | 35.00 |
| 6332 | 100.00 | 50.00 |
| 6344 SH SP | 45.00 | 22.50 |
| 6344 SH PEN | 45.00 | 22.50 |
| 6345½ SH | 125.00 | 62.50 |
| 63047 | 80.00 | 40.00 |
| 6347 SH SP | 80.00 | 40.00 |
| 6347 SH SP SS | 110.00 | 55.00 |
| 6347 SP P | 80.00 | 40.00 |
| 6375 REGULAR PULL | 125.00 | 62.50 |
| 6375 LONG PULL | 225.00 | 112.50 |
| 6380 "WHITTLER" | 135.00 | 67.50 |
| 6383 "WHITTLER" | 110.00 | 55.00 |
| 63087 SP PEN | 45.00 | 22.50 |
| 6392 | 85.00 | 42.50 |
| 6394½ LONG PULL | 600.00 | 300.00 |

## FOUR BLADE

| | | |
|---|---|---|
| 6445 R "SCOUT'S KNIFE" | 65.00 | 32.50 |
| 64047 P | 100.00 | 50.00 |

96 / CASE XX'S

| PATTERN NO. | MINT | VG |
|---|---|---|
| ☐ 64052 | 100.00 | 50.00 |
| ☐ 6488 REGULAR PULL | 150.00 | 75.00 |
| ☐ 6488 LONG PULL | 300.00 | 150.00 |

## CASE XX GREEN BONE (HONEY COMB)
### ONE BLADE
(*XX Frame; **Etched Lengthwise On Blade; "Test XX Stainless")

| | | |
|---|---|---|
| ☐ 6104 B "BUDDING KNIFE" | 175.00 | 87.50 |
| ☐ 61011 "HAWK BILL" | 75.00 | 37.50 |
| ☐ 6111½ L "LOCK BACK" | 325.00 | 162.50 |
| ☐ 6143 "DADDY BARLOW" | 110.00 | 55.00 |
| ☐ 61048 | 110.00 | 55.00 |
| ☐ C61050 SAB "BIG COKE BOTTLE" | 325.00 | 162.50 |
| ☐ 6165 "FOLDING HUNTER" BLADE FLAT GROUND | 350.00 | 175.00 |
| ☐ 6165 SAB "FOLDING HUNTER" | 275.00 | 137.50 |
| ☐ 61093 "TEXAS TOOTHPICK" | 190.00 | 95.00 |

### TWO BLADE

| | | |
|---|---|---|
| ☐ MUSKRAT | 300.00 | 150.00 |
| ☐ 6202½ | 75.00 | 37.50 |
| ☐ 6205 | 125.00 | 62.50 |
| ☐ 6205 "RAZ OR ONE ARM MAN" | 150.00 | 75.00 |
| ☐ 6207 | 130.00 | 65.00 |
| ☐ 6208 "HALF WHITTLER" | 75.00 | 37.50 |
| ☐ 62009 "BARLOW" | 110.00 | 55.00 |
| ☐ 62009 "BARLOW" "RAZ OR ONE ARM MAN" | 125.00 | 62.50 |
| ☐ 62009½ "BARLOW" | 110.00 | 55.00 |
| ☐ 62009½ "BARLOW" OLD STYLE | 140.00 | 70.00 |
| ☐ 6214 | 105.00 | 52.50 |
| ☐ 6214½ | 90.00 | 45.00 |
| ☐ 6217 "HALF HAWK BILL" | 150.00 | 75.00 |
| ☐ 6220 "PEANUT" | 150.00 | 75.00 |
| ☐ 62024½ | 55.00 | 27.50 |
| ☐ 6225½ "COKE BOTTLE" | 125.00 | 62.50 |
| ☐ 6231 | 140.00 | 70.00 |
| ☐ 6231½ | 120.00 | 60.00 |
| ☐ 62031 REGULAR PULL | 140.00 | 70.00 |
| ☐ 62031 LONG PULL | 155.00 | 77.50 |
| ☐ 62031½ | 150.00 | 75.00 |

CASE XX'S / 97

| PATTERN NO. | MINT | VG |
|---|---|---|
| ☐ 6232 | 95.00 | 47.50 |
| ☐ 6233 REGULAR PULL | 100.00 | 50.00 |
| ☐ 6233 LONG PULL | 120.00 | 60.00 |
| ☐ 6235 | 65.00 | 32.50 |
| ☐ 6235½ | 65.00 | 32.50 |
| ☐ 62042 | 50.00 | 25.00 |
| ☐ 06244 | 50.00 | 25.00 |
| ☐ 6244 | 60.00 | 30.00 |
| ☐ 06245 XX | 200.00 | 100.00 |
| ☐ 06247 PEN | 95.00 | 47.50 |
| ☐ 62048 SP | 100.00 | 50.00 |
| ☐ 6249 "COPPERHEAD OR VIETNAM" | 175.00 | 87.50 |
| ☐ 6250 "SUNFISH" | 400.00 | 200.00 |
| ☐ 62052 | 85.00 | 42.50 |
| ☐ 62055 LONG PULL | 120.00 | 60.00 |
| ☐ 06263 SS | 55.00 | 27.50 |
| ☐ 62063½ | 60.00 | 30.00 |
| ☐ 62063 | 65.00 | 32.50 |
| ☐ 6265 "FOLDING HUNTER" MASTER BLADE FLAT GROUND | 400.00 | 200.00 |
| ☐ 6265 SAB "FOLDING HUNTER" | 275.00 | 137.50 |
| ☐ 6269 REGULAR PULL | 80.00 | 40.00 |
| ☐ 6275 SP "MOOSE" LONG PULL | 250.00 | 125.00 |
| ☐ 6279 SS | 65.00 | 32.50 |
| ☐ 6279 F SS | 65.00 | 32.50 |
| ☐ 62087 | 50.00 | 25.00 |
| ☐ 6292 "TEXAS JACK" | 150.00 | 75.00 |
| ☐ 6294 LONG PULL | 400.00 | 200.00 |
| ☐ 6296X SS "CITRUS KNIFE" | 250.00 | 125.00 |
| ☐ 6299 | 190.00 | 90.00 |
| ☐ 62109X "SMALL COPPERHEAD" | 80.00 | 40.00 |

## THREE BLADE

| | | |
|---|---|---|
| ☐ 6308 "WHITTLER" | 150.00 | 75.00 |
| ☐ 6318 SP P | 130.00 | 65.00 |
| ☐ 6318 SH SP REGULAR PULL | 110.00 | 55.00 |
| ☐ 6318 SH SP LONG PULL | 140.00 | 70.00 |
| ☐ 6318 SH PEN | 120.00 | 60.00 |
| ☐ 6332 | 150.00 | 75.00 |
| ☐ 6333 | 110.00 | 55.00 |
| ☐ 6344 SH SP | 120.00 | 60.00 |
| ☐ 6344 SH PEN | 120.00 | 60.00 |

## 98 / CASE XX U.S.A.

| PATTERN NO. | MINT | VG |
|---|---|---|
| ☐ 6345½ SH | 175.00 | 87.50 |
| ☐ 6347 SH SP *REGULAR PULL* | 150.00 | 75.00 |
| ☐ 6347 SH SP *LONG PULL* | 225.00 | 112.50 |
| ☐ 6347 SP P *REGULAR PULL* | 150.00 | 75.00 |
| ☐ 6347 SP P *LONG PULL* | 225.00 | 112.50 |
| ☐ 6347 SH P *REGULAR PULL* | 150.00 | 75.00 |
| ☐ 6347 SH P *LONG PULL* | 225.00 | 112.50 |
| ☐ 63047 | 175.00 | 87.50 |
| ☐ 6375 *LONG PULL* | 300.00 | 150.00 |
| ☐ 6380 *"WHITTLER"* | 375.00 | 187.50 |
| ☐ 6383 *"WHITTLER"* | 300.00 | 150.00 |
| ☐ 63087 SP PEN | 75.00 | 37.50 |
| ☐ 6392 | 175.00 | 87.50 |
| ☐ 6394½ | 600.00 | 300.00 |

### FOUR BLADE

| | | |
|---|---|---|
| ☐ 64047 PU | 200.00 | 100.00 |
| ☐ 64052 | 200.00 | 100.00 |
| ☐ 6488 | 400.00 | 200.00 |

# CASE XX U.S.A.

## ONE BLADE

(*XX Frame; **Etched Lengthwise On Blade; "Tested XX Stainless")

| | | |
|---|---|---|
| ☐ 4100 SS *"MELON TESTER"* | 45.00 | 22.50 |
| ☐ 4100 SS *"MELON TESTER" SERRATED EDGE* | 75.00 | 37.50 |
| ☐ 2109 B *"BUDDING KNIFE"* | 100.00 | 50.00 |
| ☐ 11011 *"HAWK BILL"* | 22.00 | 11.00 |
| ☐ 6111½ *"LOCK BACK"* | 45.00 | 22.50 |
| ☐ 61011 *"HAWK BILL" LAMINATED WOOD HANDLE* | 125.00 | 62.50 |
| ☐ 61011 *"HAWK BILL"* BONE STAG HANDLE | 20.00 | 10.00 |
| ☐ 1116 SP *"BUDDING KNIFE"* | 85.00 | 42.50 |
| ☐ 31024½ | 35.00 | 17.50 |
| ☐ 61024½ | 30.00 | 15.00 |
| ☐ 11031 SH | 18.00 | 9.00 |
| ☐ 2138 *"SOD BUSTER"* | 25.00 | 12.50 |
| ☐ 6143 *"DADDY BARLOW"* | 30.00 | 15.00 |
| ☐ 31048 | 20.00 | 10.00 |
| ☐ 31048 SP | 35.00 | 17.50 |

*CASE XX U.S.A. / 99*

| PATTERN NO. | MINT | VG |
|---|---|---|
| ☐ **61048** *DELRIN HANDLE* | 20.00 | 10.00 |
| ☐ **61048** *BONE STAG HANDLE* | 25.00 | 12.50 |
| ☐ **61048 SP** *DELRIN HANDLE* | 25.00 | 12.50 |
| ☐ **61048 SP** *BONE STAG HANDLE* | 35.00 | 17.50 |
| ☐ **61048 SSP** *POLISHED BLADE* | 45.00 | 22.50 |
| ☐ **61048 SSP** *DELRIN HANDLE* | 20.00 | 10.00 |
| ☐ **\*\*61048 SSP** *BONE STAG HANDLE (FIRST MODEL)* | 50.00 | 25.00 |
| ☐ **61048 SSP** *BONE STAG HANDLE* | 30.00 | 15.00 |
| ☐ **C61050 SAB** *"BIG COKE BOTTLE" LAMINATED WOOD HANDLE* | 42.00 | 21.00 |
| ☐ **5165 SAB** *"FOLDING HUNTER" SMALL PATTERN NUMBER* | 325.00 | 162.50 |
| ☐ **5165 SAB** *"FOLDING HUNTER" LARGE PATTERN NUMBER* | 325.00 | 162.50 |
| ☐ **\*6165 SAB** *"FOLDING HUNTER" LAMINATED WOOD HANDLE, BOLSTER NOT DRILLED FOR LANYARD* | 950.00 | 475.00 |
| ☐ **6165** *BONE HANDLE LARGE STAMPING WITH SAB DELETED* | 160.00 | 80.00 |
| ☐ **\*6165 SAB DR** *"FOLDING HUNTER" LAMINATED WOOD HANDLE* | 65.00 | 32.50 |
| ☐ **6165 SAB DR** *"FOLDING HUNTER" LAMINATED WOOD HANDLE* | 35.00 | 17.50 |
| ☐ **6165 SAB DR** *LAMINATED WOOD (LETTERS SAB DR DELETED)* | 42.00 | 21.00 |

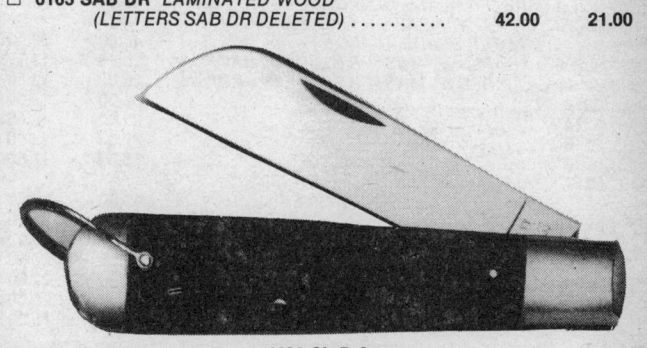

1199 Sh R Ss

100 / CASE XX U.S.A.

| PATTERN NO. | MINT | VG |
|---|---|---|
| ☐ P172 "BUFFALO" | 60.00 | 30.00 |
| ☐ 5172 "BULLDOG" | 130.00 | 65.00 |
| ☐ 5172 "BULLDOG" TRANSITION | 180.00 | 90.00 |
| ☐ 3185 "DOCTORS KNIFE" | 55.00 | 27.50 |
| ☐ 6185 "DOCTORS KNIFE" | 55.00 | 27.50 |
| ☐ 61093 "TEXAS TOOTHPICK" | 55.00 | 27.50 |
| ☐ 1199 SH R SS "GRAFTING KNIFE" | 25.00 | 12.50 |

## TWO BLADE

| | MINT | VG |
|---|---|---|
| ☐ MUSKRAT | 32.00 | 16.00 |
| ☐ 4200 SS "MELON TESTER" | 65.00 | 32.50 |
| ☐ 4200 SS "MELON TESTER" MASTER BLADE SERRATED EDGE | 90.00 | 45.00 |
| ☐ 3201 | 24.00 | 12.00 |
| ☐ 6201 | 27.00 | 13.50 |
| ☐ 9201 | 22.00 | 11.00 |
| ☐ S2 | 110.00 | 55.00 |
| ☐ 6202½ | 20.00 | 10.00 |
| ☐ 6205 "RAZ OR ONE ARM MAN" | 50.00 | 25.00 |
| ☐ 6207 | 30.00 | 15.00 |
| ☐ 6208 "HALF WHITTLER" | 22.00 | 11.00 |
| ☐ 62009 "BARLOW" MASTER BLADE IN BACK | 30.00 | 15.00 |
| ☐ 62009 "BARLOW" MASTER BLADE IN FRONT | 30.00 | 15.00 |
| ☐ 62009 "BARLOW" "RAZ OR ONE ARM MAN" MASTER BLADE IN BACK | 40.00 | 20.00 |
| ☐ 62009 "BARLOW" "RAZ OR ONE ARM MAN" MASTER BLADE IN FRONT | 40.00 | 20.00 |
| ☐ 62009½ "BARLOW" MASTER BLADE IN BACK | 25.00 | 12.50 |
| ☐ 62009½ "BARLOW" MASTER BLADE IN FRONT | 25.00 | 12.50 |
| ☐ 6214 | 35.00 | 17.50 |
| ☐ 6214½ | 25.00 | 12.50 |
| ☐ 6216 | 27.00 | 13.50 |
| ☐ 6216½ | 35.00 | 17.50 |
| ☐ 6217 "HALF HAWK BILL" LAMINATED WOOD HANDLE | 40.00 | 20.00 |
| ☐ 6217 "HALF HAWK BILL" BONE STAG HANDLE | 40.00 | 20.00 |
| ☐ 2220 "PEANUT" | 40.00 | 20.00 |
| ☐ 3220 "PEANUT" | 55.00 | 27.50 |
| ☐ 5220 "PEANUT" | 45.00 | 22.50 |
| ☐ 6220 "PEANUT" | 50.00 | 25.00 |
| ☐ 32024½ | 30.00 | 15.00 |

*CASE XX U.S.A. / 101*

| PATTERN NO. | MINT | VG |
|---|---|---|
| ☐ 62024½ | 25.00 | 12.50 |
| ☐ 6225½ "COKE BOTTLE" | 30.00 | 15.00 |
| ☐ 6227 | 22.00 | 11.00 |
| ☐ 6229½ | 45.00 | 22.50 |
| ☐ 2229½ | 50.00 | 25.00 |
| ☐ 12031 L R "ELECTRICIANS KNIFE" | 20.00 | 10.00 |
| ☐ 2231½ SAB LONG PULL STANDARD | 25.00 | 12.50 |
| ☐ 6231½ LONG PULL STANDARD | 30.00 | 15.00 |
| ☐ 5232 | 45.00 | 22.50 |
| ☐ 6232 | 20.00 | 10.00 |
| ☐ 3233 | 25.00 | 12.50 |
| ☐ 5233 | 45.00 | 22.50 |
| ☐ 6233 | 25.00 | 12.50 |
| ☐ 6233 DELRIN RARE | 35.00 | 17.50 |
| ☐ 8233 | 45.00 | 22.50 |
| ☐ 9233 | 22.00 | 11.00 |
| ☐ 6235½ MASTER BLADE IN BACK | 20.00 | 10.00 |
| ☐ 6235½ MASTER BLADE IN FRONT | 20.00 | 10.00 |
| ☐ 62042 | 20.00 | 11.00 |
| ☐ 62942 R | 25.00 | 12.50 |
| ☐ 92042 | 18.00 | 9.00 |
| ☐ 93042 R | 25.00 | 12.50 |
| ☐ 06244 | 22.00 | 11.00 |
| ☐ 6244 | 25.00 | 12.50 |
| ☐ 6246 R SS "RIGGER'S KNIFE" | 45.00 | 22.50 |
| ☐ 04247 SP | 75.00 | 37.50 |
| ☐ 05247 SP | 175.00 | 87.50 |
| ☐ 06247 PEN | 20.00 | 10.00 |
| ☐ 4247 F K "GREEN KEEPER'S" | 250.00 | 125.00 |
| ☐ 32048 SP | 25.00 | 12.50 |
| ☐ 62048 SP DELRIN HANDLE | 20.00 | 10.00 |
| ☐ 62048 SP BONE STAG HANDLE | 30.00 | 15.00 |
| ☐ 62048 SP SSP DELRIN HANDLE | 20.00 | 10.00 |
| ☐ **62048 SP SSP BONE STAG HANDLE (FIRST MODEL) | 50.00 | 25.00 |
| ☐ 62048 SP SSP BONE STAG HANDLE | 30.00 | 15.00 |
| ☐ 62048 SP SSP BONE STAG HANDLE POLISHED BLADE | 50.00 | 25.00 |
| ☐ 6249 "COPPERHEAD OR VIETNAM" | 32.00 | 16.00 |
| ☐ 6250 "SUNFISH" LAMINATED WOOD HANDLE | 45.00 | 22.50 |
| ☐ 6250 "SUNFISH" LAMINATED WOOD HANDLE | 200.00 | 100.00 |
| ☐ 62052 | 30.00 | 15.00 |

## 102 / CASE XX U.S.A.

| PATTERN NO. | MINT | VG |
|---|---|---|
| ☐ 62053 SS | 100.00 | 50.00 |
| ☐ 82053 S R SS | 45.00 | 22.50 |
| ☐ 82053 "TRAPPER" | 55.00 | 27.50 |
| ☐ 3254 FLAT YELLOW | 75.00 | 37.50 |
| ☐ 3254 "TRAPPER" MUSKRAT BLADE | 75.00 | 37.50 |
| ☐ 5254 "TRAPPER" | 75.00 | 37.50 |
| ☐ 5254 "TRAPPER" MUSKRAT BLADE | 100.00 | 50.00 |
| ☐ 5254 "TRAPPER" SECOND CUT STAG HANDLE | 500.00 | 250.00 |
| ☐ 5254 "TRAPPER" MUSKRAT BLADE SECOND CUT STAG HANDLE | 500.00 | 250.00 |
| ☐ 6254 "TRAPPER" | 55.00 | 27.50 |
| ☐ 6254 "TRAPPER" MUSKRAT BLADE | 80.00 | 40.00 |
| ☐ 6254 "TRAPPER" SECOND CUT STAG HANDLE | 400.00 | 200.00 |
| ☐ 6254 "TRAPPER" SECOND CUT STAG HANDLE MUSKRAT BLADE | 400.00 | 200.00 |
| ☐ 6254 "TRAPPER" BLADES POLISHED | 100.00 | 50.00 |
| ☐ 6254 SSP "TRAPPER" EDGE OF BLADE POLISHED | 60.00 | 30.00 |
| ☐ 6254 SSP "TRAPPER" MUSKRAT BLADE POLISHED EDGE | 100.00 | 50.00 |
| ☐ 6254 SSP BOTH BLADES STAMPED - "CASE XX STAINLESS" (ONLY A FEW EXIST) RARE | 150.00 | 75.00 |
| ☐ 6254 SSP "TRAPPER" MUSKRAT BLADE POLISHED | 125.00 | 62.50 |
| ☐ **6254 SSP "TRAPPER" (FIRST MODEL) | 120.00 | 60.00 |
| ☐ 6254 1ST MODEL MUSKRAT | 125.00 | 62.50 |
| ☐ 22055 | 145.00 | 72.50 |
| ☐ 62055 | 25.00 | 12.50 |
| ☐ 8261 | 45.00 | 22.50 |
| ☐ 9261 | 25.00 | 12.50 |
| ☐ 05263 SS | 45.00 | 22.50 |
| ☐ 06263 SS | 25.00 | 12.50 |
| ☐ 06263 F SS | 25.00 | 12.50 |
| ☐ 06263 SSP BLADE POLISHED | 25.00 | 12.50 |
| ☐ 06263 SSP EDGE OF BLADE POLISHED | 25.00 | 12.50 |
| ☐ **06263 SSP (FIRST MODEL) | 50.00 | 25.00 |
| ☐ 82063 SHAD SS | 85.00 | 42.00 |
| ☐ *5265 SAB "FOLDING HUNTER" NOT DRILLED FOR LANYARD | 125.00 | 62.50 |
| ☐ 5265 SAB DR "FOLDING HUNTER" | 70.00 | 35.00 |
| ☐ *5265 SAB DR "FOLDING HUNTER" | 95.00 | 47.50 |
| ☐ *6265 SAB "FOLDING HUNTER" NOT DRILLED FOR LANYARD | 85.00 | 42.50 |

*CASE XX U.S.A. / 103*

| PATTERN NO. | MINT | VG |
|---|---|---|
| ☐ *6265 SAB "FOLDING HUNTER" BONE STAG HANDLE NOT DRILLED FOR LANYARD | 175.00 | 87.50 |
| ☐ *6265 SAB DR "FOLDING HUNTER" LAMINATED WOOD HANDLE | 60.00 | 30.00 |
| ☐ 6265 SAB DR "FOLDING HUNTER" LAMINATED WOOD HANDLE | 35.00 | 17.50 |
| ☐ 6265 SAB DR "FOLDING HUNTER" BONE STAG HANDLE | 175.00 | 87.50 |
| ☐ MARINER'S KNIFE SET | 50.00 | 25.00 |
| ☐ 06267 | 65.00 | 32.50 |
| ☐ 6269 | 25.00 | 12.50 |
| ☐ 6275 SP "MOOSE" | 35.00 | 17.50 |
| ☐ 5279 SS | 150.00 | 75.00 |
| ☐ 6279 SS | 22.00 | 11.00 |
| ☐ 6279 SS TRANS XX TO U.S.A. | 50.00 | 25.00 |
| ☐ 82079½ SS "SLEEVE BOARD" | 45.00 | 27.50 |
| ☐ M279 SC SS "PHYSICIANS KNIFE" BRUSHED STAINLESS STEEL HANDLE | 30.00 | 15.00 |
| ☐ M279 SS "PHYSICIAN'S KNIFE" POLISHED STAINLESS STEEL HANDLE | 25.00 | 12.50 |
| ☐ M279 SS "PHYSICIAN'S KNIFE" BRUSHED STAINLESS STEEL HANDLE | 20.00 | 10.00 |
| ☐ M279 F SS "PHYSICIAN'S KNIFE" STAINLESS STEEL HANDLE | 20.00 | 10.00 |
| ☐ 22087 | 20.00 | 10.00 |
| ☐ 52087 | 45.00 | 22.50 |
| ☐ 62087 | 20.00 | 10.00 |
| ☐ 6292 "TEXAS JACK" | 25.00 | 12.50 |
| ☐ 32095 F SS "FISHERMANS KNIFE" | 26.00 | 13.00 |
| ☐ 32095 F SS "FISHERMANS KNIFE" | 26.00 | 13.00 |
| ☐ 6296X SS "CITRUS KNIFE" | 225.00 | 112.00 |
| ☐ 3299½ | 30.00 | 15.00 |
| ☐ 5299½ | 70.00 | 38.00 |
| ☐ 62109 X "SMALL COPPERHEAD" | 25.00 | 12.50 |
| ☐ 52131 "CANOE" | 80.00 | 40.00 |
| ☐ 62131 "CANOE" | 45.00 | 22.50 |

## THREE BLADE

| | | |
|---|---|---|
| ☐ 6308 "WHITTLER" | 30.00 | 15.00 |
| ☐ 3318 SH PEN | 22.00 | 11.00 |
| ☐ 4318 SH SP | 40.00 | 20.00 |
| ☐ 6318 SP P | 22.00 | 11.00 |

## 104 / CASE XX U.S.A.

| PATTERN NO. | MINT | VG |
|---|---|---|
| ☐ 6318 SH SP | 20.00 | 10.00 |
| ☐ 6318 SH PEN | 20.00 | 10.00 |
| ☐ **6318 SH SP SSP *POLISHED BLADE* | 50.00 | 25.00 |
| ☐ 6318 SH SP SSP *EDGE OF BLADE POLISHED* | 28.00 | 14.00 |
| ☐ **6318 SH SP SSP *(FIRST MODEL)* | 50.00 | 25.00 |
| ☐ 6327 SH SP | 27.00 | 13.50 |
| ☐ 9327 SH SP | 27.00 | 13.50 |
| ☐ 13031 L R *"ELECTRICIANS KNIFE"* | 40.00 | 20.00 |
| ☐ 5332 | 60.00 | 30.00 |
| ☐ 6332 | 25.00 | 12.50 |
| ☐ 6333 | 25.00 | 12.50 |
| ☐ 9333 | 22.00 | 11.00 |
| ☐ 6344 SH PEN | 30.00 | 15.00 |
| ☐ 6344 SH SP | 30.00 | 15.00 |
| ☐ 33044 SH SP *"BIRDSEYE"* | 30.00 | 15.00 |
| ☐ 2345½ SH | 175.00 | 87.50 |
| ☐ 3347 SH SP | 25.00 | 12.50 |
| ☐ 5347 SH SP | 60.00 | 30.00 |
| ☐ 5347 SH SP S | 60.00 | 30.00 |
| ☐ 53047 | 70.00 | 35.00 |
| ☐ 6347 SH P | 45.00 | 22.50 |
| ☐ 6347 SH SP | 27.00 | 13.50 |
| ☐ 6347 SH SP SS | 30.00 | 15.00 |
| ☐ 6347 SH PEN | 75.00 | 37.50 |
| ☐ 6347 SP P | 32.00 | 16.00 |
| ☐ 6347 SP PEN | 45.00 | 22.50 |
| ☐ 6347 SH SP SSP *BLADES POLISHED* | 50.00 | 25.00 |
| ☐ 6437 SH SP SSP *EDGE OF BLADE POLISHED* | 30.00 | 15.00 |
| ☐ **6347 SH SP SSP *(FIRST MODEL)* | 50.00 | 25.00 |
| ☐ 63047 | 30.00 | 15.00 |
| ☐ 8364 SCIS SS | 85.00 | 42.50 |
| ☐ 5375 | 75.00 | 37.50 |
| ☐ 5375 *SECOND CUT STAG HANDLE* | 650.00 | 325.00 |
| ☐ 6375 | 35.00 | 17.50 |
| ☐ 6380 *"WHITTLER"* | 45.00 | 22.50 |
| ☐ 2383 *"WHITTLER"* | 95.00 | 45.00 |
| ☐ 5383 *"WHITTLER"* | 80.00 | 40.00 |
| ☐ 6383 *"WHITTLER"* | 40.00 | 20.00 |
| ☐ 23087 SH PEN | 22.00 | 11.00 |
| ☐ 53087 SH PEN | 50.00 | 25.00 |
| ☐ 63087 SP PEN | 22.00 | 11.00 |
| ☐ 83089 SC F SS | 175.00 | 87.50 |

*CASE XX U.S.A. (10 DOT) / 105*

| PATTERN NO. | MINT | VG |
|---|---|---|
| ☐ 33092 "BIRDSEYE" | 35.00 | 17.50 |
| ☐ 5392 | 60.00 | 30.00 |
| ☐ 6392 | 30.00 | 15.00 |
| ☐ M3102 R SS | 30.00 | 15.00 |

## FOUR BLADE

| | | |
|---|---|---|
| ☐ CASE'S SS "FLY FISHERMAN" (U.S.A. TO 10 DOT) | 95.00 | 47.50 |
| ☐ CASE'S SS "FLY FISHERMAN" | 95.00 | 47.50 |
| ☐ 6445 R "SCOUTS KNIFE" | 35.00 | 17.50 |
| ☐ 640045 R "SCOUTS KNIFE" BROWN PLASTIC HANDLE | 22.00 | 11.00 |
| ☐ 64047 P | 30.00 | 15.00 |
| ☐ 54052 | 70.00 | 35.00 |
| ☐ 54052 (U.S.A. TO 10 DOT) | 95.00 | 47.50 |
| ☐ 64052 | 35.00 | 17.50 |
| ☐ 64052 (U.S.A. TO 10 DOT) | 75.00 | 37.50 |
| ☐ 5488 | 100.00 | 50.00 |
| ☐ 5488 (U.S.A. TO 10 DOT) | 200.00 | 100.00 |
| ☐ 5488 SECOND CUT STAG HANDLE | 400.00 | 200.00 |
| ☐ 6488 | 60.00 | 30.00 |
| ☐ 6488 (U.S.A. TO 10 DOT) | 75.00 | 37.50 |
| ☐ 6488 SECOND CUT STAG HANDLE | 350.00 | 175.00 |

# CASE XX U.S.A. (10 DOT)

## ONE BLADE

| | | |
|---|---|---|
| ☐ 11011 "HAWK BILL" | 25.00 | 12.50 |
| ☐ 61011 "HAWK BILL" LAMINATED WOOD HANDLE | 18.00 | 9.00 |
| ☐ 6111½ L "LOCK BACK" | 45.00 | 22.50 |
| ☐ 1116 SP "BUDDING KNIFE" | 30.00 | 15.00 |
| ☐ 11031 SH | 16.00 | 9.00 |
| ☐ 2137 "SOD BUSTER JR." | 45.00 | 22.50 |
| ☐ 2137 SS "SOD BUSTER JR." | 30.00 | 15.00 |
| ☐ 2138 "SOD BUSTER" | 20.00 | 10.00 |
| ☐ 2138 SS "SOD BUSTER" | 22.00 | 11.00 |
| ☐ 2138 L SS "SOD BUSTER" BLADE LOCKS OPEN | 30.00 | 15.00 |
| ☐ 6143 "DADDY BARLOW" | 30.00 | 15.00 |
| ☐ 31048 | 20.00 | 10.00 |
| ☐ 31048 SP | 30.00 | 15.00 |

## 106 / CASE XX U.S.A. (10 DOT)

| PATTERN NO. | MINT | VG |
|---|---|---|
| ☐ 61048 | 18.00 | 9.00 |
| ☐ 61048 SP | 25.00 | 12.50 |
| ☐ 61048 SSP | 20.00 | 10.00 |
| ☐ C61050 SAB "BIG COKE BOTTLE" LAMINATED WOOD HANDLE | 45.00 | 22.50 |
| ☐ 6165 SAB DR "FOLDING HUNTER" LAMINATED WOOD HANDLE | 35.00 | 17.50 |
| ☐ P172 VERY RARE | 120.00 | 60.00 |
| ☐ 3185 "DOCTORS KNIFE" | 50.00 | 25.00 |
| ☐ 6185 "DOCTORS KNIFE" | 45.00 | 22.50 |
| ☐ 61093 "TEXAS TOOTHPICK" | 60.00 | 30.00 |
| ☐ 1199 SH R SS "GRAFTING KNIFE" | 22.00 | 11.00 |

## TWO BLADE

| | MINT | VG |
|---|---|---|
| ☐ MUSKRAT | 35.00 | 17.50 |
| ☐ MUSKRAT "HAWBAKER'S SPECIAL | 175.00 | 87.50 |
| ☐ MUSKRAT "HAWBAKER'S SPECIAL" (10 DOT TO U.S.A.) | 150.00 | 75.00 |
| ☐ 4200 SS "MELON TESTER" | 65.00 | 32.50 |
| ☐ 3201 | 25.00 | 12.50 |
| ☐ 6201 | 25.00 | 12.50 |
| ☐ 9201 | 22.00 | 11.00 |
| ☐ 6202½ DELRIN HANDLE | 18.00 | 9.00 |
| ☐ 6202½ BONE STAG HANDLE | 25.00 | 12.50 |
| ☐ 6205 "RAZ OR ONE ARM MAN" | 50.00 | 25.00 |
| ☐ 6207 | 30.00 | 15.00 |
| ☐ 6208 "HALF WHITTLER" | 20.00 | 10.00 |
| ☐ 62009 "BARLOW" DELRIN HANDLE | 20.00 | 10.00 |
| ☐ 62009 "BARLOW" BONE STAG HANDLE | 24.00 | 12.00 |
| ☐ 62009 "BARLOW" "RAZ OR ONE ARM MAN" DELRIN HANDLE | 45.00 | 22.50 |
| ☐ 62009 "BARLOW" "RAZ OR ONE ARM MAN" BONE STAG HANDLE | 45.00 | 22.50 |
| ☐ 62009½ "BARLOW" DELRIN HANDLE | 20.00 | 10.00 |
| ☐ 62009½ "BARLOW" BONE STAG HANDLE | 24.00 | 12.00 |
| ☐ 6214 DELRIN HANDLE | 20.00 | 10.00 |
| ☐ 6214 BONE STAG HANDLE | 40.00 | 20.00 |
| ☐ 6214½ DELRIN HANDLE | 18.00 | 9.00 |
| ☐ 6214½ BONE STAG | 28.00 | 14.00 |
| ☐ 6217 "HALF HAWK BILL" BONE STAG HANDLE | 45.00 | 22.50 |
| ☐ 6217 "HALF HAWK BILL" LAMINATED WOOD HANDLE | 30.00 | 15.00 |

*CASE XX U.S.A. (10 DOT) / 107*

| PATTERN NO. | MINT | VG |
|---|---|---|
| ☐ 2220 "PEANUT" | 35.00 | 17.50 |
| ☐ 3220 "PEANUT" | 35.00 | 17.50 |
| ☐ 5220 "PEANUT" | 50.00 | 25.00 |
| ☐ 6220 "PEANUT" | 40.00 | 20.00 |
| ☐ 6220 DELRIN HANDLE | 50.00 | 25.00 |
| ☐ 6225½ "COKE BOTTLE" | 35.00 | 17.50 |
| ☐ 6227 DELRIN HANDLE | 30.00 | 15.00 |
| ☐ 6227 BONE STAG HANDLE | 24.00 | 12.00 |
| ☐ 12031 L R "ELECTRICIANS KNIFE" | 20.00 | 10.00 |
| ☐ 2231½ SAB LONG PULL STANDARD | 25.00 | 12.50 |
| ☐ 6231½ LONG PULL STANDARD | 30.00 | 15.00 |
| ☐ 5232 | 45.00 | 22.50 |
| ☐ 6232 | 20.00 | 10.00 |
| ☐ 3233 | 25.00 | 12.50 |
| ☐ 3233 FLAT YELLOW | 35.00 | 17.50 |
| ☐ 5233 | 45.00 | 22.50 |
| ☐ 6233 DELRIN HANDLE | 35.00 | 17.50 |
| ☐ 6233 BONE STAG HANDLE | 25.00 | 12.50 |
| ☐ 8233 | 45.00 | 22.50 |
| ☐ 9233 | 20.00 | 10.00 |
| ☐ 6235½ | 20.00 | 10.00 |
| ☐ 62042 | 20.00 | 10.00 |
| ☐ 62042 R | 24.00 | 12.00 |
| ☐ 92042 | 20.00 | 10.00 |
| ☐ 92042 R | 24.00 | 12.00 |
| ☐ 06244 DELRIN STAG HANDLE | 30.00 | 15.00 |
| ☐ 06244 BONE STAG HANDLE | 26.00 | 13.00 |
| ☐ 6244 BONE STAG HANDLE | 26.00 | 13.00 |
| ☐ 6246 R SS "RIGGER'S KNIFE" | 40.00 | 20.00 |
| ☐ 4247 F K "GREEN KEEPER'S KNIFE" | 250.00 | 125.00 |
| ☐ 06247 PEN | 20.00 | 10.00 |
| ☐ 32048 SP | 25.00 | 12.50 |
| ☐ 62048 SP DELRIN HANDLE | 18.00 | 9.00 |
| ☐ 62048 SP SSP DELRIN HANDLE | 24.00 | 12.00 |
| ☐ 6249 "COPPERHEAD OR VIETNAM" | 35.00 | 17.50 |
| ☐ 6250 "SUNFISH" LAMINATED WOOD HANDLE | 45.00 | 22.50 |
| ☐ 62052 | 27.00 | 13.50 |
| ☐ 82053 S R SS | 45.00 | 22.50 |
| ☐ 3254 "TRAPPER" | 55.00 | 27.50 |
| ☐ 3254 "TRAPPER" FLAT YELLOW | 85.00 | 42.50 |
| ☐ 5254 "TRAPPER" | 70.00 | 35.00 |
| ☐ 6254 "TRAPPER" | 55.00 | 27.50 |

## 108 / CASE XX U.S.A. (10 DOT)

| PATTERN NO. | MINT | VG |
|---|---|---|
| ☐ 6254 SSP "TRAPPER" EDGE OF BLADE POLISHED | 55.00 | 27.50 |
| ☐ 62055 | 25.00 | 12.50 |
| ☐ 8261 | 45.00 | 22.50 |
| ☐ 9261 | 22.00 | 11.00 |
| ☐ 05263 SS | 40.00 | 20.00 |
| ☐ 06263 SS | 22.00 | 11.00 |
| ☐ 06263 SSP | 22.00 | 11.00 |
| ☐ 06263 F SSP | 24.00 | 12.00 |
| ☐ 06263 F SS | 24.00 | 12.00 |
| ☐ 5265 SAB DR "FOLDING HUNTER" | 70.00 | 35.00 |
| ☐ 6265 SAB DR "FOLDING HUNTER" LAMINATED WOOD HANDLE | 30.00 | 15.00 |
| ☐ MARINER'S KNIFE SET | 50.00 | 25.00 |
| ☐ 6269 | 22.00 | 11.00 |
| ☐ 6275 SP "MOOSE" | 35.00 | 17.50 |
| ☐ 6279 SS | 20.00 | 10.00 |
| ☐ 8207 9½ SS "SLEEVE BOARD" | 45.00 | 22.50 |
| ☐ M279 SC SS "PHYSICIAN'S KNIFE" BRUSHED STAINLESS STEEL HANDLE | 20.00 | 10.00 |
| ☐ M279 F SS "PHYSICIAN'S KNIFE" BRUSHED STAINLESS STEEL HANDLE | 20.00 | 10.00 |
| ☐ M279 SS "PHYSICIAN'S KNIFE" BRUSHED STAINLESS STEEL HANDLE | 20.00 | 10.00 |
| ☐ 22087 | 20.00 | 10.00 |
| ☐ 52087 | 65.00 | 32.50 |
| ☐ 62087 DELRIN HANDLE | 20.00 | 10.00 |
| ☐ 62087 BONE STAG HANDLE | 26.00 | 13.00 |
| ☐ 6292 "TEXAS JACK" | 25.00 | 22.50 |
| ☐ 32095 F SS "FISHERMANS KNIFE" | 50.00 | 25.00 |
| ☐ 3299½ | 30.00 | 15.00 |
| ☐ 5299½ | 85.00 | 42.50 |
| ☐ 62109X "SMALL COPPERHEAD" | 28.00 | 14.00 |
| ☐ 52131 "CANOE" | 80.00 | 40.00 |
| ☐ 62131 "CANOE" | 45.00 | 22.50 |

## THREE BLADE

| | | |
|---|---|---|
| ☐ 6308 "WHITTLER" | 30.00 | 15.00 |
| ☐ 3318 SH PEN | 24.00 | 12.00 |
| ☐ 4318 SH SP | 45.00 | 22.50 |
| ☐ 6318 SP P | 25.00 | 12.50 |
| ☐ 6318 SH PEN | 25.00 | 12.50 |
| ☐ 6318 SH SP | 25.00 | 12.50 |

*CASE XX U.S.A. (10 DOT) / 109*

| PATTERN NO. | MINT | VG |
|---|---|---|
| ☐ 6318 SH SP SSP *EDGE OF BLADE POLISHED* | 28.00 | 14.00 |
| ☐ 6327 SH SP *DELRIN HANDLE* | 20.00 | 10.00 |
| ☐ 6327 SH SP *BONE STAG HANDLE* | 28.00 | 14.00 |
| ☐ 9327 SH SP | 22.00 | 11.00 |
| ☐ 13031 L R *"ELECTRICIANS KNIFE"* | 40.00 | 20.00 |
| ☐ 5332 | 60.00 | 30.00 |
| ☐ 6332 | 24.00 | 12.00 |
| ☐ 6333 *DELRIN HANDLE* | 20.00 | 10.00 |
| ☐ 6333 *BONE STAG HANDLE* | 24.00 | 12.00 |
| ☐ 9333 | 20.00 | 10.00 |
| ☐ 6344 SH PEN | 28.00 | 14.00 |
| ☐ 6344 SH PEN | 28.00 | 14.00 |
| ☐ 33044 SH SP *"BIRDSEYE"* | 26.00 | 13.00 |
| ☐ 3347 SH SP | 25.00 | 12.50 |
| ☐ 5347 SH SP | 65.00 | 32.50 |
| ☐ 5347 SH SP SS | 200.00 | 100.00 |
| ☐ 53047 | 70.00 | 35.00 |
| ☐ 6347 SH SP | 24.00 | 12.00 |
| ☐ 6347 SP P | 28.00 | 14.00 |
| ☐ 6347 SP PEN | 35.00 | 17.50 |
| ☐ 6347 SH SP SSP *EDGE OF BLADE POLISHED* | 30.00 | 15.00 |
| ☐ 63047 | 30.00 | 15.00 |
| ☐ 8364 SCIS SS | 85.00 | 42.50 |
| ☐ 5375 | 70.00 | 35.00 |
| ☐ 6375 | 35.00 | 17.50 |
| ☐ 6380 *"WHITTLER"* | 45.00 | 22.50 |
| ☐ 5383 *"WHITTLER"* | 85.00 | 42.50 |
| ☐ 6383 *"WHITTLER"* | 40.00 | 20.00 |
| ☐ 23087 SH PEN | 23.00 | 11.50 |
| ☐ 53087 SH PEN | 50.00 | 25.00 |
| ☐ 63087 SP PEN *DELRIN HANDLE* | 20.00 | 10.00 |
| ☐ 63087 SP PEN *BONE STAG HANDLE* | 28.00 | 14.00 |
| ☐ 33092 *"BIRDSEYE"* | 30.00 | 15.00 |
| ☐ 5392 | 60.00 | 30.00 |
| ☐ 6392 | 30.00 | 15.00 |
| ☐ 6392 *(10 DOT TO U.S.A.)* | 100.00 | 50.00 |
| ☐ M3102 R SS | 22.00 | 11.00 |

## FOUR BLADE

| | | |
|---|---|---|
| ☐ CASE'S SS *"FLY FISHERMAN"* | 110.00 | 50.00 |
| ☐ 6445 R *"SCOUTS KNIFE"* | 35.00 | 17.50 |
| ☐ 640045 R *"SCOUTS KNIFE"* BROWN PLASTIC HANDLE | 22.00 | 11.00 |

110 / CASE XX U.S.A. (9 DOT)

| PATTERN NO. | MINT | VG |
|---|---|---|
| ☐ 64047 P | 30.00 | 15.00 |
| ☐ 54052 *(10 DOT TO U.S.A.)* | 95.00 | 47.50 |
| ☐ 54052 | 75.00 | 37.50 |
| ☐ 64052 | 30.00 | 15.00 |
| ☐ 64052 *(10 DOT TO U.S.A.)* | 75.00 | 37.50 |
| ☐ 5488 | 150.00 | 75.00 |
| ☐ 6488 | 50.00 | 25.00 |
| ☐ 6488 *(10 DOT TO U.S.A.)* | 90.00 | 45.00 |

## CASE XX U.S.A. (9 DOT)
### ONE BLADE

| | MINT | VG |
|---|---|---|
| ☐ 4100 SS "MELON TESTER" | 45.00 | 22.50 |
| ☐ 11011 "HAWK BILL" | 22.00 | 11.00 |
| ☐ 61011 "HAWK BILL" LAMINATED WOOD HANDLE | 16.00 | 8.00 |
| ☐ 6111½ L "LOCK BACK" | 35.00 | 17.50 |
| ☐ 1116 SP "BUDDING KNIFE" | 30.00 | 15.00 |
| ☐ 11031 SH | 15.00 | 7.50 |
| ☐ 2137 "SOD BUSTER JR." | 18.00 | 9.00 |
| ☐ 2137 SS "SOD BUSTER JR." | 20.00 | 10.00 |
| ☐ 2138 "SOD BUSTER" | 18.00 | 9.00 |
| ☐ 2138 SS "SOD BUSTER" | 20.00 | 10.00 |
| ☐ 2138 L SS "SOD BUSTER" BLADE LOCKS OPEN | 25.00 | 12.50 |
| ☐ 6143 "DADDY BARLOW" | 25.00 | 12.50 |
| ☐ 6143 BONE | 30.00 | 15.00 |
| ☐ 31048 | 17.00 | 8.50 |
| ☐ 31048 SP | 28.00 | 14.00 |
| ☐ 61048 | 15.00 | 7.50 |
| ☐ 61048 SP | 22.00 | 11.00 |
| ☐ 61048 SSP | 18.00 | 9.00 |
| ☐ C61050 SAB "BIG COKE BOTTLE" LAMINATED WOOD HANDLE | 35.00 | 17.50 |
| ☐ 6165 SAB "FOLDING HUNTER" LAMINATED WOOD HANDLE | 30.00 | 15.00 |
| ☐ P172 "BUFFALO" | 50.00 | 25.00 |
| ☐ 3185 "DOCTORS KNIFE" | 45.00 | 22.50 |
| ☐ 6185 "DOCTORS KNIFE" | 45.00 | 22.50 |
| ☐ 61093 "TEXAS TOOTHPICK" | 45.00 | 22.50 |
| ☐ 61093 DELRIN | 45.00 | 22.50 |
| ☐ 1199 SH R SS "GRAFTING KNIFE" | 18.00 | 9.00 |

CASE XX U.S.A. (9 DOT) / 111

## TWO BLADE

| PATTERN NO. | MINT | VG |
|---|---|---|
| ☐ MUSKRAT | 25.00 | 12.50 |
| ☐ MUSKRAT "HAWBAKER'S SPECIAL (9 DOT TO 8 DOT) | 75.00 | 37.50 |
| ☐ MUSKRAT "HAWBAKER'S SPECIAL" | 75.00 | 37.50 |
| ☐ 4200 SS "MELON TESTER" | 60.00 | 30.00 |
| ☐ 3201 | 22.00 | 11.00 |
| ☐ 6201 | 22.00 | 11.00 |
| ☐ 9201 | 20.00 | 10.00 |
| ☐ 6202½ | 14.00 | 7.00 |
| ☐ 6205 "RAZ OR ONE ARM MAN" | 45.00 | 22.50 |
| ☐ 6207 | 25.00 | 12.50 |
| ☐ 6208 "HALF WHITTLER" | 18.00 | 9.00 |
| ☐ 62009 "BARLOW" | 20.00 | 10.00 |
| ☐ 62009 "BARLOW" "RAZ OR ONE ARM MAN" | 30.00 | 15.00 |
| ☐ 62009½ "BARLOW" | 15.00 | 7.50 |
| ☐ 6214 | 18.00 | 9.00 |
| ☐ 6214½ | 15.00 | 7.50 |
| ☐ 6217 "HALF HAWK BILL" LAMINATED WOOD HANDLE | 20.00 | 10.00 |
| ☐ 2220 "PEANUT" | 40.00 | 20.00 |
| ☐ 3220 "PEANUT" | 40.00 | 20.00 |
| ☐ 6220 "PEANUT" DELRIN HANDLE | 35.00 | 17.50 |
| ☐ 6220 "PEANUT" BONE STAG HANDLE | 75.00 | 37.50 |
| ☐ 6225½ "COKE BOTTLE" | 25.00 | 12.50 |
| ☐ 6227 | 15.00 | 7.50 |
| ☐ 2231½ SAB LONG PULL STANDARD | 20.00 | 10.00 |
| ☐ 6231½ LONG PULL STANDARD | 25.00 | 12.50 |
| ☐ 12031 L R "ELECTRICIANS KNIFE" | 18.00 | 9.00 |
| ☐ 5232 OUT OF SETS | 60.00 | 30.00 |
| ☐ 6232 | 18.00 | 9.00 |
| ☐ 3233 | 30.00 | 15.00 |
| ☐ 6233 | 20.00 | 10.00 |
| ☐ 8233 | 40.00 | 20.00 |
| ☐ 9233 | 20.00 | 10.00 |
| ☐ 6235½ | 16.00 | 8.00 |
| ☐ 62042 | 15.00 | 7.50 |
| ☐ 92042 | 15.00 | 7.50 |
| ☐ 06244 | 15.00 | 7.50 |
| ☐ 6244 | 15.00 | 7.50 |
| ☐ 6246 R SS "RIGGER'S KNIFE" | 35.00 | 17.50 |
| ☐ 06247 PEN | 18.00 | 9.00 |

## 112 / CASE XX U.S.A. (9 DOT)

| PATTERN NO. | MINT | VG |
|---|---|---|
| ☐ 32048 SP | 20.00 | 10.00 |
| ☐ 62048 SP | 18.00 | 9.00 |
| ☐ 62048 SP SSP | 20.00 | 10.00 |
| ☐ 6249 "COPPERHEAD OR VIETNAM" | 25.00 | 12.50 |
| ☐ 6250 "SUNFISH" LAMINATED WOOD HANDLE | 40.00 | 20.00 |
| ☐ 62052 | 25.00 | 12.50 |
| ☐ 82053 SR SS | 40.00 | 20.00 |
| ☐ 3254 "TRAPPER" | 50.00 | 25.00 |
| ☐ 6254 "TRAPPER" | 50.00 | 25.00 |
| ☐ 6254 SSP "TRAPPER" | 50.00 | 25.00 |
| ☐ 62055 | 20.00 | 10.00 |
| ☐ 8261 | 40.00 | 20.00 |
| ☐ 9261 | 20.00 | 10.00 |
| ☐ 06263 SSP | 18.00 | 9.00 |
| ☐ 06263 F SSP | 22.00 | 11.00 |
| ☐ 6265 SAB DR "FOLDING HUNTER" LAMINATED WOOD HANDLE | 30.00 | 15.00 |
| ☐ MARINER'S KNIFE SET | 40.00 | 20.00 |
| ☐ 6269 | 22.00 | 11.00 |
| ☐ 6275 SP "MOOSE" | 25.00 | 12.50 |
| ☐ 6279 SS | 15.00 | 7.50 |
| ☐ 6207 9½ "SLEEVE BOARD" | 35.00 | 17.50 |
| ☐ M279 SC SS "PHYSICIAN'S KNIFE" BRUSHED STAINLESS STEEL HANDLE | 18.00 | 9.00 |
| ☐ M279 F SS "PHYSICIAN'S KNIFE" BRUSHED STAINLESS STEEL HANDLE | 18.00 | 9.00 |
| ☐ M279 SS "PHYSICIAN'S KNIFE" BRUSHED STAINLESS STEEL HANDLE | 18.00 | 9.00 |
| ☐ 22087 | 16.00 | 8.00 |
| ☐ 62087 | 16.00 | 8.00 |
| ☐ 6292 "TEXAS JACK" | 20.00 | 10.00 |
| ☐ 32095 F SS "FISHERMANS KNIFE" | 25.00 | 12.50 |
| ☐ 3299½ | 25.00 | 12.50 |
| ☐ 62109X "SMALL COPPERHEAD" | 22.00 | 11.00 |
| ☐ 62131 "CANOE" | 40.00 | 20.00 |

## THREE BLADE

| | | |
|---|---|---|
| ☐ 6308 "WHITTLER" | 24.00 | 12.00 |
| ☐ 3318 SH PEN | 18.00 | 9.00 |
| ☐ 4318 SH SP | 40.00 | 20.00 |
| ☐ 4318 SH SP | 75.00 | 37.50 |
| ☐ 6318 SH SP | 18.00 | 9.00 |

*CASE XX U.S.A. (9 DOT) / 113*

| PATTERN NO. | MINT | VG |
|---|---|---|
| ☐ 6318 SH P | 18.00 | 9.00 |
| ☐ 6318 SH PEN | 18.00 | 9.00 |
| ☐ 6318 SH SP SSP *EDGE OF BLADE POLISHED* | 25.00 | 12.50 |
| ☐ 6327 SH SP | 18.00 | 9.00 |
| ☐ 9327 SH SP | 18.00 | 9.00 |
| ☐ 13031 L R *"ELECTRICIANS KNIFE"* | 30.00 | 15.00 |
| ☐ 5332 *(COLLECTORS SET)* | 65.00 | 32.50 |
| ☐ 6332 | 18.00 | 9.00 |
| ☐ 6333 | 15.00 | 7.50 |
| ☐ 9333 | 18.00 | 9.00 |
| ☐ 6344 SH PEN *DELRIN HANDLE* | 18.00 | 9.00 |
| ☐ 6344 SH PEN *BONE STAG HANDLE* | 28.00 | 14.00 |
| ☐ 6344 SH SP | 18.00 | 9.00 |
| ☐ 33044 SH SP *"BIRDSEYE"* | 22.00 | 11.00 |
| ☐ 3347 SH SP | 18.00 | 9.00 |
| ☐ 5347 SH SP *(COLLECTORS SET)* | 65.00 | 32.50 |
| ☐ 6347 SH SP | 18.00 | 9.00 |
| ☐ 6347 SP P | 22.00 | 11.00 |
| ☐ 6347 SP PEN | 25.00 | 12.50 |
| ☐ 6347 SH SP SSP | 25.00 | 12.50 |
| ☐ 63047 | 25.00 | 12.50 |
| ☐ 8364 SC SS | 75.00 | 37.50 |
| ☐ 6375 | 30.00 | 15.00 |
| ☐ 6380 *"WHITTLER"* | 35.00 | 17.50 |
| ☐ 6383 *"WHITTLER"* | 25.00 | 12.50 |
| ☐ 23087 SH PEN | 18.00 | 9.00 |
| ☐ 53087 SH PEN *(COLLECTORS SET)* | 65.00 | 32.50 |
| ☐ 63087 SP PEN | 18.00 | 9.00 |
| ☐ 6392 | 26.00 | 13.00 |
| ☐ 33092 *"BIRDSEYE"* | 22.00 | 11.00 |
| ☐ M3102 R SS | 20.00 | 10.00 |

## FOUR BLADE

| | | |
|---|---|---|
| ☐ CASE'S SS *"FLY FISHERMAN"* | 95.00 | 47.50 |
| ☐ 6445 R *"SCOUTS KNIFE"* | 32.00 | 16.00 |
| ☐ 640045 R *"SCOUTS KNIFE" BROWN PLASTIC HANDLE* | 20.00 | 10.00 |
| ☐ 64047 P | 30.00 | 15.00 |
| ☐ 64052 | 30.00 | 15.00 |

*114 / CASE XX U.S.A. (8 DOT)*

# CASE XX U.S.A. (8 DOT)

## ONE BLADE

| PATTERN NO. | MINT | VG |
|---|---|---|
| ☐ 4100 SS "MELON TESTER" | 42.00 | 21.00 |
| ☐ 11011 "HAWK BILL" | 16.00 | 8.00 |
| ☐ 61011 "HAWK BILL" LAMINATED WOOD HANDLE | 14.00 | 7.00 |
| ☐ 5111½ L SSP "CHEETAH" BLADE LOCKS OPEN, LARGE PATTERN NUMBER FROM COLLECTORS SET | 150.00 | 75.00 |
| ☐ 5111½ L SS "CHEETAH" BLADE LOCKS OPEN, SMALL PATTERN NUMBER FROM COLLECTORS SET | 150.00 | 75.00 |
| ☐ 6111½ L "LOCK BACK" | 32.00 | 16.00 |
| ☐ 11031 SH | 14.00 | 7.00 |
| ☐ 2137 "SOD BUSTER JR." | 12.00 | 6.00 |
| ☐ 2137 SS "SOD BUSTER JR." | 15.00 | 7.50 |
| ☐ 2138 "SOD BUSTER" | 15.00 | 7.50 |
| ☐ 2138 SS "SOD BUSTER" | 16.00 | 8.00 |
| ☐ 2139 L SS "SOD BUSTER" BLADE LOCKS OPEN | 20.00 | 10.00 |
| ☐ 6143 "DADDY BARLOW" BONE | 28.00 | 14.00 |
| ☐ 6143 "DADDY BARLOW" | 17.00 | 8.50 |
| ☐ 31048 | 15.00 | 7.50 |
| ☐ 61048 | 12.00 | 6.00 |
| ☐ 61048 SSP | 15.00 | 7.50 |
| ☐ C61050 SAB "BIG COKE BOTTLE" LAMINATED WOOD HANDLE | 35.00 | 17.50 |
| ☐ 6165 SAB DR "FOLDING HUNTER" LAMINATED WOOD HANDLE | 25.00 | 12.50 |
| ☐ P172 "BUFFALO" | 50.00 | 25.00 |
| ☐ 3185 "DOCTORS KNIFE" | 45.00 | 22.50 |
| ☐ 6185 "DOCTORS KNIFE" | 45.00 | 22.50 |
| ☐ 61093 "TEXAS TOOTHPICK" | 45.00 | 22.50 |
| ☐ 61093 "TEXAS TOOTHPICK" DELRIN | 30.00 | 15.00 |
| ☐ 7197 L SSP "SHARK TOOTH" LOCK BACK | 95.00 | 47.50 |
| ☐ 7197 L SSP CURLY MAPLE | 175.00 | 87.50 |
| ☐ P197 L SSP PAKKAWOOD | 50.00 | 25.00 |
| ☐ 1199 SH R SS "GRAFTING KNIFE" | 16.00 | 8.00 |

## TWO BLADE

| | MINT | VG |
|---|---|---|
| ☐ MUSKRAT | 24.00 | 12.00 |
| ☐ 4200 SS "MELON TESTER" | 60.00 | 30.00 |

*CASE XX U.S.A. (8 DOT) / 115*

| PATTERN NO. | MINT | VG |
|---|---|---|
| ☐ 3201 | 20.00 | 10.00 |
| ☐ 6201 | 22.00 | 11.00 |
| ☐ 9201 | 20.00 | 10.00 |
| ☐ 6202½ | 10.00 | 5.00 |
| ☐ 6205 "RAZ OR ONE ARM MAN" | 40.00 | 20.00 |
| ☐ 6207 | 23.00 | 11.50 |
| ☐ 6208 "HALF WHITTLER" | 16.00 | 8.00 |
| ☐ 62009 "BARLOW" | 12.00 | 6.00 |
| ☐ 62009 "BARLOW" "RAZ OR ONE ARM MAN" | 22.00 | 11.00 |
| ☐ 62009½ "BARLOW" | 10.00 | 5.00 |
| ☐ 6214 | 18.00 | 9.00 |
| ☐ 6214½ | 12.00 | 6.00 |
| ☐ 6217 "HALF HAWK BILL" LAMINATED WOOD HANDLE | 18.00 | 9.00 |
| ☐ 2220 "PEANUT" | 30.00 | 15.00 |
| ☐ 3220 "PEANUT" | 30.00 | 15.00 |
| ☐ 6220 "PEANUT" | 25.00 | 12.50 |
| ☐ 6225½ "COKE BOTTLE" | 25.00 | 12.50 |
| ☐ 6227 | 12.00 | 6.00 |
| ☐ 2231½ SAB LONG PULL STANDARD | 15.00 | 7.50 |
| ☐ 6231½ LONG PULL STANDARD | 25.00 | 12.50 |
| ☐ 12031 L R "ELECTRICIANS KNIFE" | 16.00 | 8.00 |
| ☐ 62048 SP SSP | 16.00 | 8.00 |
| ☐ 6232 | 17.00 | 8.50 |
| ☐ 3233 | 25.00 | 12.50 |
| ☐ 6233 | 15.00 | 7.50 |
| ☐ 8233 | 40.00 | 20.00 |
| ☐ 9233 | 20.00 | 10.00 |
| ☐ 6235½ | 12.00 | 6.00 |
| ☐ 62042 | 12.00 | 6.00 |
| ☐ 92042 | 14.00 | 7.00 |
| ☐ 06244 | 14.00 | 7.00 |
| ☐ 6244 | 14.00 | 7.00 |
| ☐ 6246 R SS "RIGGER'S KNIFE" | 30.00 | 15.00 |
| ☐ 06247 PEN | 16.00 | 8.00 |
| ☐ 32048 SP | 16.00 | 8.00 |
| ☐ 62048 SP | 14.00 | 7.00 |
| ☐ 62048 SP SSP | 16.00 | 8.00 |
| ☐ 6249 "COPPERHEAD OR VIETNAM" | 25.00 | 12.50 |
| ☐ 6250 "SUNFISH" LAMINATED WOOD HANDLE | 35.00 | 17.50 |
| ☐ 62052 | 22.00 | 11.00 |
| ☐ 82053 SR SS | 40.00 | 20.00 |
| ☐ 3254 "TRAPPER" | 30.00 | 15.00 |

## 116 / CASE XX U.S.A. (8 DOT)

| PATTERN NO. | MINT | VG |
|---|---|---|
| ☐ 6254 "TRAPPER" | 35.00 | 17.50 |
| ☐ 6254 SSP "TRAPPER" | 35.00 | 17.50 |
| ☐ 62055 | 20.00 | 10.00 |
| ☐ 8261 | 40.00 | 20.00 |
| ☐ 9261 | 20.00 | 10.00 |
| ☐ 06263 F SS | 20.00 | 10.00 |
| ☐ 06263 SSP | 16.00 | 8.00 |
| ☐ 6265 SAB DR "FOLDING HUNTER" LAMINATED WOOD HANDLE | 25.00 | 12.50 |
| ☐ 6265 SAB DR SSP "FOLDING HUNTER" LAMINATED WOOD HANDLE | 30.00 | 15.00 |
| ☐ MARINER'S KNIFE SET | 35.00 | 17.50 |
| ☐ MARINER'S KNIFE SET SSP | 40.00 | 20.00 |
| ☐ 6269 | 20.00 | 10.00 |
| ☐ 6275 SP "MOOSE" | 24.00 | 12.00 |
| ☐ 6279 SS | 12.00 | 6.00 |
| ☐ 6279 SS BONE | 18.00 | 9.00 |
| ☐ 82079½ SS "SLEEVE BOARD" | 40.00 | 20.00 |
| ☐ M279 SC SS "PHYSICIAN'S KNIFE" BRUSHED STAINLESS STEEL HANDLE | 16.00 | 8.00 |
| ☐ M279 F SS "PHYSICIAN'S KNIFE" BRUSHED STAINLESS STEEL HANDLE | 24.00 | 12.00 |
| ☐ M279 SS "PHYSICIAN'S KNIFE" BRUSHED STAINLESS STEEL HANDLE | 25.00 | 12.50 |
| ☐ 22087 | 15.00 | 7.50 |
| ☐ 62087 | 14.00 | 7.00 |
| ☐ 6292 "TEXAS JACK" | 18.00 | 9.00 |
| ☐ 32095 F SS "FISHERMANS KNIFE" | 20.00 | 10.00 |
| ☐ 3299½ | 25.00 | 12.50 |
| ☐ 62109X "SMALL COPPERHEAD" | 18.00 | 9.00 |
| ☐ 62131 "CANOE" BONE STAG HANDLE | 35.00 | 17.50 |

### THREE BLADE

| | | |
|---|---|---|
| ☐ 6308 "WHITTLER" | 22.00 | 11.00 |
| ☐ 3318 SH PEN | 20.00 | 10.00 |
| ☐ 4318 SH SP | 40.00 | 20.00 |
| ☐ 6318 SH SP | 16.00 | 8.00 |
| ☐ 6318 SP P | 18.00 | 9.00 |
| ☐ 6318 SH PEN | 16.00 | 8.00 |
| ☐ 6318 SH SP SSP | 20.00 | 10.00 |
| ☐ 6327 SH SP | 18.00 | 9.00 |
| ☐ 9327 SH SP | 20.00 | 10.00 |
| ☐ 13031 L R "ELECTRICIANS KNIFE" | 30.00 | 15.00 |

## CASE XX U.S.A. (7 DOT) / 117

| PATTERN NO. | MINT | VG |
|---|---|---|
| ☐ 6332 | 18.00 | 9.00 |
| ☐ 6333 | 15.00 | 7.50 |
| ☐ 9333 | 18.00 | 9.00 |
| ☐ 6344 SH PEN | 16.00 | 8.00 |
| ☐ 6344 SH SP | 16.00 | 8.00 |
| ☐ 33044 SH SP "BIRDSEYE" | 22.00 | 11.00 |
| ☐ 3347 SH SP | 22.00 | 11.00 |
| ☐ 6347 SH SP | 20.00 | 10.00 |
| ☐ 6347 SH P | 22.00 | 11.00 |
| ☐ 6347 SP PEN | 30.00 | 15.00 |
| ☐ 6347 SH SP SSP | 25.00 | 12.50 |
| ☐ 63047 | 22.00 | 11.00 |
| ☐ 8364 SC SS | 75.00 | 37.50 |
| ☐ 6375 | 25.00 | 12.50 |
| ☐ 6380 "WHITTLER" | 30.00 | 15.00 |
| ☐ 6383 "WHITTLER" | 24.00 | 12.00 |
| ☐ 23087 SH PEN | 18.00 | 9.00 |
| ☐ 63087 SP PEN | 16.00 | 8.00 |
| ☐ 6392 | 25.00 | 12.50 |
| ☐ 33092 "BIRDSEYE" | 20.00 | 10.00 |
| ☐ M3102 R SS | 20.00 | 10.00 |

## FOUR BLADE

| | MINT | VG |
|---|---|---|
| ☐ 640045 R "SCOUT'S KNIFE" BROWN PLASTIC HANDLE | 20.00 | 10.00 |
| ☐ 64047 P | 25.00 | 12.50 |
| ☐ 64052 | 30.00 | 15.00 |
| ☐ 6488 | 50.00 | 25.00 |
| ☐ CASE'S SS "FLY FISHERMAN" | 95.00 | 47.50 |
| ☐ 6445 R "SCOUT'S KNIFE" | 30.00 | 15.00 |

## CASE XX U.S.A. (7 DOT)

### ONE BLADE

| | MINT | VG |
|---|---|---|
| ☐ 4100 SS "MELON TESTER" | 42.00 | 21.00 |
| ☐ 4100 "MELON TESTER" POLISHED BLADE | 45.00 | 22.50 |
| ☐ 11011 "HAWK BILL" | 16.00 | 8.00 |
| ☐ 61011 "HAWK BILL" LAMINATED WOOD HANDLE | 14.00 | 7.00 |
| ☐ 6111½ L "LOCK BACK" BONE STAG HANDLE | 40.00 | 20.00 |
| ☐ 6111½ L "LOCK BACK" DELRIN HANDLE | 30.00 | 15.00 |

## 118 / CASE XX U.S.A. (7 DOT)

| PATTERN NO. | MINT | VG |
|---|---|---|
| ☐ 11031 SH | 12.00 | 6.00 |
| ☐ 2137 "SOD BUSTER JR." | 12.00 | 6.00 |
| ☐ 2137 SS "SOD BUSTER JR." | 14.00 | 7.00 |
| ☐ 2138 "SOD BUSTER" | 14.00 | 7.00 |
| ☐ 2138 SS "SOD BUSTER" | 16.00 | 8.00 |
| ☐ 2138 L SS "SOD BUSTER" BLADE LOCKS OPEN | 20.00 | 10.00 |
| ☐ 6143 "DADDY BARLOW" | 17.00 | 8.50 |
| ☐ 31048 | 15.00 | 7.50 |
| ☐ 61048 | 12.00 | 6.00 |
| ☐ 61048 SSP | 15.00 | 7.50 |
| ☐ C61050 SAB "BIG COKE BOTTLE" LAMINATED WOOD HANDLE | 35.00 | 17.50 |
| ☐ 6165 SAB DR "FOLDING HUNTER" LAMINATED WOOD HANDLE | 25.00 | 12.50 |
| ☐ P179 "BUFFALO" | 50.00 | 25.00 |
| ☐ 3185 "DOCTORS KNIFE" | 42.00 | 21.00 |
| ☐ 3185 "DOCTORS KNIFE" | 40.00 | 20.00 |
| ☐ 6185 "DOCTORS KNIFE" | 42.00 | 21.00 |
| ☐ 61093 "TEXAS TOOTHPICK" | 100.00 | 50.00 |
| ☐ 7197 L SSP "SHARK'S TOOTH" LOCK BACK | 95.00 | 47.50 |
| ☐ 7197 L SSP CURLY MAPLE | 140.00 | 70.00 |
| ☐ P197 L SSP PAKKAWOOD | 50.00 | 25.00 |
| ☐ 1199 SH R SS "GRAFTING KNIFE" | 15.00 | 7.50 |

## TWO BLADE

| | MINT | VG |
|---|---|---|
| ☐ MUSKRAT | 22.00 | 11.00 |
| ☐ 4200 SS "MELON TESTER" | 60.00 | 30.00 |
| ☐ 3201 | 20.00 | 10.00 |
| ☐ 6201 | 20.00 | 10.00 |
| ☐ 9201 | 18.00 | 9.00 |
| ☐ 6202½ | 10.00 | 5.00 |
| ☐ 6205 RAZ DELRIN | 30.00 | 15.00 |
| ☐ 6205 "RAZ OR ONE ARM MAN" | 40.00 | 20.00 |
| ☐ 6207 | 22.00 | 11.00 |
| ☐ 6207 DELRIN | 20.00 | 10.00 |
| ☐ 6208 "HALF WHITTLER" | 16.00 | 8.00 |
| ☐ 62009 "BARLOW" | 12.00 | 6.00 |
| ☐ 62009 "BARLOW" "RAZ OR ONE ARM MAN" | 22.00 | 11.00 |
| ☐ 62009½ "BARLOW" | 10.00 | 5.00 |
| ☐ 6214 | 14.00 | 7.00 |
| ☐ 6214½ | 12.00 | 6.00 |
| ☐ 6217 "HALF HAWK BILL" LAMINATED WOOD HANDLE | 18.00 | 9.00 |

## CASE XX U.S.A. (7 DOT) / 119

| PATTERN NO. | MINT | VG |
|---|---|---|
| ☐ 2220 "PEANUT" | 60.00 | 30.00 |
| ☐ 3220 "PEANUT" | 60.00 | 30.00 |
| ☐ 6220 "PEANUT" | 30.00 | 15.00 |
| ☐ 6225½ "COKE BOTTLE" | 20.00 | 10.00 |
| ☐ 6227 | 12.00 | 6.00 |
| ☐ 2231½ SAB LONG PULL STANDARD | 15.00 | 7.50 |
| ☐ 6231½ LONG PULL STANDARD | 22.00 | 11.00 |
| ☐ 12031 L R "ELECTRICIAN'S KNIFE" | 14.00 | 7.00 |
| ☐ 6232 | 15.00 | 7.50 |
| ☐ 3233 | 60.00 | 30.00 |
| ☐ 6233 | 20.00 | 10.00 |
| ☐ 8233 | 40.00 | 20.00 |
| ☐ 9233 | 20.00 | 10.00 |
| ☐ 6235½ | 12.00 | 6.00 |
| ☐ 62042 | 12.00 | 6.00 |
| ☐ 92042 | 12.00 | 6.00 |
| ☐ 06244 | 14.00 | 7.00 |
| ☐ 6244 | 12.00 | 6.00 |
| ☐ 6246 R SS "RIGGER'S KNIFE" | 25.00 | 12.50 |
| ☐ 06247 PEN | 15.00 | 7.50 |
| ☐ 32048 SP | 15.00 | 7.50 |
| ☐ 62048 SP | 14.00 | 7.00 |
| ☐ 61048 SP SSP | 16.00 | 8.00 |
| ☐ 6249 "COPPERHEAD OR VIETNAM" | 22.00 | 11.00 |
| ☐ 6250 "SUNFISH" LAMINATED WOOD HANDLE | 35.00 | 17.50 |
| ☐ 62052 | 22.00 | 11.00 |
| ☐ 62053 SR SS | 40.00 | 20.00 |
| ☐ 3254 "TRAPPER" | 30.00 | 15.00 |
| ☐ 6254 "TRAPPER" | 35.00 | 17.50 |
| ☐ 6254 "TRAPPER" | 45.00 | 22.50 |
| ☐ 6254 SSP "TRAPPER" | 35.00 | 17.50 |
| ☐ 6254 SSP "TRAPPER" | 45.00 | 22.50 |
| ☐ 62055 | 18.00 | 9.00 |
| ☐ 8261 | 40.00 | 20.00 |
| ☐ 9261 | 20.00 | 10.00 |
| ☐ 06263 SSP | 16.00 | 8.00 |
| ☐ 06263 F SS | 20.00 | 10.00 |
| ☐ 6265 SAB DR "FOLDING HUNTER" LAMINATED WOOD HANDLE | 25.00 | 12.50 |
| ☐ 6265 SAB DR SSP "FOLDING HUNTER" LAMINATED WOOD HANDLE | 30.00 | 15.00 |
| ☐ MARINER'S KNIFE SET | 35.00 | 17.50 |
| ☐ MARINER'S KNIFE SET SSP | 40.00 | 20.00 |

## 120 / CASE XX U.S.A. (7 DOT)

| PATTERN NO. | MINT | VG |
|---|---|---|
| ☐ 6269 | 20.00 | 10.00 |
| ☐ 6275 SP "MOOSE" | 22.00 | 11.00 |
| ☐ 6279 SS | 12.00 | 6.00 |
| ☐ M279 SC SS "PHYSICIAN'S KNIFE" BRUSHED STAINLESS STEEL HANDLE | 16.00 | 8.00 |
| ☐ M279 F SS "PHYSICIAN'S KNIFE" STAINLESS STEEL HANDLE | 16.00 | 8.00 |
| ☐ M279 SS "PHYSICIAN'S KNIFE" BRUSHED STAINLESS STEEL HANDLE | 15.00 | 7.50 |
| ☐ 82079½ SS "SLEEVE BOARD" | 35.00 | 17.50 |
| ☐ 22087 | 14.00 | 7.00 |
| ☐ 62087 | 14.00 | 7.00 |
| ☐ 6292 "TEXAS JACK" | 16.00 | 8.00 |
| ☐ 32095 F SS "FISHERMANS KNIFE" | 22.00 | 11.00 |
| ☐ 3299½ | 22.00 | 11.00 |
| ☐ 62109 X "SMALL COPPERHEAD" | 16.00 | 8.00 |
| ☐ 62131 "CANOE" BONE STAG HANDLE | 28.00 | 14.00 |
| ☐ 62131 "CANOE" DELRIN HANDLE | 50.00 | 25.00 |

## THREE BLADE

| | MINT | VG |
|---|---|---|
| ☐ 6308 "WHITTLER" | 18.00 | 9.00 |
| ☐ 3318 SH PEN | 18.00 | 9.00 |
| ☐ 4318 SH SP | 40.00 | 20.00 |
| ☐ 6318 SH SP | 16.00 | 8.00 |
| ☐ 6318 SP P | 16.00 | 8.00 |
| ☐ 6318 SH PEN | 20.00 | 10.00 |
| ☐ 6318 SH SP SSP | 20.00 | 10.00 |
| ☐ 6327 SH SP | 16.00 | 8.00 |
| ☐ 9327 SH SP | 20.00 | 10.00 |
| ☐ 13031 L R "ELECTRICIANS KNIFE" | 30.00 | 15.00 |
| ☐ 6332 | 16.00 | 8.00 |
| ☐ 6333 | 18.00 | 9.00 |
| ☐ 9333 | 18.00 | 9.00 |
| ☐ 6344 SH PEN | 15.00 | 7.50 |
| ☐ 6344 SH SP | 15.00 | 7.50 |
| ☐ 33044 SH SP "BIRDSEYE" | 20.00 | 10.00 |
| ☐ 3347 SH SP | 20.00 | 10.00 |
| ☐ 6347 SH SP | 16.00 | 8.00 |
| ☐ 6347 SP P | 20.00 | 10.00 |
| ☐ 6347 SP PEN | 22.00 | 11.00 |
| ☐ 6347 SH SP SSP | 22.00 | 11.00 |
| ☐ 63047 | 22.00 | 11.00 |
| ☐ 8364 SC SS | 75.00 | 37.50 |

*CASE XX U.S.A. (6 DOT) / 121*

| PATTERN NO. | MINT | VG |
|---|---|---|
| ☐ 6375 | 25.00 | 12.50 |
| ☐ 6380 "WHITTLER" | 30.00 | 15.00 |
| ☐ 6383 "WHITTLER" | 24.00 | 12.00 |
| ☐ 23087 SH PEN | 16.00 | 8.00 |
| ☐ 63087 SP PEN | 15.00 | 7.50 |
| ☐ 6392 | 25.00 | 12.50 |
| ☐ 33092 "BIRDSEYE" | 20.00 | 10.00 |
| ☐ M3102 R SS | 18.00 | 9.00 |

## FOUR BLADE

| | | |
|---|---|---|
| ☐ CASE'S SS "FLY FISHERMAN" | 95.00 | 47.50 |
| ☐ 6445 R "SCOUT'S KNIFE" | 30.00 | 15.00 |
| ☐ 640045 R "SCOUT'S KNIFE" BROWN PLASTIC HANDLE | 20.00 | 10.00 |
| ☐ 64047 P | 22.00 | 11.00 |
| ☐ 64052 | 25.00 | 12.50 |
| ☐ 6488 | 40.00 | 20.00 |

# CASE XX U.S.A. (6 DOT)

## ONE BLADE

| | | |
|---|---|---|
| ☐ 4100 SS "MELON TESTER" | 40.00 | 20.00 |
| ☐ 11011 "HAWK BILL" | 16.00 | 8.00 |
| ☐ 61011 "HAWK BILL" LAMINATED WOOD HANDLE | 12.00 | 6.00 |
| ☐ 6111½ L "LOCK BACK" | 40.00 | 20.00 |
| ☐ 11031 SH | 12.00 | 6.00 |
| ☐ 2137 "SOD BUSTER JR." | 12.00 | 6.00 |
| ☐ 2137 SS "SOD BUSTER JR." | 14.00 | 7.00 |
| ☐ 2138 "SOD BUSTER" | 14.00 | 7.00 |
| ☐ 2138 SS "SOD BUSTER" | 16.00 | 8.00 |
| ☐ 2138 L "SOD BUSTER" BLADE LOCK OPEN | 20.00 | 10.00 |
| ☐ 6143 "DADDY BARLOW" | 17.00 | 8.50 |
| ☐ 31048 | 12.00 | 6.00 |
| ☐ 61048 | 10.00 | 5.00 |
| ☐ 61048 SSP | 12.00 | 6.00 |
| ☐ C61050 SAB "BIG COKE BOTTLE" LAMINATED WOOD HANDLE | 35.00 | 17.50 |
| ☐ 6165 SAB DR "FOLDING HUNTER" LAMINATED WOOD HANDLE | 25.00 | 12.50 |
| ☐ P172 "BUFFALO" | 50.00 | 25.00 |
| ☐ 3185 "DOCTORS KNIFE" WITH SHIELD | 40.00 | 20.00 |

## 122 / CASE XX U.S.A. (6 DOT)

| PATTERN NO. | MINT | VG |
|---|---|---|
| ☐ 3185 "DOCTORS KNIFE" NO SHIELD | 40.00 | 20.00 |
| ☐ 6185 "DOCTORS KNIFE" | 26.00 | 13.00 |
| ☐ 61093 "TEXAS TOOTHPICK" | 28.00 | 14.00 |
| ☐ P197 L SSP "SHARK TOOTH" LOCK BACK | 60.00 | 30.00 |
| ☐ 7197 L SSP "SHARK TOOTH" LOCK BACK | 85.00 | 42.50 |
| ☐ 1199 SH R SS "GRAFTING KNIFE" | 14.00 | 7.00 |

## TWO BLADE

| | MINT | VG |
|---|---|---|
| ☐ MUSKRAT | 20.00 | 10.00 |
| ☐ 3201 | 20.00 | 10.00 |
| ☐ 6201 | 20.00 | 10.00 |
| ☐ 9201 | 18.00 | 9.00 |
| ☐ 6202½ | 10.00 | 5.00 |
| ☐ 6205 "RAZ OR ONE ARM MAN" DELRIN HANDLE | 30.00 | 15.00 |
| ☐ 6205 "RAZ OR ONE ARM MAN" BONE STAG HANDLE | 35.00 | 17.50 |
| ☐ 6207 | 20.00 | 10.00 |
| ☐ 6207 DELRIN | 20.00 | 10.00 |
| ☐ 6208 "HALF WHITTLER" | 15.00 | 7.50 |
| ☐ 62009 "BARLOW" | 12.00 | 6.00 |
| ☐ 62009 "BARLOW" "RAZ OR ONE ARM MAN" | 18.00 | 9.00 |
| ☐ 62009½ "BARLOW" | 10.00 | 5.00 |
| ☐ 6214 | 14.00 | 7.00 |
| ☐ 6214½ | 12.00 | 6.00 |
| ☐ 6217 "HALF HAWK BILL" LAMINATED WOOD HANDLE | 16.00 | 8.00 |
| ☐ 2220 "PEANUT" | 35.00 | 17.50 |
| ☐ 3220 "PEANUT" | 35.00 | 17.50 |
| ☐ 6220 "PEANUT" | 30.00 | 15.00 |
| ☐ 6225½ "COKE BOTTLE" | 18.00 | 9.00 |
| ☐ 6227 | 12.00 | 6.00 |
| ☐ 2231½ SAB | 15.00 | 7.50 |
| ☐ 6231½ | 20.00 | 10.00 |
| ☐ 12031 L R "ELECTRICIAN'S KNIFE" | 14.00 | 7.00 |
| ☐ 6232 | 14.00 | 7.00 |
| ☐ 3233 | 25.00 | 12.50 |
| ☐ 6233 | 20.00 | 10.00 |
| ☐ 8233 | 40.00 | 20.00 |
| ☐ 9233 | 20.00 | 10.00 |
| ☐ 6235½ | 12.00 | 6.00 |
| ☐ 62042 | 12.00 | 6.00 |
| ☐ 92042 | 12.00 | 6.00 |

*CASE XX U.S.A. (6 DOT) / 123*

| PATTERN NO. | MINT | VG |
|---|---|---|
| ☐ 6244 | 12.00 | 6.00 |
| ☐ 06244 | 13.00 | 6.50 |
| ☐ 6246 R SS "RIGGER'S KNIFE" | 25.00 | 12.50 |
| ☐ 06247 PEN | 14.00 | 7.00 |
| ☐ 32048 SP | 14.00 | 7.00 |
| ☐ 62048 SP | 14.00 | 7.00 |
| ☐ 62048 SP SSP | 16.00 | 8.00 |
| ☐ 6249 "COPPERHEAD OR VIETNAM" | 20.00 | 10.00 |
| ☐ 6250 "SUNFISH" LAMINATED WOOD HANDLE | 35.00 | 17.50 |
| ☐ 6250 "SUNFISH" LAMINATED WOOD HANDLE, BLADE ETCHED | 35.00 | 17.50 |
| ☐ 62052 | 20.00 | 10.00 |
| ☐ 82053 S R SS | 40.00 | 20.00 |
| ☐ 3254 "TRAPPER" | 54.00 | 22.50 |
| ☐ 6254 "TRAPPER" | 35.00 | 17.50 |
| ☐ 6254 "TRAPPER" DELRIN | 45.00 | 22.50 |
| ☐ 6254 SSP "TRAPPER" | 35.00 | 17.50 |
| ☐ 6254 SSP "TRAPPER" BONE | 50.00 | 25.00 |
| ☐ 62055 | 15.00 | 7.50 |
| ☐ 8261 | 40.00 | 20.00 |
| ☐ 9261 | 20.00 | 10.00 |
| ☐ 06263 SSP | 15.00 | 7.50 |
| ☐ 06263 F SSP | 20.00 | 10.00 |
| ☐ 6265 SAB DR "FOLDING HUNTER" LAMINATED WOOD HANDLE | 25.00 | 12.50 |
| ☐ 6265 SAB DR SSP "FOLDING HUNTER" LAMINATED WOOD HANDLE | 28.00 | 14.00 |
| ☐ MARINER'S KNIFE SET | 35.00 | 17.50 |
| ☐ MARINER'S KNIFE SET SSP | 40.00 | 20.00 |
| ☐ 6269 | 20.00 | 10.00 |
| ☐ 6275 SP "MOOSE" | 20.00 | 10.00 |
| ☐ M279 SS "PHYSICIAN KNIFE" BRUSHED STAINLESS STEEL HANDLE | 15.00 | 7.50 |
| ☐ M279SC SS "PHYSICIAN'S KNIFE" BRUSHED STAINLESS STEEL HANDLE | 15.00 | 7.50 |
| ☐ M279 F SS "PHYSICIAN'S KNIFE" BRUSHED STAINLESS STEEL HANDLE | 15.00 | 7.50 |
| ☐ 6279 SS | 12.00 | 6.00 |
| ☐ 82079½ SS "SLEEVE BOARD" | 30.00 | 15.00 |
| ☐ 22087 | 12.00 | 6.00 |
| ☐ 62087 | 12.00 | 6.00 |
| ☐ 6292 "TEXAS JACK" | 15.00 | 7.50 |
| ☐ 32095 F SS "FISHERMANS KNIFE" | 20.00 | 10.00 |

## 124 / CASE XX U.S.A. (6 DOT)

| PATTERN NO. | MINT | VG |
|---|---|---|
| ☐ 3299½ | 22.00 | 11.00 |
| ☐ 62109 X "SMALL COPPERHEAD" | 16.00 | 8.00 |
| ☐ 62131 "CANOE" BLADE ETCHED | 25.00 | 12.50 |

### THREE BLADE

| | | |
|---|---|---|
| ☐ 6308 "WHITTLER" | 15.00 | 7.50 |
| ☐ 3318 SH PEN | 15.00 | 7.50 |
| ☐ 6318 SH SP | 15.00 | 7.50 |
| ☐ 6318 SH PEN | 15.00 | 7.50 |
| ☐ 6318 SP P | 15.00 | 7.50 |
| ☐ 6318 SH SP SSP | 18.00 | 9.00 |
| ☐ 6327 SH SP | 16.00 | 8.00 |
| ☐ 13031 L R "ELECTRICIANS KNIFE" | 25.00 | 12.50 |
| ☐ 6332 | 16.00 | 8.00 |
| ☐ 6333 | 18.00 | 9.00 |
| ☐ 6344 SH PEN | 16.00 | 8.00 |
| ☐ 6344 SH SP | 16.00 | 8.00 |
| ☐ 33044 SH SP "SMALL BIRDSEYE" | 20.00 | 10.00 |
| ☐ 3347 SH SP | 16.00 | 8.00 |
| ☐ 6347 SH SP | 16.00 | 8.00 |
| ☐ 6347 SH SP SSP | 18.00 | 9.00 |
| ☐ 6347 SP PEN | 25.00 | 12.50 |
| ☐ 63047 | 20.00 | 10.00 |
| ☐ 8364 SC SS | 75.00 | 37.50 |
| ☐ 6375 | 20.00 | 10.00 |
| ☐ 6380 "WHITTLER" | 28.00 | 14.00 |
| ☐ 6383 "WHITTLER" BONE STAG HANDLE | 20.00 | 10.00 |
| ☐ 6383 "WHITTLER" DELRIN HANDLE | 20.00 | 10.00 |
| ☐ 23087 SH PEN | 15.00 | 7.50 |
| ☐ 63087 SP PEN | 15.00 | 7.50 |
| ☐ 33092 "BIRDSEYE" | 18.00 | 9.00 |
| ☐ 6392 | 20.00 | 10.00 |
| ☐ M3102 R SS | 18.00 | 9.00 |

### FOUR BLADE

| | | |
|---|---|---|
| ☐ 6445 R "SCOUTS KNIFE" | 30.00 | 15.00 |
| ☐ 640045 R "SCOUTS KNIFE" BROWN PLASTIC HANDLE | 20.00 | 10.00 |
| ☐ 64047 P | 22.00 | 11.00 |
| ☐ 64052 | 20.00 | 10.00 |
| ☐ 6488 | 35.00 | 17.50 |
| ☐ CASE'S SS "FLY FISHERMAN" | 95.00 | 47.50 |

## CASE XX U.S.A. (5 DOT)

### ONE BLADE

| PATTERN NO. | MINT | VG |
|---|---|---|
| ☐ 11011 "HAWK BILL" | 16.00 | 9.00 |
| ☐ 61011 "HAWK BILL" LAMINATED WOOD HANDLE | 12.00 | 6.00 |
| ☐ 6111½ L "LOCK BACK" | 35.00 | 17.50 |
| ☐ 11031 SH | 10.00 | 5.00 |
| ☐ 2137 "SOD BUSTER JR." | 10.00 | 5.00 |
| ☐ 2137 SS "SOD BUSTER JR." | 12.00 | 6.00 |
| ☐ 2138 "SOD BUSTER" | 12.00 | 6.00 |
| ☐ 2138 SS "SOD BUSTER" | 13.00 | 6.50 |
| ☐ 2138 L SS "SOD BUSTER" BLADE LOCKS OPEN | 18.00 | 9.00 |
| ☐ P138 L SS "ALYESKA SOD BUSTER" PACKWOOD HANDLE (500 MADE) | 125.00 | 62.50 |
| ☐ 6143 "DADDY BARLOW" | 12.00 | 6.00 |
| ☐ 31048 | 10.00 | 5.00 |
| ☐ 61048 | 10.00 | 5.00 |
| ☐ 61048 SSP | 12.00 | 6.00 |
| ☐ C61050 SAB "BIG COKE BOTTLE" LAMINATED WOOD HANDLE | 35.00 | 17.50 |
| ☐ 6165 SAB DR "FOLDING HUNTER" LAMINATED WOOD HANDLE | 22.00 | 11.00 |
| ☐ P172 "BUFFALO" | 50.00 | 25.00 |
| ☐ P197 L SSP "SHARKS TOOTH" "LOCK BACK" | 45.00 | 22.50 |
| ☐ 1199 SH R SS "GRAFTING KNIFE" | 11.00 | 6.50 |

### TWO BLADE

| | MINT | VG |
|---|---|---|
| ☐ MUSKRAT | 20.00 | 10.00 |
| ☐ 6202½ | 8.00 | 4.00 |
| ☐ 6205 "RAZOR ONE ARM MAN" | 50.00 | 25.00 |
| ☐ 6205 RAZ BONE HANDLE | 50.00 | 25.00 |
| ☐ 6207 BONE | 20.00 | 10.00 |
| ☐ 6207 DELRIN | 15.00 | 7.50 |
| ☐ 6208 "HALF WHITTLER" | 12.00 | 6.00 |
| ☐ 62009 "BARLOW" RAZOR ONE ARM MAN | 18.00 | 9.00 |
| ☐ 62009½ "BARLOW" DELRIN HANDLE | 10.00 | 5.00 |
| ☐ 62009½ "BARLOW" BONE STAG HANDLE | 30.00 | 15.00 |
| ☐ 6217 "HALF HAWK BILL" LAMINATED WOOD HANDLE | 20.00 | 10.00 |
| ☐ 6220 "PEANUT" | 20.00 | 10.00 |
| ☐ 6225½ "COKE BOTTLE" | 15.00 | 7.50 |
| ☐ 6227 | 10.00 | 5.00 |

## CASE XX U.S.A. (5 DOT)

| PATTERN NO. | MINT | VG |
|---|---|---|
| 2231½ SAB *LONG PULL STANDARD* | 15.00 | 7.50 |
| 6231½ *LONG PULL STANDARD* | 16.00 | 8.00 |
| 12031 L R *"ELECTRICIANS KNIFE"* | 12.00 | 6.00 |
| 6232 | 12.00 | 6.00 |
| 6233 | 18.00 | 9.00 |
| 9233 | 16.00 | 8.00 |
| 6235½ | 12.00 | 6.00 |
| 62042 | 12.00 | 6.00 |
| 92042 | 12.00 | 6.00 |
| 06244 | 12.00 | 6.00 |
| 6244 | 12.00 | 6.00 |
| 6246 R SS *"RIGGER'S KNIFE"* | 22.00 | 11.00 |
| 06247 PEN | 12.00 | 6.00 |
| 32048 SP | 12.00 | 6.00 |
| 62048 SP | 12.00 | 6.00 |
| 62048 SP SSP | 14.00 | 7.00 |
| 6249 *"COPPERHEAD OR VIETNAM"* | 15.00 | 7.50 |
| 6250 *"SUNFISH"* LAMINATED WOOD HANDLE, BLADE ETCHED | 25.00 | 12.50 |
| 62052 | 18.00 | 9.00 |
| 3254 *"TRAPPER"* | 30.00 | 15.00 |
| 6254 *"TRAPPER"* | 30.00 | 15.00 |
| 6254 SSP *"TRAPPER"* | 30.00 | 15.00 |
| 62055 *DELRIN* | 12.00 | 6.00 |
| 62055 *BONE* | 16.00 | 8.00 |
| 06263 SSP | 11.00 | 5.50 |
| 6265 SAB DR *"FOLDING HUNTER"* LAMINATED WOOD HANDLE | 22.00 | 11.00 |
| 6265 SAB DR SSP *"FOLDING HUNTER"* LAMINATED WOOD HANDLE | 25.00 | 12.50 |
| MARINER'S KNIFE SET | 35.00 | 17.50 |
| MARINER'S KNIFE SET SSP | 40.00 | 20.00 |
| 6269 | 16.00 | 8.00 |
| 6275 SP *"MOOSE"* | 18.00 | 8.00 |
| 6279 SS | 10.00 | 5.00 |
| M279 SS *"PHYSICIAN'S KNIFE"* BRUSHED STAINLESS STEEL HANDLE | 12.00 | 6.00 |
| M279 F SS *"PHYSICIAN'S KNIFE"* BRUSHED STAINLESS STEEL HANDLE | 12.00 | 6.00 |
| 22087 | 11.00 | 5.50 |
| 62087 | 11.00 | 5.50 |
| 6292 *"TEXAS JACK"* | 15.00 | 7.50 |
| 32095 F SS *"FISHERMANS KNIFE"* | 15.00 | 7.50 |

*CASE XX U.S.A. (5 DOT) / 127*

| PATTERN NO. | MINT | VG |
|---|---|---|
| ☐ 3299½ | 20.00 | 10.00 |
| ☐ 62109 X "SMALL COPPERHEAD" | 12.00 | 6.00 |
| ☐ 62131 "CANOE" ETCHED BLADE | 25.00 | 12.50 |

## THREE BLADE

| | | |
|---|---|---|
| ☐ 6308 "WHITTLER" | 18.00 | 9.00 |
| ☐ 3318 SH PEN | 15.00 | 7.50 |
| ☐ 6318 SH PEN | 16.00 | 8.00 |
| ☐ 6318 SP P | 16.00 | 8.00 |
| ☐ 6318 SH SP | 16.00 | 8.00 |
| ☐ 6318 SH SP SSP | 16.00 | 8.00 |
| ☐ 6327 SH SP | 12.00 | 6.00 |
| ☐ 6332 | 18.00 | 9.00 |
| ☐ 6333 | 12.00 | 6.00 |
| ☐ 6344 SH PEN | 12.00 | 6.00 |
| ☐ 6344 SH SP | 12.00 | 6.00 |
| ☐ 33044 SH SP "BIRDSEYE" | 20.00 | 10.00 |
| ☐ 3347 SH SP | 14.00 | 7.50 |
| ☐ 6347 SH SP SSP | 20.00 | 10.00 |
| ☐ 6347 SP PEN | 25.00 | 12.50 |
| ☐ 6347 SH SP | 18.00 | 9.00 |
| ☐ 63047 | 22.00 | 11.00 |
| ☐ 6375 | 22.00 | 11.00 |
| ☐ 6380 "WHITTLER" | 28.00 | 14.00 |
| ☐ 6383 "WHITTLER" | 22.00 | 11.00 |
| ☐ 23087 SH PEN | 12.00 | 6.00 |
| ☐ 63087 SP PEN | 12.00 | 6.00 |
| ☐ 33092 "BIRDSEYE" | 16.00 | 8.00 |
| ☐ 6392 | 20.00 | 10.00 |

## FOUR BLADE

| | | |
|---|---|---|
| ☐ 640045 R "SCOUT KNIFE" BROWN PLASTIC HANDLE | 17.00 | 8.50 |
| ☐ 6445 R "SCOUT KNIFE" | 27.00 | 13.50 |
| ☐ 64047 P | 26.00 | 13.00 |
| ☐ 64052 | 30.00 | 15.00 |
| ☐ 6488 | 35.00 | 17.50 |

*128 / CASE XX U.S.A. (4 DOT)*

# CASE XX U.S.A. (4 DOT)

## ONE BLADE

| PATTERN NO. | MINT | VG |
|---|---|---|
| ☐ 6111½ L "LOCK BACK" | 30.00 | 15.00 |
| ☐ 61011½ "HAWK BILL" | | |
|     *LAMINATED WOOD HANDLE* | 10.00 | 5.00 |
| ☐ 11031 SH | 10.00 | 5.00 |
| ☐ 2137 "SOD BUSTER JR." | 10.00 | 5.00 |
| ☐ 2137 SS "SOD BUSTER JR." | 11.00 | 5.50 |
| ☐ 2138 "SOD BUSTER" | 11.00 | 5.50 |
| ☐ 2138 SS "SOD BUSTER" | 12.00 | 6.00 |
| ☐ 6143 "DADDY BARLOW" | 12.00 | 6.00 |
| ☐ 31048 | 9.00 | 4.50 |
| ☐ 61048 | 9.00 | 4.50 |
| ☐ 61048 SSP | 10.00 | 5.00 |
| ☐ C61050 SAB "BIG COKE BOTTLE" | | |
|     *LAMINATED WOOD HANDLE* | 30.00 | 15.00 |
| ☐ 21051 L SSP "HORNET" LOCK BACK | 20.00 | 10.00 |
| ☐ 61051 L SSP "HORNET" LOCK BACK | 25.00 | 12.50 |
| ☐ 6165 SAB DR "FOLDING HUNTER" | | |
|     *LAMINATED WOOD HANDLE* | 20.00 | 10.00 |
| ☐ 5165 "AMERICAN SPIRIT" | 175.00 | 87.50 |
| ☐ P172 "BUFFALO" | 45.00 | 22.50 |
| ☐ 5172 SSP "BULLDOG PATTERN" (NO BOX) | 55.00 | 27.50 |
| ☐ P197 L SSP "SHARK TOOTH" LOCK BACK | 50.00 | 25.00 |
| ☐ 1199 SH R SS "GRAFTING KNIFE" | 11.00 | 5.50 |

## TWO BLADE

| | | |
|---|---|---|
| ☐ MUSKRAT | 20.00 | 10.00 |
| ☐ 6202½ *DISC DELRIN* | 10.00 | 5.00 |
| ☐ 6205 "RAZ OR ONE ARM MAN KNIFE" | 30.00 | 15.00 |
| ☐ 6205 *RAZ OR DELRIN DISC* | 25.00 | 17.50 |
| ☐ 6207 | 20.00 | 10.00 |
| ☐ 6207 *BONE* | 15.00 | 7.50 |
| ☐ 6208 "HALF WHITTLER" | 15.00 | 7.50 |
| ☐ 62009½ "BARLOW" | 10.00 | 5.00 |
| ☐ 6217 "HALF HAWK BILL" | | |
|     *LAMINATED WOOD HANDLE* | 16.00 | 8.00 |
| ☐ 6220 "PEANUT" | 20.00 | 10.00 |
| ☐ 6225½ "COKE BOTTLE" | 12.00 | 6.00 |
| ☐ 6227 | 10.00 | 5.00 |
| ☐ 2231½ **SAB** *LONG PULL STANDARD* | 15.00 | 7.50 |

## CASE XX U.S.A. (4 DOT) / 129

| PATTERN NO. | MINT | VG |
|---|---|---|
| ☐ 6231½ LONG PULL STANDARD | 15.00 | 7.50 |
| ☐ 12031 L R "ELECTRICIANS KNIFE" | 14.00 | 7.00 |
| ☐ 6232 | 14.00 | 7.00 |
| ☐ 6233 | 15.00 | 7.50 |
| ☐ 62033 | 10.00 | 5.00 |
| ☐ 9233 | 10.00 | 5.00 |
| ☐ 5233 SSP | 35.00 | 17.50 |
| ☐ 6235½ | 12.00 | 6.00 |
| ☐ 62042 | 10.00 | 5.00 |
| ☐ 92042 | 12.00 | 6.00 |
| ☐ 06244 | 12.00 | 6.00 |
| ☐ 6244 | 10.00 | 5.00 |
| ☐ 6246 R SS "RIGGERS KNIFE" | 25.00 | 12.50 |
| ☐ 06247 PEN | 15.00 | 7.50 |
| ☐ 32048 SP | 12.00 | 6.00 |
| ☐ 62048 SP | 12.00 | 6.00 |
| ☐ 62048 SP SSP | 14.00 | 7.00 |
| ☐ 6249 "COPPERHEAD"/"VIETNAM" | 18.00 | 9.00 |
| ☐ 6250 "SUN FISH" LAMINATED WOOD HANDLE BLADE ETCHED | 30.00 | 15.00 |
| ☐ 62052 | 18.00 | 9.00 |
| ☐ 3254 "TRAPPER" | 25.00 | 12.50 |
| ☐ 5254 SSP "TRAPPER" | 45.00 | 22.50 |
| ☐ 6254 "BONE" | 30.00 | 15.00 |
| ☐ 6254 "DELRIN" | 45.00 | 22.50 |
| ☐ 6254 "TRAPPER" | 30.00 | 15.00 |
| ☐ 6254 "TRAPPER" | 45.00 | 22.00 |
| ☐ 62055 | 15.00 | 7.50 |
| ☐ 06263 SSP | 11.00 | 5.50 |
| ☐ 5265 SSP "FOLDING HUNTER" | 55.00 | 27.50 |
| ☐ 6265 SAB DR "FOLDING HUNTER" LAMINATED WOOD HANDLE | 22.00 | 11.00 |
| ☐ 6265 SAB DR SSP "FOLDING HUNTER" LAMINATED WOOD HANDLE | 25.00 | 12.50 |
| ☐ MARINER'S KNIFE SET | 23.00 | 11.50 |
| ☐ MARINER'S KNIFE SET | 25.00 | 12.50 |
| ☐ 6269 | 16.00 | 8.00 |
| ☐ 6275 SP "MOOSE" | 18.00 | 9.00 |
| ☐ M279 SS "PHYSICIAN'S KNIFE" | 10.00 | 5.00 |
| ☐ M279 F SS "PHYSICIAN'S KNIFE" | 12.00 | 6.00 |
| ☐ M279 SS BARK HANDLE (NO DOT SHOWING, PROTOTYPE) | 40.00 | 20.00 |

## 130 / CASE XX U.S.A. (4 DOT)

| PATTERN NO. | MINT | VG |
|---|---|---|
| ☐ M279 F SS BARK HANDLE (NO DOT SHOWING, PROTOTYPE) | 40.00 | 20.00 |
| ☐ M279 SS JEWLER'S HANDLE (NO DOT SHOWING, PROTOTYPE) | 40.00 | 20.00 |
| ☐ M279 F SS JEWLER'S HANDLE (DO DOT SHOWING, PROTOTYPE) | 40.00 | 20.00 |
| ☐ 6279 SS | 10.00 | 5.00 |
| ☐ 22087 | 10.00 | 5.00 |
| ☐ 52087 SSP | 35.00 | 17.50 |
| ☐ 62087 | 10.00 | 5.00 |
| ☐ 6292 "TEXAS JACK" | 16.00 | 8.00 |
| ☐ 32095 F SS "FISHERMAN'S KNIFE" | 14.00 | 7.00 |
| ☐ 3299½ | 20.00 | 10.00 |
| ☐ 62109 X "SMALL COPPERHEAD" | 15.00 | 7.50 |
| ☐ 62131 "CANOE ETCHED BLADE" | 25.00 | 12.50 |

### THREE BLADE

| PATTERN NO. | MINT | VG |
|---|---|---|
| ☐ 6308 "WHITTLER" | 18.00 | 9.00 |
| ☐ 3318 SH PEN | 15.00 | 12.50 |
| ☐ 6318 SH SP | 18.00 | 9.00 |
| ☐ 6318 SH SP SSP | 18.00 | 9.00 |
| ☐ 6318 SH PEN | 18.00 | 9.00 |
| ☐ 6318 SP P | 18.00 | 9.00 |
| ☐ 6327 SH SP | 12.00 | 6.00 |
| ☐ 6332 | 20.00 | 10.00 |
| ☐ 6333 | 12.00 | 6.00 |
| ☐ 6344 SH PEN | 12.00 | 6.00 |
| ☐ 6344 SH SP | 15.00 | 7.50 |
| ☐ 33044 SH SP "BIRDSEYE" | 20.00 | 10.00 |
| ☐ 3347 SH SP | 12.00 | 6.00 |
| ☐ 5347 SH SP SSP | 40.00 | 20.00 |
| ☐ 6347 SH SP SSP | 18.00 | 9.00 |
| ☐ 6347 SH SP | 15.00 | 7.50 |
| ☐ 63047 | 22.00 | 11.00 |
| ☐ 6375 | 20.00 | 10.00 |
| ☐ 6380 "WHITTLER" | 28.00 | 14.00 |
| ☐ 6383 "WHITTLER" | 22.00 | 11.00 |
| ☐ 23087 SH PEN | 12.00 | 6.00 |
| ☐ 63087 SP PEN | 12.00 | 6.00 |
| ☐ 33092 "BIRDSEYE" | 15.00 | 7.50 |
| ☐ 6392 | 20.00 | 10.00 |

*CASE XX U.S.A. (3 DOT) / 131*

## FOUR BLADE

| PATTERN NO. | MINT | VG |
|---|---|---|
| ☐ 640045 R "SCOUT'S KNIFE" BROWN PLASTIC HANDLE | 12.00 | 6.00 |
| ☐ 6445 R "SCOUT KNIFE" | 27.00 | 13.50 |
| ☐ 64052 | 30.00 | 15.00 |
| ☐ 64047 P | 26.00 | 13.00 |
| ☐ 6488 *BONE* | 35.00 | 17.50 |
| ☐ 6488 *DELRIN* | 25.00 | 12.50 |

# CASE XX U.S.A. (3 DOT)

## ONE BLADE

| | | |
|---|---|---|
| ☐ 61011 "HAWK BILL" LAMINATED WOOD HANDLE | 10.00 | 5.00 |
| ☐ 6111½ L "LOCK BACK" | 30.00 | 15.00 |
| ☐ 5111½ L SSP "LOCK BACK" | 50.00 | 25.00 |
| ☐ 11031 SH | 10.00 | 5.00 |
| ☐ 2137 SS "SOD BUSTER JR." | 11.00 | 5.50 |
| ☐ 2137 "SOD BUSTER JR." | 10.00 | 5.00 |
| ☐ 2138 "SOD BUSTER" | 11.00 | 5.50 |
| ☐ 2138 SS "SOD BUSTER" | 12.00 | 6.00 |
| ☐ 2138 L SS "SOD BUSTER" | 18.00 | 9.00 |
| ☐ 6143 "DADDY BARLOW" | 10.00 | 5.00 |
| ☐ 31048 | 9.00 | 4.50 |
| ☐ 61048 | 9.00 | 4.50 |
| ☐ 61048 SSP | 10.00 | 5.00 |
| ☐ C61050 SAB "BIG COKE BOTTLE" LAMINATED WOOD HANDLE | 30.00 | 15.00 |
| ☐ M1051 L SSP "HORNET" LOCK BACK | 16.00 | 8.00 |
| ☐ 21051 L SSP "HORNET" LOCK BACK | 22.00 | 11.00 |
| ☐ 61051 L SSP "HORNET" LOCK BACK | 22.00 | 11.00 |
| ☐ 6165 SAB DR L SSP "FOLDING HUNTER" LOCK BACK LAMINATED WOOD HANDLE | 25.00 | 12.50 |
| ☐ 6165 SAB SSP "MOBY DICK" "FOLDING HUNTER" (LIMITED EDITION) | 175.00 | 87.50 |
| ☐ 6165 SAB DR "FOLDING HUNTER" LAMINATED WOOD HANDLE | 22.00 | 11.00 |
| ☐ 5172 "BULLDOG PATTERN" (NO BOX) | 55.00 | 27.50 |
| ☐ P172 "BUFFALO" | 45.00 | 22.50 |

## 132 / CASE XX U.S.A. (3 DOT)

| PATTERN NO. | MINT | VG |
|---|---|---|
| ☐ P197 L SSP "SHARKS TOOTH" LOCK BACK | 47.00 | 23.50 |
| ☐ 1199 SH R SS "GRAFTING KNIFE" | 11.00 | 5.50 |

## TWO BLADE

| | MINT | VG |
|---|---|---|
| ☐ MUSKRAT | 18.00 | 9.00 |
| ☐ 6202½ | 10.00 | 5.00 |
| ☐ 6205 RAZ "RAZ"/"ONE ARM MAN" | 25.00 | 12.50 |
| ☐ 6207 BONE | 20.00 | 10.00 |
| ☐ 6207 DELRIN | 15.00 | 7.50 |
| ☐ 6208 "HALF WHITTLER" | 15.00 | 7.50 |
| ☐ 6209½ "BARLOW" | 10.00 | 5.00 |
| ☐ 6217 "HALF HAWK BILL" LAMINATED WOOD HANDLE | 15.00 | 7.50 |
| ☐ 6220 "PEANUT" | 18.00 | 9.00 |
| ☐ 6225½ "COKE BOTTLE" | 12.00 | 6.00 |
| ☐ 6227 | 10.00 | 5.00 |
| ☐ 62027 | 10.00 | 5.00 |
| ☐ 12031 L HR "ELECTRICIANS KNIFE" | 14.00 | 7.00 |
| ☐ 12031 LR "ELECTRICIANS KNIFE" | 15.00 | 7.50 |
| ☐ 2231½ SAB LONG PULL STANDARD | 15.00 | 7.50 |
| ☐ 6231½ LONG PULL STANDARD | 15.00 | 7.50 |
| ☐ 6232 | 13.00 | 6.50 |
| ☐ 5233 SSP | 35.00 | 17.50 |
| ☐ 62033 | 10.00 | 5.00 |
| ☐ 9233 | 10.00 | 5.00 |
| ☐ 92033 CRACKED ICE HANDLE | 15.00 | 7.50 |
| ☐ 6235½ | 10.00 | 5.00 |
| ☐ 62042 | 10.00 | 5.00 |
| ☐ 92042 | 12.00 | 6.00 |
| ☐ 6244 | 10.00 | 5.00 |
| ☐ 06244 | 12.00 | 6.00 |
| ☐ 6246 R SS "RIGGER'S KNIFE" | 20.00 | 10.00 |
| ☐ 06247 PEN | 12.00 | 6.00 |
| ☐ 32048 SP | 12.00 | 6.00 |
| ☐ 62048 SP | 12.00 | 6.00 |
| ☐ 62048 SP SSP | 14.00 | 7.00 |
| ☐ 6249 "COPPERHEAD"/"VIETNAM" | 18.00 | 9.00 |
| ☐ 6250 "SUNFISH" LAMINATED WOOD HANDLE, BLADE ETCHED | 30.00 | 15.00 |
| ☐ 62052 | 18.00 | 9.00 |
| ☐ 3254 "TRAPPER" | 22.00 | 11.00 |
| ☐ 5254 SSP "TRAPPER" | 45.00 | 22.50 |
| ☐ 6254 "TRAPPER" | 25.00 | 12.50 |

*CASE XX U.S.A. (3 DOT) / 133*

| PATTERN NO. | MINT | VG |
|---|---|---|
| ☐ 6254 SSP "TRAPPER" | 25.00 | 12.50 |
| ☐ 62055 | 15.00 | 7.50 |
| ☐ 06263 SSP | 12.00 | 6.00 |
| ☐ 5265 SAB SSP "FOLDING HUNTER" | 55.00 | 27.50 |
| ☐ 6265 SAB DR "FOLDING HUNTER" LAMINATED WOOD HANDLE | 22.00 | 11.00 |
| ☐ 6265 SAB DR SSP "FOLDING HUNTER" LAMINATED WOOD HANDLE | 25.00 | 12.50 |
| ☐ MARINER'S KNIFE SET | 22.00 | 11.00 |
| ☐ MARINER'S KNIFE SET SSP | 25.00 | 12.50 |
| ☐ 6269 | 16.00 | 8.00 |
| ☐ 6275 SP "MOOSE" | 18.00 | 9.00 |
| ☐ M279 SS "PHYSICIAN'S KNIFE" BRUSHED STAINLESS STEEL HANDLE | 10.00 | 5.00 |
| ☐ M279 F SS "PHYSICIAN'S KNIFE" BRUSHED STAINLESS STEEL HANDLE | 12.00 | 6.00 |
| ☐ 6279 SS | 10.00 | 5.00 |
| ☐ 22087 | 10.00 | 5.00 |
| ☐ 52087 SSP | 32.00 | 16.00 |
| ☐ 62087 | 10.00 | 5.00 |
| ☐ 6292 "TEXAS JACK" | 15.00 | 7.50 |
| ☐ 32095 F SS "FISHERMANS KNIFE" | 16.00 | 8.00 |
| ☐ 3299½ | 20.00 | 10.00 |
| ☐ 62109 X "SMALL COPPERHEAD" | 15.00 | 7.50 |
| ☐ 52131 SSP | 50.00 | 25.00 |
| ☐ 62131 "CANOE" BLADE ETCHED | 25.00 | 12.50 |

## THREE BLADE

| | | |
|---|---|---|
| ☐ 6308 "WHITTLER" | 18.00 | 9.00 |
| ☐ 3318 SH PEN | 15.00 | 7.50 |
| ☐ 6318 SH PEN | 18.00 | 9.00 |
| ☐ 6318 SPP | 18.00 | 9.00 |
| ☐ 6318 SH SP SSP | 20.00 | 10.00 |
| ☐ 6318 SH SP | 18.00 | 9.00 |
| ☐ 63027 SH SP | 12.00 | 6.00 |
| ☐ 6327 SH SP | 14.00 | 7.00 |
| ☐ 6332 | 14.00 | 7.00 |
| ☐ 63032 | 14.00 | 7.00 |
| ☐ 6333 | 12.00 | 6.00 |
| ☐ 63033 | 12.00 | 6.00 |
| ☐ 33044 SH SP "BIRDSEYE" | 20.00 | 10.00 |
| ☐ 6344 SH PEN | 12.00 | 6.00 |
| ☐ 6344 SH SP | 15.00 | 7.50 |

134 / CASE XX U.S.A. (2 DOT)

| PATTERN NO. | MINT | VG |
|---|---|---|
| ☐ 3347 SH SP | 12.00 | 6.00 |
| ☐ 5347 SH SSP | 40.00 | 20.00 |
| ☐ 6347 SH SP | 15.00 | 7.50 |
| ☐ 6347 SH SP SSP | 18.00 | 9.00 |
| ☐ 63047 | 22.00 | 11.00 |
| ☐ 6375 | 22.00 | 11.00 |
| ☐ 6380 "WHITTLER" | 28.00 | 14.00 |
| ☐ 6383 "WHITTLER" | 22.00 | 11.00 |
| ☐ 23087 SH PEN | 12.00 | 6.00 |
| ☐ 63087 SP PEN | 12.00 | 6.00 |
| ☐ 33092 "BIRDSEYE" | 15.00 | 7.50 |
| ☐ 6392 | 20.00 | 10.00 |

## FOUR BLADE

| | MINT | VG |
|---|---|---|
| ☐ 6445 R "SCOUT KNIFE" | 27.00 | 13.50 |
| ☐ 640045 R "SCOUT KNIFE" | 12.00 | 6.00 |
| ☐ 64047 P | 26.00 | 13.00 |
| ☐ 64052 | 30.00 | 15.00 |
| ☐ 6488 BONE | 35.00 | 17.50 |
| ☐ 6488 DELRIN | 25.00 | 12.50 |

# CASE XX U.S.A. (2 DOT)

## ONE BLADE

| | MINT | VG |
|---|---|---|
| ☐ 61011 "HAWK BILL" LAMINATED WOOD HANDLE | 10.00 | 5.00 |
| ☐ 6111½ L "LOCK BACK" | 30.00 | 15.00 |
| ☐ 2137 SS "SOD BUSTER JR." | 11.00 | 5.50 |
| ☐ 2137 "SOD BUSTER JR." | 10.00 | 5.00 |
| ☐ 2138 "SOD BUSTER" | 11.00 | 5.50 |
| ☐ 2138 SS "SOD BUSTER" | 12.00 | 6.00 |
| ☐ 2138 L SS "SOD BUSTER" | 18.00 | 9.00 |
| ☐ 6143 "DADDY BARLOW" | 12.00 | 6.00 |
| ☐ 31048 | 9.00 | 4.50 |
| ☐ 61048 | 9.00 | 4.50 |
| ☐ 61048 SSP | 10.00 | 5.00 |
| ☐ M1051 L SSP "HORNET" LOCK BACK | 14.00 | 7.00 |
| ☐ 21051 L SSP "HORNET" LOCK BACK | 20.00 | 10.00 |
| ☐ 61051 L SSP "HORNET" LOCK BACK | 22.00 | 11.00 |
| ☐ P158 L SSP "MAKO" LOCK BACK | 30.00 | 15.00 |
| ☐ P159 L SSP "HAMMERHEAD" LOCK BACK | 35.00 | 17.50 |

*CASE XX U.S.A. (2 DOT) / 135*

| PATTERN NO. | MINT | VG |
|---|---|---|
| ☐ 6165 SAB DR L SSP "FOLDING HUNTER" LOCK BACK LAMINATED WOOD | 25.00 | 12.50 |
| ☐ W165 SAB SSP "MOBBY DICK" FOLDING HUNTER (LIMITED EDT) | 175.00 | 87.50 |
| ☐ 6165 SAB DR "FOLDING HUNTER" LAMINATED WOOD HANDLE | 20.00 | 10.00 |
| ☐ P172 "BUFFALO" | 45.00 | 22.50 |
| ☐ P197 L SSP "SHARKS TOOTH" LOCK BACK | 45.00 | 22.50 |
| ☐ 1199 SH R SS "GRAFTING KNIFE" | 11.00 | 5.50 |

## TWO BLADE

| | MINT | VG |
|---|---|---|
| ☐ MUSKRAT SSP *STAG DISC* | 35.00 | 17.50 |
| ☐ MUSKRAT | 20.00 | 10.00 |
| ☐ 6207 | 20.00 | 10.00 |
| ☐ 6208 "HALF WHITTLER" | 15.00 | 7.50 |
| ☐ 62009½ "BARLOW" | 10.00 | 5.00 |
| ☐ 6217 "HALF HAWK BILL" LAMINATED WOOD HANDLE | 15.00 | 7.50 |
| ☐ 6220 "PEANUT" | 14.00 | 7.00 |
| ☐ 5220 SSP DISC | 30.00 | 15.00 |
| ☐ 6225½ "COKE BOTTLE" | 12.00 | 6.00 |
| ☐ 62027 | 10.00 | 5.00 |
| ☐ 12031 L HR "ELECTRICIANS KNIFE" | 14.00 | 7.00 |
| ☐ 12031 LR "ELECTRICIANS KNIFE" | 15.00 | 7.50 |
| ☐ 2231½ SAB *LONG PULL STANDARD* | 15.00 | 7.50 |
| ☐ 6231½ *LONG PULL STANDARD* | 15.00 | 7.50 |
| ☐ 6232 | 13.00 | 6.50 |
| ☐ 52032 SSP DISC | 30.00 | 15.00 |
| ☐ 62033 | 10.00 | 5.00 |
| ☐ 92033 *CRACKED ICE HANDLE* | 15.00 | 7.50 |
| ☐ 6235½ | 10.00 | 5.00 |
| ☐ 62042 | 10.00 | 5.00 |
| ☐ 92042 | 12.00 | 6.00 |
| ☐ 6244 | 10.00 | 5.00 |
| ☐ 06244 | 12.00 | 6.00 |
| ☐ 6246 R SS "RIGGER'S KNIFE" | 20.00 | 10.00 |
| ☐ 06247 PEN | 12.00 | 6.00 |
| ☐ 32048 SP | 12.00 | 6.00 |
| ☐ 62048 SP | 12.00 | 6.00 |
| ☐ 62048 SP SSP | 14.00 | 7.00 |
| ☐ 6249 "COPPERHEAD/VIETNAM" | 18.00 | 9.00 |

## 136 / CASE XX U.S.A. (2 DOT)

| PATTERN NO. | MINT | VG |
|---|---|---|
| ☐ 6250 "SUNFISH" LAMINATED WOOD HANDLE, BLADE ETCHED | 30.00 | 15.00 |
| ☐ 3254 "TRAPPER" | 20.00 | 10.00 |
| ☐ 5254 SSP REP *ETCHING DISC* | 45.00 | 22.50 |
| ☐ 6254 "TRAPPER" | 20.00 | 10.00 |
| ☐ 6254 SSP "TRAPPER" | 20.00 | 10.00 |
| ☐ 06263 SSP | 11.00 | 5.50 |
| ☐ 6265 SAB DR "FOLDING HUNTER" | 22.00 | 11.00 |
| ☐ 6265 SAB DR SSP "FOLDING HUNTER" | 25.00 | 12.50 |
| ☐ MARINER'S KNIFE SET SSP | 22.00 | 11.00 |
| ☐ MARINER'S KNIFE SET | 25.00 | 12.50 |
| ☐ 6275 SS "MOOSE" | 20.00 | 10.00 |
| ☐ M279 SS "PHYSICIANS KNIFE" BRUSHED STAINLESS STEEL HANDLE | 10.00 | 5.00 |
| ☐ M279 F SS "PHYSICIANS KNIFE" BRUSHED STAINLESS STEEL HANDLE | 12.00 | 6.00 |
| ☐ 5279 SSP DISC | 28.00 | 14.00 |
| ☐ 6279 SS | 10.00 | 5.00 |
| ☐ 22087 | 10.00 | 5.00 |
| ☐ 52087 SSP DISC *RED ETCHED* | 30.00 | 15.00 |
| ☐ 52087 SSP *BLUE SCROLL (RARE)* | 60.00 | 30.00 |
| ☐ 62087 | 10.00 | 5.00 |
| ☐ 6292 "TEXAS JACK" | 15.00 | 7.50 |
| ☐ 32095 F SS "FISHERMANS KNIFE" | 15.00 | 7.50 |
| ☐ 62109 X "SMALL COPPERHEAD" | 15.00 | 7.50 |
| ☐ 62131 "CANOE" BLADE ETCHED | 25.00 | 12.50 |

### THREE BLADE

| | MINT | VG |
|---|---|---|
| ☐ 6308 "WHITTLER" | 18.00 | 9.00 |
| ☐ 3318 SH PEN | 15.00 | 7.50 |
| ☐ 6318 SH PEN | 18.00 | 9.00 |
| ☐ 6318 SP P | 18.00 | 9.00 |
| ☐ 6318 SH SP SSP | 18.00 | 9.00 |
| ☐ 6318 SH SP | 18.00 | 9.00 |
| ☐ 63027 SH SP | 12.00 | 6.00 |
| ☐ 6332 | 20.00 | 10.00 |
| ☐ 63032 | 18.00 | 9.00 |
| ☐ 63033 | 12.00 | 6.00 |
| ☐ 6344 SH PEN | 12.00 | 6.00 |
| ☐ 6344 SH SP | 15.00 | 7.50 |
| ☐ 3344 SH SP | 15.00 | 7.50 |
| ☐ 5347 SSP DISC | 40.00 | 20.00 |
| ☐ 6347 SH SP | 20.00 | 10.00 |

## CASE XX U.S.A. (10 & 9 DOT) LIGHTNING "S" / 137

| PATTERN NO. | MINT | VG |
|---|---|---|
| ☐ 6347 SH SP SSP | 22.00 | 11.00 |
| ☐ 63047 | 22.00 | 11.00 |
| ☐ 6375 | 22.00 | 11.00 |
| ☐ 6380 "WHITTLER" | 27.00 | 13.50 |
| ☐ 6383 "WHITTLER" | 22.00 | 11.00 |
| ☐ 23087 SH PEN | 12.00 | 6.00 |
| ☐ 63087 SP PEN | 12.00 | 6.00 |
| ☐ 33092 "BIRDS EYE" | 13.00 | 6.00 |
| ☐ 6392 | 18.00 | 9.00 |

### FOUR BLADE

| | MINT | VG |
|---|---|---|
| ☐ 640045 R "SCOUTS KNIFE" BROWN PLASTIC HANDLE | 12.00 | 6.00 |
| ☐ 64047 P | 20.00 | 10.00 |
| ☐ 64052 | 20.00 | 10.00 |
| ☐ 6488 | 25.00 | 12.50 |

## CASE XX U.S.A. (10 & 9 DOT) LIGHTNING "S"
### ONE BLADE

| | MINT | VG |
|---|---|---|
| ☐ 61011 DISC. | 16.00 | 8.00 |
| ☐ 11011 DISC. | 12.00 | 6.00 |
| ☐ 6111½ DISC. | 36.00 | 18.00 |
| ☐ 5120R SSP *Without Shield* | 25.00 | 12.50 |
| ☐ 5120R SSP *With Shield* | 35.00 | 17.50 |
| ☐ 2137 | 10.00 | 5.00 |
| ☐ 2137 SS | 11.00 | 5.50 |
| ☐ 2138 | 11.00 | 5.50 |
| ☐ 2138 SS | 12.00 | 6.00 |
| ☐ 2138 L SS | 18.00 | 9.00 |
| ☐ 6143 DISC | 16.00 | 8.00 |
| ☐ 31048 | 9.00 | 4.50 |
| ☐ 61048 | 9.00 | 4.50 |
| ☐ 61048 SSP | 12.00 | 6.00 |
| ☐ 21051 L SSP | 16.00 | 8.00 |
| ☐ 061050 L SSP DISC | 16.00 | 8.00 |
| ☐ 61051 L SSP DISC | 16.00 | 8.00 |
| ☐ M1051 L SSP | 16.00 | 8.00 |
| ☐ M1057 L SSP | 14.00 | 7.00 |
| ☐ 5158 L SSP | 65.00 | 32.50 |
| ☐ P158 SSP | 40.00 | 20.00 |

## 138 / CASE XX U.S.A. (10 & 9 DOT) LIGHTNING "S"

| PATTERN NO. | MINT | VG |
|---|---|---|
| ☐ 2159 L SSP | 30.00 | 15.00 |
| ☐ 5159 L SSP | 75.00 | 37.50 |
| ☐ P159 L SSP | 35.00 | 17.50 |
| ☐ 6165 SAB DR DISC | 22.00 | 11.00 |
| ☐ 6165 DR L SSP SAB | 30.00 | 15.00 |
| ☐ P172 DISC | 50.00 | 25.00 |
| ☐ P172 L SSP | 50.00 | 25.00 |
| ☐ P197 L SSP | 50.00 | 25.00 |
| ☐ 5197 L SSP | 70.00 | 35.00 |
| ☐ 1199 SH R SS | 14.00 | 7.00 |

## TWO BLADE

| | MINT | VG |
|---|---|---|
| ☐ 6201 R SS | 11.00 | 5.50 |
| ☐ 9201 R SS | 11.00 | 5.50 |
| ☐ TEXAS LOCKHORN | 45.00 | 22.50 |
| ☐ 6207 SP SSP | 18.00 | 9.00 |
| ☐ A6208 | 15.00 | 7.50 |
| ☐ 6208 DISC | 15.00 | 7.50 |
| ☐ A6209½ | 15.00 | 7.50 |
| ☐ 6209½ DISC | 12.00 | 6.00 |
| ☐ 6217 DISC | 15.00 | 7.50 |
| ☐ SR 6220 | 15.00 | 7.50 |
| ☐ 6220 DISC | 10.00 | 5.00 |
| ☐ SR 6225½ | 16.00 | 8.00 |
| ☐ 6225½ DISC | 12.00 | 6.00 |
| ☐ SR 62027 | 15.00 | 7.50 |
| ☐ 62027 DISC | 14.00 | 7.00 |
| ☐ 6231½ | 14.00 | 7.00 |
| ☐ 12031 L H R | 14.00 | 7.00 |
| ☐ 12031 LR | 14.00 | 7.00 |
| ☐ 62032 | 14.00 | 7.00 |
| ☐ 52033 R SSP | 25.00 | 12.50 |
| ☐ A62033 | 14.00 | 7.00 |
| ☐ 62033 DISC | 10.00 | 5.00 |
| ☐ 92033 | 12.00 | 6.00 |
| ☐ A6235½ | 14.00 | 7.00 |
| ☐ 62042 | 14.00 | 7.00 |
| ☐ 52042 R SSP | 25.00 | 12.50 |
| ☐ 92042 R SSP | 14.00 | 7.00 |
| ☐ 62042 DISC | 10.00 | 5.00 |
| ☐ 92042 | 14.00 | 7.00 |
| ☐ 03244 | 14.00 | 7.00 |
| ☐ SR 6244 | 16.00 | 8.00 |

## CASE XX U.S.A. (10 & 9 DOT) LIGHTNING "S" / 139

| PATTERN NO. | MINT | VG |
|---|---|---|
| ☐ 03244R | 14.00 | 7.00 |
| ☐ 6246 R SS DISC | 20.00 | 10.00 |
| ☐ 6246 R L SS | 18.00 | 9.00 |
| ☐ 06247 PEN | 16.00 | 8.00 |
| ☐ 32048 SP | 12.00 | 6.00 |
| ☐ 62048 SP | 12.00 | 6.00 |
| ☐ 62048 SP SSP | 14.00 | 7.00 |
| ☐ 6249 | 18.00 | 9.00 |
| ☐ 6250 *BRADFORD BON.* | 30.00 | 15.00 |
| ☐ 3254 | 15.00 | 7.50 |
| ☐ 6254 | 18.00 | 9.00 |
| ☐ 06263 R SSP | 25.00 | 12.50 |
| ☐ 6265 SAB DR | 22.00 | 11.00 |
| ☐ 6265 SAB DR SSP | 26.00 | 13.00 |
| ☐ 6275 SP | 18.00 | 9.00 |
| ☐ E278 SS | 14.00 | 7.00 |
| ☐ I278 SS | 14.00 | 7.00 |
| ☐ IS278 SS | 14.00 | 7.00 |
| ☐ S278 SS | 15.00 | 7.50 |
| ☐ M279 R SS | 14.00 | 7.00 |
| ☐ M279 SS | 14.00 | 7.00 |
| ☐ M279 F SS | 14.00 | 7.00 |
| ☐ 6279 SS | 12.00 | 6.00 |
| ☐ 22087 | 12.00 | 6.00 |
| ☐ 62087 | 12.00 | 6.00 |
| ☐ 6292 | 16.00 | 8.00 |
| ☐ 32095 F SS DISC | 16.00 | 8.00 |
| ☐ 62109X | 16.00 | 8.00 |
| ☐ 62131 | 25.00 | 12.50 |
| ☐ MARINER'S KNIFE SET | 30.00 | 15.00 |
| ☐ MARINER'S KNIFE SET SS | 32.00 | 16.00 |
| ☐ MUSKRAT | 20.00 | 10.00 |
| ☐ 6308 | 18.00 | 9.00 |
| ☐ 3318 SH PEN | 15.00 | 7.50 |
| ☐ 6318 SH SP | 18.00 | 9.00 |
| ☐ 6318 SH SP SSP | 18.00 | 9.00 |
| ☐ 6318 SH PEN | 18.00 | 9.00 |
| ☐ 6318 SP P | 18.00 | 9.00 |
| ☐ 63027 SH SP | 15.00 | 7.50 |

### THREE BLADE

| | | |
|---|---|---|
| ☐ 6347 SH SP SSP | 20.00 | 10.00 |
| ☐ 6375 | 22.00 | 11.00 |

## 140 / CASE XX U.S.A. (8 DOT) LIGHTNING "S"

| PATTERN NO. | MINT | VG |
|---|---|---|
| ☐ 63033 | 14.00 | 7.00 |
| ☐ 6344 SH PEN | 15.00 | 7.50 |

### FOUR BLADE

| | | |
|---|---|---|
| ☐ 640045 R | 12.00 | 6.00 |
| ☐ 64052 DISC | 28.00 | 14.00 |

## CASE XX USA (8 DOT) LIGHTNING "S"

### ONE BLADE

| | | |
|---|---|---|
| ☐ 61011 DISC | 12.00 | 6.00 |
| ☐ 6111½ L DISC | 30.00 | 15.00 |
| ☐ 5120 R SSP | 25.00 | 12.50 |
| ☐ 2137 | 11.00 | 5.50 |
| ☐ 2137 SS | 12.00 | 6.00 |
| ☐ 2138 | 12.00 | 6.00 |
| ☐ 2138 SS | 15.00 | 7.50 |
| ☐ 6143 DISC | 18.00 | 9.00 |
| ☐ 31048 | 10.00 | 5.00 |
| ☐ 61048 | 10.00 | 5.00 |
| ☐ 61048 SSP | 12.00 | 6.00 |
| ☐ M1051L SSP | 16.00 | 8.00 |
| ☐ 51051L SSP | 28.00 | 14.00 |
| ☐ P10051L SSP | 18.00 | 9.00 |
| ☐ P1051½ L SSP | 18.00 | 9.00 |
| ☐ M1057L SSP | 16.00 | 8.00 |
| ☐ P158L SSP | 35.00 | 17.50 |
| ☐ P159L SSP DISC | 45.00 | 22.50 |
| ☐ 6165 SAB DR DISC | 25.00 | 12.50 |
| ☐ 6165 SAB DRL SSP | 28.00 | 14.00 |
| ☐ P172 DISC | 50.00 | 25.00 |
| ☐ P172L SSP | 50.00 | 25.00 |
| ☐ P197L SSP | 50.00 | 25.00 |
| ☐ 1199 SH R SS | 14.00 | 7.00 |
| ☐ SIDEWINDER | 55.00 | 27.50 |

### TWO BLADE

| | | |
|---|---|---|
| ☐ 6201 R SS | 11.00 | 5.50 |
| ☐ 9201 R SS | 11.00 | 5.50 |
| ☐ 6207 SP SSP *"MINI TRAPPER"* | 18.00 | 9.00 |
| ☐ A6208 | 15.00 | 7.50 |
| ☐ A62009½ | 15.00 | 7.50 |

## CASE XX U.S.A. (8 DOT) LIGHTNING "S" / 141

| PATTERN NO. | MINT | VG |
|---|---|---|
| ☐ SR 6220 | 15.00 | 7.50 |
| ☐ SR 6225½ | 16.00 | 8.00 |
| ☐ SR 62027 DISC | 15.00 | 7.50 |
| ☐ 12031 LR DISC | 14.00 | 7.00 |
| ☐ 12031 LHR | 14.00 | 7.00 |
| ☐ 6231½ DISC | 14.00 | 7.00 |
| ☐ 62032 | 14.00 | 7.00 |
| ☐ 52033 R SSP | 25.00 | 17.50 |
| ☐ A62033 | 14.00 | 7.00 |
| ☐ 92033 | 12.00 | 6.00 |
| ☐ A6235½ | 14.00 | 7.00 |
| ☐ A62042 | 14.00 | 7.00 |
| ☐ 92042 | 14.00 | 7.00 |
| ☐ 52042 R SSP | 25.00 | 12.50 |
| ☐ SR6244 | 16.00 | 8.00 |
| ☐ 03244 | 14.00 | 7.00 |
| ☐ 03244 R DISC | 14.00 | 7.00 |
| ☐ 6246 LR SS | 18.00 | 9.00 |
| ☐ 06247 PEN | 16.00 | 8.00 |
| ☐ 32048 SP | 12.00 | 6.00 |
| ☐ 62048 SP | 12.00 | 6.00 |
| ☐ 61048 SP SSP | 14.00 | 7.00 |
| ☐ 6249 | 18.00 | 9.00 |
| ☐ 6250 "BRADFORD BONANZA" DISC | 30.00 | 15.00 |
| ☐ 3254 | 15.00 | 7.50 |
| ☐ 6254 | 18.00 | 9.00 |
| ☐ 6254 SSP | 20.00 | 10.00 |
| ☐ 05263 R SSP | 25.00 | 12.50 |
| ☐ 06263 SSP | 12.00 | 6.00 |
| ☐ 6265 SAB DR | 22.00 | 11.00 |
| ☐ 6265 SAB DR SSP | 26.00 | 13.00 |
| ☐ 6275 SP | 18.00 | 9.00 |
| ☐ E278 SS | 14.00 | 7.00 |
| ☐ I278 SS | 14.00 | 7.00 |
| ☐ IS278 SS | 14.00 | 7.00 |
| ☐ S278 SS | 15.00 | 7.50 |
| ☐ M279 SS | 14.00 | 7.00 |
| ☐ M279 R SS DISC | 14.00 | 7.00 |
| ☐ M279 F SS | 14.00 | 7.00 |
| ☐ M279 FR SS DISC | 14.00 | 7.00 |
| ☐ 6279 SS DISC | 12.00 | 6.00 |
| ☐ 22087 SS | 12.00 | 6.00 |
| ☐ 62087 SS | 14.00 | 7.00 |

## 142 / CASE XX U.S.A. (8 DOT) LIGHTNING "S"

| PATTERN NO. | MINT | VG |
|---|---|---|
| ☐ 6292 | 16.00 | 8.00 |
| ☐ 32095 F SS DISC | 20.00 | 10.00 |
| ☐ 62109 X | 16.00 | 8.00 |
| ☐ 62131 | 25.00 | 12.50 |
| ☐ MARINER'S KNIFE SET | 30.00 | 15.00 |
| ☐ MARINER'S KNIFE SET SS | 32.00 | 16.00 |
| ☐ MUSKRAT | 20.00 | 10.00 |
| ☐ TEXAS LOCKHORN | 45.00 | 22.50 |

### THREE BLADE

| | | |
|---|---|---|
| ☐ 6308 | 18.00 | 9.00 |
| ☐ 3318 SH PEN DISC | 15.00 | 7.50 |
| ☐ 6318 SH SP | 18.00 | 9.00 |
| ☐ 6318 SH SP SSP | 20.00 | 10.00 |
| ☐ 6318 SH PEN DISC | 18.00 | 9.00 |
| ☐ 6318 SP P DISC | 18.00 | 9.00 |
| ☐ 63027 SH SP DISC | 15.00 | 7.50 |
| ☐ 63032 | 18.00 | 9.00 |
| ☐ 63033 | 12.00 | 6.00 |
| ☐ 6344 SH PEN | 14.00 | 7.00 |
| ☐ 3347 SH SP | 14.00 | 7.00 |
| ☐ 6347 SH SP | 18.00 | 9.00 |
| ☐ 6347 SH SP SS | 20.00 | 10.00 |
| ☐ SR6347½ DISC | 22.00 | 11.00 |
| ☐ 6375 | 22.00 | 11.00 |
| ☐ 6383 DISC | 22.00 | 11.00 |
| ☐ 63087 SH PEN | 12.00 | 6.00 |
| ☐ 63087 SP PEN SS | 15.00 | 7.50 |
| ☐ 23087 SH PEN | 12.00 | 6.00 |
| ☐ 6392 | 18.00 | 9.00 |
| ☐ 33092 DISC | 18.00 | 9.00 |

### FOUR BLADE

| | | |
|---|---|---|
| ☐ 640045 R | 12.00 | 6.00 |
| ☐ 64052 DISC | 25.00 | 12.50 |

# KABAR

## KA-BAR SHIELDS

Ka-Bar used a number of different shield designs and styles of lettering, of which the following is a selection. The most famous Ka-Bar shield is the Dog's Head, which in style S11 carries no lettering. Another version of this shield, style S10, reads "KA-BAR" in inverted lettering. Dates of usage have not been established.

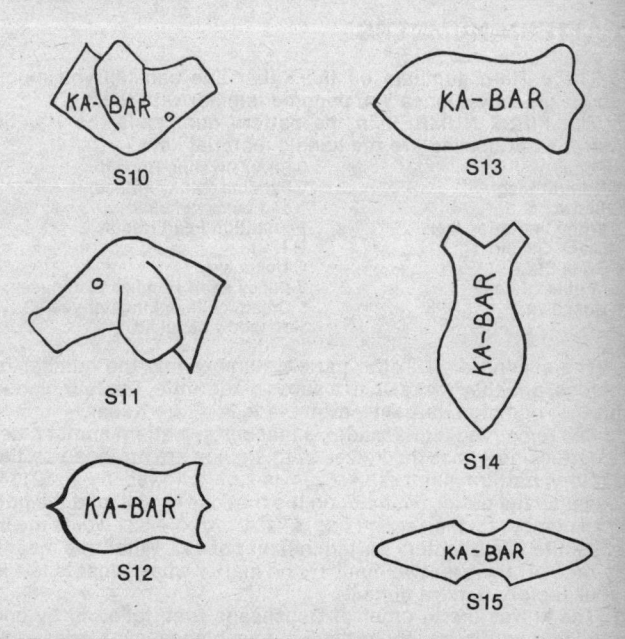

## KA-BAR

**S16**

**S18** (Kabar)

**S17** (KA-BAR)

**S19** (KA-BAR)

## PATTERN NUMBERS

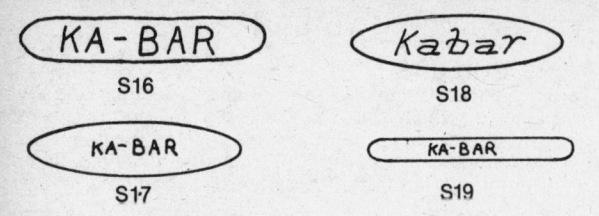

The pattern numbers on the Kabar line can tell you much about the knives once you become familiar with them.

The FIRST NUMBER in the pattern number is the Handle Material. Following are the handle material keys.

1-Ebony
2-Natural Stag
3-Redwood
4-White Imatation Ivory
4-Clack Celluloid
6-Bone Stag
7-Mother of Pearl
8-Unknown
9-Silver Pyraline Handle
0-Pyraline (candy striped) and fancy celluloid
P-Imitation Pearl Handle
H-Horn
C-Unknown
T-Fancy Pearl Handles (early use) Cream celluloid in later years.
R-Rainbow celluloid

The second digit in the pattern number told the number of blades, and they make up to a seven blade knife. The four blades are not common, but any seven blade is a rare Kabar.

The remaining digits made up the factory pattern number. Let us stress here that the knives in this guide are arranged by the factory pattern number. A 6234 is not followed by a 62134, because the pattern number on the first one is "34" and the pattern number on the second one is "134". Also, a 531 would mean the knife has a factory pattern number of "1". What this means is take off the first two numbers no matter what. What is left is your factory pattern number.

The knives are in order of Dogsheads first, followed by one blades, two blades, three blades, four blades, six blades, and seven blades.

There is one major drawback, and if you have had any experience with Kabars you already know what it is. Unlike many of the other manufacturers of the time, few Kabars had the pattern numbers stamped on them, therefore to use this guide effectively it is important that you study the styles of knives more than the pattern numbers.

## TANG STAMPINGS

Kabar has reported that they have over 200 different tang stampings over the years, but through our research so far we have uncovered the following.

*U-R Co.* Tidioute PA
*Union Razor Co.* Tidioute, Pa
*Union Cutlery Co.* Tidioute Pa
*Union Cut. Co.* Tidioute
*Union* inside a North American shield
(The Union Cut. Co.) stamping was
adopted in 1909.
*Union Cut. Co.* Olean N. Y.
*Union Cut. Co.*

*KA-BAR*
*KA-BAR,* Olean N. Y.
*Ka-Bar* Stainless
*Ka-Bar* Olean N. Y.
*Kabar* Stainless
*Kabar* (pattern no.) USA (current stamping
*Olcut*
*Keenwell*
*VikingU-C Co. Olean,* N. Y. USA
*John Jay* Made in USA

## KA-BAR DOGSHEAD SECTION

|  | MINT | VG |
|---|---|---|
| ☐ **22 BULLET** *KA-BAR Union Cut on Rear Tang or on Second Blade, Genuine Stag* | 850.00 | 425.00 |
| ☐ **62 BULLET** *KA-BAR Union Cut on Rear Tang or on Second Blade, Bone Stag* | 700.00 | 350.00 |
| ☐ **6191 LG** *KA-BAR Union Cut on Rear Tang or on Second Blade, Bone Stag* | 700.00 | 350.00 |
| ☐ **P191 LG** *KA-BAR Union Cut on Rear Tang or on Second Blade, Imitation Pearl* | 650.00 | 325.00 |
| ☐ **6291 KF** *Union in North American Shield, Bone Stag* | 600.00 | 300.00 |
| ☐ **6291 KF** *Union Cut Co. Straightline Mark, Bone Stag.* | 550.00 | 275.00 |
| ☐ **2291 KF** *Union Cut Co. Straightline Mark, Genuine Stag.* | 600.00 | 300.00 |
| ☐ **6291 KF** *KA-BAR Union Cut on Rear Tang or on Second Blade, Bone Stag* | 500.00 | 250.00 |

## 146 / KA-BAR

| | MINT | VG |
|---|---:|---:|
| ☐ **6391 K-F-S** *KA-BAR Union Cut on Rear Tang or on Second Blade, Bone Stag* | 650.00 | 325.00 |
| ☐ **61106 LG** *Union in North American Shield, Bone Stag* | 1000.00 | 500.00 |
| ☐ **61106 LG** *Union Cut Co. Circle Marking, Bone Stag* | 750.00 | 375.00 |
| ☐ **61106 LG** *Union Cut Co. Straightline Mark, Bone Stag* | 750.00 | 375.00 |
| ☐ **61106 LG** *KA-BAR Union Cut on Rear Tang or on Second Blade, Bone Stag* | 725.00 | 375.00 |
| ☐ **61106** *Union in North American Shield, Bone Stag* | 850.00 | 425.00 |
| ☐ **61106** *Union Cut Co. Circle Marking, Bone Stag* | 700.00 | 350.00 |
| ☐ **61106** *Union Cut Co. Straightline Mark, Bone Stag* | 700.00 | 350.00 |
| ☐ **21106** *KA-BAR Union Cut on Rear Tang or on Second Blade, Genuine Stag* | 800.00 | 400.00 |
| ☐ **61106** *KA-BAR Union Cut on Rear Tang or on Second Blade, Bone Stag* | 650.00 | 325.00 |
| ☐ **P1106** *KA-BAR Union Cut on Rear Tang or on Second Blade, Pearl Celluloid* | 465.00 | 238.00 |
| ☐ **21107** *Union Cut Co. Straightline Mark, Genuine Stag* | 600.00 | 300.00 |
| ☐ **21107** *KA-BAR Union Cut on Rear Tang or on Second Blade, Genuine Stag* | 500.00 | 250.00 |
| ☐ **21107** *Current Model Dated, Genuine Stag* | 80.00 | 40.00 |

**21107**

# KA-BAR / 147

| | MINT | VG |
|---|---|---|
| ☐ 22107 Union Cut Co. Straightline Mark, Genuine Stag | 550.00 | 275.00 |
| ☐ 22107 KA-BAR Union Cut on Rear Tang or on Second Blade, Genuine Stag | 500.00 | 250.00 |
| ☐ 22107 KA-BAR OLEAN, N.Y. in small letters, Genuine Stag | 450.00 | 225.00 |
| ☐ 22107 Current Model Dated, Genuine Stag | 80.00 | 40.00 |
| ☐ 61107 LG KA-BAR Union Cut on Rear Tang or on Second Blade, Bone Stag | 850.00 | 425.00 |
| ☐ 21107 LG KA-BAR Union Cut on Rear Tang or on Second Blade, Genuine Stag | 900.00 | 450.00 |
| ☐ T1107 LG KA-BAR Union Cut on Rear Tang or on Second Blade, Cream Celluloid | 650.00 | 325.00 |
| ☐ 61107 Union in North American Shield, Bone Stag | 800.00 | 400.00 |
| ☐ 61107 Union Cut Co. Straightline Mark, Bone Stag | 575.00 | 288.00 |
| ☐ 61107 KA-BAR Union Cut on Rear Tang or on Second Blade, Bone Stag | 475.00 | 238.00 |
| ☐ 62107 Union Cut Co. Straightline Mark, Bone Stag | 550.00 | 275.00 |
| ☐ 62107 KA-BAR Union Cut on Rear Tang or on Second Blade, Bone Stag | 475.00 | 238.00 |
| ☐ 62107 KA-BAR OLEAN, N.Y. in small letters, Bone Stag | 425.00 | 213.00 |
| ☐ 61110 Union in North American Shield, Bone Stag | 650.00 | 325.00 |
| ☐ 02118 Bicentennial Model, Red, White & Blue Overlay Celluloid | 75.00 | 33.00 |
| ☐ 61126 L Union Cut Co. Circle Marking, Bone Stag | 1000.00 | 500.00 |
| ☐ 22156 Union in North American Shield, Genuine Stag | 800.00 | 400.00 |
| ☐ 22156 UNION CUT CO. Straightline Mark, Genuine Stag | 600.00 | 300.00 |
| ☐ 62156 Union in North American Shield, Bone Stag | 700.00 | 350.00 |
| ☐ 62156 UNION CUT CO. Straightline Mark, Bone Stag | 550.00 | 275.00 |

148 / KA-BAR

02118

# KA-BAR ONE-BLADE SECTION

|  | MINT | VG |
|---|---|---|
| ☐ **Cigar Cutter** *UNION CUT CO., Cream Celluloid* . . | 45.00 | 23.00 |
| ☐ **T-19** *KA-BAR Stainless, Cream Celluloid* . . . . . . . | 30.00 | 15.00 |
| ☐ **6111** *UNION CUT CO., Bone Stag* . . . . . . . . . . . . . | 100.00 | 50.00 |
| ☐ **0111** *UNION CUT CO., Pyraline* . . . . . . . . . . . . . . | 75.00 | 38.00 |
| ☐ **6112** *UNION CUT CO., Bone Stag* . . . . . . . . . . . . . | 70.00 | 35.00 |
| ☐ **0112** *UNION CUT CO., Pyraline* . . . . . . . . . . . . . . | 60.00 | 30.00 |
| ☐ **6112** *KA-BAR, Bone Stag* . . . . . . . . . . . . . . . . . . | 60.00 | 30.00 |
| ☐ **0112** *KA-BAR, Pyraline* . . . . . . . . . . . . . . . . . . . | 55.00 | 28.00 |
| ☐ **6112** *kabar, Rough Black* . . . . . . . . . . . . . . . . . . | 35.00 | 18.00 |
| ☐ **T112** *kabar, Cream Celluloid* . . . . . . . . . . . . . . . | 30.00 | 15.00 |
| ☐ **T118** *KA-BAR, Cream Celluloid* . . . . . . . . . . . . . | 30.00 | 15.00 |
| ☐ **3163** *UNION CUT CO., Redwood* . . . . . . . . . . . . . | 35.00 | 18.00 |
| ☐ **6163** *UNION CUT CO., Bone Stag* . . . . . . . . . . . . . | 55.00 | 28.00 |
| ☐ **6165** *UNION CUT CO., Bone Stag* . . . . . . . . . . . . . | 90.00 | 45.00 |
| ☐ **0165** *UNION CUT CO., Fancy Celluloid* . . . . . . . . | 80.00 | 40.00 |

## KA-BAR / 149

| | MINT | VG |
|---|---|---|
| ☐ 6165 LG UNION CUT CO., Bone Stag | 175.00 | 83.00 |
| ☐ 6165 LG KA-BAR, Bone Stag | 140.00 | 70.00 |
| ☐ 2165 LG kabar, Genuine Stag | 85.00 | 43.00 |
| ☐ 6165 LG kabar, Rough Black Composition | 50.00 | 25.00 |
| ☐ 6165 LG kabar computer number USA, Imitation Bone Delrin | 10.00 | 5.00 |
| ☐ 3170 UNION CUT CO., Redwood | 90.00 | 45.00 |
| ☐ 3174 UNION CUT CO., Redwood | 30.00 | 15.00 |
| ☐ 6174 UNION CUT CO., Bone Stag | 45.00 | 23.00 |
| ☐ 3174 KA-BAR, Redwood | 25.00 | 13.00 |
| ☐ 6174 KA-BAR, Bone Stag | 40.00 | 20.00 |
| ☐ 6175 RG UNION CUT CO., Bone Stag | 50.00 | 25.00 |
| ☐ 2179-L Grizzley KA-BAR, Genuine Stag | 1500.00 | 750.00 |
| ☐ T179 KA-BAR, Cream Celluloid | 400.00 | 200.00 |
| ☐ 9179 KA-BAR, Silver Pyraline | 600.00 | 300.00 |
| ☐ 6191 L UNION CUT CO., Bone Stag | 600.00 | 300.00 |
| ☐ 6191 L UNION CUT CO., Genuine Stag | 750.00 | 375.00 |
| ☐ 61103 UNION CUT CO., Bone Stag | 70.00 | 35.00 |
| ☐ 01103 UNION CUT CO., Fancy Celluloid | 55.00 | 28.00 |
| ☐ 71103 UNION CUT CO., Pearl | 85.00 | 43.00 |
| ☐ 61103 KA-BAR, Bone Stag | 70.00 | 35.00 |
| ☐ 01103 KA-BAR, Fancy Celluloid | 50.00 | 25.00 |
| ☐ 21105 UNION CUT CO., Genuine Stag | 500.00 | 250.00 |
| ☐ 21105 KA-BAR, Genuine Stag | 400.00 | 200.00 |
| ☐ 61105 UNION CUT CO., Bone Stag | 400.00 | 200.00 |
| ☐ T1105 KA-BAR, Cream Celluloid | 350.00 | 175.00 |
| ☐ 61106 UNION CUT CO., Bone Stag | 300.00 | 150.00 |
| ☐ 61106 KA-BAR, Bone Stag | 250.00 | 125.00 |
| ☐ T1106 KA-BAR, Cream Celluloid | 175.00 | 88.00 |
| ☐ 61106 L UNION CUT CO., Bone Stag | 450.00 | 225.00 |
| ☐ 21107 LG Little Grizzly KA-BAR, Genuine Stag | 1500.00 | 750.00 |
| ☐ 61107 UNION CUT CO., Bone Stag | 300.00 | 150.00 |
| ☐ 61107 KA-BAR, Bone Stag | 250.00 | 125.00 |
| ☐ 61107 KA-BAR, Rough Black | 125.00 | 63.00 |
| ☐ P-1107 KA-BAR, Imitation Pearl | 150.00 | 75.00 |
| ☐ 61107 kabar, Rough Black | 75.00 | 38.00 |
| ☐ 31108 kabar, Redwood | 30.00 | 15.00 |
| ☐ 31108 kabar computer number USA, Redwood | 15.00 | 7.00 |
| ☐ 61110 UNION CUT CO., Bone Stag | 95.00 | 48.00 |
| ☐ 61118 UNION CUT CO., Bone Stag | 200.00 | 100.00 |
| ☐ 01118 UNION CUT CO., Fancy Celluloid | 140.00 | 70.00 |
| ☐ 61125 L UNION CUT CO., Bone Stag | 275.00 | 138.00 |
| ☐ 61126 L UNION CUT CO., Bone Stag | 600.00 | 300.00 |

## 150 / KA-BAR

| | MINT | VG |
|---|---|---|
| ☐ 61129 UNION CUT CO., Bone Stag | 125.00 | 63.00 |
| ☐ G1129 UNION CUT CO., Pyraline | 90.00 | 45.00 |
| ☐ 61129 KA-BAR, Bone Stag | 90.00 | 45.00 |
| ☐ K1129 KA-BAR, Fancy Celluloid | 90.00 | 45.00 |
| ☐ T1129 KA-BAR, Cream Celluloid | 75.00 | 38.00 |
| ☐ 31130 kabar, Redwood | 15.00 | 7.00 |
| ☐ 31130 kabar computer number USA, Redwood | 10.00 | 5.00 |
| ☐ 31131 UNION CUT CO., Redwood | 50.00 | 25.00 |
| ☐ 31131 KA-BAR, Redwood | 40.00 | 20.00 |
| ☐ 61132 UNION CUT CO., Bone Stag | 250.00 | 125.00 |
| ☐ 11132 UNION CUT CO., Ebony | 150.00 | 75.00 |
| ☐ 91132 UNION CUT CO., Silver Pyraline | 200.00 | 100.00 |
| ☐ 61132 KA-BAR, Bone Stag | 200.00 | 100.00 |
| ☐ P-1147 KA-BAR, Imitation Pearl | 50.00 | 25.00 |
| ☐ T-1147 KA-BAR, Cream Celluloid | 50.00 | 25.00 |
| ☐ P 1154 UNION CUT CO., Fancy Celluloid | 175.00 | 88.00 |
| ☐ P-1154 KA-BAR, Fancy Celluloid | 140.00 | 70.00 |
| ☐ 71155 UNION CUT CO., Genuine Pearl | 75.00 | 38.00 |
| ☐ X 1157 UNION CUT CO., Metal | 125.00 | 63.00 |
| ☐ X 1157 KA-BAR, Metal | 100.00 | 50.00 |
| ☐ R-1160 UNION CUT CO., Fancy Celluloid | 50.00 | 25.00 |
| ☐ 61161 UNION CUT CO., Bone Stag | 200.00 | 100.00 |
| ☐ 61161-BAIL KA-BAR, Bone Stag | 175.00 | 88.00 |
| ☐ T-1161 KA-BAR, Cream Celluloid | 225.00 | 117.00 |
| ☐ 61169 KA-BAR, Bone Stag | 150.00 | 75.00 |
| ☐ T-1175 KA-BAR, Cream Celluloid | 45.00 | 23.00 |
| ☐ 21187 KA-BAR, Genuine Stag | 350.00 | 175.00 |
| ☐ 61187 KA-BAR, Bone Stag | 290.00 | 145.00 |
| ☐ 31187 KA-BAR, Red Wood | 175.00 | 88.00 |
| ☐ 61187 UNION CUT CO., Smooth Bone | 125.00 | 63.00 |
| ☐ 61187 KA-BAR, Smooth Bone | 100.00 | 50.00 |
| ☐ 51187 kabar, Slick Black Composition | 40.00 | 20.00 |
| ☐ 51187 kabar computer number USA, Black Celluloid | 10.00 | 5.00 |
| ☐ 51198 kabar, Black Celluloid | 20.00 | 10.00 |
| ☐ 51198 kabar computer number USA, Black Celluloid | 10.00 | 5.00 |

# KA-BAR TWO-BLADE SECTION

|  | MINT | VG |
|---|---|---|
| ☐ 42027 S UNION CUT CO., Imitation Ivory | 80.00 | 40.00 |
| ☐ 5-29 KA-BAR, Black Celluloid | 35.00 | 18.00 |
| ☐ T-29 KA-BAR, Cream Celluloid | 25.00 | 13.00 |
| ☐ R-29 KA-BAR, Red Celluloid | 25.00 | 13.00 |
| ☐ T-29 kabar, Cream Celluloid | 12.00 | 6.00 |
| ☐ R-29 kabar, Red Celluloid | 12.00 | 6.00 |
| ☐ T-29 kabar computer number USA, Cream Celluloid | 8.00 | 4.00 |
| ☐ 6200 UNION CUT CO., Bone Stag | 45.00 | 23.00 |
| ☐ T 200 UNION CUT CO., Cream Celluloid | 25.00 | 13.00 |
| ☐ T 200 RG UNION CUT CO., Cream Celluloid | 25.00 | 13.00 |
| ☐ T 200 RG UNION CUT CO., Genuine Pearl | 50.00 | 25.00 |
| ☐ R 200 RG KA-BAR, Rainbow Celluloid | 30.00 | 15.00 |
| ☐ 6200 KA-BAR, Bone Stag | 50.00 | 25.00 |
| ☐ 6201 T UNION CUT CO., Bone Stag | 45.00 | 23.00 |
| ☐ 7201 T UNION CUT CO., Genuine Pearl | 70.00 | 35.00 |
| ☐ 6201 KA-BAR, Bone Stag | 40.00 | 20.00 |
| ☐ 6202 UNION CUT CO., Bone Stag | 45.00 | 23.00 |
| ☐ 7202 UNION CUT CO., Genuine Pearl | 45.00 | 23.00 |
| ☐ 6202 KA-BAR, Bone Stag | 40.00 | 20.00 |
| ☐ 7202 KA-BAR, Genuine Pearl | 70.00 | 35.00 |
| ☐ 6203½ UNION CUT CO., Bone Stag | 40.00 | 20.00 |
| ☐ 0203½ UNION CUT CO., Fancy Pyraline | 45.00 | 23.00 |
| ☐ 7203½ UNION CUT CO., Genuine Pearl | 70.00 | 35.00 |
| ☐ 6204 UNION CUT CO., Bone Stag | 50.00 | 25.00 |
| ☐ 7204 UNION CUT CO., Genuine Pearl | 70.00 | 35.00 |
| ☐ 6204 KA-BAR, Bone Stag | 45.00 | 23.00 |
| ☐ 6204 KA-BAR, Rough Black | 25.00 | 13.00 |
| ☐ 6205 UNION CUT CO., Bone Stag | 50.00 | 25.00 |
| ☐ 6205 KA-BAR, Bone Stag | 40.00 | 20.00 |
| ☐ 1206 UNION CUT CO., Ebony | 30.00 | 15.00 |
| ☐ 2206 UNION CUT CO., Genuine Stag | 45.00 | 23.00 |
| ☐ 6206 UNION CUT CO., Bone Stag | 40.00 | 20.00 |
| ☐ 7206 UNION CUT CO., Genuine Pearl | 65.00 | 33.00 |
| ☐ 9206 UNION CUT CO., Silver Pyraline | 35.00 | 18.00 |
| ☐ 2206 KA-BAR, Genuine Stag | 40.00 | 20.00 |
| ☐ 6206 KA-BAR, Bone Stag | 40.00 | 20.00 |
| ☐ P206 KA-BAR, Imitation Pearl | 35.00 | 18.00 |
| ☐ 2206 kabar, Genuine Stag | 30.00 | 15.00 |
| ☐ 6206 kabar, Bone Stag | 25.00 | 13.00 |

## 152 / KA-BAR

| | MINT | VG |
|---|---|---|
| ☐ **P206** *kabar, Pearl Celluloid* | 20.00 | 10.00 |
| ☐ **7206** *kabar, Genuine Pearl* | 40.00 | 20.00 |
| ☐ **6206** *kabar computer number USA, Delrin* | 5.00 | 2.50 |
| ☐ **6209¼** *UNION CUT CO., Bone Stag* | 125.00 | 63.00 |
| ☐ **6210** *UNION CUT CO., Bone Stag* | 120.00 | 60.00 |
| ☐ **6210** *KA-BAR, Bone Stag* | 95.00 | 48.00 |
| ☐ **6212 J** *UNION CUT CO., Bone Stag* | 75.00 | 38.00 |
| ☐ **0212 J** *UNION CUT CO., Pyraline* | 55.00 | 28.00 |
| ☐ **6212 J** *KA-BAR, Bone Stag* | 65.00 | 33.00 |
| ☐ **6212 J** *kabar, Bone Stag* | 50.00 | 25.00 |
| ☐ **5212 J** *kabar, Black Celluloid* | 25.00 | 13.00 |
| ☐ **6213 J** *UNION CUT CO., Bone Stag* | 135.00 | 68.00 |
| ☐ **2213 J** *UNION CUT CO., Genuine Stag* | 145.00 | 73.00 |
| ☐ **6213 J** *KA-BAR, Bone Stag* | 120.00 | 60.00 |
| ☐ **1215** *UNION CUT CO., Ebony* | 80.00 | 40.00 |
| ☐ **6215** *UNION CUT CO., Bone Stag* | 140.00 | 70.00 |
| ☐ **6215 PU** *UNION CUT CO., Bone Stag* | 130.00 | 65.00 |
| ☐ **6215** *KA-BAR, Bone Stag* | 110.00 | 55.00 |
| ☐ **6215½** *KA-BAR, Bone Stag* | 110.00 | 55.00 |
| ☐ **6215 & 15½** *kabar, Bone Stag* | 80.00 | 40.00 |
| ☐ **6215 & 15½** *kabar, Rough Black* | 40.00 | 20.00 |
| ☐ **6215** *kabar computer number USA, Delrin* | 10.00 | 5.00 |
| ☐ **1218** *UNION CUT CO., Ebony* | 50.00 | 25.00 |
| ☐ **2218** *UNION CUT CO., Genuine Stag* | 90.00 | 45.00 |
| ☐ **6218** *UNION CUT CO., Bone Stag* | 75.00 | 38.00 |
| ☐ **7218** *UNION CUT CO., Pearl* | 120.00 | 60.00 |
| ☐ **1218** *KA-BAR, Ebony* | 40.00 | 20.00 |
| ☐ **6218** *KA-BAR, Bone Stag* | 75.00 | 38.00 |
| ☐ **6219½** *UNION CUT CO., Bone Stag* | 65.00 | 33.00 |
| ☐ **6220 J** *UNION CUT CO., Bone Stag* | 95.00 | 48.00 |
| ☐ **2220 J** *KA-BAR, Genuine Stag* | 100.00 | 50.00 |
| ☐ **6220 J** *KA-BAR, Bone Stag* | 85.00 | 43.00 |
| ☐ **7220 J** *KA-BAR, Genuine Pearl* | 135.00 | 68.00 |
| ☐ **6221** *UNION CUT CO., Bone Stag* | 65.00 | 33.00 |
| ☐ **6221** *KA-BAR, Bone Stag* | 50.00 | 25.00 |
| ☐ **6221** *kabar, Rough Black* | 25.00 | 13.00 |
| ☐ **T 221** *kabar, Cream Composition* | 20.00 | 10.00 |
| ☐ **1222 T** *UNION CUT CO., Ebony* | 40.00 | 20.00 |
| ☐ **6222 T** *UNION CUT CO., Bone Stag* | 65.00 | 33.00 |
| ☐ **7222 T** *UNION CUT CO., Genuine Pearl* | 90.00 | 45.00 |
| ☐ **9222 T** *UNION CUT CO., Silver Pyraline* | 60.00 | 30.00 |
| ☐ **6223 EX** *CANOE, UNION CUT CO., Bone Stag* | 175.00 | 83.00 |
| ☐ **P223 EX** *UNION CUT CO., Imitation Pearl* | 140.00 | 70.00 |

KA-BAR / 153

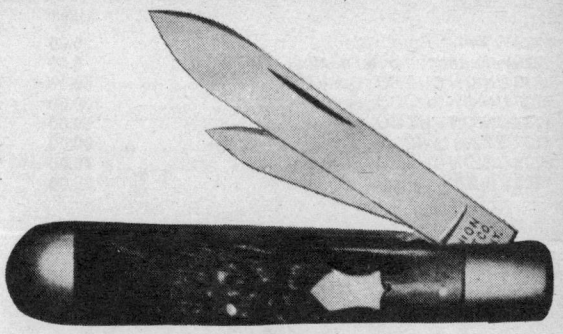

1218

| | | MINT | VG |
|---|---|---|---|
| ☐ | 5223 BARLOW, KA-BAR, Black Composition ... | 60.00 | 30.00 |
| ☐ | 6223 KA-BAR, Smooth Bone ................ | 90.00 | 45.00 |
| ☐ | 6223½ KA-BAR, Smooth Bone .............. | 90.00 | 45.00 |
| ☐ | 5223 SH kabar, Black Composition ......... | 40.00 | 20.00 |
| ☐ | 5223 kabar, Black Composition............ | 30.00 | 15.00 |
| ☐ | 5223½ kabar, Black Composition........... | 30.00 | 15.00 |
| ☐ | 6223 kabar computer number USA, Delrin ... | 10.00 | 5.00 |
| ☐ | 6223½ kabar computer number USA, Delrin ... | 10.00 | 5.00 |
| ☐ | 6224 UNION CUT CO., Bone Stag ........... | 55.00 | 28.00 |
| ☐ | 6224 KA-BAR, Bone Stag .................. | 45.00 | 23.00 |
| ☐ | P 225 UNION CUT CO., Imitation Pearl ...... | 70.00 | 35.00 |
| ☐ | 6225½ KA-BAR, Bone Stag ................ | 125.00 | 63.00 |
| ☐ | 6225 KA-BAR, Bone Stag ................. | 125.00 | 63.00 |
| ☐ | 5226 Emb UNION CUT CO., Black Pyraline .. | 35.00 | 18.00 |
| ☐ | 7226 Emb UNION CUT CO., Genuine Pearl ... | 65.00 | 33.00 |
| ☐ | 6226 KA-BAR, Bone Stag ................. | 50.00 | 25.00 |
| ☐ | 7226 KA-BAR, Genuine Pearl .............. | 60.00 | 30.00 |
| ☐ | 1228 EO UNION CUT CO., Ebony ........... | 90.00 | 45.00 |
| ☐ | 2228 EO UNION CUT CO., Genuine Stag...... | 150.00 | 75.00 |
| ☐ | 6228 EO UNION CUT CO., Bone Stag ....... | 110.00 | 55.00 |
| ☐ | 6228 EO UNION CUT CO., Bone Stag ....... | 130.00 | 63.00 |
| ☐ | 9228 EO UNION CUT CO., Silver Pyraline ... | 115.00 | 58.00 |
| ☐ | 6229 UNION CUT CO., Bone Stag .......... | 55.00 | 28.00 |
| ☐ | 6229½ UNION CUT CO., Bone Stag ......... | 55.00 | 28.00 |
| ☐ | 6229 KA-BAR, Bone Stag ................. | 50.00 | 25.00 |

## 154 / KA-BAR

|  | MINT | VG |
|---|---|---|
| ☐ **6229½ kabar**, Rough Black | 25.00 | 13.00 |
| ☐ **6229½ kabar computer number USA**, Delrin | 8.00 | 4.00 |
| ☐ **6230** UNION CUT CO., Bone Stag | 60.00 | 30.00 |
| ☐ **7230** UNION CUT CO., Genuine Pearl | 100.00 | 50.00 |
| ☐ **1232** UNION CUT CO., Ebony | 50.00 | 25.00 |
| ☐ **6232 & 32½** UNION CUT CO., Bone Stag | 90.00 | 45.00 |
| ☐ **9232** UNION CUT CO., Silver Pyraline | 70.00 | 35.00 |
| ☐ **1232** KA-BAR, Ebony | 35.00 | 18.00 |

**1232**

|  | MINT | VG |
|---|---|---|
| ☐ **6232 & 32½** KA-BAR | 75.00 | 38.00 |
| ☐ **6232 & 32½ kabar**, Rough Black | 30.00 | 15.00 |
| ☐ **6232½ kabar computer number USA**, Delrin | 8.00 | 4.00 |
| ☐ **1233** UNION CUT CO., Ebony | 90.00 | 45.00 |
| ☐ **2233** UNION CUT CO., Genuine Stag | 130.00 | 65.00 |
| ☐ **6233** UNION CUT CO., Bone Stag | 120.00 | 60.00 |
| ☐ **9233** UNION CUT CO., Silver Pyraline | 105.00 | 52.00 |
| ☐ **2233** KA-BAR, Genuine Stag | 115.00 | 58.00 |
| ☐ **6233** KA-BAR, Bone Stag | 100.00 | 50.00 |
| ☐ **6236 LL** KA-BAR, Bone Stag | 60.00 | 30.00 |
| ☐ **6236 LL kabar**, Rough Black | 25.00 | 13.00 |
| ☐ **Gunstock 6237** UNION CUT CO., Bone Stag | 135.00 | 68.00 |
| ☐ **Gunstock P237** UNION CUT CO., Imitation Pearl | 110.00 | 55.00 |
| ☐ **Gunstock 6237** KA-BAR, Bone Stag | 115.00 | 58.00 |

## KA-BAR / 155

| | MINT | VG |
|---|---|---|
| ☐ **Gunstock 2237** *KA-BAR, Genuine Stag* | 135.00 | 68.00 |
| ☐ **Gunstock 7237** *KA-BAR, Genuine Pearl* | 160.00 | 80.00 |
| ☐ **Gunstock P237** *KA-BAR, Imitation Pearl* | 100.00 | 50.00 |
| ☐ **6239** *UNION CUT CO., Bone Stag* | 45.00 | 23.00 |
| ☐ **9239** *UNION CUT CO., Fancy Celluloid* | 40.00 | 20.00 |
| ☐ **6240 J** *UNION CUT CO., Bone Stag* | 120.00 | 60.00 |
| ☐ **6240 J** *KA-BAR, Bone Stag* | 95.00 | 48.00 |
| ☐ **6241** *UNION CUT CO., Bone Stag* | 40.00 | 20.00 |
| ☐ **7241** *UNION CUT CO., Genuine Pearl* | 50.00 | 25.00 |
| ☐ **P-241** *KA-BAR, Pearl Celluloid* | 20.00 | 10.00 |
| ☐ **6241** *KA-BAR, Bone Stag* | 30.00 | 15.00 |
| ☐ **7241 RG** *KA-BAR, Genuine Pearl* | 35.00 | 18.00 |
| ☐ **P-241** *kabar, Pearl Celluloid* | 15.00 | 13.00 |
| ☐ **2241** *kabar, Genuine Stag* | 30.00 | 15.00 |
| ☐ **6242** *UNION CUT CO., Bone Stag* | 55.00 | 28.00 |
| ☐ **6242** *KA-BAR, Bone Stag* | 65.00 | 33.00 |
| ☐ **T 242** *KA-BAR, Cream Celluloid* | 50.00 | 25.00 |
| ☐ **6242** *kabar, Bone Stag* | 50.00 | 25.00 |
| ☐ **6244** *UNION CUT CO., Bone Stag* | 150.00 | 75.00 |
| ☐ **7244** *UNION CUT CO., Genuine Pearl* | 175.00 | 88.00 |
| ☐ **1246** *UNION CUT CO., Ebony* | 80.00 | 40.00 |
| ☐ **2246** *UNION CUT CO., Genuine Stag* | 150.00 | 75.00 |
| ☐ **6246** *UNION CUT CO., Bone Stag* | 140.00 | 70.00 |
| ☐ **P246** *UNION CUT CO., Imitation Pearl* | 110.00 | 55.00 |
| ☐ **2246** *KA-BAR, Genuine Stag* | 135.00 | 68.00 |
| ☐ **6246** *KA-BAR, Bone Stag* | 120.00 | 60.00 |
| ☐ **6247** *UNION CUT CO., Bone Stag, Iron Bolsters* | 65.00 | 33.00 |
| ☐ **6249** *UNION CUT CO., Bone Stag* | 120.00 | 60.00 |
| ☐ **6250** *UNION CUT CO., Bone Stag* | 350.00 | 175.00 |
| ☐ **R250** *UNION CUT CO., Rainbow Celluloid* | 275.00 | 138.00 |
| ☐ **6250** *KA-BAR, Bone Stag* | 275.00 | 138.00 |
| ☐ **6251** *KA-BAR, Bone Stag* | 135.00 | 68.00 |
| ☐ **6251½** *KA-BAR, Bone Stag* | 135.00 | 68.00 |
| ☐ **1252** *UNION CUT CO., Ebony* | 65.00 | 33.00 |
| ☐ **2252½** *UNION CUT CO., Genuine Stag* | 130.00 | 65.00 |
| ☐ **6252 & 52½** *UNION CUT CO., Bone Stag* | 110.00 | 55.00 |
| ☐ **6252 Saber** *UNION CUT CO., Bone Stag* | 125.00 | 63.00 |
| ☐ **2253** *UNION CUT CO., Genuine Stag* | 60.00 | 30.00 |
| ☐ **7253** *UNION CUT CO., Genuine Pearl* | 75.00 | 38.00 |
| ☐ **2253** *KA-BAR, Genuine Stag* | 65.00 | 33.00 |
| ☐ **3253** *KA-BAR, Redwood* | 35.00 | 18.00 |
| ☐ **6253** *KA-BAR, Bone Stag* | 55.00 | 28.00 |
| ☐ **7253** *KA-BAR, Genuine Pearl* | 75.00 | 38.00 |

## 156 / KA-BAR

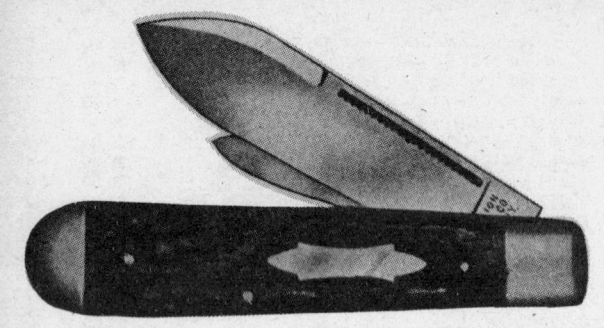

**1252**

|  | MINT | VG |
|---|---|---|
| ☐ **T253** *KA-BAR, Cream Celluloid* | 40.00 | 20.00 |
| ☐ **6253** *kabar, Rough Black* | 25.00 | 13.00 |
| ☐ **T253** *kabar, Celluloid* | 20.00 | 10.00 |
| ☐ **2255** *UNION CUT CO., Genuine Stag* | 85.00 | 43.00 |
| ☐ **6255** *UNION CUT CO., Bone Stag* | 80.00 | 40.00 |
| ☐ **7255** *UNION CUT CO., Genuine Pearl* | 120.00 | 60.00 |
| ☐ **9255** *UNION CUT CO., Fancy Celluloid* | 60.00 | 30.00 |
| ☐ **6255** *KA-BAR, Bone Stag* | 70.00 | 35.00 |
| ☐ **7255** *KA-BAR, Genuine Pearl* | 100.00 | 50.00 |
| ☐ **6255** *kabar, Rough Black* | 30.00 | 15.00 |
| ☐ **T255** *kabar, Cream Celluloid* | 25.00 | 13.00 |
| ☐ **6256 J** *UNION CUT CO., Bone Stag* | 75.00 | 38.00 |
| ☐ **7256 J** *UNION CUT CO., Genuine Pearl* | 110.00 | 55.00 |
| ☐ **R256 J** *UNION CUT CO., Imitation Pearl* | 60.00 | 30.00 |
| ☐ **6256 J** *KA-BAR, Bone Stag* | 65.00 | 33.00 |
| ☐ **2256 J** *KA-BAR, Genuine Stag* | 75.00 | 38.00 |
| ☐ **7256 J** *KA-BAR, Genuine Pearl* | 100.00 | 50.00 |
| ☐ **P256 J** *KA-BAR, Imitation Pearl* | 50.00 | 25.00 |
| ☐ **6256 J** *kabar, Bone Stag* | 45.00 | 23.00 |
| ☐ **2256 J** *kabar, Genuine Stag* | 50.00 | 25.00 |
| ☐ **T256 J** *kabar, Cream Celluloid* | 25.00 | 13.00 |
| ☐ **6256** *kabar computer number USA, Delrin* | 9.00 | 4.50 |
| ☐ **6257 mu** *KA-BAR, Bone Stag* | 120.00 | 60.00 |
| ☐ **6257 mu** *kabar, Imitation Bone, Rough Black* | 60.00 | 30.00 |
| ☐ **2257 mu** *kabar, Genuine Stag* | 85.00 | 43.00 |

## KA-BAR / 157

| | | MINT | VG |
|---|---|---|---|
| ☐ 2260 | **K&F** UNION CUT CO., Genuine Stag | 145.00 | 73.00 |
| ☐ 6260 | **K&F** UNION CUT CO., Bone Stag | 130.00 | 65.00 |
| ☐ 6260 | **K&F** KA-BAR, Bone Stag | 100.00 | 50.00 |
| ☐ T260 | **K&F** KA-BAR, Cream Celluloid | 80.00 | 40.00 |
| ☐ 6261 | UNION CUT CO., Bone Stag | 150.00 | 75.00 |
| ☐ 6261 | KA-BAR, Bone Stag | 120.00 | 60.00 |
| ☐ 6261 | KA-BAR, Rough Black | 60.00 | 30.00 |
| ☐ 6261 | kabar, Rough Black | 40.00 | 20.00 |
| ☐ 6263 | UNION CUT CO., Bone Stag | 60.00 | 30.00 |
| ☐ 6263 **PU** | UNION CUT CO., Bone Stag | 60.00 | 30.00 |
| ☐ 6263 | KA-BAR, Bone Stag | 50.00 | 25.00 |
| ☐ 6263 | kabar, Rough Black | 20.00 | 10.00 |
| ☐ 6263 | kabar computer number USA, Delrin | 7.00 | 3.50 |
| ☐ 6265 | UNION CUT CO., Bone Stag | 200.00 | 100.00 |
| ☐ 0265 | UNION CUT CO., Fancy Celluloid | 160.00 | 80.00 |
| ☐ 6265 & 65½ | KA-BAR, Bone Stag | 170.00 | 88.00 |
| ☐ 2266 **J** | UNION CUT CO., Genuine Stag | 275.00 | 133.00 |
| ☐ 6266 **J** | UNION CUT CO., Bone Stag | 250.00 | 125.00 |
| ☐ 2266 **J** | KA-BAR, Genuine Stag | 240.00 | 120.00 |
| ☐ 6266 **J** | KA-BAR, Bone Stag | 210.00 | 105.00 |
| ☐ 6267 | UNION CUT CO., Bone Stag | 250.00 | 125.00 |
| ☐ 6267 | KA-BAR, Bone Stag | 210.00 | 105.00 |
| ☐ P269 **J** | UNION CUT CO., Imitation Pearl | 80.00 | 40.00 |
| ☐ 2269 **J** | UNION CUT CO., Genuine Stag | 140.00 | 70.00 |
| ☐ 6269 **J** | UNION CUT CO., Bone Stag | 120.00 | 60.00 |
| ☐ P269 **J** | KA-BAR, Imitation Pearl | 60.00 | 30.00 |
| ☐ 2269 **J** | KA-BAR, Genuine Stag | 110.00 | 55.00 |
| ☐ 6269 **J** | KA-BAR, Bone Stag | 95.00 | 48.00 |
| ☐ 5269 **J** | KA-BAR, Black Celluloid | 35.00 | 18.00 |
| ☐ 6270 | UNION CUT CO., Bone Stag | 150.00 | 75.00 |
| ☐ 2270½ | KA-BAR, Genuine Stag | 130.00 | 63.00 |
| ☐ 6270½ | KA-BAR, Bone Stag | 110.00 | 55.00 |
| ☐ 1270½ | kabar, Second Cut Stag | 85.00 | 43.00 |
| ☐ 2270½ | kabar, Genuine Stag | 70.00 | 35.00 |
| ☐ 6270½ | kabar, Delrin | 30.00 | 15.00 |
| ☐ 6271 **J** | UNION CUT CO., Bone Stag | 110.00 | 55.00 |
| ☐ 2271 | UNION CUT CO., Genuine Stag | 135.00 | 68.00 |
| ☐ 6271 | (Blade each end), UNION CUT CO., Bone Stag | 130.00 | 65.00 |
| ☐ 6271 **J** | KA-BAR, Bone Stag | 95.00 | 48.00 |
| ☐ 2271 **J** | KA-BAR, Genuine Stag | 115.00 | 58.00 |
| ☐ 3273 | UNION CUT CO., Redwood | 30.00 | 15.00 |
| ☐ 3273 | KA-BAR, Redwood | 35.00 | 18.00 |

158 / KA-BAR

|  | MINT | VG |
|---|---|---|
| ☐ TL-29 Model KA-BAR, Redwood | 35.00 | 18.00 |
| ☐ 5273 kabar computer number USA, Black Celluloid | 8.00 | 4.00 |
| ☐ T275 KA-BAR, Cream Celluloid | 20.00 | 10.00 |
| ☐ T275 kabar, Cream Celluloid | 15.00 | 7.50 |
| ☐ 7285 and 86 UNION CUT CO., Genuine Pearl | 75.00 | 38.00 |
| ☐ 7285 Emblem UNION CUT CO., Genuine Pearl | 95.00 | 48.00 |
| ☐ 7286 RG UNION CUT CO., Genuine Pearl | 75.00 | 38.00 |
| ☐ 6288 UNION CUT CO., Bone Stag | 175.00 | 88.00 |
| ☐ 6288 KA-BAR, Bone Stag | 150.00 | 75.00 |
| ☐ 7289 R KA-BAR, Genuine Pearl | 120.00 | 60.00 |
| ☐ 6290 UNION CUT CO., Bone Stag | 70.00 | 35.00 |

6290

|  | MINT | VG |
|---|---|---|
| ☐ 2291 K&F UNION CUT CO., Genuine Stag | 350.00 | 175.00 |
| ☐ 6291 K&F UNION CUT CO., Bone Stag | 300.00 | 150.00 |
| ☐ 7291 K&F UNION CUT CO., Genuine Pearl | 450.00 | 225.00 |
| ☐ 0291 K&F UNION CUT CO., Fancy Celluloid | 250.00 | 125.00 |
| ☐ 6291 K&F KA-BAR, Bone Stag | 225.00 | 113.00 |
| ☐ 6295 EX UNION CUT CO., Bone Stag | 140.00 | 70.00 |
| ☐ 9295 EX UNION CUT CO., Silver Pyraline | 105.00 | 52.00 |
| ☐ 6295 EX KA-BAR, Bone Stag | 110.00 | 55.00 |
| ☐ 9295 EX KA-BAR, Silver Pyraline | 80.00 | 40.00 |
| ☐ 6296 UNION CUT CO., Bone Stag | 90.00 | 45.00 |
| ☐ 7296 UNION CUT CO., Genuine Pearl | 130.00 | 65.00 |
| ☐ 2296 KA-BAR, Genuine Stag | 120.00 | 60.00 |
| ☐ 6296 KA-BAR, Bone Stag | 90.00 | 45.00 |

KA-BAR / 159

|  | MINT | VG |
|---|---|---|
| ☐ T-298 UNION CUT CO., Fancy Pearl | 125.00 | 63.00 |
| ☐ 7298 UNION CUT CO., Genuine Pearl | 90.00 | 45.00 |
| ☐ 6298 UNION CUT CO., Bone Stag | 60.00 | 30.00 |
| ☐ 6298 KA-BAR, Bone Stag | 45.00 | 23.00 |
| ☐ 6299 UNION CUT CO., Bone Stag | 80.00 | 40.00 |
| ☐ 7299 UNION CUT CO., Genuine Pearl | 110.00 | 55.00 |
| ☐ 22100 UNION CUT CO., Genuine Stag | 110.00 | 55.00 |
| ☐ 62100 UNION CUT CO., Bone Stag | 90.00 | 45.00 |
| ☐ 62100 KA-BAR, Bone Stag | 80.00 | 40.00 |
| ☐ 22106-Cleaver KA-BAR, Genuine Stag | 475.00 | 238.00 |
| ☐ 62107 UNION CUT CO., Bone Stag | 275.00 | 138.00 |
| ☐ 62107 KA-BAR, Bone Stag | 225.00 | 113.00 |
| ☐ 62107 KA-BAR, Rough Black | 125.00 | 63.00 |
| ☐ P2107 KA-BAR, Imitation Pearl | 125.00 | 63.00 |
| ☐ 22107 kabar, Genuine Stag | 80.00 | 40.00 |
| ☐ 62107 kabar, Rough Black | 45.00 | 23.00 |
| ☐ 62107 kabar, Aster Felts Model | 100.00 | 50.00 |
| ☐ 22107 kabar computer number USA, Imitation Stag | 15.00 | 7.50 |
| ☐ 22107 kabar computer number USA, Imitation Stag Serrated | 15.00 | 7.50 |
| ☐ P-2109 UNION CUT CO., Imitation Pearl | 45.00 | 23.00 |

P-2109

| ☐ 72109, UNION CUT CO., Genuine Pearl | 95.00 | 48.00 |
|---|---|---|
| ☐ 52109 KA-BAR, Black Celluloid | 35.00 | 18.00 |
| ☐ 02109 KA-BAR, Fancy Celluloid (Gold Metalic or Christmas Tree) | 75.00 | 38.00 |

## 160 / KA-BAR

| | MINT | VG |
|---|---|---|
| ☐ **72110** UNION CUT CO., Abalone Pearl | 175.00 | 88.00 |
| ☐ **72111** UNION CUT CO., Abalone Pearl | 175.00 | 88.00 |
| ☐ **62118** UNION CUT CO., Bone Stag | 250.00 | 125.00 |
| ☐ **22118** KA-BAR, Genuine Stag | 225.00 | 113.00 |
| ☐ **62118** KA-BAR, Bone Stag | 200.00 | 100.00 |
| ☐ **P2118** KA-BAR, Imitation Pearl | 200.00 | 100.00 |
| ☐ **R2118** KA-BAR, Rainbow Celluloid | 200.00 | 100.00 |
| ☐ **22118** kabar, Genuine Stag | 80.00 | 40.00 |
| ☐ **62118** kabar, Bone Stag | 120.00 | 60.00 |
| ☐ **62118** kabar, Rough Black | 60.00 | 30.00 |
| ☐ **T2118** kabar, Cream Composition | 45.00 | 23.00 |
| ☐ **62118** kabar computer number USA, Delrin | 12.00 | 6.00 |
| ☐ **T2118** kabar computer number USA, Cream Composition | 15.00 | 7.50 |
| ☐ **52118** kabar computer number USA, Chattahoochee Knife | 50.00 | 25.00 |
| ☐ **72124 RG** UNION CUT CO., Genuine Pearl | 60.00 | 30.00 |
| ☐ **P2127** UNION CUT CO., Imitation Pearl | 60.00 | 30.00 |
| ☐ **R2127** UNION CUT CO., Rainbow Celluloid | 70.00 | 35.00 |
| ☐ **52127** KA-BAR, Black Celluloid | 55.00 | 28.00 |
| ☐ **P-2127** KA-BAR, Imitation Pearl | 55.00 | 28.00 |
| ☐ **62128-F** UNION CUT CO., Bone Stag | 75.00 | 38.00 |
| ☐ **62128** BOY SCOUT, UNION CUT CO., Bone Stag | 100.00 | 50.00 |
| ☐ **62128** BOY SCOUT, KA-BAR, Bone Stag | 75.00 | 38.00 |
| ☐ **62132** UNION CUT CO., Bone Stag | 225.00 | 113.00 |

62132

| | | |
|---|---|---|
| ☐ **T2132** KA-BAR, Cream Celluloid | 150.00 | 75.00 |
| ☐ **62133** UNION CUT CO., Bone Stag | 50.00 | 25.00 |
| ☐ **72133** UNION CUT CO., Genuine Pearl | 70.00 | 35.00 |
| ☐ **R2133** UNION CUT CO., Rainbow Celluloid | 40.00 | 20.00 |

KA-BAR / 161

| | MINT | VG |
|---|---|---|
| ☐ 62133 KA-BAR, Bone Stag | 45.00 | 23.00 |
| ☐ 72133 KA-BAR, Genuine Pearl | 65.00 | 33.00 |
| ☐ 62133 kabar, Bone Stag | 30.00 | 15.00 |
| ☐ T2133 kabar, Cream Composition | 20.00 | 10.00 |
| ☐ P2133 kabar, Pearl Celluloid | 20.00 | 10.00 |
| ☐ 62134 UNION CUT CO., Bone Stag | 175.00 | 88.00 |
| ☐ 62134 KA-BAR, Bone Stag | 160.00 | 80.00 |
| ☐ 62135 UNION CUT CO., Bone Stag | 60.00 | 30.00 |
| ☐ B2135 UNION CUT CO., Goldstone Celluloid | 50.00 | 25.00 |
| ☐ 72135 KA-BAR, Genuine Pearl | 90.00 | 45.00 |
| ☐ 62140 UNION CUT CO., Bone Stag | 80.00 | 40.00 |
| ☐ 72140 UNION CUT CO., Genuine Pearl | 110.00 | 55.00 |
| ☐ H2140 UNION CUT CO., Horn | 65.00 | 33.00 |
| ☐ 62140 KA-BAR, Bone Stag | 65.00 | 33.00 |
| ☐ 62141 PEANUT, UNION CUT CO., Bone Stag | 80.00 | 40.00 |
| ☐ 72141 UNION CUT CO., Genuine Pearl | 110.00 | 55.00 |
| ☐ 62141 KA-BAR, Bone Stag | 75.00 | 38.00 |
| ☐ T2141 KA-BAR, Cream Celluloid | 45.00 | 23.00 |
| ☐ 62141 kabar, Rough Black | 30.00 | 15.00 |
| ☐ T2141 kabar, Cream Celluloid | 30.00 | 15.00 |
| ☐ 62141 kabar computer number USA, Delrin | 8.00 | 4.00 |
| ☐ 62142 UNION CUT CO., Bone Stag | 70.00 | 35.00 |
| ☐ 72142 UNION CUT CO., Genuine Pearl | 95.00 | 48.00 |
| ☐ 62142 KA-BAR, Bone Stag | 60.00 | 30.00 |
| ☐ 72142 KA-BAR, Genuine Pearl | 85.00 | 43.00 |
| ☐ 62143 UNION CUT CO., Bone Stag | 75.00 | 38.00 |
| ☐ 72143 UNION CUT CO., Genuine Pearl | 120.00 | 60.00 |
| ☐ 62143 KA-BAR, Bone Stag | 70.00 | 35.00 |
| ☐ 72143 KA-BAR, Pearl | 110.00 | 55.00 |
| ☐ 92143 KA-BAR, Silver Pyraline | 80.00 | 40.00 |
| ☐ 22144 UNION CUT CO., Genuine Stag | 150.00 | 75.00 |
| ☐ 62144 UNION CUT CO., Bone Stag | 150.00 | 75.00 |
| ☐ 72144 UNION CUT CO., Genuine Pearl | 200.00 | 100.00 |
| ☐ 22144 KA-BAR, Genuine Stag | 150.00 | 75.00 |
| ☐ 62144 KA-BAR, Bone Stag | 150.00 | 75.00 |
| ☐ 72144 KA-BAR, Genuine Pearl | 200.00 | 100.00 |
| ☐ 62145 UNION CUT CO., Bone Stag | 50.00 | 25.00 |
| ☐ 72145 UNION CUT CO., Genuine Pearl | 90.00 | 45.00 |
| ☐ 62145 KA-BAR, Bone Stag | 45.00 | 23.00 |
| ☐ 72145 KA-BAR, Genuine Pearl | 80.00 | 40.00 |
| ☐ 92145 KA-BAR, Fancy Celluloid | 75.00 | 38.00 |
| ☐ 22146 UNION CUT CO., Genuine Stag | 65.00 | 33.00 |
| ☐ 62146 UNION CUT CO., Bone Stag | 55.00 | 28.00 |

## KA-BAR

| | MINT | VG |
|---|---|---|
| ☐ 72146 and 46 EX *UNION CUT CO.*, Genuine Pearl | 90.00 | 45.00 |
| ☐ P2146 EX *(No Bolster), UNION CUT CO., Fancy Celluloid* | 60.00 | 30.00 |
| ☐ H2147 *UNION CUT CO.*, Horn Celluloid | 35.00 | 18.00 |
| ☐ 62147 *UNION CUT CO.*, Bone Stag | 50.00 | 25.00 |
| ☐ 72147 *UNION CUT CO.*, Genuine Pearl | 75.00 | 38.00 |
| ☐ 62147 *KA-BAR*, Bone Stag | 75.00 | 38.00 |
| ☐ M2147 *KA-BAR*, Metal Handle | 50.00 | 25.00 |
| ☐ P2147 *kabar*, Pearl Celluloid | 30.00 | 15.00 |
| ☐ T2147 *kabar*, Cream Celluloid | 30.00 | 15.00 |
| ☐ 62148 *UNION CUT CO.*, Bone Stag | 85.00 | 43.00 |
| ☐ 72148 *UNION CUT CO.*, Genuine Pearl | 120.00 | 60.00 |
| ☐ 62148 *KA-BAR*, Bone Stag | 70.00 | 35.00 |
| ☐ 72148 *KA-BAR*, Genuine Pearl | 100.00 | 50.00 |
| ☐ 62149 *UNION CUT CO.*, Bone Stag | 70.00 | 35.00 |
| ☐ 72149 *UNION CUT CO.*, Genuine Pearl | 90.00 | 45.00 |
| ☐ P2149 *KA-BAR*, Imitation Pearl | 45.00 | 23.00 |
| ☐ 22150 *UNION CUT CO.*, Genuine Stag Spear | 140.00 | 70.00 |
| ☐ 22150 R *UNION CUT CO.*, Genuine Stag Razor | 160.00 | 80.00 |
| ☐ 22150½ *UNION CUT CO.*, Genuine Stag Clip | 120.00 | 60.00 |
| ☐ 22150 *KA-BAR*, Genuine Pearl | 115.00 | 58.00 |
| ☐ 220151 *UNION CUT CO.*, Genuine Stag | 175.00 | 88.00 |
| ☐ 620151 *UNION CUT CO.*, Bone Stag | 150.00 | 75.00 |
| ☐ 22151 *UNION CUT CO.*, Stag | 200.00 | 100.00 |
| ☐ 62151 *UNION CUT CO.*, Bone Stag | 175.00 | 88.00 |
| ☐ 02151 *UNION CUT CO.*, Fancy Celluloid | 150.00 | 75.00 |
| ☐ 22151 *KA-BAR*, Stag | 175.00 | 88.00 |
| ☐ 62151 *KA-BAR*, Bone Stag | 150.00 | 75.00 |
| ☐ 72151 *KA-BAR*, Genuine Pearl | 200.00 | 100.00 |
| ☐ 62152 *UNION CUT CO.*, Bone Stag | 150.00 | 75.00 |
| ☐ 62152 *KA-BAR*, Bone Stag | 135.00 | 68.00 |
| ☐ 62153 *UNION CUT CO.*, Bone Stag | 160.00 | 80.00 |
| ☐ 62153 *KA-BAR*, Bone Stag | 150.00 | 75.00 |
| ☐ 62156 *UNION CUT CO.*, Bone Stag | 175.00 | 88.00 |
| ☐ 62156 *KA-BAR*, Bone Stag | 150.00 | 75.00 |
| ☐ 62156 *KA-BAR*, Boy Scout Model | 190.00 | 95.00 |
| ☐ 52198 *KA-BAR*, Black Celluloid | 40.00 | 20.00 |
| ☐ 52198 *kabar*, Black Celluloid | 25.00 | 13.00 |
| ☐ T2217 *KA-BAR*, Cream Celluloid | 75.00 | 38.00 |
| ☐ T2217 *kabar*, Cream Celluloid | 55.00 | 28.00 |
| ☐ 52217 *kabar*, Black Composition | 30.00 | 15.00 |
| ☐ 52217 *kabar computer number USA, Black Composition* | 15.00 | 7.50 |

# KA-BAR THREE-BLADE SECTION

|  | MINT | VG |
|---|---|---|
| ☐ **ARMY KNIFE** *UNION CUT CO., Ebony* | 125.00 | 63.00 |
| ☐ **T-33** *KA-BAR, Cream Celluloid* | 75.00 | 38.00 |
| ☐ **T-33** *kabar, Cream Celluloid* | 60.00 | 30.00 |
| ☐ **6306 WHITTLER,** *UNION CUT CO., Bone Stag* | 200.00 | 100.00 |
| ☐ **6306** *KA-BAR, Bone Stag* | 180.00 | 140.00 |
| ☐ **2307** *UNION CUT CO., Genuine Stag* | 70.00 | 35.00 |
| ☐ **7307** *UNION CUT CO., Genuine Pearl* | 120.00 | 60.00 |
| ☐ **T 307** *UNION CUT CO., Abalone Pearl* | 175.00 | 88.00 |
| ☐ **1309½** *UNION CUT CO., Ebony* | 200.00 | 100.00 |
| ☐ **6309 (Wharnc Life Blade),** *UNION CUT CO., Bone Stag* | 300.00 | 150.00 |
| ☐ **6313 F** *UNION CUT CO., Bone Stag* | 160.00 | 80.00 |
| ☐ **9313 F** *UNION CUT CO., Silver Pyraline* | 145.00 | 73.00 |
| ☐ **6314** *UNION CUT CO., Bone Stag* | 225.00 | 113.00 |
| ☐ **6314** *KA-BAR, Bone Stag* | 190.00 | 95.00 |
| ☐ **2314 EX PU** *UNION CUT CO., Genuine Stag* | 700.00 | 350.00 |
| ☐ **6314 EX** *UNION CUT CO., Bone Stag* | 600.00 | 300.00 |
| ☐ **6314 PU (Bolsters Not Extended),** *UNION CUT CO.* | 225.00 | 113.00 |
| ☐ **6314 PU** *KA-BAR, Bone Stag* | 200.00 | 100.00 |
| ☐ **2320½** *UNION CUT CO., Genuine Stag* | 300.00 | 150.00 |
| ☐ **6320½** *UNION CUT CO., Bone Stag* | 275.00 | 138.00 |
| ☐ **7320½** *UNION CUT CO., Genuine Pearl* | 400.00 | 200.00 |
| ☐ **2320½** *KA-BAR, Genuine Stag* | 250.00 | 125.00 |
| ☐ **6320½** *KA-BAR, Bone Stag* | 225.00 | 125.00 |
| ☐ **7320½** *KA-BAR, Genuine Pearl* | 350.00 | 175.00 |
| ☐ **6322 T** *UNION CUT CO., Bone Stag* | 275.00 | 138.00 |
| ☐ **6324 RG** *KA-BAR, Bone Stag* | 80.00 | 40.00 |
| ☐ **6326** *KA-BAR, Bone Stag* | 180.00 | 90.00 |
| ☐ **P326** *kabar, Imitation Pearl* | 125.00 | 113.00 |
| ☐ **6331 EX PU** *UNION CUT CO., Bone Stag* | 600.00 | 300.00 |
| ☐ **7331 EX PU** *UNION CUT CO., Genuine Pearl* | 900.00 | 450.00 |
| ☐ **6331 EX PU** *KA-BAR, Bone Stag* | 600.00 | 300.00 |
| ☐ **6340½ WHITTLER,** *UNION CUT CO., Bone Stag* | 250.00 | 125.00 |
| ☐ **7340½** *KA-BAR, Genuine Pearl* | 300.00 | 150.00 |
| ☐ **2345** *UNION CUT CO., Genuine Stag* | 110.00 | 55.00 |
| ☐ **7345** *UNION CUT CO., Genuine Pearl* | 140.00 | 70.00 |
| ☐ **6349** *UNION CUT CO., Bone Stag* | 375.00 | 188.00 |
| ☐ **6349½** *KA-BAR, Bone Stag* | 325.00 | 163.00 |
| ☐ **T3256 CC** *KA-BAR, Cream Celluloid* | 90.00 | 45.00 |
| ☐ **T3256 CC** *kabar, Cream Celluloid* | 50.00 | 25.00 |

## 164 / KA-BAR

| | MINT | VG |
|---|---|---|
| ☐ 6356 UNION CUT CO., Bone Stag | 135.00 | 65.00 |
| ☐ 7356 UNION CUT CO., Genuine Pearl | 175.00 | 88.00 |
| ☐ 6356 KA-BAR, Bone Stag | 120.00 | 60.00 |
| ☐ 2356 kabar, Genuine Stag | 60.00 | 30.00 |
| ☐ 6356 kabar, Bone Stag | 50.00 | 25.00 |
| ☐ P356 kabar, Imitation Pearl | 35.00 | 18.00 |
| ☐ 6356 kabar computer number USA, Delrin | 10.00 | 5.00 |
| ☐ T3257 CC KA-BAR, Cream Celluloid | 120.00 | 60.00 |
| ☐ T3257 CC kabar, Cream Celluloid | 60.00 | 30.00 |
| ☐ 2357 UNION CUT CO., Genuine Stag | 160.00 | 80.00 |
| ☐ 6357 UNION CUT CO., Bone Stag | 150.00 | 75.00 |
| ☐ 9357 UNION CUT CO., Fancy Celluloid | 125.00 | 113.00 |
| ☐ 2357 KA-BAR, Genuine Stag | 135.00 | 118.00 |
| ☐ 6357 KA-BAR, Bone Stag | 120.00 | 60.00 |
| ☐ 9357 KA-BAR, Fancy Celluloid | 110.00 | 55.00 |
| ☐ 2357 kabar, Genuine Stag | 60.00 | 30.00 |
| ☐ 6357 kabar, Rough Black | 40.00 | 20.00 |
| ☐ P357 kabar, Imitation Pearl | 40.00 | 20.00 |
| ☐ 6357 kabar computer number USA, Delrin | 8.00 | 4.00 |
| ☐ 2360 UNION CUT CO., Genuine Stag | 140.00 | 70.00 |
| ☐ 9360 UNION CUT CO., Rainbow Stag | 120.00 | 60.00 |
| ☐ 6360 KA-BAR, Bone Stag | 120.00 | 60.00 |
| ☐ 2366 EX UNION CUT CO., Genuine Stag | 750.00 | 375.00 |
| ☐ 6366 EX UNION CUT CO., Bone Stag | 700.00 | 350.00 |
| ☐ 2366 EX KA-BAR, Genuine Stag | 650.00 | 325.00 |
| ☐ 6366 EX KA-BAR, Bone Stag | 600.00 | 300.00 |
| ☐ 2367 UNION CUT CO., Genuine Stag | 700.00 | 350.00 |
| ☐ 6367 UNION CUT CO., Bone Stag | 600.00 | 300.00 |
| ☐ 2369 UNION CUT CO., Genuine Stag | 175.00 | 88.00 |
| ☐ 6369 UNION CUT CO., Bone Stag | 160.00 | 80.00 |
| ☐ 6369 PU UNION CUT CO., Bone Stag | 165.00 | 83.00 |
| ☐ P367 PU UNION CUT CO., Imitation Pearl | 130.00 | 65.00 |
| ☐ 2369 KA-BAR, Genuine Stag | 150.00 | 75.00 |
| ☐ 2369 KA-BAR, Second Cut Stag | 175.00 | 88.00 |
| ☐ 6369 KA-BAR, Bone Stag | 135.00 | 63.00 |
| ☐ P369 KA-BAR, Imitation Pearl | 100.00 | 50.00 |
| ☐ 2369 kabar, Genuine Stag | 75.00 | 38.00 |
| ☐ 6369 kabar, Bone Stag | 70.00 | 35.00 |
| ☐ 6369 kabar, Rough Black | 45.00 | 23.00 |
| ☐ P369 kabar, Imitation Pearl | 40.00 | 20.00 |
| ☐ 6369 kabar computer number USA, Delrin | 10.00 | 5.00 |
| ☐ 2371 UNION CUT CO., Genuine Stag | 250.00 | 125.00 |
| ☐ 6371 UNION CUT CO., Bone Stag | 225.00 | 113.00 |

KA-BAR / 165

| | MINT | VG |
|---|---|---|
| ☐ 2371 KA-BAR, Genuine Stag | 225.00 | 113.00 |
| ☐ 6371 KA-BAR, Bone Stag | 200.00 | 100.00 |
| ☐ 9371 KA-BAR, Fancy Celluloid | 180.00 | 90.00 |
| ☐ T371 kabar, Cream Celluloid | 45.00 | 23.00 |
| ☐ 2381 UNION CUT CO., Genuine Stag | 95.00 | 48.00 |
| ☐ 7381 UNION CUT CO., Genuine Pearl | 125.00 | 113.00 |
| ☐ 7381 KA-BAR, Genuine Pearl | 110.00 | 55.00 |
| ☐ P381 KA-BAR, Imitation Pearl | 60.00 | 30.00 |
| ☐ 6390 KA-BAR, Bone Stag | 70.00 | 35.00 |
| ☐ P390 KA-BAR, Cream Celluloid | 45.00 | 23.00 |
| ☐ 6390 kabar, Rough Black | 30.00 | 15.00 |
| ☐ P390 kabar, Cream Celluloid | 30.00 | 15.00 |
| ☐ 6390 kabar computer number USA, Delrin | 6.00 | 3.00 |
| ☐ 6397 UNION CUT CO., Bone Stag | 400.00 | 200.00 |
| ☐ 6397 KA-BAR, Bone Stag | 300.00 | 150.00 |
| ☐ 23101 UNION CUT CO., Genuine Stag | 55.00 | |
| ☐ 73101 UNION CUT CO., Genuine Pearl | 100.00 | |
| ☐ 73101 KA-BAR, Genuine Pearl | 90. | |
| ☐ 73101 UNION CUT CO., Abalone Pearl | 190. | |
| ☐ 63104 UNION CUT CO., Bone Stag | 800 | |
| ☐ 73104 UNION CUT CO., Genuine Pearl | 1200.00 | 600.00 |
| ☐ P3104 UNION CUT CO., Imitation Pearl | 650.00 | 325.00 |
| ☐ 63111 UNION CUT CO., Bone Stag | 190.00 | 95.00 |
| ☐ P3111 UNION CUT CO., Imitation Pearl | 150.00 | 75.00 |
| ☐ P3111 PU UNION CUT CO., Imitation Pearl | 150.00 | 75.00 |
| ☐ 63111 KA-BAR, Bone Stag | 160.00 | 80.00 |
| ☐ P3111 KA-BAR, Imitation Pearl | 120.00 | 60.00 |
| ☐ P3111 PU KA-BAR, Imitation Pearl | 120.00 | 60.00 |
| ☐ 23116 UNION CUT CO., Genuine Stag | 175.00 | 88.00 |
| ☐ 63116 UNION CUT CO., Bone Stag | 160.00 | 80.00 |
| ☐ P3116 UNION CUT CO., Imitation Pearl | 110.00 | 55.00 |
| ☐ 23116 KA-BAR, Genuine Stag | 150.00 | 75.00 |
| ☐ 63116 KA-BAR, Bone Stag | 130.00 | 65.00 |
| ☐ P3116 KA-BAR, Imitation Pearl | 90.00 | 45.00 |
| ☐ 23116 kabar, Genuine Stag | 65.00 | 33.00 |
| ☐ 63116 kabar, Rough Black | 45.00 | 23.00 |
| ☐ 63116 kabar computer number USA, Delrin | 10.00 | 5.00 |
| ☐ 63118 UNION CUT CO., Bone Stag | 300.00 | 150.00 |
| ☐ 63152 UNION CUT CO., Bone Stag | 200.00 | 100.00 |
| ☐ W3152 UNION CUT CO., Golden Celluloid | 180.00 | 90.00 |
| ☐ 63152 KA-BAR, Bone Stag | 175.00 | 88.00 |
| ☐ 62163 KA-BAR, Bone Stag | 120.00 | 60.00 |
| ☐ 62195 TJ KA-BAR, Bone Stag | 90.00 | 45.00 |

166 / KA-BAR

| | MINT | VG |
|---|---|---|
| ☐ 62195 TJ KA-BAR, Rough Black | 45.00 | 23.00 |
| ☐ T2195 TJ KA-BAR, Cream Celluloid | 40.00 | 20.00 |
| ☐ 62195 TJ kabar, Rough Black | 35.00 | 18.00 |
| ☐ T2195 TJ kabar, Cream Celluloid | 30.00 | 15.00 |
| ☐ 62195 TJ kabar computer number USA, Delrin | 12.00 | 6.00 |
| ☐ 63195 KA-BAR, Bone Stag | 150.00 | 75.00 |
| ☐ 23195 kabar, Genuine Stag | 75.00 | 38.00 |
| ☐ 63195 kabar, Bone Stag | 70.00 | 35.00 |
| ☐ 63195 kabar, Rough Black | 40.00 | 20.00 |
| ☐ 63195 kabar computer number USA, Delrin | 10.00 | 5.00 |

## KA-BAR MULTI-BLADE SECTION

| | MINT | VG |
|---|---|---|
| ☐ 6401 T UNION CUT CO., Bone Stag | 200.00 | 100.00 |
| ☐ 7401 T UNION CUT CO., Genuine Pearl | 275.00 | 138.00 |
| ☐ R466 KAMP KNIFE KA-BAR, Fibroid Handle | 125.00 | 63.00 |
| ☐ T4107 KA-BAR, Cream Celluloid | 1000.00 | 500.00 |
| ☐ 64107 KA-BAR, Green Bone | 1500.00 | 750.00 |
| ☐ 24107 KA-BAR, Genuine Stag | 2000.00 | 1000.00 |
| ☐ 6415 RG UNION CUT CO., Bone Stag | 100.00 | 50.00 |
| ☐ 6415 RG KA-BAR, Bone Stag | 80.00 | 40.00 |
| ☐ P415 RG KA-BAR, Imitation Pearl | 90.00 | 45.00 |
| ☐ 6415 RG kabar, Rough Black | 20.00 | 10.00 |
| ☐ 6415 RG kabar computer number USA, Rough Black | 8.00 | 4.00 |
| ☐ 6421 UNION CUT CO., Bone Stag | 250.00 | 125.00 |
| ☐ 6421 KA-BAR, Bone Stag | 225.00 | 113.00 |
| ☐ 6426 UNION CUT CO., Bone Stag | 140.00 | 120.00 |
| ☐ 7426 UNION CUT CO., Genuine Pearl | 180.00 | 140.00 |
| ☐ 7426 KA-BAR, Genuine Pearl | 160.00 | 130.00 |
| ☐ 7455 UNION CUT CO., Genuine Pearl | 225.00 | 113.00 |
| ☐ 7455 KA-BAR, Genuine Pearl | 225.00 | 113.00 |
| ☐ 6460 UNION CUT CO., Bone Stag | 150.00 | 75.00 |
| ☐ 6460 KA-BAR, Bone Stag | 135.00 | 63.00 |
| ☐ 2461 PU UNION CUT CO., Genuine Stag | 250.00 | 125.00 |
| ☐ 6461 PU UNION CUT CO., Bone Stag | 240.00 | 120.00 |
| ☐ 6461 PU KA-BAR, Bone Stag | 225.00 | 113.00 |
| ☐ 2461 kabar, Genuine Stag | 100.00 | 50.00 |
| ☐ 6461 kabar, Rough Black | 75.00 | 38.00 |
| ☐ 2462 UNION CUT CO., Genuine Stag | 200.00 | 100.00 |
| ☐ 6766 KA-BAR, Bone Stag | 2500.00 | 1250.00 |
| ☐ T766 KA-BAR, Cream Celluloid | 2000.00 | 1000.00 |

*KA-BAR / 167*

| | MINT | VG |
|---|---|---|
| ☐ **6469 PU** *UNION CUT CO., Bone Stag* | 250.00 | 125.00 |
| ☐ **5480** *UNION CUT CO., Black Celluloid* | 125.00 | 113.00 |
| ☐ **P480** *UNION CUT CO., Imitation Pearl* | 125.00 | 113.00 |
| ☐ **P480** *KA-BAR, Imitation Pearl* | 110.00 | 55.00 |
| ☐ **7487** *UNION CUT CO., Genuine Pearl* | 150.00 | 75.00 |

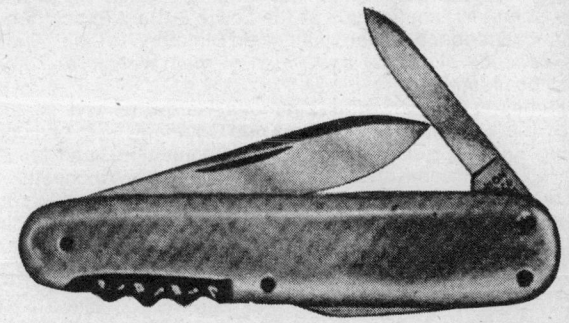

**7487**

| | | |
|---|---|---|
| ☐ **T487** *UNION CUT CO., Abalone Pearl* | 175.00 | 88.00 |
| ☐ **2488** *UNION CUT CO., Genuine Stag* | 325.00 | 163.00 |
| ☐ **6488** *UNION CUT CO., Bone Stag* | 300.00 | 150.00 |
| ☐ **2488** *KA-BAR, Genuine Stag* | 250.00 | 125.00 |
| ☐ **6488** *KA-BAR, Bone Stag* | 250.00 | 125.00 |
| ☐ **7489** *UNION CUT CO., Genuine Pearl* | 200.00 | 100.00 |
| ☐ **7489** *KA-BAR, Genuine Pearl* | 175.00 | 88.00 |
| ☐ **24100** *UNION CUT CO., Genuine Stag* | 225.00 | 113.00 |
| ☐ **64100** *UNION CUT CO., Bone Stag* | 225.00 | 113.00 |
| ☐ **66158** *KA-BAR, Bone Stag* | 150.00 | 75.00 |
| ☐ **24163** *UNION CUT CO., Genuine Stag* | 175.00 | 88.00 |
| ☐ **64163** *UNION CUT CO., Bone Stag* | 175.00 | 88.00 |
| ☐ **74163** *UNION CUT CO., Genuine Pearl* | 250.00 | 125.00 |
| ☐ **64168** *KA-BAR, Bone Stag* | 85.00 | 43.00 |
| ☐ **54202** *KA-BAR, Black Celluloid* | 90.00 | 45.00 |
| ☐ **T4202** *KA-BAR, Cream Celluloid* | 120.00 | 60.00 |
| ☐ **M4202** *KA-BAR, Metal Handles* | 110.00 | 55.00 |
| ☐ **54202** *kabar, Black Celluloid* | 80.00 | 40.00 |
| ☐ **T4202** *kabar, Cream Celluloid* | 80.00 | 40.00 |

## KEEN KUTTER
### ST. LOUIS, MISSOURI

The "Keen Kutter" was a brand of E. C. Simmons Hardware, and was used on tools as well as cutlery. The stamping was used beginning around 1870.

Simmons Hardware owned controlling interest in Walden Knife Company, and in 1905 at the Lewis & Clark Exposition in Portland, Oregon, an award was given Simmons for the *"Superior excellence of quality and finish of their Walden and Keen Kutter pocketknives"*.

Winchester merged with Simmons Hardware and in 1923 moved the equipment of Walden Knife Company, who had been making Keen Kutter, to New Haven, Connecticut, and for the next 10 years Keen Kutter knives were made by Winchester.

Later, the Simmons Hardware and Winchester merger split, and in 1940, Shapleigh Hardware bought the assets (including the controlling interest in Walden Knife Company) of Simmons Hardware. All Simmons brands were continued by Shapleigh.

| PATTERN NO. | MINT | VG | PATTERN NO. | MINT | VG |
|---|---|---|---|---|---|
| ☐ K7WCCE | 60.00 | 30.00 | ☐ K0195 3/4P | 40.00 | 20.00 |
| ☐ K7WCS | 60.00 | 30.00 | ☐ K0196 | 50.00 | 25.00 |
| ☐ K7WPC | 120.00 | 60.00 | ☐ K0197 3/4K | 60.00 | 30.00 |
| ☐ K013 | 35.00 | 18.00 | ☐ K0198 | 50.00 | 25.00 |
| ☐ K013/S | 50.00 | 25.00 | ☐ K0198 3/4 | 40.00 | 20.00 |
| ☐ K38 3/4 | 175.00 | 88.00 | ☐ K0207R | 30.00 | 15.00 |
| ☐ K50 | 45.00 | 23.00 | ☐ K0109R | 80.00 | 40.00 |
| ☐ K50K | 65.00 | 33.00 | ☐ K0214 | 30.00 | 15.00 |
| ☐ K50 3/4K | 65.00 | 33.00 | ☐ K0214K | 35.00 | 18.00 |
| ☐ K51 3/4 | 45.00 | 23.00 | ☐ K0214TC | 30.00 | 15.00 |
| ☐ K53 | 45.00 | 23.00 | ☐ K0247 | 100.00 | 50.00 |
| ☐ K53 3/4 | 45.00 | 23.00 | ☐ K0256 | 45.00 | 23.00 |
| ☐ K080 | 60.00 | 30.00 | ☐ K0258 | 45.00 | 23.00 |
| ☐ K083T | 90.00 | 45.00 | ☐ K2654 | 35.00 | 18.00 |
| ☐ K094T | 70.00 | 35.00 | ☐ K264 3/4 | 70.00 | 35.00 |
| ☐ K099T | 110.00 | 55.00 | ☐ K0281T | 40.00 | 20.00 |
| ☐ K0147 3/4 | 150.00 | 75.00 | ☐ K309R | 80.00 | 40.00 |
| ☐ K0151 | 60.00 | 30.00 | ☐ K0333 | 80.00 | 40.00 |
| ☐ K0153 | 60.00 | 30.00 | ☐ K341 | 80.00 | 40.00 |
| ☐ K153 | 70.00 | 35.00 | ☐ K343 | 70.00 | 35.00 |
| ☐ K0195 3/4K | 40.00 | 20.00 | ☐ K0348 | 60.00 | 30.00 |

## KEEN KUTTER / 169

| PATTERN NO. | MINT | VG | PATTERN NO. | MINT | VG |
|---|---|---|---|---|---|
| ☐ K356 | 90.00 | 45.00 | ☐ K02238 | 80.00 | 40.00 |
| ☐ K357 | 120.00 | 60.00 | ☐ K02239 | 95.00 | 48.00 |
| ☐ K0388/S | 95.00 | 45.00 | ☐ K02423 | 50.00 | 25.00 |
| ☐ K443 | 120.00 | 60.00 | ☐ K02436 3/4 | 60.00 | 30.00 |
| ☐ K0486 | 25.00 | 13.00 | ☐ K02437 3/4 | 45.00 | 23.00 |
| ☐ K0488 | 50.00 | 25.00 | ☐ K02463 | 80.00 | 40.00 |
| ☐ K0498 | 50.00 | 25.00 | ☐ K02527 | 30.00 | 15.00 |
| ☐ K0499 | 90.00 | 45.00 | ☐ K02529 | 45.00 | 23.00 |
| ☐ K0529 | 45.00 | 23.00 | ☐ K02529/S | 45.00 | 23.00 |
| ☐ K0612R | 60.00 | 30.00 | ☐ K2720 | 35.00 | 18.00 |
| ☐ K0643 | 80.00 | 40.00 | ☐ K2723 | 35.00 | 18.00 |
| ☐ K0698 | 80.00 | 40.00 | ☐ K02736 | 45.00 | 23.00 |
| ☐ K711 | 90.00 | 45.00 | ☐ K02878 | 60.00 | 30.00 |
| ☐ K711G | 35.00 | 18.00 | ☐ K2878 3/4 | 60.00 | 30.00 |
| ☐ K711/SC | 35.00 | 18.00 | ☐ K3036T | 90.00 | 45.00 |
| ☐ K713 | 35.00 | 18.00 | ☐ K3037T | 70.00 | 35.00 |
| ☐ K713 3/4 | 35.00 | 18.00 | ☐ K3070J | 120.00 | 60.00 |
| ☐ K713 3/4A | 100.00 | 50.00 | ☐ K3070FK | 120.00 | 60.00 |
| ☐ 735 3/4A | 100.00 | 50.00 | ☐ K3070FL | 100.00 | 50.00 |
| ☐ K735 3/4 | 100.00 | 50.00 | ☐ K3071F | 100.00 | 50.00 |
| ☐ K737 3/4 | 100.00 | 50.00 | ☐ K3071 1/4 | 120.00 | 60.00 |
| ☐ K738 3/4 | 175.00 | 88.00 | ☐ K3071 1/2 | 120.00 | 60.00 |
| ☐ K0797 | 30.00 | 15.00 | ☐ K3073 | 150.00 | 75.00 |
| ☐ K0798 | 50.00 | 25.00 | ☐ K3215 3/4G | 120.00 | 60.00 |
| ☐ K0799 | 40.00 | 20.00 | ☐ K3218 3/4 | 110.00 | 55.00 |
| ☐ K0814 | 30.00 | 15.00 | ☐ K3278 | 120.00 | 60.00 |
| ☐ K0815/S | 30.00 | 15.00 | ☐ K3305RJ | 90.00 | 45.00 |
| ☐ K0878 | 50.00 | 25.00 | ☐ K3307R | 120.00 | 60.00 |
| ☐ K0883 | 110.00 | 55.00 | ☐ K3310 | 120.00 | 60.00 |
| ☐ K1704 1/4 | 20.00 | 10.00 | ☐ K03311 | 75.00 | 38.00 |
| ☐ K1734 1/2 | 75.00 | 38.00 | ☐ K3311 1/4 | 125.00 | 63.00 |
| ☐ K01880A | 40.00 | 20.00 | ☐ K3316 | 160.00 | 80.00 |
| ☐ K0188OR | 40.00 | 20.00 | ☐ K3317 | 125.00 | 63.00 |
| ☐ K01881 | 35.00 | 18.00 | ☐ K0334 | 50.00 | 25.00 |
| ☐ K01884 | 30.00 | 15.00 | ☐ K03342J | 30.00 | 15.00 |
| ☐ K0207OM | 30.00 | 15.00 | ☐ K03342K | 30.00 | 15.00 |
| ☐ K02071 | 30.00 | 15.00 | ☐ K03344/S | 35.00 | 18.00 |
| ☐ K02074 | 60.00 | 30.00 | ☐ K3430 | 125.00 | 63.00 |
| ☐ K02074L | 40.00 | 20.00 | ☐ K03433 | 90.00 | 45.00 |
| ☐ K02120 | 40.00 | 20.00 | ☐ K3433 | 125.00 | 63.00 |
| ☐ K02220 | 40.00 | 20.00 | ☐ K3433 1/4 | 120.00 | 60.00 |
| ☐ K02235N | 80.00 | 40.00 | ☐ K03471 | 45.00 | 23.00 |
| ☐ K02237 | 45.00 | 23.00 | ☐ K3472 | 90.00 | 45.00 |

## 170 / KEEN KUTTER

| PATTERN NO. | MINT | VG | PATTERN NO. | MINT | VG |
|---|---|---|---|---|---|
| ☐ K3483 | 1209.00 | 604.00 | ☐ K23628 3/4 | 40.00 | 20.00 |
| ☐ K3527 | 120.00 | 60.00 | ☐ K27122 | 40.00 | 20.00 |
| ☐ K3553 | 110.00 | 55.00 | ☐ K27233 3/4 | 350.00 | 175.00 |
| ☐ K3599T | 150.00 | 75.00 | ☐ K32436 3/4 | 90.00 | 45.00 |
| ☐ K3619 | 175.00 | 88.00 | ☐ K32437 | 100.00 | 50.00 |
| ☐ K3681T | 120.00 | 60.00 | ☐ K33251 | 50.00 | 25.00 |
| ☐ K3698 3/4 | 120.00 | 60.00 | ☐ K33253 | 140.00 | 70.00 |
| ☐ K3705 1/4D | 115.00 | 58.00 | ☐ K33433 | 125.00 | 63.00 |
| ☐ K03706 | 40.00 | 20.00 | ☐ K33720R | 90.00 | 45.00 |
| ☐ K3706 1/2 | 90.00 | 45.00 | ☐ K33721 | 90.00 | 45.00 |
| ☐ K03706 1/4 | 40.00 | 20.00 | ☐ K33732K | 90.00 | 45.00 |
| ☐ K03707 | 40.00 | 20.00 | ☐ K37334 | 90.00 | 45.00 |
| ☐ K3708 1/4 | 150.00 | 75.00 | ☐ K72286 | 20.00 | 10.00 |
| ☐ K3732 | 90.00 | 45.00 | ☐ K72288 3/4 | 20.00 | 10.00 |
| ☐ K3733 | 90.00 | 45.00 | ☐ K72423 | 65.00 | 33.00 |
| ☐ K3825 | 125.00 | 63.00 | ☐ K72783 | 65.00 | 33.00 |
| ☐ K3825H | 90.00 | 45.00 | ☐ K72783 3/4 | 65.00 | 33.00 |
| ☐ K3826 | 110.00 | 55.00 | ☐ K73310 1/4R | 150.00 | 75.00 |
| ☐ K3828 | 120.00 | 60.00 | ☐ K73311 1/4 | 50.00 | 25.00 |
| ☐ K3878 3/4 | 140.00 | 70.00 | ☐ K73433 1/4 | 140.00 | 70.00 |
| ☐ K3908/S | 140.00 | 70.00 | ☐ K73477 3/4 | 140.00 | 70.00 |
| ☐ K4208 | 120.00 | 60.00 | ☐ K73553 3/4 | 90.00 | 45.00 |
| ☐ K4428 | 150.00 | 75.00 | ☐ K73265G | 90.00 | 45.00 |
| ☐ K04527 | 110.00 | 55.00 | ☐ K73628 | 90.00 | 45.00 |
| ☐ K4527 | 120.00 | 60.00 | ☐ K73706 | 110.00 | 55.00 |
| ☐ K04529 | 120.00 | 60.00 | ☐ K73706 1/4 | 110.00 | 55.00 |
| ☐ K4843 | 110.00 | 55.00 | ☐ K73733 | 130.00 | 65.00 |
| ☐ K5328 | 150.00 | 75.00 | ☐ K73828 | 130.00 | 65.00 |
| ☐ K5738/S | 60.00 | 30.00 | ☐ K73845 1/4D | 150.00 | 75.00 |
| ☐ K06256F | 60.00 | 30.00 | ☐ K73845 1/4L | 150.00 | 75.00 |
| ☐ K6353 | 70.00 | 35.00 | ☐ K73848 | 90.00 | 45.00 |
| ☐ K6559 | 70.00 | 35.00 | ☐ K73848 1/4 | 135.00 | 68.00 |
| ☐ K07243 | 90.00 | 45.00 | ☐ K73875 3/4P | 125.00 | 63.00 |
| ☐ K7433 | 120.00 | 60.00 | ☐ K73878 1/4 | 125.00 | 63.00 |
| ☐ K7530J | 115.00 | 58.00 | ☐ K73878 3/4 | 125.00 | 63.00 |
| ☐ K7733 | 75.00 | 38.00 | ☐ K74825E | 150.00 | 75.00 |
| ☐ K7733 3/4 | 75.00 | 38.00 | ☐ K74828 | 150.00 | 75.00 |
| ☐ K8464 1/4 | 140.00 | 70.00 | | | |

# PARKER CUTLERY

James F. Parker was a popular name in the knife business long before the formation of Parker Cutlery. He was one of the first mail order dealers in antique pocketknives, and his reputation as one of the most reputable dealers in the business led to rapid growth of his business.

He formed Parker Dist. Company in 1970. James F. Parker Co. Inc. was chartered in 1974. From 1976-1978 Parker was a partner in a commemorative knife manufacturing firm, "Parker-Frost" Parker bought the entire company in 1978.

The trademark of Parker Cutlery's Eagle brand knives is an eagle with widespread wings. It was adopted by the suggestion of a New York cutlery salesman who had the same eagle carved in wood.

Parker pioneered the Japanese import market after testing his own brand being manufactured by an American cutlery firm, with his private label.

At his insistence the Japanese began a massive program to upgrade their quality, resulting in the top quality Japanese knives available today.

Parker's line is constantly changing, giving the variety collector a wide range to choose from. The knives marked with the Parker-Frost tang stamping are already sought after collector's items.

Parker offers a catalog for $3.00 refundable with the first order and is co-compiler of the OFFICIAL PRICE GUIDE TO COLLECTOR KNIVES.

The following is a list of all items made with the Parker-Frost Eagle Brand Trademark. This trademark was first used in 1975. On some of the earlier knives only the Eagle Trademark appeared on the blade and not the name Parker-Frost. In most instances we were able to list the quantities made of the items.

|  | MINT | VG |
|---|---|---|
| ☐ **American Bicentennial Clasp Knives,** *1500 released, Tang marked America. Back of blade marked made especially for Parker-Frost Cutlery by Alcoa, 5½ inches.* | 250.00 | 125.00 |

## 172 / PARKER

| | MINT | VG |
|---|---|---|
| ☐ **American Eagle Bicentennial Series**, *12,000 released, 5 different knives: Patrick Henry, John Adams, Nathan Hale, Thomas Jefferson and George Washington models, 4 inches.* | 175.00 | 87.50 |
| ☐ **Big Grizzly**, *24,000 released, Pakkawood, 4¾ inches.* | 35.00 | 17.50 |
| ☐ **Bobcat**, *12,000 released, Wood Insert, 3 inches.* | 12.00 | 6.00 |
| ☐ **Boone and Crockett Commemorative Set**, *1,000 released, German made Stag lockback, 3 color etching on blades, 5½ inches.* | 150.00 | 75.00 |
| ☐ **Brahma**, *4,800 released, Smoothbone, 3 blade stock, 4 inches.* | 30.00 | 15.00 |
| ☐ **Bull**, *4,800 released, Smoothbone, 3 blade, 3⅜ inches.* | 25.00 | 12.50 |
| ☐ **Bulldog**, *3,000 released, Fleur De Lis lockback, 2⁷⁄₁₆ inches.* | 15.00 | 7.50 |
| ☐ **Canoe**, *12,000 released, Regular Christmas Tree, Back of Tang marked Rodgers-Wostenholm, 3¾ inches.* | 35.00 | 17.50 |
| ☐ **Canoe**, *1,000 released, Tiger Eye, Back of Tang marked Rodgers-Wostenholm, 3¾ inches.* | 50.00 | 25.00 |
| ☐ **Canoe**, *1,000 released, Christmas of 41, Back of Tang marked Rodgers-Wostenholm, 3¾ inches.* | 50.00 | 25.00 |
| ☐ **Canoe**, *12,000 released, Red and Brown Bone, Back of Tang marked Rodgers-Wostenholm, 3¾ inches.* | 40.00 | 20.00 |
| ☐ **Canoe**, *6,000 released, Genuine Stag, Back of Tang marked Rodgers-Wostenholm, 3¾ inches.* | 50.00 | 25.00 |
| ☐ **Coffin Pearl**, *1,200 released, Mother of Pearl, 3¾ inches.* | 70.00 | 35.00 |
| ☐ **Colony Bicentennial**, *3,000 released, Sculptured knives with Eagle Stamp. The center knife marked Schrade. Center knife is Genuine Stag, Sizes different on 14 knives.* | 550.00 | 275.00 |
| ☐ **Colt**, *Lock available in same handle as Little Mustang, 2⁹⁄₁₆ inches.* | 12.00 | 6.00 |
| ☐ **Cub Model #1**, *3,600 released, Etched Cub on front of Blade. Smoothbone and Pickbone, 3⅛ inches.* | 30.00 | 15.00 |
| ☐ **Cub Model #2**, *3,600 released, Picture of Cub Bear climbing on back of blade. Smoothbone and Pickbone, 3⅛ inches.* | 30.00 | 15.00 |

PARKER / 173

|  | MINT | VG |
|---|---|---|
| ☐ **Cub Model #3,** Picture of bear cub on front of blade. Smoothbone and Pickbone, 3 1/8 inches.... | 25.00 | 12.50 |
| ☐ **Deerslayer,** 1,000 released, Clasp knife, Back of blade marked made especially for Parker-Frost, 5 1/2 inches. | 50.00 | 25.00 |
| ☐ **Eagle Display Knives,** 25 released, Blade identical to the American Eagle Bicentennial series, 12 inches. ............................................ea. | 500.00 | 250.00 |
| ☐ **El Diablo,** 4,800 released, Smoothbone, 4 inches. | 40.00 | 20.00 |
| ☐ **El Diablo,** 4,800 released, Stag, 4 inches. ....... | 55.00 | 27.50 |
| ☐ **Football Knives,** 600 released, SEC Teams Wildcats, Vols, Tide, War Eagles, Bulldogs, Commodores, Bengal Tigers, Mississippi Bulldogs, Rebels All Teams, Wake Forest Deacons, 3 1/4 inches. | 15.00 | 7.00 |
| ☐ **Football Knives,** 1,200 released, SEC Team N.C. State Wolfpack, 3 1/4 inches. | 15.00 | 7.00 |
| ☐ **Football Knives,** 6,000 released, SEC Team N.C. Tarheels, 3 1/4 inches. | 15.00 | 7.00 |
| ☐ **Football Knives,** 600 released, SEC Team Duke Blue Devils, 3 1/4 inches. | 15.00 | 7.00 |
| ☐ **Football Knives,** 600 released, SEC Team Clemson Tigers, 3 1/4 inches. | 15.00 | 7.00 |
| ☐ **Football Knives,** 600 released, SEC Team S.C. Gamecocks, 3 1/4 inches. | 15.00 | 7.00 |
| ☐ **Football Knives,** 6,000 released, Each SEC, 3 1/4 inches. ............................................ea. | 30.00 | 10.00 |
| ☐ **Hawg,** 3,600 released, Lockback canoe, Wood, 3 5/8 inches. | 30.00 | 15.00 |
| ☐ **Husky,** 4,800 released, Smoothbone, 3 inches. .. | 25.00 | 12.50 |
| ☐ **IM-100,** 1,164 released, Pakkawood, 3 inches. .... | 20.00 | 10.00 |
| ☐ **IM-200,** 600 released, Pakkawood, 4 inches. .... | 30.00 | 15.00 |
| ☐ **IM-300,** 960 released, Pakkawood, 4 inches. .... | 35.00 | 17.50 |
| ☐ **Indian Series II,** 1,200 released, Same as #1 but different Indians, 3 3/4 inches. | 90.00 | 45.00 |
| ☐ **Jaquar,** 6,000 released, Wood, 3 1/4 inches. ...... | 18.00 | 9.00 |
| ☐ **Kayak,** 2,400 released, Wood, 3 3/4 inches. ...... | 20.00 | 10.00 |
| ☐ **Kayak,** 12,000 released, Smoothbone, 3 3/4 inches. | 25.00 | 12.50 |
| ☐ **Kayak,** 6,000 released, Pickbone, 3 3/4 inches. ... | 25.00 | 12.50 |
| ☐ **Kentucky Thorobred and Tennessee Walking Horse Set,** 1,000 released, German made, Stag handle, Lockback, 3 color etching on blade, 5 1/4 inches. | 150.00 | 75.00 |

## 174 / PARKER

|  | MINT | VG |
|---|---|---|
| ☐ **Leopard,** 6,000 released, Wood, 3¾ inches. | 25.00 | 12.50 |
| ☐ **Leopard,** 6,000 released, White Delrin, 3¾ inches. | 25.00 | 12.50 |
| ☐ **Leopard,** 24,000 released, Pickbone. | 25.00 | 12.50 |
| ☐ **Leopard,** 24,000 released, Smoothbone. | 25.00 | 12.50 |
| ☐ **Leopard,** 6,000 released, Imitation Tortoise Shell. | 25.00 | 12.50 |
| ☐ **Leopard,** 600 released, Genuine Mother of Pearl. | 60.00 | 30.00 |
| ☐ **Little Bandit,** 36,000 released, Pickbone, 4 inches. | 25.00 | 12.50 |
| ☐ **Little Doagie,** 7,200 released, Peanut Smoothbone, 2¾ inches. | 20.00 | 10.00 |
| ☐ **Little Grizzly,** 6,000 released, Pakkawood, 4⅛ inches. | 25.00 | 12.50 |
| ☐ **Little Kayak,** 12,000 released, Wood, 3 inches. | 21.00 | 10.50 |
| ☐ **Little Mink,** 12,000 released, Smoothbone, 2⅞ inches. | 15.00 | 7.50 |
| ☐ **Little Mustang,** 6,000 released, Brown Micarta, 2½ inches. | 12.00 | 6.00 |
| ☐ **Little Mustang,** 6,000 released, Green Micarta, 2½ inches. | 15.00 | 7.50 |
| ☐ **Little Mustang,** 6,000 released, Pakkawood, 2½ inches. | 15.00 | 7.50 |
| ☐ **Little Mustang,** 6,000 released, Sandalwood, 2½ inches. | 15.00 | 7.50 |
| ☐ **Little Mustang,** 6,000 released, Imitation Pearl, 2½ inches. | 15.00 | 7.50 |
| ☐ **Little Mustang,** 12,000 released, Smoothbone, 2½ inches. | 20.00 | 10.00 |
| ☐ **Little Mustang,** 3,000 released, Genuine Pearl, 2½ inches. | 30.00 | 15.00 |
| ☐ **Longhorn,** 7,200 released, Smoothbone, No lanyard hole, 3¾ inches. | 35.00 | 17.50 |
| ☐ **Longhorn,** 1,200 released, Mother of Pearl, 3¾ inches. | 60.00 | 30.00 |
| ☐ **Mustang,** 24,000 released, White Delrin, 3½ inches. | 20.00 | 10.00 |
| ☐ **Mustang,** 12,000 released, Black Pakkawood, 3½ inches. | 20.00 | 10.00 |
| ☐ **Mustang,** 24,000 released, Smoothbone, 3½ inches. | 25.00 | 12.50 |
| ☐ **Mustang,** 24,000 released, Pickbone, 3½ inches. | 25.00 | 12.50 |

| | MINT | VG |
|---|---|---|
| ☐ **North American Whittler Commemorative Set,** *1,500 released, Set of 4, Genuine Stag, Whittlers.* | 250.00 | 125.00 |
| ☐ **Parker Frost American,** *1,000 released, Made by Schrade for Parker Frost in 1978. Back of Tang marked #1978-1 through 1978-14, 1978-1 Stag etched Tennessee Stockman, 4 inches. . . . . . . .* | 60.00 | 30.00 |
| ☐ **Parker Frost American,** *1,000 released, 1978-1 Stag etched Kentucky Stockman, 4 inches. . . . . .* | 60.00 | 30.00 |
| ☐ **Parker Frost American,** *12,000 released, 1978-2 Bone, 3 blade stockman, 4 inches. . . . . . . . . . . . .* | 30.00 | 15.00 |
| ☐ **Parker Frost American,** *12,000 released, 1978-3 Bone, 2 blade Muskrat, 4 inches. . . . . . . . . . . . . . .* | 25.00 | 12.50 |
| ☐ **Parker Frost American,** *12,000 released, 1978-4 Bone, Trapper Pattern, 3⅞ inches. . . . . . . . . . . . . .* | 28.00 | 14.00 |
| ☐ **Parker Frost American,** *12,000 released, 1978-5 Bone, 1 blade lockback, 3⅞ inches. . . . . . . . . . . . .* | 25.00 | 12.50 |
| ☐ **Parker Frost American,** *12,000 released, 1978-6 Stainless Steel lockback, 4 inches. . . . . . . . . . . .* | 20.00 | 10.00 |
| ☐ **Parker Frost American,** *6,000 released, 1978-7 Black Sawcut 2 blade Muskrat, 4 inches. . . . . . . .* | 20.00 | 10.00 |
| ☐ **Parker Frost American,** *12,000 released, 1978-8 2 blade folding hunter scrimshaw, 5¼ inches. . . . .* | 35.00 | 17.50 |
| ☐ **Parker Frost American,** *12,000 released, 1978-9 3 blade Stocknife, Black Sawcut, 4 inches. . . . . .* | 20.00 | 10.00 |
| ☐ **Parker Frost American,** *12,000 released, 1978-10 2 blade Trapper, Black Sawcut, 3⅞ inches. . . . . . .* | 20.00 | 10.00 |
| ☐ **Parker Frost American,** *12,000 released, 1978-11 3 blade stock knife, black sawcut, 3 5/16 inches. . .* | 18.00 | 9.00 |
| ☐ **Parker Frost American,** *12,000 released, 1978-12 2 blade Peanut style black sawcut, 3⅛ inches. . .* | 15.00 | 7.50 |
| ☐ **Parker Frost American,** *6,000 released, 1978-13 Scrimshaw drop point, 7¼ inches. . . . . . . . . . . .* | 30.00 | 15.00 |
| ☐ **Parker Frost American,** *6,000 released, 1978-14 Scrimshaw sharp point, 7¼ inches. . . . . . . . . . . .* | 30.00 | 15.00 |
| ☐ **Parker Frost Canoes,** *2,400 released, Wood, 3¾ inches. . . . . . . . . . . . . . . . . . . . . . . . . . . . . . .* | 20.00 | 10.00 |
| ☐ **Parker Frost Canoes,** *6,000 released, Smooth Brown Bone, 3¾ inches. . . . . . . . . . . . . . . . . . .* | 25.00 | 12.50 |
| ☐ **Parker Frost Canoes,** *6,000 released, Red Pickbone, 3¾ inches. . . . . . . . . . . . . . . . . . . . . . .* | 25.00 | 12.50 |
| ☐ **Parker Frost Deerskinner,** *600 released, Stag German made 3 colors, etching on blade, 4¼ inches. . . . . . . . . . . . . . . . . . . . . . . . . . . . . . .* | 60.00 | 30.00 |

## 176 / PARKER

|  | MINT | VG |
|---|---|---|
| ☐ **Parker Frost 3 Dot Crowbar,** *600 released, Wood with 3 metal dots, 4½ inches.* | 25.00 | 12.50 |
| ☐ **Parker Frost Gentlemen's,** *1,200 released, Pearl, Blade, File and Scissors, German made, 3 inches.* | 45.00 | 22.50 |
| ☐ **Parker Frost Indian Series I,** *1,200 released, 4 Trapper Knives in Case, 2 Bone, 2 Imitation Tortoise Shell, 3¾ inches.* | 100.00 | 50.00 |
| ☐ **Smoky Mountain Toothpick,** *12,000 released, 3 different varieties: Fancy etch, Regular etch, no etch, 9½ inches.* | 25.00 | 12.50 |
| ☐ **Stallion,** *24,000 released, Pickbone and Smoothbone, 3¾ inches.* | 20.00 | 10.00 |
| ☐ **Tennessee and Kentucky Copperhead Set,** *1,200 released, Genuine Stag, 3¾ inches.* | 150.00 | 75.00 |
| ☐ **Tiger,** *4,800 released, Wood insert, 4½ inches.* | 15.00 | 7.50 |
| ☐ **Timberwolf,** *2,400 released, Pakkawood, 4 inches.* | 25.00 | 12.50 |
| ☐ **Timberwolf,** *2,400 released, White Delrin, 4 inches.* | 25.00 | 12.50 |
| ☐ **Wildcat,** *3,000 released, Sandalwood, 3 inches.* | 20.00 | 10.00 |
| ☐ **Wildcat,** *12,000 released, Smoothbone, 3 inches.* | 25.00 | 12.50 |
| ☐ **Wildcat,** *6,000 released, Pickbone, 3 inches.* | 25.00 | 12.50 |
| ☐ **Wildcat,** *600 released, Genuine Mother of Pearl, 2 inches.* | 60.00 | 30.00 |
| ☐ **Wolverine,** *4,800 released, 3 blade stock amber, 4 inches.* | 18.00 | 9.00 |
| ☐ **U.S. Armed Forces 3 knife Commemorative Set,** *3,000 released, Has Eagle Stamp, 4 inches.* | 45.00 | 22.50 |

Parker Cutlery Company. The following knives were made with Parker Cutlery Co. Eagle Brand Logo. The knives are identified with either etching on front of blade or number on rear tang. Knives that are marked discontinued will have quantity manufactured. If they are still currently manufactured no quantity will be shown. Keep in mind that even if 6,000 of a knife is manufactured, 90% to 95% of them are used so after a few years, it is hard to find a mint or near mint specimen.

|  | MINT | VG |
|---|---|---|
| ☐ **AK-341** *Genuine Stag, 3 inches.* | 20.00 | 10.00 |
| ☐ **American Lockback Whittler,** *Disc., 6,000 released, Pickbone, 4 inches.* | 45.00 | 22.50 |

PARKER / 177

| | MINT | VG |
|---|---|---|
| ☐ **American Lockback Whittler,** *6,000 released, Smoothbone, 4 inches.* | 45.00 | 22.50 |
| ☐ **Angel of Mercy,** *Bronzed Brass, 7¼ inches.* | 19.00 | 9.50 |
| ☐ **Apache Teardrop,** *Disc., 12,000 released, Smoothbone, 3⅞ inches.* | 20.00 | 10.00 |

**Apache Teardrop**

| | | |
|---|---|---|
| ☐ **Armadillo,** *Disc., 2,400 released, Smoothbone, 3⅞ inches.* | 25.00 | 12.50 |
| ☐ **Art Noveau,** *Brass, 3 inches.* | 8.00 | 4.00 |

**Art Noveau**

## 178 / PARKER

| | MINT | VG |
|---|---|---|
| ☐ **Bald Eagle,** *Smoothbone, 3½ inches.* | 17.00 | 8.50 |
| ☐ **Barlow,** *Disc., 1,200 released, Mother of Pearl, 3¾ inches.* | 40.00 | 20.00 |
| ☐ **Barlow - Dogleg,** *Pickbone, 3¾ inches.* | 17.00 | 8.50 |
| ☐ **Barlow - Dogleg,** *Smoothbone, 3¾ inches.* | 17.00 | 8.50 |
| ☐ **Battle of Lookout Mountain,** *Disc., 1,200 released, Pickbone, 4 inches.* | 50.00 | 25.00 |

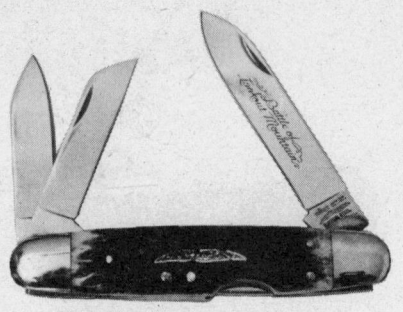

**Battle Of Lookout Mountain**

| | | |
|---|---|---|
| ☐ **Battle of Lookout Mountain,** *Disc., 2,400 released, Smoothbone.* | 45.00 | 22.50 |

**Battle Of Lookout Mountain**

PARKER / 179

|  | MINT | VG |
|---|---|---|
| ☐ **Bearclaw,** Mother of Pearl, 2 inches. | 19.00 | 9.50 |
| ☐ **Bearclaw,** Smoothbone, 2 inches. | 15.00 | 7.50 |
| ☐ **Beavertail,** 4 different varieties, 600 each released, Christmas Tree, Disc., 3⅛ inches. | 20.00 | 10.00 |
| ☐ **Beavertail,** Mother of Pearl, 3⅛ inches. | 45.00 | 22.50 |
| ☐ **Beavertail,** Smoothbone, 3⅛ inches. | 21.00 | 10.50 |

**Beavertail**

| | | |
|---|---|---|
| ☐ **Big Canittler,** Disc., 2,400 released, Christmas Tree, 3½ inches. | 20.00 | 10.00 |
| ☐ **Big Canittler,** Disc., 1,200 released, Mother of Pearl, 3½ inches. | 35.00 | 17.50 |
| ☐ **Big Canittler,** Disc., 4,800 released, Smoothbone, 3½ inches. | 22.00 | 11.00 |
| ☐ **Big Copperhead,** 1,200 released, Mother of Pearl, 3¾ inches. | 45.00 | 22.50 |
| ☐ **Big Copperhead,** Smoothbone, 3¾ inches. | 20.00 | 10.00 |
| ☐ **Big Copperhead II Lock,** Smoothbone, 3¾ inches. | 22.00 | 11.00 |
| ☐ **Big Horn,** Disc., 6,000 released, Smoothbone, 4¾ inches. | 30.00 | 15.00 |
| ☐ **Big Low - 1980,** Disc., 48,000 released, Smoothbone, 5¼ inches. | 30.00 | 15.00 |
| ☐ **Big Lou K-138 Gunstock,** 2,400 released, Smoothbone, 5 inches. | 27.00 | 13.50 |
| ☐ **Big Mouth Bass,** Disc., 1,200 released, Micarta, 8½ inches. | 20.00 | 10.00 |

180 / PARKER

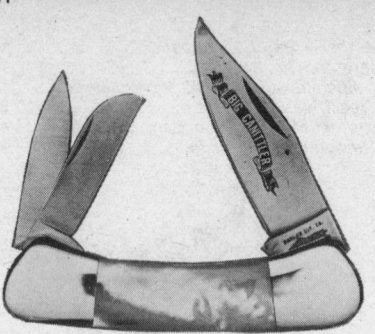

**Big Canittler**

**Big Horn**

|  | MINT | VG |
|---|---|---|
| ☐ **Big Smoky,** *Metal Survival, 11⅞ inches.* | 35.00 | 17.50 |
| ☐ **Bird and Trout Knife,** *Parker Skinner Micarta, 6 inches.* | 12.00 | 6.00 |
| ☐ **Black Beauty,** *Disc., 1,200 released, Metal with etched blade, 7¼ inches.* | 35.00 | 17.50 |

PARKER / 181

**Big Lou**

|  | MINT | VG |
|---|---|---|
| ☐ **Black Beauty,** *Disc., 4,800 released, Not Etched, 7¼ inches*. | 30.00 | 15.00 |
| ☐ **Bobcat,** *Genuine Indian Stag, 3 inches.* | 20.00 | 10.00 |
| ☐ **Bobcat,** *Sandalwood, 3 inches.* | 10.00 | 5.00 |
| ☐ **Bobcat,** *Smoothbone, 3 inches.* | 12.00 | 6.00 |
| ☐ **Boothill,** *Abalone Pearl, 2 inches.* | 20.00 | 10.00 |
| ☐ **Boothill,** *Mother of Pearl, 2 inches.* | 20.00 | 10.00 |
| ☐ **Born Leaders,** *All Metal, Etched, 4 inches.* | 18.00 | 9.00 |
| ☐ **Brahma,** *2,400 released, Genuine Stag, Disc., 4 inches.* | 35.00 | 17.50 |
| ☐ **Brahma,** *Imitation Jade, 4 inches.* | 16.00 | 8.00 |
| ☐ **Brahma,** *Imitation Tortoise Shell, 4 inches.* | 16.00 | 8.00 |
| ☐ **Brahma,** *Sandalwood, 4 inches.* | 16.00 | 8.00 |
| ☐ **Brahma,** *Smoothbone, 4 inches.* | 20.00 | 10.00 |
| ☐ **Brass Novelty,** *12 different varieties, 2½ to 3 inches.* | 9.00 | 8.00 |
| ☐ **Bream,** *Disc., 600 released, Mother of Pearl, 2⅞ inches.* | 35.00 | 17.50 |
| ☐ **Buckskinner,** *Pakkawood, 7½ inches.* | 22.00 | 11.00 |
| ☐ **Buckskinner,** *Smoothbone, 7½ inches.* | 25.00 | 12.50 |
| ☐ **Bull,** *2,400 released, Genuine Stag, Disc., 3⅜ inches.* | 30.00 | 15.00 |
| ☐ **Bull,** *Smoothbone, 3⅜ inches.* | 18.00 | 9.00 |
| ☐ **Bulldog,** *Metal Fleur-De-Lis, 2⁷⁄₁₆ inches.* | 11.00 | 5.50 |

## 182 / PARKER

|  | MINT | VG |
|---|---|---|
| ☐ **Bullet,** 1,200 released, 4 different handles, Christmas Tree, Disc., 3½ inches. | 20.00 | 10.00 |
| ☐ **Bullet,** *Engraved, 300 released, Christmas - 1982, Mother of Pearl, 3½ inches.* | 120.00 | 60.00 |
| ☐ **Bullet,** 6,000 released, Pickbone, Disc., 3½ inches. | 22.00 | 11.00 |
| ☐ **Bullet,** *Smoothbone, 3½ inches.* | 20.00 | 10.00 |
| ☐ **Buzztail,** *Disc., 3,600 released, Genuine Stag, 3½ inches.* | 25.00 | 12.50 |

**Buzztail**

|  |  |  |
|---|---|---|
| ☐ **Celebrated Dirk,** 2,400 released, Mother of Pearl, Disc., 4 inches. | 90.00 | 45.00 |
| ☐ **Chattanooga Coca Cola,** *Mother of Pearl, 3 inches.* | 25.00 | 12.50 |
| ☐ **Chickamauga,** 1,200 released, Mother of Pearl, 4 inches. | 40.00 | 20.00 |
| ☐ **Chickamauga,** *Smoothbone, 4 inches.* | 21.00 | 10.50 |
| ☐ **Chinchilla,** *Black Moroccan, 2¾ inches.* | 6.00 | 3.00 |
| ☐ **Chinchilla,** *Brown Moroccan, 2¾ inches.* | 6.00 | 3.00 |
| ☐ **Chinchilla,** *All Stainless, 2¾ inches.* | 6.00 | 3.00 |
| ☐ **Colt,** *Abalone, 2³⁄₁₆ inches.* | 24.00 | 12.00 |
| ☐ **Colt,** *Black Pakkawood, 2³⁄₁₆ inches.* | 10.00 | 5.00 |
| ☐ **Colt,** 4 different varieties, 1,200 each released, Christmas Tree, 2³⁄₁₆ inches. | 12.00 | 6.00 |

PARKER / 183

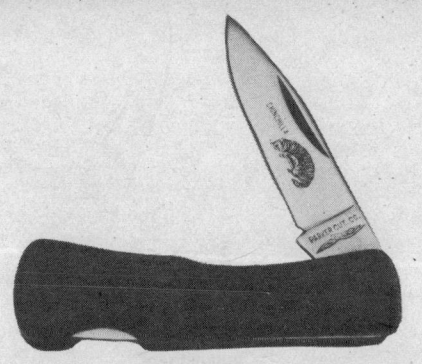

**Chinchilla**

|  | MINT | VG |
|---|---|---|
| ☐ **Colt,** *Imitation Pearl, 2 3/16 inches.* | 10.00 | 5.00 |
| ☐ **Colt,** *6,000 released, Micarta Brown and Green, Disc., 2 3/16 inches.* | 12.00 | 6.00 |
| ☐ **Colt,** *Mother of Pearl, 2 3/16 inches.* | 24.00 | 12.00 |
| ☐ **Colt,** *Sandalwood, 2 3/16 inches.* | 10.00 | 5.00 |
| ☐ **Colt,** *Smoothbone, 2 3/16 inches.* | 12.00 | 6.00 |
| ☐ **Conquistador,** *Disc., 200 released, Abalone, 5 1/4 inches.* | 100.00 | 50.00 |
| ☐ **Conquistador,** *200 released, Black Pearl, 5 1/4 inches.* | 100.00 | 50.00 |
| ☐ **Conquistador,** *200 released, Mother of Pearl, 5 1/4 inches.* | 100.00 | 50.00 |
| ☐ **Countess,** *Mother of Pearl, 2 1/4 inches.* | 20.00 | 10.00 |
| ☐ **Country Doctor,** *1,200 released, Abalone, Disc., 3 1/4 inches.* | 35.00 | 17.50 |
| ☐ **Country Doctor,** *1,200 released, Genuine Stag, Disc., 3 1/4 inches.* | 30.00 | 15.00 |
| ☐ **Country Doctor,** *1,200 released, Mother of Pearl, Disc., 3 1/4 inches.* | 35.00 | 17.50 |
| ☐ **Country Doctor,** *Pickbone, 3 1/4 inches.* | 20.00 | 10.00 |
| ☐ **Country Doctor,** *Smoothbone, 3 1/4 inches.* | 20.00 | 10.00 |
| ☐ **Coyote,** *Smoothbone, 3 3/4 inches.* | 20.00 | 10.00 |
| ☐ **Cub,** *Disc., 3,600 released, Pickbone, 3 1/8 inches.* | 20.00 | 10.00 |

184 / PARKER

**Conquistador**

| | MINT | VG |
|---|---|---|
| ☐ **Cub,** *Smoothbone, 3⅛ inches.* | 20.00 | 10.00 |

**Cub**

PARKER / 185

| | MINT | VG |
|---|---|---|
| ☐ **Desperado,** *1,200 released, Mother of Pearl, Disc., 4 inches.* | 45.00 | 22.50 |
| ☐ **Desperado,** *Smoothbone, 4 inches.* | 21.00 | 10.50 |
| ☐ **Doc's Whittlin,** *Smoothbone, 3⅞ inches.* | 20.00 | 10.00 |
| ☐ **Duchess Set,** *1,000 released, Six Knives in box, 2 inches.* | 120.00 | 60.00 |
| ☐ **Dugout,** *Disc., 1,200 released, Ebony Wood, 3⅛ inches.* | 18.00 | 9.00 |
| ☐ **Dugout,** *Disc., 2,400 released, Imitation Pearl, 3⅛ inches.* | 18.00 | 9.00 |
| ☐ **Dugout,** *Disc., 2,400 released, Japanese Ivory, 3⅛ inches.* | 18.00 | 9.00 |
| ☐ **Dugout,** *Disc., 3,600 released, Sandalwood, 3⅛ inches.* | 18.00 | 9.00 |
| ☐ **Dugout,** *Disc., 7,200 released, Smoothwood, 3⅛ inches.* | 21.00 | 10.50 |
| ☐ **Eagle Beak,** *Abalone, 1½ inches.* | 22.00 | 11.00 |
| ☐ **Eagle Beak,** *Mother of Pearl, 1½ inches.* | 22.00 | 11.00 |
| ☐ **Eagle Coffin,** *Metal, 3¾ inches.* | 20.00 | 10.00 |
| ☐ **Eagle Improved Muskrat,** *Genuine Stag, 4 inches.* | 35.00 | 17.50 |
| ☐ **Eagle Improved Musrat,** *300 released, Mother of Pearl, 4 inches.* | 50.00 | 25.00 |
| ☐ **Eagle Improved Muskrat,** *Pick and Smoothbone, 4 inches.* | 22.00 | 11.00 |
| ☐ **Eagle Razor,** *Smoothbone, 3 inches.* | 13.00 | 6.50 |
| ☐ **Eagle Skinner I,** *Disc., 1,200 released, Genuine Stag, 6¾ inches.* | 35.00 | 17.50 |
| ☐ **Eagle Skinner II,** *Disc., 1,200 released, Genuine Stag, 7 inches.* | 35.00 | 17.50 |
| ☐ **Eagle Skinner III,** *Smoothbone, 5 inches.* | 25.00 | 12.50 |
| ☐ **Eagle Skinner IV,** *Genuine Stag, 5½ inches.* | 27.00 | 13.50 |
| ☐ **Eagle Pocket Skinner,** *Smoothbone, 4½ inches.* | 23.00 | 11.50 |
| ☐ **Eaglet,** *Smoothbone, 3 inches.* | 13.00 | 6.50 |
| ☐ **Easylock,** *Disc., 1,200 released, Smoothbone, 3½ inches.* | 35.00 | 17.50 |
| ☐ **El Diablo,** *Genuine Stag, 4 inches.* | 50.00 | 25.00 |
| ☐ **El Diablo,** *Pickbone, 4 inches.* | 35.00 | 17.50 |
| ☐ **El Diablo,** *Smoothbone, 4 inches.* | 35.00 | 17.50 |
| ☐ **Excalibur,** *Disc., 200 released, Abalone, 4⅝ inches.* | 150.00 | 75.00 |
| ☐ **Excalibur,** *Disc., 1,000 released, Black Pearl, 4⅝ inches.* | 120.00 | 60.00 |

| | | MINT | VG |
|---|---|---|---|
| ☐ | **Excalibur,** *Disc., 200 released, Mother of Pearl, 4⅝ inches.* | 150.00 | 75.00 |

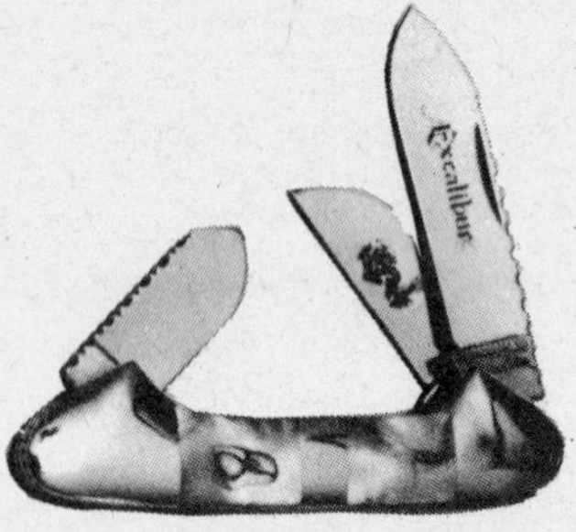


**Excalibur**

| | | MINT | VG |
|---|---|---|---|
| ☐ | **Filet I,** *Herculon, 7⅝ inches.* | 9.00 | 4.50 |
| ☐ | **Filet II,** *Herculon, 7⅝ inches.* | 8.00 | 4.00 |
| ☐ | **Filly,** *Smoothbone, 2⅛ inches.* | 11.00 | 5.50 |
| ☐ | **First Monday,** *Genuine Stag, 3¾ inches.* | 30.00 | 15.00 |
| ☐ | **First Monday,** *Mother of Pearl, 3¾ inches.* | 40.00 | 20.00 |
| ☐ | **First Monday,** *Disc., 1,200 released, Pickbone, 3¾ inches.* | 25.00 | 12.50 |
| ☐ | **First Monday,** *Smoothbone, 3¾ inches.* | 20.00 | 10.00 |
| ☐ | **Gentleman - 2 Bl,** *All Metal, 2¼ inches.* | 9.00 | 4.50 |
| ☐ | **Gentleman - 3 Bl,** *All Metal, 2¼ inches.* | 12.00 | 6.00 |
| ☐ | **Gentleman - 3 Bl,** *Mother of Pearl, 2¼ inches.* | 30.00 | 15.00 |
| ☐ | **Gentleman - 6 Bl,** *All Metal, 2¼ inches.* | 17.00 | 8.50 |
| ☐ | **Gentleman Fancy,** *Wood Insert, 2¾ inches.* | 12.00 | 6.00 |
| ☐ | **Gentleman Stock,** *Smoothbone, 3¼ inches.* | 16.00 | 8.00 |
| ☐ | **Gettysburg,** *1,200 released, Mother of Pearl, 3⅞ inches.* | 40.00 | 20.00 |
| ☐ | **Gettysburg,** *Smoothbone, 3⅞ inches.* | 20.00 | 10.00 |
| ☐ | **Golden Eagle,** *1,200 released, Micarta, Disc., 4 inches.* | 30.00 | 15.00 |
| ☐ | **Golden Eagle,** *Smoothbone, 4 inches.* | 27.00 | 13.50 |
| ☐ | **Great Conflict Set,** *400 released, 4 Whittlers.* | 150.00 | 75.00 |
| ☐ | **Gone With Wind,** *200 released, Abalone, 3⅞ inches.* | 120.00 | 60.00 |

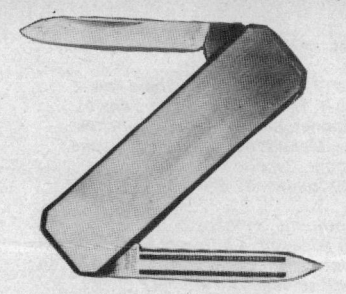

**Gentleman - 2 Blade**

|  | MINT | VG |
|---|---|---|
| ☐ **Gone With Wind,** *200 released, Black Pearl, 3⅞ inches.* | 120.00 | 60.00 |
| ☐ **Gone With Wind,** *200 released, Mother of Pearl, 3⅞ inches.* | 120.00 | 60.00 |
| ☐ **Gray Ghost,** *Graystone, 3⅞ inches.* | 22.00 | 11.00 |
| ☐ **Gray Ghost,** *Imitation Tortoise Shell, 3⅞ inches.* | 20.00 | 10.00 |
| ☐ **Gray Ghost,** *Smoothbone, 3⅞ inches.* | 21.00 | 10.50 |
| ☐ **Gunfighter 1,** *1,200 released, three knives in display.* | 80.00 | 40.00 |
| ☐ **Gunfighter 2,** *1,200 released, three knives in display.* | 80.00 | 40.00 |
| ☐ **Gunfighter 3,** *1,200 released, three knives in display.* | 60.00 | 30.00 |
| ☐ **Gunfighter 4,** *1,200 released, three knives in display.* | 50.00 | 25.00 |
| ☐ **Hercules,** *200 released, Abalone, 3 inches.* | 60.00 | 30.00 |
| ☐ **Hercules,** *200 released, Black Pearl, 3 inches.* | 60.00 | 30.00 |
| ☐ **Hercules,** *200 released, Mother of Pearl, 3 inches.* | 60.00 | 30.00 |
| ☐ **Hillbilly,** *All Metal, 4½ inches.* | 30.00 | 15.00 |
| ☐ **Hunter Pride,** *Disc., 1,200 released, Japanese Ivory, 3 inches.* | 24.00 | 12.00 |
| ☐ **Hunter,** *Genuine Stag, 5¼ inches.* | 40.00 | 20.00 |
| ☐ **Hunter I,** *Smoothbone Etched, 5¼ inches.* | 30.00 | 15.00 |
| ☐ **Hunter II,** *Smoothbone No Etch, 5¼ inches.* | 27.00 | 13.50 |
| ☐ **Husky,** *Genuine Stag, 3 inches.* | 23.00 | 11.50 |
| ☐ **Husky,** *Smoothbone, 3 inches.* | 18.00 | 9.00 |

## 188 / PARKER

|  | MINT | VG |
|---|---|---|
| ☐ **Indian Series III,** *1,200 released, three knives bone.* | 60.00 | 30.00 |
| ☐ **Indian Series IV,** *1,200 released, three knives* | 50.00 | 25.00 |
| ☐ **Indian Series V,** *1,200 released, three knives.* | 50.00 | 25.00 |
| ☐ **Invincible Skinner,** *Smoothbone, 3¾ inches.* | 23.00 | 11.50 |
| ☐ **Jaquar,** *Disc., Metal Wood Insert, 3¼ inches.* | 20.00 | 10.00 |
| ☐ **Kayak,** *Pickbone, 3 inches.* | 17.00 | 8.50 |
| ☐ **Kayak,** *1,200 released, Sandalwood, Disc., 3 inches.* | 20.00 | 10.00 |
| ☐ **Kayak,** *Smoothbone, 3 inches.* | 17.00 | 8.50 |
| ☐ **Kayak,** *1,200 released, 4 different knives, Christmas Tree, Disc., 3¾ inches.* ............ea. | 20.00 | 10.00 |
| ☐ **Kayak,** *1,200 released, Japanese Ivory, 3¾ inches.* | 23.00 | 11.50 |
| ☐ **Kayak,** *Pickbone, 3¾ inches.* | 21.00 | 10.50 |
| ☐ **Kayak,** *Smoothbone, 3¾ inches.* | 21.00 | 10.50 |
| ☐ **King of Beast,** *Pakkawood, 8¼ inches.* | 25.00 | 12.50 |
| ☐ **King of Beast,** *Smoothwood, 8¼ inches.* | 28.00 | 14.00 |
| ☐ **King Cobra,** *Disc., 600 released, Abalone, 2½ inches.* | 24.00 | 12.00 |
| ☐ **King Cobra,** *Disc., 12,000 released, Japanese Ivory, 2½ inches.* | 9.00 | 4.50 |
| ☐ **King Cobra,** *Disc., 36,000 released, Sandalwood, 2½ inches.* | 9.00 | 4.50 |
| ☐ **King of the Woods,** *3,600 released, White Delrin, Disc., 3½ inches.* | 20.00 | 10.00 |
| ☐ **K-236,** *Smoothbone, 4¼ inches.* | 30.00 | 15.00 |
| ☐ **K-344,** *Disc., 2,400 released, Smoothbone, 3⅞ inches.* | 24.00 | 12.00 |
| ☐ **K-345,** *Disc., 2,400 released, Smoothbone, 4 inches.* | 22.00 | 11.00 |
| ☐ **K-355,** *Smoothbone, 7⅞ inches.* | 30.00 | 15.00 |
| ☐ **K-401 Clasp,** *1,000 released, Signature, Smoothbone, 5 inches.* | 35.00 | 17.50 |
| ☐ **K-234,** *Disc., 3,600 released, Genuine Stag, 4 inches.* | 29.00 | 14.50 |
| ☐ **K-832,** *Disc., 3,600 released, Genuine Stag, 3 inches.* | 35.00 | 17.50 |
| ☐ **Knife Ax Combo,** *600 released, Pickbone, 10½ inches.* | 80.00 | 40.00 |
| ☐ **Knife Ax Combo,** *600 released, Second Cut Stag, 10½ inches.* | 90.00 | 45.00 |

|  | MINT | VG |
|---|---|---|
| ☐ **Knife Ax Combo,** *600 released, Smoothbone, 10½ inches.* | 80.00 | 40.00 |
| ☐ **Knife Ax Combo,** *600 released, Tiger Micarta, 10½ inches.* | 80.00 | 40.00 |
| ☐ **Leopard,** *600 released, Abalone, Disc., 3¾ inches.* | 45.00 | 22.50 |
| ☐ **Leopard,** *1,200 released, 4 different knives, Christmas Tree, Disc., 3¾ inches.* | 22.00 | 11.00 |
| ☐ **Leopard,** *600 released, Black Handles, Abalone Eagle Inlay, Disc., 3¾ inches.* | 65.00 | 32.50 |
| ☐ **Leopard,** *600 released, Mother of Pearl, Full, 3¾ inches.* | 60.00 | 30.00 |
| ☐ **Leopard,** *600 released, Mother of Pearl, Divided Handle, 3¾ inches.* | 45.00 | 22.50 |
| ☐ **Leopard,** *Pickbone, 3¾ inches.* | 21.00 | 10.50 |
| ☐ **Leopard,** *Smoothbone, 3¾ inches.* | 21.00 | 10.50 |
| ☐ **Lipstick,** *All Metal, 2 inches.* | 10.00 | 5.00 |
| ☐ **Little Bandit,** *Genuine Stag, 4 inches.* | 28.00 | 14.00 |
| ☐ **Little Bandit,** *Long Groove Pick, 4 inches.* | 22.00 | 11.00 |
| ☐ **Little Bandit,** *Pickbone, 4 inches.* | 22.00 | 11.00 |
| ☐ **Little Bandit,** *Smoothbone, 4 inches.* | 22.00 | 11.00 |
| ☐ **Little Bandit,** *White Micarta, 4 inches.* | 22.00 | 11.00 |
| ☐ **Little Canittler,** *Disc., 1,200 released, Christmas Tree, 2½ inches.* | 20.00 | 10.00 |
| ☐ **Little Canittler,** *Disc., 1,200 released, Mother of Pearl, 2½ inches.* | 35.00 | 17.50 |
| ☐ **Little Canittler,** *Disc., 1,200 released, Smoothbone, 2½ inches.* | 20.00 | 10.00 |
| ☐ **Little Doagie,** *Genuine Stag, 2¾ inches.* | 23.00 | 11.50 |
| ☐ **Little Doagie,** *1,200 released, Mother of Pearl, 2¾ inches.* | 27.00 | 13.50 |
| ☐ **Little Doagie,** *Smoothbone, 2¾ inches.* | 14.00 | 7.00 |
| ☐ **Little Eagle,** *Disc., 3,600 released, Genuine Stag, 3¼ inches.* | 26.00 | 13.00 |
| ☐ **Little Eagle,** *Disc., 3,600 released, Smoothbone, 3¼ inches.* | 19.00 | 9.50 |
| ☐ **Little Grizzly,** *4,800 released, Pakkawood, Disc., 4⅛ inches.* | 22.00 | 11.00 |
| ☐ **Little Grizzly,** *Smoothbone, 4⅛ inches.* | 22.00 | 11.00 |
| ☐ **Little Hunter,** *Micarta, 5½ inches.* | 20.00 | 10.00 |
| ☐ **Little John Set,** *1,200 released, 4 knives in Display, 1¾ inches.* | 60.00 | 30.00 |

## 190 / PARKER

|  | MINT | VG |
|---|---|---|
| ☐ **Little Mink,** 1,200 released, Japanese Ivory, Disc., 2⅞ inches. | 15.00 | 7.50 |
| ☐ **Little Mink,** Smoothbone, 2⅞ inches. | 10.00 | 5.00 |
| ☐ **Little Mustang,** 2,400 released, Abalone, 2½ inches. | 28.00 | 14.00 |
| ☐ **Little Mustang,** 1,200 released, 4 different knives, Christmas Tree, Disc., 2½ inches. | 15.00 | 7.50 |
| ☐ **Little Mustang,** Imitation Pearl, 2½ inches. | 14.00 | 7.00 |
| ☐ **Little Mustang,** 1,200 each released, Micarta, Green and Brown, 2½ inches. | 12.00 | 6.00 |
| ☐ **Little Mustang,** 2,400 released, Mother of Pearl, 2½ inches. | 28.00 | 14.00 |
| ☐ **Little Mustang,** Pakkawood, 2½ inches. | 14.00 | 7.00 |
| ☐ **Little Mustang,** Sandalwood, 2½ inches. | 14.00 | 7.00 |
| ☐ **Little Mustang,** Smoothbone, 2½ inches. | 14.00 | 7.00 |
| ☐ **Little Pillbuster Set,** 1,000 released, 7 knives Serial Numbered. | 100.00 | 50.00 |
| ☐ **Little Pillbuster,** 600 released, Mother of Pearl, 3⅝ inches. | 35.00 | 17.50 |
| ☐ **Little Pillbuster,** Pickbone, 3⅝ inches. | 19.00 | 9.50 |
| ☐ **Little Pillbuster,** Smoothbone, 3⅝ inches. | 19.00 | 9.50 |
| ☐ **Little Smoky,** All Metal, 7 inches. | 19.00 | 9.50 |
| ☐ **Locking Bandit,** Disc., 2,400 released, Christmas Tree, 4 inches. | 24.00 | 12.00 |
| ☐ **Locking Bandit,** Disc., 4,800 released, Smoothbone, 4 inches. | 35.00 | 7.50 |
| ☐ **Longhorn,** 3,600 released, Japanese Ivory, Disc., 3½ inches. | 20.00 | 10.00 |
| ☐ **Longhorn,** Smoothbone, 3½ inches. | 23.00 | 11.50 |
| ☐ **Mallard,** Disc., 2,400 released, Genuine Stag, 3½ inches. | 35.00 | 17.50 |
| ☐ **Maverick,** Disc., 6,000 released, Smoothbone, 3¼ inches. | 25.00 | 12.50 |
| ☐ **Maverick II,** Disc., 1,200 released, Smoothbone, 4 inches. | 40.00 | 20.00 |
| ☐ **Miniature Bowie,** Abalone, 2 inches. | 17.00 | 8.50 |
| ☐ **Miniature Bowie,** Black Pearl, 2 inches. | 17.00 | 8.50 |
| ☐ **Miniature Bowie,** Imitation Pearl, 2 inches. | 11.00 | 5.50 |
| ☐ **Miniature Bowie,** Mother of Pearl, 2 inches. | 17.00 | 8.50 |
| ☐ **Miniature Bowie,** Smoothbone, 2 inches. | 12.00 | 6.00 |
| ☐ **Miniature-Mini-Lock,** Abalone, 1½ inches. | 17.00 | 8.50 |
| ☐ **Miniature-Mini-Lock,** Black Pearl, 1½ inches. | 17.00 | 8.50 |
| ☐ **Miniature-Mini-Lock,** Mother of Pearl, 1½ inches | 17.00 | 8.50 |

PARKER / 191

| | MINT | VG |
|---|---|---|
| ☐ **Money Clip,** *Stainless Steel, 2¼ inches.* | 9.00 | 4.50 |
| ☐ **Muskrat,** *1,000 released, Genuine Stag, Disc., 4 inches.* | 35.00 | 17.50 |
| ☐ **Muskrat,** *Pickbone, Serrated Blade, 4 inches.* | 19.00 | 9.50 |
| ☐ **Muskrat,** *Smoothbone, 4 inches.* | 19.00 | 9.50 |
| ☐ **Mustang,** *1,200 each released, Christmas Tree, Disc., 3½ inches.* | 20.00 | 10.00 |
| ☐ **Mustang,** *Ebonite, Black, 4 inches.* | 12.00 | 6.00 |

**Mustang**

| | | |
|---|---|---|
| ☐ **Mustang,** *Pickbone, Green, 3½ inches.* | 25.00 | 12.50 |
| ☐ **Mustang,** *Pickbone, Red, 3½ inches.* | 20.00 | 10.00 |
| ☐ **Mustang,** *Smoothbone, 3½ inches.* | 20.00 | 10.00 |
| ☐ **Mustang,** *White Delrin, 3½ inches.* | 18.00 | 9.00 |
| ☐ **Nazi Whittler,** *Nickel Silver, 3¾ inches.* | 20.00 | 10.00 |
| ☐ **Nehi Knife,** *Nickel Silver, 3 inches.* | 12.00 | 6.00 |
| ☐ **Old Remington,** *3,000 released, Pickbone, Disc., 3¾ inches.* | 40.00 | 20.00 |
| ☐ **Old Remington,** *3,000 released, Smoothbone, Disc., 3¾ inches.* | 40.00 | 20.00 |
| ☐ **Old Trapper,** *600 released, Genuine Stag, 3¼ inches.* | 30.00 | 15.00 |
| ☐ **Old Trapper,** *Pickbone, 3¼ inches.* | 17.00 | 8.50 |
| ☐ **Old Trapper,** *Smoothbone, 3¼ inches.* | 17.00 | 8.50 |
| ☐ **One Arm Pillbuster,** *Smoothbone 1 Blade, 3⅞ inches.* | 18.00 | 9.00 |

192 / PARKER

**One Arm Pillbuster**

|  | MINT | VG |
|---|---|---|
| ☐ **One Arm Pillbuster,** *Locking Blade, 1 Blade, 3⅞ inches.* | 21.00 | 10.50 |
| ☐ **One Arm Pillbuster,** *Disc., 1,200 released, 4 different knives, 2 Blade Christmas Tree, 3⅞ inches.* ............ ea. | 23.00 | 11.50 |
| ☐ **One Arm Pillbuster,** *Genuine Stag, 3⅞ inches.* | 30.00 | 15.00 |
| ☐ **One Arm Pillbuster,** *Disc., 1,200 released, Japanese Ivory, 3⅞ inches.* | 21.00 | 10.50 |
| ☐ **One Arm Pillbuster,** *2,400 released, Mother of Pearl, 3⅞ inches.* | 45.00 | 22.50 |
| ☐ **One Arm Pillbuster,** *Pickbone, 3⅞ inches.* | 24.00 | 12.00 |
| ☐ **One Arm Pillbuster,** *Smoothbone, 3⅞ inches.* | 24.00 | 12.00 |
| ☐ **Packrat,** *Smoothbone, 3 inches.* | 19.00 | 9.50 |
| ☐ **Packrat Custom,** *200 released, Genuine Stag, 9¼ inches.* | 60.00 | 30.00 |
| ☐ **Packrat Custom,** *200 released, Crown Stag, 9¼ inches.* | 75.00 | 37.50 |
| ☐ **Packrat Custom,** *400 released, Micarta, Signed Ichiro, 9¼ inches.* | 60.00 | 30.00 |
| ☐ **Parker Gem,** *Abalone, 3½ inches.* | 50.00 | 25.00 |
| ☐ **Parker Gem,** *Mother of Pearl, 3½ inches.* | 50.00 | 25.00 |
| ☐ **Parker Christmas Knife - 1979,** *1,000 released, Mother of Pearl, 3¾ inches.* | 75.00 | 37.50 |
| ☐ **Parker Christmas Knife - 1980,** *1,800 released, Surgical Steel, 3 inches.* | 30.00 | 15.00 |
| ☐ **Parker Christmas Knife - 1980,** *100 released, Mother of Pearl, Whittler, 4 inches.* | 100.00 | 50.00 |

## PARKER / 193

| | MINT | VG |
|---|---|---|
| ☐ **Parker Christmas Knife - 1981,** *1,000 released, Stag Clasp Knife, 5½ inches.* | 100.00 | 50.00 |
| ☐ **Parker Christmas Knife - 1982,** *2,000 released, Smoothbone, Worker Bolster, 3½ inches.* | 40.00 | 20.00 |
| ☐ **Parker Custom,** *Graystone, 4¼ inches.* | 45.00 | 22.50 |
| ☐ **Parker Custom,** *Smoothbone, 4¼ inches.* | 45.00 | 22.50 |
| ☐ **Pigeon Forge Fats,** *Disc., 1,200 released, Abalone, 2¼ inches.* | 20.00 | 10.00 |
| ☐ **Pigeon Forge Fats,** *Disc., 1,200 released, Mother of Pearl, 2¼ inches.* | 20.00 | 10.00 |
| ☐ **Pigeon Forge Fats,** *Disc., Smoothbone, 2¼ inches.* | 14.00 | 7.00 |
| ☐ **Parker Pen,** *All Surgical, 4¼ inches.* | 18.00 | 9.00 |
| ☐ **Parker Pen Locking,** *All Surgical, 4½ inches.* | 20.00 | 10.00 |
| ☐ **Porky,** *Smoothbone, 2⅜ inches.* | 14.00 | 7.00 |
| ☐ **Princess Set,** *1,000 released, Six Knives in Case, 2 inches.* | 120.00 | 60.00 |
| ☐ **Python,** *Clear Gold Celluloid, 2⅜ inches.* | 8.00 | 4.00 |
| ☐ **Railsplitter I,** *Smoothbone, 3¼ inches.* | 22.00 | 11.00 |
| ☐ **Railsplitter II,** *600 released, Mother of Pearl, 3¼ inches.* | 40.00 | 20.00 |
| ☐ **Railsplitter II,** *Smoothbone, 3¼ inches.* | 22.00 | 11.00 |
| ☐ **Redneck,** *Brass Etched, 4 inches.* | 20.00 | 10.00 |
| ☐ **Redneck II,** *Stainless Etched, 3¾ inches.* | 18.00 | 9.00 |
| ☐ **Red Tail Hawk,** *Smoothbone, 3⅞ inches.* | 20.00 | 10.00 |
| ☐ **Remember The Alamo,** *Disc., 600 released, Mother of Pearl, 3¼ inches.* | 45.00 | 22.50 |
| ☐ **Remember The Alamo,** *Disc., 3,600 released, Smoothbone, 3¼ inches.* | 25.00 | 12.50 |
| ☐ **Remington Derringer,** *Antique Copper on Brass, 5 inches.* | 17.00 | 8.50 |
| ☐ **Rough and Ready,** *Pickbone, 3⅜ inches.* | 19.00 | 9.50 |
| ☐ **Rough and Ready,** *Smoothbone, 3⅜ inches.* | 19.00 | 9.50 |
| ☐ **Saturday Night Special,** *1,000 released, Set of 9 in Case, 5 inches.* | 190.00 | 95.00 |
| ☐ **Saturday Night Special,** *Disc., 1,200 each released, 4 different knives, Christmas Tree, 5 inches.* | 25.00 | 12.50 |
| ☐ **Saturday Night Special,** *600 released, Abalone and Pearl, 5 inches.* | 50.00 | 25.00 |
| ☐ **Saturday Night Special,** *Genuine Stag, 5 inches.* | 28.00 | 14.00 |
| ☐ **Saturday Night Special,** *600 released, Mother of Pearl, 5 inches.* | 45.00 | 22.50 |
| ☐ **Saturday Night Special,** *Pickbone, 5 inches.* | 20.00 | 10.00 |

| | MINT | VG |
|---|---|---|
| ☐ **Saturday Night Special,** *Smoothbone, 5 inches.* | 20.00 | 10.00 |
| ☐ **Scorpion,** *Disc., 1,200 released, Mother of Pearl, 2¼ inches.* | 30.00 | 15.00 |
| ☐ **Scorpion,** *Disc., Smoothbone, 2¼ inches.* | 16.00 | 8.00 |
| ☐ **Scout,** *Smoothbone, 3 inches.* | 15.00 | 7.50 |
| ☐ **Shiloh,** *Imitation Jade, 4 inches.* | 29.00 | 14.50 |
| ☐ **Shiloh,** *Smoothbone, 4 inches.* | 32.00 | 16.00 |
| ☐ **Sidewinder,** *Japanese Ivory, 3 inches.* | 16.00 | 8.00 |
| ☐ **Sidewinder,** *Smoothbone, 3 inches.* | 20.00 | 10.00 |
| ☐ **Signature Skinner,** *All Metal, 9 inches.* | 20.00 | 10.00 |
| ☐ **Silver Fox,** *All Surgical Steel, 3⅜ inches.* | 15.00 | 7.50 |
| ☐ **Smoky Mountain Skeleton,** *All Surgical Steel, 7 inches.* | 15.00 | 7.50 |
| ☐ **Smoky Mountain Slim,** *All Metal, 7¼ inches.* | 16.00 | 8.00 |
| ☐ **Smoky Mountain Survivor,** *All Metal, 9½ inches.* | 29.00 | 14.50 |
| ☐ **Smoky Mountain Toothpick,** *All Metal, 9½ inches.* | 22.00 | 11.00 |
| ☐ **Smoky Mountain Ultra Lite,** *All Metal, 9½ inches.* | 19.00 | 9.50 |
| ☐ **Southern Belle,** *Mother of Pearl, 2½ inches.* | 20.00 | 10.00 |
| ☐ **Sowbelly I,** *Pickbone, 4¼ inches.* | 22.00 | 11.00 |
| ☐ **Sowbelly I,** *Smoothbone, 4¼ inches.* | 22.00 | 11.00 |
| ☐ **Sowbelly III,** *Pickbone, 4¼ inches.* | 26.00 | 13.00 |
| ☐ **Sowbelly III,** *Smoothbone, 4¼ inches.* | 26.00 | 13.00 |
| ☐ **Sowbelly V,** *Pickbone, 4¼ inches.* | 35.00 | 17.50 |
| ☐ **Sowbelly V,** *Second Cut, 4¼ inches.* | 40.00 | 20.00 |
| ☐ **Sowbelly V,** *Smoothbone, 4¼ inches.* | 35.00 | 17.50 |
| ☐ **Space Shuttle,** *6,000 released, Delrin.* | 20.00 | 10.00 |
| ☐ **Space Shuttle,** *600 released, Black Pearl.* | 40.00 | 20.00 |
| ☐ **Space Shuttle,** *600 released, Mother of Pearl.* | 40.00 | 20.00 |
| ☐ **Stallion,** *Disc., 3,600 released, Pickbone, 4 inches.* | 18.00 | 9.00 |
| ☐ **Stallion,** *Disc., 7,200 released, Smoothbone, 4 inches.* | 18.00 | 9.00 |
| ☐ **Stock Knife,** *Genuine Stag, 4 inches.* | 30.00 | 15.00 |
| ☐ **Stock Knife,** *Pickbone, 4 inches.* | 20.00 | 10.00 |
| ☐ **Stock Knife,** *Smoothbone, 4 inches.* | 20.00 | 10.00 |
| ☐ **Survival I,** *Survival Knife, 9¼ inches.* | 12.00 | 6.00 |
| ☐ **Survival Bowie,** *All Metal, 10 inches.* | 29.00 | 14.50 |
| ☐ **Survival Skinner,** *All Metal, 9½ inches.* | 27.00 | 13.50 |
| ☐ **Survival Tool Large,** *All Metal, 2¾ inches.* | 12.00 | 6.00 |
| ☐ **Survival Tool Small,** *All Metal, 2 inches.* | 8.00 | 4.00 |

PARKER / 195

| | MINT | VG |
|---|---|---|
| ☐ **Survivor,** 7,200 released, Linen Micarta, 3¾ inches. | 15.00 | 7.50 |
| ☐ **Tadpole,** Black Pearl, 2¼ inches. | 19.00 | 9.50 |
| ☐ **Tadpole,** Mother of Pearl, 2¼ inches. | 19.00 | 9.50 |
| ☐ **The Stagge,** Green Pickbone, 4¼ inches. | 22.00 | 11.00 |
| ☐ **The Trapper,** Disc., 2,400 released, Genuine Stag, 4½ inches. | 40.00 | 20.00 |
| ☐ **The Trapper,** Smoothbone, 4½ inches. | 32.00 | 16.00 |
| ☐ **Throwing Knife,** 3 different knives, All Metal, 9 inches. | 16.00 | 8.00 |
| ☐ **Timber Wolf,** Pakkawood, 4 inches. | 18.00 | 9.00 |
| ☐ **Thorobred,** Disc., 4,800 released, Genuine Stag, 4 inches. | 30.00 | 15.00 |
| ☐ **Trapper I,** Pickbone, 4 inches. | 21.00 | 10.50 |
| ☐ **Trapper I,** Smoothbone, 4 inches. | 21.00 | 10.50 |
| ☐ **Trapper II,** 1,200 released, Mother of Pearl, 3½ inches. | 40.00 | 20.00 |
| ☐ **Trapper II,** Pickbone, 3½ inches. | 18.00 | 9.00 |
| ☐ **Trapper II,** Smoothbone, 3½ inches. | 18.00 | 9.00 |
| ☐ **Unique,** 1,200 released, Abalone, Disc., 2½ inches. | 28.00 | 14.00 |
| ☐ **Unique,** 1,200 released, Mother of Pearl, Disc., 2½ inches. | 28.00 | 14.00 |
| ☐ **Unique,** Smoothbone, 2½ inches. | 14.00 | 7.00 |
| ☐ **Viper,** Micarta, 3⅛ inches. | 12.00 | 6.00 |

**Viper**

196 / PARKER

|  | MINT | VG |
|---|---|---|
| ☐ **Viper,** *Smoothbone, 3⅛ inches.* | 16.00 | 8.00 |
| ☐ **Viper,** *Surgical Steel, 3⅛ inches.* | 14.00 | 7.00 |
| ☐ **Viper,** *Football Etchings, 3⅛ inches.* | 16.00 | 8.00 |
| ☐ **Warrior,** *Smoothbone, 4 inches.* | 19.00 | 9.50 |

**Warrior**

|  | | |
|---|---|---|
| ☐ **Wedge,** *Micarta, 7¾ inches.* | 27.00 | 13.50 |
| ☐ **Widow Maker,** *Push Dagger, All Metal, 6½ inches.* | 24.00 | 12.00 |
| ☐ **Wild Boar,** *Smoothbone, 4¼ inches.* | 18.00 | 9.00 |
| ☐ **Wildcat,** *Genuine Stag, 3¼ inches.* | 25.00 | 12.50 |
| ☐ **Wildcat,** *Disc., Imitation Pearl, 3¼ inches.* | 18.00 | 9.00 |
| ☐ **Wildcat,** *Disc., Mother of Pearl, 3¼ inches.* | 45.00 | 22.50 |
| ☐ **Wildcat,** *Pickbone, 3¼ inches.* | 20.00 | 10.00 |
| ☐ **Wildcat,** *Sandalwood, 3¼ inches.* | 18.00 | 9.00 |
| ☐ **Wildcat,** *Smoothbone, 3¼ inches.* | 20.00 | 10.00 |
| ☐ **Wolfhead,** *Smoothbone, 4¼ inches.* | 18.00 | 9.00 |
| ☐ **World Fair,** *Brass, 3 inches.* | 9.00 | 4.50 |

Parker Brothers Eagle Brand. A partnership of Mack V. Parker and James F. Parker manufacturing high quality Eagle Brand knives. Started in 1978.

|  | | |
|---|---|---|
| ☐ **Big Colt,** *Disc., 2,400 released, Micarta, 4½ inches.* | 35.00 | 17.50 |
| ☐ **Gunboat,** *Smoothbone, 4 inches.* | 22.00 | 11.00 |

PARKER / 197

|  | MINT | VG |
|---|---|---|
| ☐ **Invincible Skinner,** *Disc., 4,800 released, Smoothbone, 4 inches.* | 30.00 | 15.00 |
| ☐ **K-74,** *Disc., 7,200 released, Genuine Stag, 3½ inches.* | 30.00 | 15.00 |
| ☐ **K-115,** *Disc., 4,800 released, Genuine Stag, 5 inches.* | 40.00 | 20.00 |
| ☐ **K-116,** *Disc., 4,800 released, Genuine Stag, 4 inches.* | 35.00 | 17.50 |
| ☐ **K-118,** *Disc., 1,200 released, Genuine Stag, 4¼ inches.* | 40.00 | 20.00 |

K-118

| | | |
|---|---|---|
| ☐ **K-118,** *Disc., 1,200 released, Smoothbone, 4¼ inches.* | 35.00 | 17.50 |
| ☐ **K-119,** *Disc., 1,200 released, Genuine Stag, 5¼ inches.* | 50.00 | 25.00 |
| ☐ **K-119,** *Disc., 1,200 released, Smoothbone, 5¼ inches.* | 40.00 | 20.00 |
| ☐ **K-122,** *Disc., 2,400 released, Genuine Stag, 3¾ inches.* | 30.00 | 15.00 |
| ☐ **K-123,** *Disc., 2,400 released, Genuine Stag, 4 inches.* | 35.00 | 17.50 |
| ☐ **K-124,** *Disc., 2,400 released, Genuine Stag, 3½ inches.* | 25.00 | 12.50 |

198 / PARKER

K-122

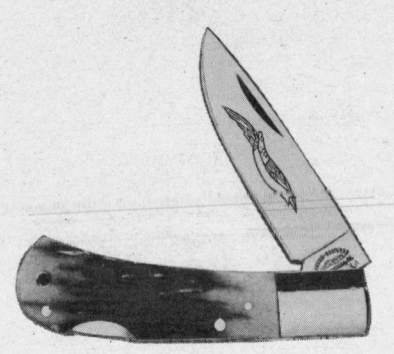

K-123

|  | MINT | VG |
|---|---|---|
| ☐ **K-126,** *Disc., 2,400 released, Genuine Stag, 3¾ inches.* | 30.00 | 15.00 |
| ☐ **K-128,** *Disc., 2,400 released, Genuine Stag, 4 inches.* | 30.00 | 15.00 |

PARKER / 199

K-124

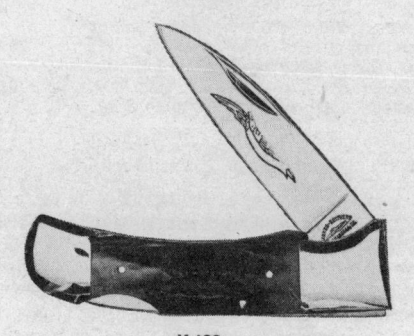

K-128

|  | MINT | VG |
|---|---|---|
| ☐ K-133, Disc., 2,400 released, Genuine Stag, 2⅞ inches. | 20.00 | 10.00 |
| ☐ K-247, Disc., 6,000 released, Genuine Stag, 3 inches. | 25.00 | 12.50 |
| ☐ K-248, Disc., 6,000 released, Genuine Stag, 3½ inches. | 30.00 | 15.00 |

## 200 / PARKER

|  | MINT | VG |
|---|---|---|
| ☐ **K-249,** Disc., 2,400 released, Genuine Stag, 4¼ inches. | 40.00 | 20.00 |
| ☐ **K-250,** Disc., 2,400 released, Genuine Stag, 5 inches. | 50.00 | 25.00 |
| ☐ **K-266,** Disc., 2,400 released, Genuine Stag, 4 inches. | 40.00 | 20.00 |
| ☐ **K-266,** Disc., 2,400 released, Genuine Stag, 5 inches. | 50.00 | 25.00 |
| ☐ **Little Colt,** Disc., 4,800 released, Micarta, 3¼ inches. | 25.00 | 12.50 |
| ☐ **Little Congress,** Disc., 1,800 released, Genuine Stag, 3⅛ inches. | 32.00 | 16.00 |
| ☐ **Little Congress,** Disc., 1,200 released, Mother of Pearl, 3⅛ inches. | 45.00 | 22.50 |
| ☐ **Little Congress,** Disc., 600 released, Pickbone, 3⅛ inches. | 30.00 | 15.00 |
| ☐ **Little Congress,** Disc., 3,600 released, Smoothbone, 3⅛ inches. | 25.00 | 12.50 |
| ☐ **Silver Fox,** Disc., 7,200 released, All Surgical Steel, 3⅜ inches. | 18.00 | 9.00 |
| ☐ **Trapper,** Disc., 3,600 released, Genuine Stag, 4 inches. | 35.00 | 17.50 |
| ☐ **Trojan,** Disc., 2,400 released, Abalone, 3 inches.. | 35.00 | 17.50 |
| ☐ **Trojan,** Disc., 4,800 released, Smoothbone, 3 inches. | 22.00 | 11.00 |

Parker & Son Trademark. 1982 was designated by the National Wildlife Federation as the "Year of the Eagle," honoring the 200th anniversary of the bald eagle as the national bird.

Eagle Brand Knives issued a very special series of knives, each etched on the blade "Year of the Eagle," featuring the new Parker & Son trademark and the rare long discontinued handle material, second cut stag.

Eagle Brand Knives donated five per cent of the net proceeds of these knives to the National Wildlife Federation and the North Carolina Wildlife Resources Commission. There is a very limited quantity available due to the shortage of the handle material.

| | | |
|---|---|---|
| ☐ **K-401,** 3,000 released, Second Cut Stag, 4⅞ inches. | 35.00 | 17.50 |

*PARKER / 201*

| | MINT | VG |
|---|---|---|
| ☐ **K-404,** *3,000 released, Second Cut Stag,* 5 inches. | 26.00 | 13.00 |
| ☐ **K-405,** *3,000 released, Second Cut Stag,* 5 inches. | 30.00 | 15.00 |
| ☐ **K-406,** *3,000 released, Second Cut Stag,* 4 inches. | 27.00 | 13.50 |
| ☐ **K-407,** *3,000 released, Second Cut Stag,* 4½ inches. | 32.00 | 16.00 |
| ☐ **K-409,** *3,000 released, Second Cut Stag,* 5 inches. | 35.00 | 17.50 |
| ☐ **K-410,** *3,000 released, Second Cut Stag,* 4½ inches. | 35.00 | 17.50 |
| ☐ **K-411,** *3,000 released, Second Cut Stag,* 3½ inches. | 26.00 | 13.00 |
| ☐ **K-412,** *3,000 released, Second Cut Stag,* 3½ inches. | 26.00 | 13.00 |
| ☐ **K-416,** *6,000 released, Second Cut Stag,* 3½ inches. | 24.00 | 12.00 |
| ☐ **K-418,** *3,000 released, Second Cut Stag,* 4¼ inches. | 35.00 | 17.50 |
| ☐ **K-419,** *3,000 released, Second Cut Stag,* 5¼ inches. | 40.00 | 20.00 |
| ☐ **K-422,** *3,000 released, Second Cut Stag,* 3½ inches. | 23.00 | 11.50 |
| ☐ **K-423,** *3,000 released, Second Cut Stag,* 4¼ inches. | 28.00 | 14.00 |
| ☐ **K-424,** *3,000 released, Second Cut Stag,* 4¾ inches. | 35.00 | 17.50 |
| ☐ **K-427,** *3,000 released, Second Cut Stag,* 4½ inches. | 45.00 | 22.50 |
| ☐ **K-431,** *6,000 released, Second Cut Stag,* 3 inches. | 20.00 | 10.00 |
| ☐ **K-443,** *3,000 released, Second Cut Stag,* 4½ inches. | 40.00 | 20.00 |
| ☐ **K-452,** *3,000 released, Second Cut Stag,* 4 inches. | 30.00 | 15.00 |
| ☐ **Set of Second Cut Stag Year of The Eagle.** *300 serial numbered sets of 19 — assembled in solid frame.* | 600.00 | 300.00 |
| ☐ **New Orleans Knife,** *Bronzed Art Handle,* 9½ inches. | 28.00 | 14.00 |

## 202 / PARKER

Parker-Imai (pronounced E-my-i). This trademark was introduced by Eagle Brand in late 1982. This trademark replaced many of the Parker Brothers Knives. Parker invested in the Imai factory, enlarged it, and instituted strict quality controls. When this line of knives was introduced, the knife buying public could not believe the value and quality they were receiving. For this reason, Parker-Imai Eagle Brand knives are highly collectible.

| | MINT | VG |
|---|---|---|
| ☐ K-47, *Genuine Stag, 4½ inches.* | 50.00 | 25.00 |
| ☐ K-74, *Second Cut Stag, 3½ inches.* | 22.00 | 11.00 |
| ☐ K-77, *Second Cut Stag, 4½ inches.* | 30.00 | 15.00 |
| ☐ K-77, *Genuine Stag, 4½ inches.* | 40.00 | 20.00 |
| ☐ K-78, *Second Cut Stag, 5¼ inches.* | 32.00 | 16.00 |
| ☐ K-78, *Genuine Stag, 5¼ inches.* | 42.00 | 21.00 |
| ☐ K-86, *Second Cut Stag, 4 inches.* | 20.00 | 10.00 |
| ☐ K-115, *Second Cut Stag, 4¾ inches.* | 27.00 | 13.50 |
| ☐ K-115, *Genuine Stag, 4¾ inches.* | 37.00 | 18.50 |
| ☐ K-116, *Second Cut Stag, 4 inches.* | 23.00 | 11.50 |
| ☐ K-116, *Genuine Stag, 4 inches.* | 33.00 | 16.50 |
| ☐ K-139, *Second Cut Stag, 5 inches.* | 30.00 | 15.00 |
| ☐ K-139, *Smoothbone, 5 inches.* | 27.00 | 13.50 |
| ☐ K-236, *Smoothbone, 4½ inches.* | 30.00 | 15.00 |
| ☐ K-247, *Genuine Stag, 3 inches.* | 25.00 | 12.50 |
| ☐ K-247, *Second Cut Stag, 3 inches.* | 22.00 | 11.00 |
| ☐ K-248, *Genuine Stag, 3½ inches.* | 30.00 | 15.00 |
| ☐ K-249, *Genuine Stag, 4¼ inches.* | 36.00 | 18.00 |
| ☐ K-249, *Second Cut Stag, 4¼ inches.* | 33.00 | 16.50 |
| ☐ K-250, *Genuine Stag, 5 inches.* | 40.00 | 20.00 |
| ☐ K-250, *Second Cut Stag, 5 inches.* | 35.00 | 17.50 |
| ☐ K-266, *Genuine Stag, 4 inches.* | 35.00 | 17.50 |
| ☐ K-266, *Second Cut Stag, 4 inches.* | 30.00 | 15.00 |
| ☐ K-267, *Genuine Stag, 5 inches.* | 40.00 | 20.00 |
| ☐ K-267, *Second Cut Stag, 5 inches.* | 35.00 | 17.50 |
| ☐ K-295 **Muskrat**, *Second Cut Stag, 4 inches.* | 23.00 | 11.50 |
| ☐ K-296 **Stock**, *Genuine Stag, 4 inches.* | 30.00 | 15.00 |
| ☐ K-296 **Stock**, *Second Cut Stag, 4 inches.* | 25.00 | 12.50 |
| ☐ K-298 **4-Blade Congress**, *Genuine Stag, 3⅛ inches.* | 30.00 | 15.00 |
| ☐ K-298 **4-Blade Congress**, *Second Cut Stag, 3⅛ inches.* | 25.00 | 12.50 |
| ☐ K-416, *Second Cut Stag, 3½ inches.* | 22.00 | 11.00 |
| ☐ K-424, *Second Cut Stag, 5 inches.* | 32.00 | 16.00 |

# REMINGTON

Remington stamped pattern numbers on the reverse side of the tang, using an R before the pattern number to indicate a pocketknife and the last digit indicated the handle material. They were:

| | | |
|---|---|---|
| 1-Redwood | 5-Pyremite | 9-Metal |
| 2-Black | 6-Genuine Stag | 0-Buffalo Horn |
| 3-Bone | 7-Ivory or White Bone | Ch-after the numbers |
| 4-Pearl | 8-Cocobolo | means a chain attached |

Three stampings were used by Remington: "Remington" stamped horizontally on the tang (this is called a "straightline"), "Remington" inside a circle with "Made in USA" around the outside and UMC also on the inside, and the "Remington" inside a circle with Made in USA around the outside without UMC. The circle was supposed to look like the end of a cartridge.

Remington's most sought after line is the knives with the shield in the shape of a bullet. These knives are scarce and command a top price.

| PATTERN NO. | MINT | VG | PATTERN NO. | MINT | VG |
|---|---|---|---|---|---|
| ☐ R-1 | 60.00 | 30.00 | ☐ R-25 | 80.00 | 40.00 |
| ☐ R-2 | 60.00 | 30.00 | ☐ R-31 | 80.00 | 40.00 |
| ☐ R-2 | 75.00 | 38.00 | ☐ R-32 | 80.00 | 40.00 |
| ☐ R-01 | 60.00 | 30.00 | ☐ R-33 | 100.00 | 50.00 |
| ☐ R-02 | 60.00 | 30.00 | ☐ R-35 | 100.00 | 50.00 |
| ☐ R-03 | 75.00 | 38.00 | ☐ R-B040 (B) | 75.00 | 38.00 |
| ☐ R-A1 | 60.00 | 30.00 | ☐ R-041 (B) | 74.00 | 38.00 |
| ☐ R-C5 | 60.00 | 30.00 | ☐ R-B43 (B) | 100.00 | 50.00 |
| ☐ R-C6 | 60.00 | 30.00 | ☐ R-B44 (B) | 100.00 | 50.00 |
| ☐ R-C7 | 55.00 | 28.00 | ☐ R-B45 (B) | 130.00 | 65.00 |
| ☐ R-C8 | 55.00 | 28.00 | ☐ R-B44W (B) | 75.00 | 38.00 |
| ☐ R-C9 | 55.00 | 28.00 | ☐ R-B46 (B) | 90.00 | 45.00 |
| ☐ R-15 (L.K.) | 100.00 | 50.00 | ☐ R-B47 (B) | 130.00 | 65.00 |
| ☐ R-015 | 75.00 | 38.00 | ☐ R-51 | 80.00 | 40.00 |
| ☐ R-17 | 45.00 | 23.00 | ☐ R-71 | 75.00 | 38.00 |
| ☐ R-21 | 80.00 | 40.00 | ☐ R-72 | 85.00 | 43.00 |
| ☐ R-21ch | 100.00 | 50.00 | ☐ R-73 | 110.00 | 55.00 |
| ☐ R-22 | 80.00 | 40.00 | ☐ R-75 | 95.00 | 48.00 |
| ☐ R-23 | 100.00 | 50.00 | ☐ R-81 | 75.00 | 38.00 |
| ☐ R-23ch | 110.00 | 55.00 | ☐ R-82 | 85.00 | 43.00 |

## 204 / REMINGTON

| PATTERN NO. | MINT | VG | PATTERN NO. | MINT | VG |
|---|---|---|---|---|---|
| ☐ R-83 | 110.00 | 55.00 | ☐ R-183 (T) | 200.00 | 100.00 |
| ☐ R-85 | 95.00 | 48.00 | ☐ R-185 (T) | 165.00 | 83.00 |
| ☐ R-C090 | 70.00 | 35.00 | ☐ R-191 (T) | 150.00 | 75.00 |
| ☐ R-C091 | 70.00 | 35.00 | ☐ R-192 (T) | 150.00 | 75.00 |
| ☐ R-91 | 100.00 | 50.00 | ☐ R-193 (T) | 200.00 | 100.00 |
| ☐ R-103 | 145.00 | 73.00 | ☐ R-195 (T) | 175.00 | 88.00 |
| ☐ R-103ch | 160.00 | 80.00 | ☐ R-201 (E.O.) | 160.00 | 80.00 |
| ☐ R-105 | 125.00 | 63.00 | ☐ R-202 (E.O.) | 160.00 | 80.00 |
| ☐ R-105A | 125.00 | 63.00 | ☐ R-203 (E.O.) | 200.00 | 100.00 |
| ☐ R-105B | 125.00 | 63.00 | ☐ R-205 (E.O.) | 180.00 | 90.00 |
| ☐ R-108ch | 120.00 | 60.00 | ☐ R-211 (E.O.) | 150.00 | 75.00 |
| ☐ R-111 | 100.00 | 50.00 | ☐ R-212 (E.O.) | 150.00 | 75.00 |
| ☐ R-112 | 100.00 | 50.00 | ☐ R-213 (E.O.) | 200.00 | 100.00 |
| ☐ R-113 | 135.00 | 68.00 | ☐ R-219 (E.O.) | 100.00 | 50.00 |
| ☐ R-115 | 115.00 | 58.00 | ☐ R-222 (T) | 140.00 | 70.00 |
| ☐ R-122 | 120.00 | 60.00 | ☐ R-223 (T) | 190.00 | 95.00 |
| ☐ R-123 | 160.00 | 80.00 | ☐ R-225 (T) | 160.00 | 80.00 |
| ☐ R-125 | 140.00 | 70.00 | ☐ R-228 (T) | 140.00 | 70.00 |
| ☐ R-131 | 120.00 | 60.00 | ☐ R-232 (T) | 140.00 | 70.00 |
| ☐ R-132 | 120.00 | 60.00 | ☐ R-233 (T) | 210.00 | 105.00 |
| ☐ R-133 | 160.00 | 80.00 | ☐ R-235 (T) | 175.00 | 88.00 |
| ☐ R-135 | 140.00 | 70.00 | ☐ R-238 (T) | 140.00 | 70.00 |
| ☐ R-141 | 120.00 | 60.00 | ☐ R-242 (E.O.) | 185.00 | 93.00 |
| ☐ R-142 | 120.00 | 60.00 | ☐ R-243 (E.O.) | 220.00 | 110.00 |
| ☐ R-143 | 160.00 | 80.00 | ☐ R-245 (E.O.) | 185.00 | 93.00 |
| ☐ R-145 | 140.00 | 70.00 | ☐ R-248 (E.O.) | 160.00 | 80.00 |
| ☐ R-151 | 120.00 | 60.00 | ☐ R-252 | 150.00 | 75.00 |
| ☐ R-152 | 120.00 | 60.00 | ☐ R-253 (T) | 200.00 | 100.00 |
| ☐ R-153 | 160.00 | 80.00 | ☐ R-255 (T) | 175.00 | 88.00 |
| ☐ R-155 | 140.00 | 70.00 | ☐ R-258 (T) | 150.00 | 75.00 |
| ☐ R-155B | 140.00 | 70.00 | ☐ R-262 | 125.00 | 63.00 |
| ☐ R-155M | 140.00 | 70.00 | ☐ R-263 | 175.00 | 88.00 |
| ☐ R-155Z | 140.00 | 70.00 | ☐ R-265 | 150.00 | 75.00 |
| ☐ R-161 | 120.00 | 60.00 | ☐ R-272 | 140.00 | 70.00 |
| ☐ R-162 | 120.00 | 60.00 | ☐ R-273 | 200.00 | 100.00 |
| ☐ R-163 | 160.00 | 80.00 | ☐ R-275 | 160.00 | 80.00 |
| ☐ R-165 | 140.00 | 70.00 | ☐ R-282 | 125.00 | 63.00 |
| ☐ R-171 (T) | 140.00 | 70.00 | ☐ R-283 | 185.00 | 93.00 |
| ☐ R-172 (T) | 140.00 | 70.00 | ☐ R-293 (S.T.) | 250.00 | 125.00 |
| ☐ R-173 (T) | 200.00 | 100.00 | ☐ R-293 (S.T.2) | 350.00 | 175.00 |
| ☐ R-175 (T) | 160.00 | 80.00 | ☐ R-293 (L.B.) | 1500.00 | 750.00 |
| ☐ R-181 (T) | 160.00 | 80.00 | ☐ R-303 | 135.00 | 68.00 |
| ☐ R-182 (T) | 160.00 | 80.00 | ☐ R-305 | 110.00 | 55.00 |

*REMINGTON / 205*

| PATTERN NO. | MINT | VG | PATTERN NO. | MINT | VG |
|---|---|---|---|---|---|
| ☐ R-313 | 200.00 | 100.00 | ☐ R-473 | 165.00 | 83.00 |
| ☐ R-315 | 125.00 | 63.00 | ☐ R-475 | 125.00 | 63.00 |
| ☐ R-322 | 160.00 | 80.00 | ☐ R-482 | 125.00 | 63.00 |
| ☐ R-323 | 200.00 | 100.00 | ☐ R-483 | 160.00 | 80.00 |
| ☐ R-325 | 175.00 | 88.00 | ☐ R-485 | 125.00 | 63.00 |
| ☐ R-328 | 160.00 | 80.00 | ☐ R-488 | 125.00 | 63.00 |
| ☐ R-333 | 175.00 | 88.00 | ☐ R-493 | 165.00 | 82.00 |
| ☐ R-341 | 175.00 | 88.00 | ☐ R-495 | 125.00 | 63.00 |
| ☐ R-342 | 175.00 | 88.00 | ☐ R-503 | 160.00 | 80.00 |
| ☐ R-343 | 225.00 | 113.00 | ☐ R-505 | 125.00 | 63.00 |
| ☐ R-352 | 150.00 | 75.00 | ☐ R-512 | 135.00 | 68.00 |
| ☐ R-353 | 200.00 | 100.00 | ☐ R-513 | 175.00 | 88.00 |
| ☐ R-355 | 175.00 | 88.00 | ☐ R-515 | 135.00 | 68.00 |
| ☐ R-358 | 150.00 | 75.00 | ☐ R-523 | 200.00 | 100.00 |
| ☐ R-363 | 225.00 | 113.00 | ☐ R-525 | 160.00 | 80.00 |
| ☐ R-365 | 175.00 | 88.00 | ☐ R-551 | 125.00 | 63.00 |
| ☐ R-365 | 175.00 | 88.00 | ☐ R-552 | 125.00 | 63.00 |
| ☐ R-372 | 160.00 | 80.00 | ☐ R-553 | 160.00 | 80.00 |
| ☐ R-373 | 200.00 | 100.00 | ☐ R-555 | 125.00 | 63.00 |
| ☐ R-375 | 180.00 | 90.00 | ☐ R-563 | 150.00 | 75.00 |
| ☐ R-378 | 160.00 | 80.00 | ☐ R-572 | 125.00 | 63.00 |
| ☐ R-383 | 200.00 | 100.00 | ☐ R-573 | 160.00 | 80.00 |
| ☐ R-391 (T) | 135.00 | 68.00 | ☐ R-575 | 125.00 | 63.00 |
| ☐ R-392 (T) | 135.00 | 68.00 | ☐ R-583 | 150.00 | 75.00 |
| ☐ R-393 (T) | 175.00 | 88.00 | ☐ R-585 | 125.00 | 63.00 |
| ☐ R-395 (T) | 145.00 | 73.00 | ☐ R-590 | 150.00 | 75.00 |
| ☐ R-402 (E.O.) | 150.00 | 75.00 | ☐ R-593 | 175.00 | 88.00 |
| ☐ R-403 (E.O.) | 200.00 | 100.00 | ☐ R-595 | 150.00 | 75.00 |
| ☐ R-405 (E.O.) | 175.00 | 88.00 | ☐ R-603 | 160.00 | 80.00 |
| ☐ R-410 | 150.00 | 75.00 | ☐ R-605 | 135.00 | 68.00 |
| ☐ R-412 (E.O.) | 150.00 | 75.00 | ☐ R-605 | 135.00 | 68.00 |
| ☐ R-413 (E.O.) | 200.00 | 100.00 | ☐ R-609 | 150.00 | 75.00 |
| ☐ R-415 (E.O.) | 175.00 | 88.00 | ☐ R-613 | 200.00 | 100.00 |
| ☐ R-423 | 140.00 | 70.00 | ☐ R-615 | 95.00 | 48.00 |
| ☐ R-432 (D.K.) | 125.00 | 63.00 | ☐ R-622 | 110.00 | 55.00 |
| ☐ R-433 (D.K.) | 165.00 | 82.00 | ☐ R-623 | 125.00 | 63.00 |
| ☐ R-435 (D.K.) | 125.00 | 63.00 | ☐ R-625 | 110.00 | 55.00 |
| ☐ R-443 (D.K.) | 175.00 | 88.00 | ☐ R-633 | 100.00 | 50.00 |
| ☐ R-444 (D.K.) | 225.00 | 113.00 | ☐ R-635 | 100.00 | 50.00 |
| ☐ R-453 (D.K.) | 225.00 | 113.00 | ☐ R-635 | 130.00 | 65.00 |
| ☐ R-455 (D.K.) | 165.00 | 82.00 | ☐ R-643 (F) | 135.00 | 72.00 |
| ☐ R-463 | 150.00 | 75.00 | ☐ R-645 (F) | 85.00 | 42.00 |
| ☐ R-465 | 125.00 | 63.00 | ☐ R-645 (F2) | 200.00 | 100.00 |

## 206 / REMINGTON

| PATTERN NO. | MINT | VG | PATTERN NO. | MINT | VG |
|---|---|---|---|---|---|
| ☐ R-653 (F) | 150.00 | 75.00 | ☐ R-813 | 225.00 | 113.00 |
| ☐ R-655 (F) | 85.00 | 42.00 | ☐ R-823 | 160.00 | 80.00 |
| ☐ R-655 (S) | 225.00 | 113.00 | ☐ R-825 | 125.00 | 63.00 |
| ☐ R-662 | 250.00 | 125.00 | ☐ R-833 | 100.00 | 50.00 |
| ☐ R-663 | 350.00 | 175.00 | ☐ R-835 | 80.00 | 40.00 |
| ☐ R-668 | 300.00 | 150.00 | ☐ R-843 | 100.00 | 50.00 |
| ☐ R-672 (D) | 85.00 | 42.00 | ☐ R-845 | 80.00 | 40.00 |
| ☐ R-673 (D) | 110.00 | 55.00 | ☐ R-853 | 100.00 | 50.00 |
| ☐ R-674 (D) | 200.00 | 100.00 | ☐ R-855 | 80.00 | 40.00 |
| ☐ R-675 (D) | 85.00 | 42.00 | ☐ R-863 | 200.00 | 100.00 |
| ☐ R-677 | 85.00 | 42.00 | ☐ R-865 | 175.00 | 88.00 |
| ☐ R-679 (D) | 85.00 | 42.00 | ☐ R-873 | 80.00 | 40.00 |
| ☐ R-682 (G) | 200.00 | 100.00 | ☐ R-874 | 80.00 | 40.00 |
| ☐ R-683 (G) | 275.00 | 138.00 | ☐ R-875 | 80.00 | 40.00 |
| ☐ R-684 (G) | 325.00 | 163.00 | ☐ R-881 | 100.00 | 50.00 |
| ☐ R-685 (G) | 200.00 | 100.00 | ☐ R-882 | 100.00 | 50.00 |
| ☐ R-693 (HA) | 85.00 | 42.00 | ☐ R-883 | 135.00 | 68.00 |
| ☐ R-698 (HA) | 60.00 | 30.00 | ☐ R-892 (E.O.) | 150.00 | 75.00 |
| ☐ R-703 (HA) | 80.00 | 40.00 | ☐ R-893 (E.O.) | 200.00 | 100.00 |
| ☐ R-706 (HA) | 60.00 | 30.00 | ☐ R-895 (E.O.) | 175.00 | 88.00 |
| ☐ R-708 (HA) | 60.00 | 30.00 | ☐ R-901 | 145.00 | 72.00 |
| ☐ R-713 (HA) | 125.00 | 63.00 | ☐ R-913 | 225.00 | 113.00 |
| ☐ R-718 (HA) | 100.00 | 50.00 | ☐ R-921 | 80.00 | 40.00 |
| ☐ R-723 (HA) | 110.00 | 55.00 | ☐ R-932 (T.T.) | 250.00 | 125.00 |
| ☐ R-728 (HA) | 85.00 | 42.00 | ☐ R-933 (T.T.) | 225.00 | 113.00 |
| ☐ R-732 | 120.00 | 60.00 | ☐ R-935 (T.T.) | 300.00 | 150.00 |
| ☐ R-733 | 160.00 | 80.00 | ☐ R-942 (T.T.) | 250.00 | 125.00 |
| ☐ R-735 | 140.00 | 70.00 | ☐ R-943 (T.T.) | 300.00 | 150.00 |
| ☐ R-738 | 120.00 | 60.00 | ☐ R-945 (T.T.) | 250.00 | 125.00 |
| ☐ R-743 | 160.00 | 80.00 | ☐ R-C953 (T.T.) | 175.00 | 88.00 |
| ☐ R-745 | 140.00 | 70.00 | ☐ R-953 (T.T.) | 175.00 | 88.00 |
| ☐ R-753 | 160.00 | 80.00 | ☐ R-955 (T.T.) | 200.00 | 100.00 |
| ☐ R-755 | 140.00 | 70.00 | ☐ R-962 (E.O.) | 175.00 | 88.00 |
| ☐ R-756 | 130.00 | 62.00 | ☐ R-963 (E.O.) | 225.00 | 113.00 |
| ☐ R-763 | 160.00 | 80.00 | ☐ R-965 (E.O.) | 150.00 | 75.00 |
| ☐ R-772 (T) | 165.00 | 82.00 | ☐ R-971 (C.S.) | 125.00 | 63.00 |
| ☐ R-773 (T) | 200.00 | 100.00 | ☐ R-982 (D) | 65.00 | 33.00 |
| ☐ R-775 (T) | 165.00 | 82.00 | ☐ R-983 (D) | 100.00 | 50.00 |
| ☐ R-783 (T) | 200.00 | 100.00 | ☐ R-985 (D) | 65.00 | 33.00 |
| ☐ R-793 | 225.00 | 113.00 | ☐ R-992 | 40.00 | 20.00 |
| ☐ R-803 | 100.00 | 50.00 | ☐ R-993 | 110.00 | 55.00 |
| ☐ R-805 | 100.00 | 50.00 | ☐ R-995 | 80.00 | 40.00 |
| ☐ R-C803 | 50.00 | 25.00 | ☐ R-1002 | 85.00 | 42.00 |

REMINGTON / 207

| PATTERN NO. | MINT | VG | PATTERN NO. | MINT | VG |
|---|---|---|---|---|---|
| ☐ R-1003 | 125.00 | 63.00 | ☐ R-1202 | 135.00 | 68.00 |
| ☐ R-1005 | 85.00 | 42.00 | ☐ R-1203 | 150.00 | 75.00 |
| ☐ R-1012 | 150.00 | 75.00 | ☐ R-1212 | 150.00 | 75.00 |
| ☐ R-1013 | 165.00 | 82.00 | ☐ R-1213 | 250.00 | 125.00 |
| ☐ R-1022 | 250.00 | 125.00 | ☐ R-1222 | 250.00 | 125.00 |
| ☐ R-1023 | 300.00 | 150.00 | ☐ R-1223 | 175.00 | 88.00 |
| ☐ R-1032 | 80.00 | 40.00 | ☐ R-1225W (L.C.) | 175.00 | 88.00 |
| ☐ R-1033 | 125.00 | 63.00 | ☐ R-1232 | 150.00 | 75.00 |
| ☐ R-1035 | 80.00 | 40.00 | ☐ R-1233 | 190.00 | 95.00 |
| ☐ R-1042 | 100.00 | 50.00 | ☐ R-1240 (D.B.) | 200.00 | 100.00 |
| ☐ R-1043 | 135.00 | 68.00 | ☐ R-1241 (D.B.) | 200.00 | 100.00 |
| ☐ R-1045 | 100.00 | 50.00 | ☐ R-1242 (D.B.) | 250.00 | 125.00 |
| ☐ R-1051 | 75.00 | 38.00 | ☐ R-1243 (D.B.) | 250.00 | 125.00 |
| ☐ R-1053 | 90.00 | 45.00 | ☐ R-1253 (BL) | 1000.00 | 500.00 |
| ☐ R-1055 | 90.00 | 45.00 | ☐ R-1263 (BL) | 1200.00 | 600.00 |
| ☐ R-1061 | 80.00 | 40.00 | ☐ R-1273 (BL) | 2000.00 | 1000.00 |
| ☐ R-1062 | 80.00 | 40.00 | ☐ R-1283 | 80.00 | 40.00 |
| ☐ R-1063 | 110.00 | 55.00 | ☐ R-1284 | 200.00 | 100.00 |
| ☐ R-1065W | 80.00 | 40.00 | ☐ R-1285 | 75.00 | 38.00 |
| ☐ R-1071 | 80.00 | 40.00 | ☐ R-1293 | 150.00 | 75.00 |
| ☐ R-1072 | 80.00 | 40.00 | ☐ R-1295 (TP) | 225.00 | 113.00 |
| ☐ R-1073 | 100.00 | 50.00 | ☐ R-1303 (BL) | 1200.00 | 600.00 |
| ☐ R-1075 | 80.00 | 40.00 | ☐ R-1306 (BL) | 1000.00 | 500.00 |
| ☐ R-1082 | 65.00 | 32.00 | ☐ R-1315 | 150.00 | 75.00 |
| ☐ R-1083 | 85.00 | 42.00 | ☐ R-1323 (D) | 90.00 | 45.00 |
| ☐ R-1085 | 60.00 | 30.00 | ☐ R-1324 (D) | 150.00 | 75.00 |
| ☐ R-1092 | 65.00 | 32.00 | ☐ R-1325 (D) | 80.00 | 40.00 |
| ☐ R-1093 | 85.00 | 42.00 | ☐ R-1333 | 150.00 | 75.00 |
| ☐ R-1102 | 75.00 | 38.00 | ☐ R-1343 | 200.00 | 100.00 |
| ☐ R-1103 | 100.00 | 50.00 | ☐ R-1353 | 125.00 | 63.00 |
| ☐ R-1112 | 75.00 | 38.00 | ☐ R-1363 | 150.00 | 75.00 |
| ☐ R-1113 | 110.00 | 55.00 | ☐ R-1373 | 300.00 | 150.00 |
| ☐ R-1123 (BL) | 700.00 | 350.00 | ☐ R-1379 | 85.00 | 42.00 |
| ☐ R-1128 (BL) | 400.00 | 200.00 | ☐ R-1383 | 125.00 | 63.00 |
| ☐ R-1133 | 160.00 | 80.00 | ☐ R-1383 (FSL) | 200.00 | 100.00 |
| ☐ R-1143 | 165.00 | 82.00 | ☐ R-1389 | 85.00 | 42.00 |
| ☐ R-1153 | 200.00 | 100.00 | ☐ R-1399 | 85.00 | 42.00 |
| ☐ R-1163 | 200.00 | 100.00 | ☐ R-1409 | 100.00 | 50.00 |
| ☐ R-1173 (BL) | 1500.00 | 750.00 | ☐ R-1413 | 100.00 | 50.00 |
| ☐ R-1182 | 125.00 | 62.00 | ☐ R-1423 | 110.00 | 55.00 |
| ☐ R-1183 | 170.00 | 82.00 | ☐ R-1437 | 130.00 | 68.00 |
| ☐ R-1192 | 100.00 | 50.00 | ☐ R-1447 | 130.00 | 68.00 |
| ☐ R-1193 | 120.00 | 60.00 | ☐ R-1457 | 150.00 | 75.00 |

## 208 / REMINGTON

| PATTERN NO. | MINT | VG | PATTERN NO. | MINT | VG |
|---|---|---|---|---|---|
| ☐ R-1465 (BU) | 160.00 | 80.00 | ☐ R-1753 | 100.00 | 50.00 |
| ☐ R-1477 | 130.00 | 68.00 | ☐ R-1755 | 85.00 | 42.00 |
| ☐ R-1483 | 130.00 | 68.00 | ☐ R-1763 | 125.00 | 63.00 |
| ☐ R-1485 | 110.00 | 55.00 | ☐ R-1772 | 120.00 | 60.00 |
| ☐ R-1493 | 130.00 | 68.00 | ☐ R-1773 | 125.00 | 63.00 |
| ☐ R-1495 | 110.00 | 55.00 | ☐ R-1782 | 110.00 | 55.00 |
| ☐ R-1535 (FL) | 100.00 | 50.00 | ☐ R-1783 | 125.00 | 63.00 |
| ☐ R-1545 | 100.00 | 50.00 | ☐ R-1785 | 100.00 | 50.00 |
| ☐ R-1555 | 130.00 | 68.00 | ☐ R-1803 | 100.00 | 50.00 |
| ☐ R-1568 | 120.00 | 60.00 | ☐ R-1823 | 110.00 | 55.00 |
| ☐ R-1572 | 90.00 | 45.00 | ☐ R-1825 | 125.00 | 63.00 |
| ☐ R-1573 | 90.00 | 45.00 | ☐ R-1833 | 140.00 | 70.00 |
| ☐ R-1573ch | 110.00 | 55.00 | ☐ R-1853 | 90.00 | 45.00 |
| ☐ R-1582 | 90.00 | 45.00 | ☐ R-1855M | 70.00 | 35.00 |
| ☐ R-1592 | 100.00 | 50.00 | ☐ R-1863 | 110.00 | 55.00 |
| ☐ R-1593 | 100.00 | 50.00 | ☐ R-1873 | 100.00 | 50.00 |
| ☐ R-1595 | 100.00 | 50.00 | ☐ R-1882B | 90.00 | 45.00 |
| ☐ R-1608 (B.K.) | 50.00 | 25.00 | ☐ R-1903 | 85.00 | 42.00 |
| ☐ R-1613 (BL) | 1500.00 | 750.00 | ☐ R-1905 | 80.00 | 40.00 |
| ☐ R-1615 | 250.00 | 125.00 | ☐ R-1913 | 120.00 | 60.00 |
| ☐ R-1615 (R.B.) | 600.00 | 300.00 | ☐ R-1915 | 100.00 | 50.00 |
| ☐ R-1622 | 100.00 | 50.00 | ☐ R-1962 | 100.00 | 50.00 |
| ☐ R-1623 | 110.00 | 55.00 | ☐ R-1973 (E) | 125.00 | 63.00 |
| ☐ R-1623ch | 115.00 | 58.00 | ☐ R-1995 (BG) | 110.00 | 55.00 |
| ☐ R-1630L (D.B.) | 350.00 | 175.00 | ☐ R-2043 | 65.00 | 32.00 |
| ☐ R-1643 | 125.00 | 63.00 | ☐ R-2045 | 65.00 | 32.00 |
| ☐ R-1644 | 200.00 | 100.00 | ☐ R-2053 | 65.00 | 32.00 |
| ☐ R-1645 | 95.00 | 48.00 | ☐ R-2055 | 60.00 | 30.00 |
| ☐ R-1653 (P) | 125.00 | 63.00 | ☐ R-2063 | 60.00 | 30.00 |
| ☐ R-1655 | 100.00 | 50.00 | ☐ R-2065 | 55.00 | 28.00 |
| ☐ R-1668 | 150.00 | 75.00 | ☐ R-2073 | 65.00 | 32.00 |
| ☐ R-1671 (BK) | 70.00 | 35.00 | ☐ R-2075 | 55.00 | 28.00 |
| ☐ R-1673 (BK) | 90.00 | 45.00 | ☐ R-2083 | 65.00 | 32.00 |
| ☐ R-1685 | 100.00 | 50.00 | ☐ R-2085 | 55.00 | 28.00 |
| ☐ R-1687 | 100.00 | 50.00 | ☐ R-2093 | 75.00 | 32.00 |
| ☐ R-1688 (BK) | 100.00 | 50.00 | ☐ R-2093 | 75.00 | 32.00 |
| ☐ R-1697 (BK) | 100.00 | 50.00 | ☐ R-2095 | 60.00 | 30.00 |
| ☐ R-1707 (BK) | 100.00 | 50.00 | ☐ R-2103 | 75.00 | 38.00 |
| ☐ R-1715 (BK) | 70.00 | 35.00 | ☐ R-2105MW | 60.00 | 30.00 |
| ☐ R-1717 (BK) | 100.00 | 50.00 | ☐ R-2111 | | |
| ☐ R-1723 | 140.00 | 70.00 | (elec) (E) | 70.00 | 35.00 |
| ☐ R-1751 | 85.00 | 42.00 | ☐ R-2203 | 100.00 | 50.00 |
| ☐ R-1752 | 85.00 | 42.00 | ☐ R-2205D | 60.00 | 30.00 |

REMINGTON / 209

| PATTERN NO. | MINT | VG | PATTERN NO. | MINT | VG |
|---|---|---|---|---|---|
| ☐ R-2213 | 60.00 | 30.00 | ☐ R-3133 | 325.00 | 163.00 |
| ☐ R-2215M | 60.00 | 30.00 | ☐ R-3143 (BL.S.) | 1000.00 | 500.00 |
| ☐ R-2223 | 60.00 | 30.00 | ☐ R-3153 (C) | 225.00 | 113.00 |
| ☐ R-2303 (S) | 250.00 | 125.00 | ☐ R-3155 (C) | 175.00 | 88.00 |
| ☐ R-2403 (S) | 350.00 | 175.00 | ☐ R-3155b (C) | 175.00 | 88.00 |
| ☐ R-2503 | 60.00 | 30.00 | ☐ R-P (C) | 175.00 | 88.00 |
| ☐ R-2505B | 60.00 | 30.00 | ☐ R-3163 (C) | 225.00 | 113.00 |
| ☐ R-2505M | 60.00 | 30.00 | ☐ R-3165T (C) | 150.00 | 75.00 |
| ☐ R-2505R | 60.00 | 30.00 | ☐ R-3173 (C) | 225.00 | 113.00 |
| ☐ R-2603 | 65.00 | 32.00 | ☐ R-3183 (C) | 225.00 | 113.00 |
| ☐ R-2605B | 65.00 | 32.00 | ☐ R-3185 (C) | 150.00 | 75.00 |
| ☐ R-3003 | 225.00 | 113.00 | ☐ R-3193 | 225.00 | 113.00 |
| ☐ R-3005 | 185.00 | 92.00 | ☐ R-3202 | 200.00 | 100.00 |
| ☐ R-3013 | 225.00 | 113.00 | ☐ R-3203 | 225.00 | 113.00 |
| ☐ R-3015 | 185.00 | 92.00 | ☐ R-3212 | 200.00 | 100.00 |
| ☐ R-3033 | 225.00 | 113.00 | ☐ R-3213 | 300.00 | 150.00 |
| ☐ R-3035 | 185.00 | 92.00 | ☐ R-3215 | 250.00 | 125.00 |
| ☐ R-3050 |  |  | ☐ R-3222 | 200.00 | 100.00 |
| Buf (ST) | 225.00 | 113.00 | ☐ R-3223 | 250.00 | 125.00 |
| ☐ R-3053 (ST) | 190.00 | 95.00 | ☐ R-3225 | 225.00 | 113.00 |
| ☐ R-3054 (ST) | 300.00 | 150.00 | ☐ R-3232 | 200.00 | 100.00 |
| ☐ R-3055 (ST) | 200.00 | 100.00 | ☐ R-3233 | 275.00 | 138.00 |
| ☐ R-3056 (ST) | 300.00 | 150.00 | ☐ R-3235 | 240.00 | 120.00 |
| ☐ R-3059 (ST) | 200.00 | 100.00 | ☐ R-3242 | 275.00 | 138.00 |
| ☐ R-3062 (ST) | 200.00 | 100.00 | ☐ R-3243 | 225.00 | 113.00 |
| ☐ R-3063 (ST) | 250.00 | 125.00 | ☐ R-3245 | 250.00 | 125.00 |
| ☐ R-3064 (ST) | 400.00 | 200.00 | ☐ R-3253 | 250.00 | 125.00 |
| ☐ R-3065B (ST) | 200.00 | 100.00 | ☐ R-3255 | 225.00 | 113.00 |
| ☐ R-3065M (ST) | 200.00 | 100.00 | ☐ R-3263 | 250.00 | 125.00 |
| ☐ R-3065R (ST) | 200.00 | 100.00 | ☐ R-3265 | 225.00 | 113.00 |
| ☐ R-3070 | 250.00 | 125.00 | ☐ R-3273 (C) | 275.00 | 138.00 |
| ☐ R-3073 | 225.00 | 113.00 | ☐ R-3274 (C) | 375.00 | 168.00 |
| ☐ R-3075 | 200.00 | 100.00 | ☐ R-3275 (C) | 250.00 | 125.00 |
| ☐ R-3083 (ST) | 250.00 | 125.00 | ☐ R-3283 | 225.00 | 113.00 |
| ☐ R-3085 (ST) | 200.00 | 100.00 | ☐ R-3285 | 200.00 | 100.00 |
| ☐ R-3093 (ST) | 250.00 | 125.00 | ☐ R-3293 | 240.00 | 120.00 |
| ☐ R-3095 (ST) | 175.00 | 88.00 | ☐ R-3295 | 215.00 | 107.00 |
| ☐ R-3103 (ST) | 200.00 | 100.00 | ☐ R-3302 | 375.00 | 168.00 |
| ☐ R-3105 (ST) | 175.00 | 88.00 | ☐ R-3303 | 375.00 | 168.00 |
| ☐ R-3113 | 175.00 | 88.00 | ☐ R-3305d | 300.00 | 150.00 |
| ☐ R-3115G | 150.00 | 75.00 | ☐ R-3312 | 300.00 | 150.00 |
| ☐ R-3115IW | 150.00 | 75.00 | ☐ R-3313 | 400.00 | 200.00 |
| ☐ R-3123 (M) | 200.00 | 100.00 | ☐ R-3315B | 350.00 | 175.00 |

## 210 / REMINGTON

| PATTERN NO. | MINT | VG | PATTERN NO. | MINT | VG |
|---|---|---|---|---|---|
| ☐ R-3322 (SC) | 125.00 | 68.00 | ☐ R-3494 | 300.00 | 150.00 |
| ☐ R-S3333 (O-SC) | 150.00 | 75.00 | ☐ R-3495M | 150.00 | 75.00 |
| ☐ R-3333 (SC) | 125.00 | 68.00 | ☐ R-3499 | 130.00 | 68.00 |
| ☐ R-3335 | 150.00 | 75.00 | ☐ R-3500 | 125.00 | 62.00 |
| ☐ R-3352 | 175.00 | 88.00 | ☐ R-3503 | 165.00 | 82.00 |
| ☐ R-3353 | 225.00 | 113.00 | ☐ R-3504 | 300.00 | 150.00 |
| ☐ R-3363 | 225.00 | 113.00 | ☐ R-3505 | 125.00 | 62.00 |
| ☐ R-3372 | 150.00 | 75.00 | ☐ R-3513 (W) | 175.00 | 88.00 |
| ☐ R-3373 | 200.00 | 100.00 | ☐ R-3514 (W) | 300.00 | 150.00 |
| ☐ R-3375 | 175.00 | 88.00 | ☐ R-3515 (W) | 140.00 | 70.00 |
| ☐ R-3382 | 175.00 | 88.00 | ☐ R-3520 (W) | 135.00 | 68.00 |
| ☐ R-3383 | 225.00 | 113.00 | ☐ R-3523 (W) | 165.00 | 82.00 |
| ☐ R-3385S | 200.00 | 100.00 | ☐ R-3524 (W) | 300.00 | 150.00 |
| ☐ R-3393 | 200.00 | 100.00 | ☐ R-3525 (W) | 125.00 | 62.00 |
| ☐ R-3395T | 175.00 | 88.00 | ☐ R-3533 | 170.00 | 85.00 |
| ☐ R-3403 | 250.00 | 125.00 | ☐ R-3535 | 125.00 | 62.00 |
| ☐ R-3405J | 225.00 | 113.00 | ☐ R-3545 | 140.00 | 70.00 |
| ☐ R-3413 | 165.00 | 82.00 | ☐ R-3553 (ST) | 225.00 | 113.00 |
| ☐ R-3414 | 300.00 | 150.00 | ☐ R-3554 (ST) | 350.00 | 175.00 |
| ☐ R-3415 | 140.00 | 70.00 | ☐ R-3555G (ST) | 200.00 | 100.00 |
| ☐ R-3415H | 140.00 | 70.00 | ☐ R-3555IW (ST) | 200.00 | 100.00 |
| ☐ R-3423 | 225.00 | 113.00 | ☐ R-3563 (ST) | 225.00 | 113.00 |
| ☐ R-3424 (W) | 325.00 | 168.00 | ☐ R-3565D (ST) | 200.00 | 100.00 |
| ☐ R-3425P (W) | 165.00 | 88.00 | ☐ R-3573 (W) | 145.00 | 72.00 |
| ☐ R-3432 | 140.00 | 70.00 | ☐ R-3575 | 130.00 | 68.00 |
| ☐ R-3433 | 160.00 | 80.00 | ☐ R-3580 | 130.00 | 68.00 |
| ☐ R-3435 | 140.00 | 70.00 | ☐ R-3583 | 145.00 | 72.00 |
| ☐ R-3442 | 150.00 | 75.00 | ☐ R-3585 | 130.00 | 68.00 |
| ☐ R-3443 | 160.00 | 80.00 | ☐ R-3593 | 325.00 | 162.00 |
| ☐ R-3445B | 130.00 | 62.00 | ☐ R-3595 | 300.00 | 150.00 |
| ☐ R-3453 (W) | 200.00 | 100.00 | ☐ R-3596 | 375.00 | 182.00 |
| ☐ R-3455 (W) | 175.00 | 88.00 | ☐ R-3600 | 125.00 | 62.00 |
| ☐ R-3463 (W) | 275.00 | 138.00 | ☐ R-3603 | 140.00 | 70.00 |
| ☐ R-3465B (W) | 225.00 | 113.00 | ☐ R-3604 | 250.00 | 150.00 |
| ☐ R-3475K (W) | 200.00 | 100.00 | ☐ R-3605 | 125.00 | 62.00 |
| ☐ R-3475G (W) | 200.00 | 100.00 | ☐ R-3613 | 140.00 | 70.00 |
| ☐ R-3480 | 160.00 | 80.00 | ☐ R-3615 | 130.00 | 68.00 |
| ☐ R-3483 | 190.00 | 95.00 | ☐ R-3620 | 130.00 | 68.00 |
| ☐ R-3484 | 300.00 | 150.00 | ☐ R-3623 | 160.00 | 80.00 |
| ☐ R-3485J | 160.00 | 80.00 | ☐ R-3625 | 135.00 | 69.00 |
| ☐ R-3489 | 140.00 | 70.00 | ☐ R-3633 | 150.00 | 75.00 |
| ☐ R-3493 | 175.00 | 88.00 | ☐ R-3635 | 135.00 | 69.00 |
| | | | ☐ R-3643 | 150.00 | 75.00 |

REMINGTON / 211

| PATTERN NO. | MINT | VG | PATTERN NO. | MINT | VG |
|---|---|---|---|---|---|
| ☐ R-3644 | 225.00 | 113.00 | ☐ R-3953 | 225.00 | 113.00 |
| ☐ R-3645 | 135.00 | 68.00 | ☐ R-3955 | 200.00 | 100.00 |
| ☐ R-3653 | 160.00 | 80.00 | ☐ R-3962 | 165.00 | 82.00 |
| ☐ R-3655 | 150.00 | 75.00 | ☐ R-3963 | 200.00 | 100.00 |
| ☐ R-3665 | 300.00 | 150.00 | ☐ R-3965 | 165.00 | 82.00 |
| ☐ R-3675 | 300.00 | 150.00 | ☐ R-3973 (ST) | 200.00 | 100.00 |
| ☐ R-3683 | 225.00 | 113.00 | ☐ R-3975 (ST) | 175.00 | 88.00 |
| ☐ R-3685 | 175.00 | 88.00 | ☐ R-3983 (W) | 160.00 | 80.00 |
| ☐ R-3693 (W) | 500.00 | 250.00 | ☐ R-3985 (W) | 125.00 | 63.00 |
| ☐ R-3695G | 400.00 | 200.00 | ☐ R-3993 (ST) | 200.00 | 100.00 |
| ☐ R-3700Buf | 185.00 | 98.00 | ☐ R-3995 (ST) | 160.00 | 80.00 |
| ☐ R-3703 | 200.00 | 100.00 | ☐ R-4003 | 165.00 | 82.00 |
| ☐ R-3704 | 375.00 | 182.00 | ☐ R-4005 | 135.00 | 68.00 |
| ☐ R-3705 | 185.00 | 92.00 | ☐ R-4013 (M) | 200.00 | 100.00 |
| ☐ R-3710Buf | 200.00 | 100.00 | ☐ R-4015 (M) | 160.00 | 80.00 |
| ☐ R-3713 | 225.00 | 113.00 | ☐ R-4023 | 160.00 | 80.00 |
| ☐ R-3714 | 375.00 | 182.00 | ☐ R-4025 | 130.00 | 68.00 |
| ☐ R-3715F | 185.00 | 92.00 | ☐ R-4033 | 125.00 | 63.00 |
| ☐ R-3722 (W) | 300.00 | 150.00 | ☐ R-4035 | 90.00 | 45.00 |
| ☐ R-3723 (W) | 500.00 | 250.00 | ☐ R-4043 | 160.00 | 80.00 |
| ☐ R-3725 | 350.00 | 175.00 | ☐ R-4045 | 135.00 | 68.00 |
| ☐ R-3732 | 350.00 | 175.00 | ☐ R-4053 | 165.00 | 82.00 |
| ☐ R-3733 | 400.00 | 200.00 | ☐ R-4055 | 135.00 | 68.00 |
| ☐ R-3735 | 350.00 | 175.00 | ☐ R-4063 | 175.00 | 88.00 |
| ☐ R-3843 (SC) | 170.00 | 85.00 | ☐ R-4065 | 140.00 | 70.00 |
| ☐ R-3853 (PR) | 225.00 | 113.00 | ☐ R-4073 | 175.00 | 88.00 |
| ☐ R-3855 | 200.00 | 100.00 | ☐ R-4075 | 160.00 | 80.00 |
| ☐ R-3858 | 200.00 | 100.00 | ☐ R-4083 | 175.00 | 88.00 |
| ☐ R-3863 (SC) | 125.00 | 63.00 | ☐ R-4085 | 150.00 | 75.00 |
| ☐ R-3870 (ST) | 225.00 | 113.00 | ☐ R-4093 | 165.00 | 82.00 |
| ☐ R-3873 (ST) | 200.00 | 100.00 | ☐ R-4095 | 150.00 | 75.00 |
| ☐ R-3874 (ST) | 300.00 | 150.00 | ☐ R-4103 | 150.00 | 75.00 |
| ☐ R-3875A (ST) | 175.00 | 88.00 | ☐ R-4105 | 125.00 | 63.00 |
| ☐ R-3883 | 200.00 | 100.00 | ☐ R-4113 (ST) | 200.00 | 100.00 |
| ☐ R-3885 | 185.00 | 92.00 | ☐ R-4114 (ST) | 350.00 | 175.00 |
| ☐ R-3893 | 140.00 | 70.00 | ☐ R-4123 (ST) | 300.00 | 150.00 |
| ☐ R-3895 | 125.00 | 62.00 | ☐ R-4124 (ST) | 350.00 | 175.00 |
| ☐ R-3903 (M) | 140.00 | 70.00 | ☐ R-4133 | 160.00 | 80.00 |
| ☐ R-3926 | 225.00 | 113.00 | ☐ R-4134 | 225.00 | 113.00 |
| ☐ R-3932 (W) | 425.00 | 213.00 | ☐ R-4135 | 165.00 | 68.00 |
| ☐ R-3933 (W) | 500.00 | 250.00 | ☐ R-4143 | 100.00 | 50.00 |
| ☐ R-3935 | 425.00 | 213.00 | ☐ R-4144 | 250.00 | 125.00 |
| ☐ R-3952 | 175.00 | 88.00 | ☐ R-4145 | 85.00 | 42.00 |

## 212 / REMINGTON

| PATTERN NO. | MINT | VG |
|---|---|---|
| ☐ R-4163 | 175.00 | 88.00 |
| ☐ R-4173 | 175.00 | 88.00 |
| ☐ R-4175 | 175.00 | 88.00 |
| ☐ R-4200 | 225.00 | 113.00 |
| ☐ R-4203 | 175.00 | 88.00 |
| ☐ R-4213 | 250.00 | 125.00 |
| ☐ R-4223 (C) | 175.00 | 88.00 |
| ☐ R-4225 | 150.00 | 75.00 |
| ☐ R-4233 (SC) | 125.00 | 68.00 |
| ☐ R-S4233 (O-SC2) | 180.00 | 90.00 |
| ☐ R-4234 (SC) | 250.00 | 125.00 |
| ☐ R-4235 (SC) | 175.00 | 88.00 |
| ☐ R-4243 (BL) | 800.00 | 400.00 |
| ☐ R-4253 | 200.00 | 100.00 |
| ☐ R-4263 (H) | 300.00 | 150.00 |
| ☐ R-4273 (H) | 350.00 | 175.00 |
| ☐ R-4274 (H) | 200.00 | 100.00 |
| ☐ R-4283 (H2) | 1500.00 | 750.00 |
| ☐ R-4293 | 125.00 | 68.00 |
| ☐ R-4303 | 125.00 | 68.00 |
| ☐ R-4313 | 175.00 | 88.00 |
| ☐ R-4323 (O.G.S.) | 75.00 | 38.00 |
| ☐ R-4323 (ST) | 250.00 | 125.00 |
| ☐ R-4334 (BR) | 200.00 | 100.00 |
| ☐ R-4336 (BR) | 175.00 | 88.00 |
| ☐ R-4343 | 200.00 | 100.00 |
| ☐ R-4345 | 250.00 | 125.00 |
| ☐ R-4353 (R.G.) | 1000.00 | 500.00 |
| ☐ R-4353 (BL) | 1400.00 | 700.00 |
| ☐ R-4363 | 300.00 | 150.00 |
| ☐ R-4365 | 300.00 | 150.00 |
| ☐ R-4373 (O.G.S.) | 175.00 | 88.00 |
| ☐ R-4375 | 150.00 | 75.00 |
| ☐ R-4383 | 150.00 | 75.00 |
| ☐ R-4384 | 325.00 | 163.00 |
| ☐ R-4394 | 300.00 | 150.00 |
| ☐ R-4403 | 125.00 | 63.00 |
| ☐ R-4405 | 95.00 | 48.00 |
| ☐ R-4413 | 140.00 | 70.00 |
| ☐ R-4423 | 150.00 | 75.00 |
| ☐ R-4425 | 130.00 | 65.00 |
| ☐ R-4433 (W) | 225.00 | 113.00 |
| ☐ R-4443 | 125.00 | 63.00 |
| ☐ R-4466 (BL) | 1800.00 | 900.00 |
| ☐ R-4473 | 120.00 | 60.00 |
| ☐ R-4483 (C) | 250.00 | 125.00 |
| ☐ R-4493 | 200.00 | 100.00 |
| ☐ R-4495 | 100.00 | 50.00 |
| ☐ R-4495 | 150.00 | 75.00 |
| ☐ R-4505 | 140.00 | 70.00 |
| ☐ R-4506 | 200.00 | 100.00 |
| ☐ R-4513 | 300.00 | 150.00 |
| ☐ R-4523 (OSS) | 200.00 | 100.00 |
| ☐ R-4533 (SS) | 200.00 | 100.00 |
| ☐ R-4548 (E) | 120.00 | 60.00 |
| ☐ R-4555 | 200.00 | 100.00 |
| ☐ R-4563 | 170.00 | 85.00 |
| ☐ R-4573 | 200.00 | 100.00 |
| ☐ R-4583 | 175.00 | 88.00 |
| ☐ R-4593 (MSB) | 200.00 | 100.00 |
| ☐ R-4593 (MRB) | 225.00 | 113.00 |
| ☐ R-4603 | 165.00 | 68.00 |
| ☐ R-4605 | 130.00 | 65.00 |
| ☐ R-4613 | 150.00 | 75.00 |
| ☐ R-4623 (W) | 175.00 | 88.00 |
| ☐ R-4625 (W) | 170.00 | 82.00 |
| ☐ R-4633 | 100.00 | 50.00 |
| ☐ R-4635G | 95.00 | 48.00 |
| ☐ R-4643 | 140.00 | 70.00 |
| ☐ R-4679 | 115.00 | 63.00 |
| ☐ R-4683 | 165.00 | 82.00 |
| ☐ R-4685 | 135.00 | 68.00 |
| ☐ R-4695 | 225.00 | 113.00 |
| ☐ R-4702 | 130.00 | 65.00 |
| ☐ R-4703 (M) | 175.00 | 88.00 |
| ☐ R-4713 | 150.00 | 75.00 |
| ☐ R-4723 (O.G.S.) | 75.00 | 38.00 |
| ☐ R-4733 (D.G.) | 175.00 | 88.00 |
| ☐ R-4783 (SC) | 150.00 | 75.00 |
| ☐ R-4813 | 125.00 | 63.00 |
| ☐ R-4815 | 100.00 | 50.00 |
| ☐ R-4823 | 90.00 | 45.00 |

REMINGTON / 213

| PATTERN NO. | MINT | VG | PATTERN NO. | MINT | VG |
|---|---|---|---|---|---|
| ☐ R-4825 ...... | 90.00 | 45.00 | ☐ R-6194 ...... | 175.00 | 88.00 |
| ☐ R-4833 ...... | 85.00 | 42.00 | ☐ R-6195 ...... | 100.00 | 50.00 |
| ☐ R-4835 ...... | 85.00 | 42.00 | ☐ R-6203 ...... | 90.00 | 45.00 |
| ☐ R-4843 ...... | 80.00 | 40.00 | ☐ R-6204 ...... | 160.00 | 80.00 |
| ☐ R-4845 ...... | 80.00 | 40.00 | ☐ R-6205 ...... | 75.00 | 38.00 |
| ☐ R-4853 ...... | 90.00 | 45.00 | ☐ R-6213 (W) ... | 125.00 | 63.00 |
| ☐ R-4855 ...... | 85.00 | 42.00 | ☐ R-6214 ...... | 200.00 | 100.00 |
| ☐ R-4863 ...... | 85.00 | 42.00 | ☐ R-6515 ...... | 100.00 | 50.00 |
| ☐ R-4865 ...... | 80.00 | 40.00 | ☐ R-6223 (W) ... | 125.00 | 63.00 |
| ☐ R-6013 ...... | 160.00 | 80.00 | ☐ R-6224 (W) ... | 175.00 | 88.00 |
| ☐ R-6014 ...... | 225.00 | 113.00 | ☐ R-6225 (W) ... | 100.00 | 50.00 |
| ☐ R-6015 ...... | 125.00 | 63.00 | ☐ R-6233 ...... | 125.00 | 63.00 |
| ☐ R-6023 (W) ... | 200.00 | 100.00 | ☐ R-6234 ...... | 200.00 | 100.00 |
| ☐ R-6024 (W) ... | 300.00 | 150.00 | ☐ R-6235 ...... | 100.00 | 50.00 |
| ☐ R-6025 ...... | 160.00 | 80.00 | ☐ R-6243 (L) ... | 90.00 | 45.00 |
| ☐ R-6032 (CO) .. | 250.00 | 125.00 | ☐ R-6244 (L) ... | 100.00 | 50.00 |
| ☐ R-6033 (CO) .. | 250.00 | 125.00 | ☐ R-6245 (L) ... | 75.00 | 38.00 |
| ☐ R-6034 (CO) .. | 500.00 | 250.00 | ☐ R-6249 ...... | 65.00 | 32.00 |
| ☐ R-6043 (CO) .. | 250.00 | 125.00 | ☐ R-6255 (L) ... | 60.00 | 30.00 |
| ☐ R-6053 (CO) .. | 250.00 | 125.00 | ☐ R-6259 (L) ... | 60.00 | 30.00 |
| ☐ R-6063 (CO) .. | 185.00 | 142.00 | ☐ R-6265 (W) ... | 150.00 | 75.00 |
| ☐ R-6073 (CO) .. | 200.00 | 100.00 | ☐ R-6275 (W) ... | 350.00 | 175.00 |
| ☐ R-6083 (CO) .. | 200.00 | 100.00 | ☐ R-6285 (W) ... | 350.00 | 175.00 |
| ☐ R-6093 (CO2) . | 125.00 | 63.00 | ☐ R-6295 (W) ... | 350.00 | 175.00 |
| ☐ R-6103 ...... | 100.00 | 50.00 | ☐ R-6303 ...... | 100.00 | 50.00 |
| ☐ R-6104 ...... | 175.00 | 88.00 | ☐ R-6313 (W) ... | 225.00 | 113.00 |
| ☐ R-6105 ...... | 80.00 | 40.00 | ☐ R-6323 (W) ... | 225.00 | 113.00 |
| ☐ R-6113 (CO) .. | 225.00 | 113.00 | ☐ R-6325 (W) ... | 190.00 | 95.00 |
| ☐ R-6123 (CO) .. | 135.00 | 82.00 | ☐ R-6330 (W) ... | 125.00 | 63.00 |
| ☐ R-6133 (W) ... | 250.00 | 125.00 | ☐ R-6333 (W) ... | 125.00 | 63.00 |
| ☐ R-6143 ...... | 100.00 | 50.00 | ☐ R-6334 (W) ... | 125.00 | 63.00 |
| ☐ R-6145 ...... | 80.00 | 40.00 | ☐ R-6335 (W) ... | 170.00 | 83.00 |
| ☐ R-6153 ...... | 100.00 | 50.00 | ☐ R-6340Buf (W) | 175.00 | 88.00 |
| ☐ R-6155 ...... | 75.00 | 38.00 | ☐ R-6340 (W) ... | 175.00 | 88.00 |
| ☐ R-6163 ...... | 125.00 | 63.00 | ☐ R-6343 (W) ... | 225.00 | 113.00 |
| ☐ R-6175W (O.K.) ......... | 100.00 | 50.00 | ☐ R-6344 (W) ... | 325.00 | 163.00 |
| ☐ R-6182 ...... | 70.00 | 35.00 | ☐ R-6345T (W) ... | 175.00 | 88.00 |
| ☐ R-6183 ...... | 90.00 | 45.00 | ☐ R-6350 (W) ... | 200.00 | 100.00 |
| ☐ R-6184 ...... | 150.00 | 75.00 | ☐ R-6353 (W) ... | 235.00 | 118.00 |
| ☐ R-6185 ...... | 90.00 | 45.00 | ☐ R-6355G (W) . | 235.00 | 118.00 |
| ☐ R-6192 ...... | 100.00 | 50.00 | ☐ R-6362 ...... | 90.00 | 45.00 |
| ☐ R-6193 ...... | 125.00 | 63.00 | ☐ R-6363 ...... | 125.00 | 63.00 |
| | | | ☐ R-6365A (W) . | 90.00 | 45.00 |

## 214 / REMINGTON

| PATTERN NO. | MINT | VG |
|---|---|---|
| ☐ R-6390 (W) | 135.00 | 68.00 |
| ☐ R-6393 (W) | 275.00 | 138.00 |
| ☐ R-6394 (W) | 325.00 | 168.00 |
| ☐ R-6395G (W) | 135.00 | 68.00 |
| ☐ R-6400 (W) | 125.00 | 63.00 |
| ☐ R-6403 (W) | 125.00 | 63.00 |
| ☐ R-6404 (W) | 325.00 | 168.00 |
| ☐ R-6405 (W) | 175.00 | 88.00 |
| ☐ R-6423 | 75.00 | 38.00 |
| ☐ R-6424 | 100.00 | 50.00 |
| ☐ R-6429 | 65.00 | 32.00 |
| ☐ R-6433 | 75.00 | 38.00 |
| ☐ R-6434 | 100.00 | 50.00 |
| ☐ R-6439 | 65.00 | 32.00 |
| ☐ R-6443 | 80.00 | 40.00 |
| ☐ R-6444 | 90.00 | 45.00 |
| ☐ R-6445 | 55.00 | 28.00 |
| ☐ R-6448 | 55.00 | 28.00 |
| ☐ R-6454 (L.W.) | 165.00 | 82.00 |
| ☐ R-6456 (L.W.) | 140.00 | 70.00 |
| ☐ R-6463 | 70.00 | 35.00 |
| ☐ R-6464 | 90.00 | 45.00 |
| ☐ R-6465 | 60.00 | 30.00 |
| ☐ R-6463 | 75.00 | 38.00 |
| ☐ R-6464 | 120.00 | 60.00 |
| ☐ R-6465 | 75.00 | 38.00 |
| ☐ R-6473 | 90.00 | 45.00 |
| ☐ R-6474 | 120.00 | 60.00 |
| ☐ R-6483 | 100.00 | 50.00 |
| ☐ R-6484 | 100.00 | 50.00 |
| ☐ R-6494 | 95.00 | 48.00 |
| ☐ R-6495 | 55.00 | 28.00 |
| ☐ R-6499 | 60.00 | 30.00 |
| ☐ R-6504 | 100.00 | 50.00 |
| ☐ R-6505 | 65.00 | 32.00 |
| ☐ R-6513 | 75.00 | 38.00 |
| ☐ R-6514 | 120.00 | 60.00 |
| ☐ R-6519 | 90.00 | 45.00 |
| ☐ R-6520 (W) | 150.00 | 75.00 |
| ☐ R-6523 (W) | 130.00 | 65.00 |
| ☐ R-6524 (W) | 225.00 | 113.00 |
| ☐ R-6533 (W) | 230.00 | 115.00 |
| ☐ R-6534 (W) | 130.00 | 65.00 |
| ☐ R-6535 (W) | 130.00 | 65.00 |
| ☐ R-6542 | 145.00 | 72.00 |
| ☐ R-6543 | 200.00 | 100.00 |
| ☐ R-6545 | 135.00 | 68.00 |
| ☐ R-6554 (L) | 65.00 | 32.00 |
| ☐ R-6559 | 90.00 | 45.00 |
| ☐ R-6563 | 100.00 | 50.00 |
| ☐ R-6565 | 90.00 | 45.00 |
| ☐ R-6573 | 100.00 | 50.00 |
| ☐ R-6575 | 75.00 | 38.00 |
| ☐ R-6583 | 100.00 | 50.00 |
| ☐ R-6585 | 80.00 | 40.00 |
| ☐ R-6585 | 75.00 | 38.00 |
| ☐ R-6593 (W) | 135.00 | 68.00 |
| ☐ R-6595 (W) | 100.00 | 50.00 |
| ☐ R-6603 (W) | 125.00 | 63.00 |
| ☐ R-6604 (W) | 200.00 | 100.00 |
| ☐ R-6605 (W) | 100.00 | 50.00 |
| ☐ R-6613 (W) | 150.00 | 75.00 |
| ☐ R-6615 | 125.00 | 63.00 |
| ☐ R-6623 | 90.00 | 45.00 |
| ☐ R-6624 | 160.00 | 80.00 |
| ☐ R-6625 | 80.00 | 40.00 |
| ☐ R-6633 | 90.00 | 45.00 |
| ☐ R-6634 | 100.00 | 50.00 |
| ☐ R-6635 | 90.00 | 45.00 |
| ☐ R-6643 | 110.00 | 55.00 |
| ☐ R-6644 | 160.00 | 80.00 |
| ☐ R-6645 | 80.00 | 40.00 |
| ☐ R-6653 | 100.00 | 50.00 |
| ☐ R-6654 | 175.00 | 88.00 |
| ☐ R-6655 | 85.00 | 42.00 |
| ☐ R-6663 | 100.00 | 50.00 |
| ☐ R-6664 | 200.00 | 100.00 |
| ☐ R-6673 (CO) | 124.00 | 72.00 |
| ☐ R-6674 (CO) | 250.00 | 125.00 |
| ☐ R-6683 (CO) | 130.00 | 65.00 |
| ☐ R-6693 (CO) | 175.00 | 88.00 |
| ☐ R-6694 (CO) | 225.00 | 113.00 |
| ☐ R-6695 (CO) | 125.00 | 63.00 |
| ☐ R-6703 | 130.00 | 65.00 |
| ☐ R-6704 | 175.00 | 88.00 |
| ☐ R-6705Q | 100.00 | 50.00 |

*REMINGTON / 215*

| PATTERN NO. | MINT | VG | PATTERN NO. | MINT | VG |
|---|---|---|---|---|---|
| ☐ R-6713 | 130.00 | 65.00 | ☐ R-6893 (W) | 185.00 | 92.00 |
| ☐ R-6714 | 170.00 | 85.00 | ☐ R-6894 (W) | 250.00 | 125.00 |
| ☐ R-6723 (W) | 175.00 | 88.00 | ☐ R-6895 (W) | 150.00 | 75.00 |
| ☐ R-6724 (W) | 300.00 | 150.00 | ☐ R-6903 | 40.00 | 20.00 |
| ☐ R-6725F (W) | 125.00 | 63.00 | ☐ R-6904 | 50.00 | 25.00 |
| ☐ R-6733 (E.E.) | 125.00 | 63.00 | ☐ R-6905 | 35.00 | 18.00 |
| ☐ R-6735 (E.E.) | 80.00 | 40.00 | ☐ R-6905 | 35.00 | 18.00 |
| ☐ R-6744 | 90.00 | 45.00 | ☐ R-6914 | 75.00 | 38.00 |
| ☐ R-6745F | 90.00 | 45.00 | ☐ R-6919 | 40.00 | 20.00 |
| ☐ R-6754 (W) | 190.00 | 85.00 | ☐ R-6923 | 125.00 | 63.00 |
| ☐ R-6755A (W) | 135.00 | 68.00 | ☐ R-6924 | 175.00 | 88.00 |
| ☐ R-6763 (W) | 165.00 | 82.00 | ☐ R-6925 | 65.00 | 32.00 |
| ☐ R-6764 (W) | 275.00 | 138.00 | ☐ R-6933 (CO) | 165.00 | 82.00 |
| ☐ R-6765A (W) | 160.00 | 80.00 | ☐ R-6934 (CO) | 225.00 | 113.00 |
| ☐ R-6773 (W) | 250.00 | 125.00 | ☐ R-6949 | 75.00 | 38.00 |
| ☐ R-6775 (W) | 100.00 | 50.00 | ☐ R-6954 (W) | 260.00 | 130.00 |
| ☐ R-6781 | 100.00 | 50.00 | ☐ R-6956 (W) | 175.00 | 88.00 |
| ☐ R-6785 (O.K.) | 100.00 | 50.00 | ☐ R-6964 (W) | 240.00 | 120.00 |
| ☐ R-6793 | 100.00 | 50.00 | ☐ R-6966 (W) | 165.00 | 82.00 |
| ☐ R-6795 | 85.00 | 42.00 | ☐ R-6973 | 200.00 | 100.00 |
| ☐ R-6803 (W) | 160.00 | 80.00 | ☐ R-6974 | 400.00 | 200.00 |
| ☐ R-6805 (W) | 160.00 | 80.00 | ☐ R-6984 (W.B.) | 550.00 | 275.00 |
| ☐ R-6816 (L.W.) | 1000.00 | 500.00 | ☐ R-6993 | 170.00 | 85.00 |
| ☐ R-6823 (W) | 400.00 | 200.00 | ☐ R-6994 | 250.00 | 125.00 |
| ☐ R-6825 (W) | 300.00 | 150.00 | ☐ R-6995 | 160.00 | 80.00 |
| ☐ R-6834 (W) | 500.00 | 250.00 | ☐ R-7003 (W) | 250.00 | 125.00 |
| ☐ R-6835 (W) | 250.00 | 125.00 | ☐ R-7004 (W) | 300.00 | 150.00 |
| ☐ R-6836 (W) | 300.00 | 150.00 | ☐ R-7005 (W) | 200.00 | 100.00 |
| ☐ R-6835 | 250.00 | 125.00 | ☐ R-7023 (W) | 100.00 | 50.00 |
| ☐ R-6843 | 50.00 | 25.00 | ☐ R-7024 | 200.00 | 100.00 |
| ☐ R-6844 | 65.00 | 32.00 | ☐ R-7026 (W) | 100.00 | 50.00 |
| ☐ R-6845 | 40.00 | 20.00 | ☐ R-7034 (W) | 100.00 | 50.00 |
| ☐ R-6854 | 65.00 | 32.00 | ☐ R-7044 | 75.00 | 38.00 |
| ☐ R-6859 | 50.00 | 25.00 | ☐ R-7045 | 60.00 | 30.00 |
| ☐ R-6863 | 45.00 | 23.00 | ☐ R-7039/5 | 75.00 | 38.00 |
| ☐ R-6864 | 60.00 | 30.00 | ☐ R-/6 | 75.00 | 38.00 |
| ☐ R-6865 | 40.00 | 20.00 | ☐ R-/7 | 75.00 | 38.00 |
| ☐ R-6872 | 40.00 | 20.00 | ☐ R-/8 | 75.00 | 38.00 |
| ☐ R-6873 | 55.00 | 28.00 | ☐ R-7044 | 90.00 | 45.00 |
| ☐ R-6874 | 100.00 | 50.00 | ☐ R-G7049/21 | 75.00 | 38.00 |
| ☐ R-6875 | 40.00 | 20.00 | ☐ R-/22 | 75.00 | 38.00 |
| ☐ R-6883 | 160.00 | 80.00 | ☐ R-/23 | 75.00 | 38.00 |
| ☐ R-6885 | 125.00 | 63.00 | ☐ R-/24 | 75.00 | 38.00 |

## 216 / REMINGTON

| PATTERN NO. | MINT | VG |
|---|---|---|
| ☐ R-G7054 | 90.00 | 45.00 |
| ☐ R-G7059/17 | 75.00 | 38.00 |
| ☐ R-/18 | 75.00 | 38.00 |
| ☐ R-/19 | 75.00 | 38.00 |
| ☐ R-/20 | 75.00 | 38.00 |
| ☐ R-/39 | 75.00 | 38.00 |
| ☐ R-/40 | 75.00 | 38.00 |
| ☐ R-7064 | 75.00 | 38.00 |
| ☐ R-7069/25 | 75.00 | 38.00 |
| ☐ R-/26 | 75.00 | 38.00 |
| ☐ R-/27 | 75.00 | 38.00 |
| ☐ R-/28 | 75.00 | 38.00 |
| ☐ R-7074 | 90.00 | 45.00 |
| ☐ R-G7079/10 | 75.00 | 38.00 |
| ☐ R-/11 | 75.00 | 38.00 |
| ☐ R-/12 | 75.00 | 38.00 |
| ☐ R-/36 | 75.00 | 38.00 |
| ☐ R-/37 | 75.00 | 38.00 |
| ☐ R-7084 | 90.00 | 45.00 |
| ☐ R-G7089/13 | 75.00 | 38.00 |
| ☐ R-/14 | 75.00 | 38.00 |
| ☐ R-/15 | 75.00 | 38.00 |
| ☐ R-/32 | 75.00 | 38.00 |
| ☐ R-/33 | 75.00 | 38.00 |
| ☐ R-/34 | 75.00 | 38.00 |
| ☐ R-7090 | 100.00 | 50.00 |
| ☐ R-7091 | 100.00 | 60.00 |
| ☐ R-7094 | 100.00 | 50.00 |
| ☐ R-G7099/1 | 100.00 | 50.00 |
| ☐ R-/2 | 100.00 | 50.00 |
| ☐ R-/3 | 100.00 | 50.00 |
| ☐ R-/4 | 100.00 | 50.00 |
| ☐ R-/29 | 100.00 | 50.00 |
| ☐ R-/30 | 100.00 | 50.00 |
| ☐ R-/31 | 100.00 | 50.00 |
| ☐ R-T7099 | 90.00 | 45.00 |
| ☐ R-7103 | 75.00 | 38.00 |
| ☐ R-7104 | 90.00 | 45.00 |
| ☐ R-7114 (W) | 100.00 | 50.00 |
| ☐ R-7116 (W) | 75.00 | 38.00 |
| ☐ R-7124 | 165.00 | 82.00 |
| ☐ R-7126 | 100.00 | 50.00 |
| ☐ R-7134 | 165.00 | 82.00 |
| ☐ R-7144 | 250.00 | 125.00 |
| ☐ R-7146 | 175.00 | 88.00 |
| ☐ R-7153 | 150.00 | 75.00 |
| ☐ R-7163 | 140.00 | 70.00 |
| ☐ R-7176 | 175.00 | 88.00 |
| ☐ R-7183 (W) | 250.00 | 125.00 |
| ☐ R-7196 (W) | 225.00 | 113.00 |
| ☐ R-7203 (W) | 275.00 | 138.00 |
| ☐ R-7216 | 275.00 | 138.00 |
| ☐ R-7223 | 150.00 | 75.00 |
| ☐ R-7224 | 200.00 | 100.00 |
| ☐ R-7225 | 140.00 | 70.00 |
| ☐ R-7234 | 90.00 | 45.00 |
| ☐ R-7236 | 75.00 | 38.00 |
| ☐ R-7243 (W) | 125.00 | 63.00 |
| ☐ R-7244 (W) | 300.00 | 150.00 |
| ☐ R-7246 (W) | 200.00 | 100.00 |
| ☐ R-7254 | 80.00 | 40.00 |
| ☐ R-7264 | 75.00 | 38.00 |
| ☐ R-7274 | 75.00 | 38.00 |
| ☐ R-7284 (L) | 80.00 | 40.00 |
| ☐ R-7293 (W) | 200.00 | 100.00 |
| ☐ R-7284 | 100.00 | 50.00 |
| ☐ R-7284-6 | 100.00 | 50.00 |
| ☐ R-7293 (W) | 200.00 | 100.00 |
| ☐ R-7309 | 75.00 | 38.00 |
| ☐ R-7319 | 75.00 | 38.00 |
| ☐ R-7329 | 55.00 | 28.00 |
| ☐ R-7335 | 40.00 | 20.00 |
| ☐ R-7339 | 40.00 | 20.00 |
| ☐ R-7343 | 65.00 | 32.00 |
| ☐ R-7344 | 65.00 | 32.00 |
| ☐ R-7353 | 80.00 | 40.00 |
| ☐ R-7366 | 90.00 | 45.00 |
| ☐ R-7374 | 90.00 | 45.00 |
| ☐ R-7375 | 90.00 | 45.00 |
| ☐ R-7384 | 90.00 | 45.00 |
| ☐ R-7394 (L) | 100.00 | 50.00 |
| ☐ R-7396 | 60.00 | 30.00 |
| ☐ R-7403 | 75.00 | 38.00 |
| ☐ R-7404 | 110.00 | 55.00 |
| ☐ R-7414 | 110.00 | 55.00 |
| ☐ R-7423 | 60.00 | 30.00 |

REMINGTON / 217

| PATTERN NO. | MINT | VG | PATTERN NO. | MINT | VG |
|---|---|---|---|---|---|
| ☐ R-7425 | 95.00 | 48.00 | ☐ R-7684 | 90.00 | 45.00 |
| ☐ R-7433 (W) | 150.00 | 75.00 | ☐ R-7696 (W) | 150.00 | 75.00 |
| ☐ R-7443 | 70.00 | 35.00 | ☐ R-7706 | 80.00 | 40.00 |
| ☐ R-7453 | 65.00 | 32.00 | ☐ R-7713 | 55.00 | 28.00 |
| ☐ R-7463 | 75.00 | 38.00 | ☐ R-7725 (BU.K) | 55.00 | 28.00 |
| ☐ R-7465 | 70.00 | 35.00 | ☐ R-7734 | 70.00 | 35.00 |
| ☐ R-7473 | 75.00 | 38.00 | ☐ R-7744 | 70.00 | 35.00 |
| ☐ R-7475 | 70.00 | 35.00 | ☐ R-7756 | 500.00 | 250.00 |
| ☐ R-7483 (W) | 200.00 | 100.00 | ☐ R-7766 | 500.00 | 250.00 |
| ☐ R-7485 (W) | 200.00 | 100.00 | ☐ R-7772 | 50.00 | 25.00 |
| ☐ R-7495 (W) | 275.00 | 138.00 | ☐ R-7773 | 60.00 | 30.00 |
| ☐ R-7500Buf (W) | 130.00 | 65.00 | ☐ R-7783 (W) | 90.00 | 45.00 |
| ☐ R-7503 | 110.00 | 55.00 | ☐ R-7785 | 120.00 | 60.00 |
| ☐ R-7513 (W) | 160.00 | 80.00 | ☐ R-7793 | 70.00 | 35.00 |
| ☐ R-7526 | 120.00 | 60.00 | ☐ R-7795 | 75.00 | 38.00 |
| ☐ R-7536 | 110.00 | 55.00 | ☐ R-7803 | 130.00 | 65.00 |
| ☐ R-7544 | 80.00 | 40.00 | ☐ R-7805 | 150.00 | 75.00 |
| ☐ R-7546 | 65.00 | 32.00 | ☐ R-7813 | 75.00 | 38.00 |
| ☐ R-7554 | 100.00 | 50.00 | ☐ R-7814 | 110.00 | 55.00 |
| ☐ R-7564 | 100.00 | 50.00 | ☐ R-7823 | 90.00 | 45.00 |
| ☐ R-7566 | 65.00 | 32.00 | ☐ R-7825 | 90.00 | 45.00 |
| ☐ R-7573 | 65.00 | 32.00 | ☐ R-7833 | 225.00 | 113.00 |
| ☐ R-7574 | 90.00 | 45.00 | ☐ R-7853 | 60.00 | 30.00 |
| ☐ R-7576 | 70.00 | 35.00 | ☐ R-C7853 | 75.00 | 38.00 |
| ☐ R-7584 (W) | 200.00 | 100.00 | ☐ R-7854 | 60.00 | 30.00 |
| ☐ R-7586 (W) | 150.00 | 75.00 | ☐ R-7863 | 75.00 | 38.00 |
| ☐ R-7593 | 100.00 | 50.00 | ☐ R-7873 | 75.00 | 38.00 |
| ☐ R-7596 | 125.00 | 63.00 | ☐ R-7895 | 60.00 | 30.00 |
| ☐ R-7603 | 100.00 | 50.00 | ☐ R-7925 | 50.00 | 25.00 |
| ☐ R-7604 | 175.00 | 88.00 | ☐ R-7985 | 90.00 | 45.00 |
| ☐ R-7606 | 150.00 | 75.00 | ☐ R-7993 (BR) | 60.00 | 30.00 |
| ☐ R-7613 | 75.00 | 38.00 | ☐ R-7995 (BR) | 65.00 | 32.00 |
| ☐ R-7614 | 75.00 | 38.00 | ☐ R-8003 | 65.00 | 32.00 |
| ☐ R-7624 | 90.00 | 45.00 | ☐ R-8004 | 70.00 | 35.00 |
| ☐ R-7633 (W) | 160.00 | 80.00 | ☐ R-8013 | 55.00 | 28.00 |
| ☐ R-7643 | 75.00 | 38.00 | ☐ R-8023 (W) | 125.00 | 63.00 |
| ☐ R-7645 | 75.00 | 38.00 | ☐ R-8039 (BR) | 60.00 | 30.00 |
| ☐ R-7653 (W) | 170.00 | 85.00 | ☐ R-8044 (L) | 90.00 | 45.00 |
| ☐ R-7654 (W) | 210.00 | 105.00 | ☐ R-8055 (S) | 100.00 | 50.00 |
| ☐ R-7663 (W) | 175.00 | 88.00 | ☐ R-8059 (BR) | 60.00 | 30.00 |
| ☐ R-7664 (W) | 250.00 | 125.00 | ☐ R-8063 (S) | 150.00 | 75.00 |
| ☐ R-7674 | 75.00 | 38.00 | ☐ R-8065 (S) | 120.00 | 60.00 |
| ☐ R-7683 | 60.00 | 30.00 | ☐ R-8069 (S) | 120.00 | 60.00 |

# SCHRADE

*SCHRADE HAD ITS OWN PATTERN NUMBER SYSTEM, BUT NOT EVERY SCHRADE KNIFE YOU SEE WILL BE STAMPED. We would advise you to become familiar with this system, since we will have a much expanded section on Schrade in next year's edition.*

**THE FIRST DIGIT**-The number of blades in the knife.
- *1*-1 Blade
- *2*-2 Blades, both blades in one end
- *3*-3 Blades, all 3 blades in one end
- *7*-2 Blade Knife, 1 blade in each end
- *8*-3 Blade Knife, 2 blades in one end and 1 blade in the other end
- *9*-4 Blade Knife, 2 blades in each end

**THE SECOND AND THIRD DIGITS**-The factory pattern number. For example 2011, the "01" will always mean an easy open.

**THE LAST FIGURE**-Handle material.
- *1*-Cocobola
- *2*-Ebony
- *3*-Bone Stag
- *4*-Celluloid
- *5*-White Bone
- *6*-Mother of Pearl
- *7*-Stained Bone
- *8*-Buffalo Horn
- *9*-Miscellaneous

| PATTERN NO. | MINT | VG | PATTERN NO. | MINT | VG |
|---|---|---|---|---|---|
| ☐ 24143 | 45.00 | 22.50 | ☐ 37203 | 60.00 | 30.00 |
| ☐ 34173 | 70.00 | 35.00 | ☐ 37283 | 45.00 | 22.50 |
| ☐ 34263 | 95.00 | 47.50 | ☐ 44133 | 70.00 | 35.00 |
| ☐ 37153 | 40.00 | 20.00 | ☐ 46163 | 50.00 | 25.00 |
| ☐ 37193 | 200.00 | 100.00 | ☐ 47283 | 50.00 | 25.00 |

## SCHRADE KNIVES
### (CURRENT PRODUCTION)

| PATTERN NO. | MINT | VG | PATTERN NO. | MINT | VG |
|---|---|---|---|---|---|
| ☐ 80T | 16.00 | 8.00 | ☐ 510T | 34.00 | 17.00 |
| ☐ 180T | 9.00 | 4.50 | ☐ 610T | 17.00 | 8.50 |
| ☐ 260T | 26.00 | 13.00 | ☐ 770T | 14.00 | 7.00 |
| ☐ 330T | 10.00 | 5.00 | ☐ 940T | 15.00 | 7.50 |
| ☐ 340T | 14.00 | 7.00 | ☐ 1080T | 13.00 | 6.50 |

## SCHRADE / 219

| PATTERN NO. | MINT | VG |
|---|---|---|
| ☐ 1250T | 23.00 | 11.50 |
| ☐ 1940T | 12.00 | 6.00 |
| ☐ 8580T | 24.00 | 12.00 |
| ☐ 130T | 35.00 | 17.50 |
| ☐ 140T | 35.00 | 17.50 |
| ☐ 150T | 27.00 | 13.50 |
| ☐ 1520T | 18.00 | 9.00 |
| ☐ 1540T | 18.00 | 9.00 |
| ☐ 1560T | 22.00 | 11.00 |
| ☐ 1650T | 32.00 | 16.00 |

### UNCLE HENRY

| PATTERN NO. | MINT | VG |
|---|---|---|
| ☐ LB-1 | 20.00 | 10.00 |
| ☐ LB-5 | 30.00 | 15.00 |
| ☐ LB-7 | 35.00 | 17.50 |
| ☐ LB-8 | 40.00 | 20.00 |
| ☐ 197UH | 40.00 | 20.00 |
| ☐ 285UH | 40.00 | 20.00 |
| ☐ 885UH | 15.00 | 7.50 |
| ☐ 897UH | 18.00 | 9.00 |
| ☐ 127UH | 27.00 | 13.50 |
| ☐ 227UH | 33.00 | 16.50 |
| ☐ 144UH | 45.00 | 22.50 |
| ☐ 153UH | 38.00 | 19.00 |
| ☐ 171UH | 45.00 | 22.50 |

### SCHRADE SCRIMSHAWS

| PATTERN NO. | MINT | VG |
|---|---|---|
| ☐ 503SC | 18.00 | 9.00 |
| ☐ 505SC | 21.00 | 10.50 |
| ☐ 506SC | 19.00 | 9.50 |
| ☐ 500SC | 29.00 | 14.50 |
| ☐ 508SC | 35.00 | 17.50 |
| ☐ 502SC | 25.00 | 12.50 |
| ☐ 507SC | 40.00 | 20.00 |
| ☐ 509SC | 30.00 | 15.00 |

### SCHRADE OPEN STOCK

| PATTERN NO. | MINT | VG |
|---|---|---|
| ☐ 136 | 16.00 | 8.00 |
| ☐ 186 | 16.00 | 8.00 |
| ☐ 206 | 16.00 | 8.00 |
| ☐ 293 | 13.00 | 6.50 |
| ☐ 708 | 12.00 | 6.00 |
| ☐ 787 | 12.00 | 6.00 |
| ☐ 808 | 12.00 | 6.00 |
| ☐ 834 | 12.00 | 6.00 |
| ☐ 835Y | 14.00 | 7.00 |
| ☐ 863 | 13.00 | 6.50 |
| ☐ 881 | 14.00 | 7.00 |
| ☐ 881Y | 15.00 | 7.50 |
| ☐ 896K | 14.00 | 7.00 |
| ☐ 899 | 14.00 | 7.00 |
| ☐ 175RB | 12.00 | 6.00 |
| ☐ 778RB | 16.00 | 8.00 |
| ☐ 825RB | 17.00 | 8.50 |

### SCHRADE WALDEN POCKETKNIVES

| PATTERN NO. | MINT | VG |
|---|---|---|
| ☐ C3-150 | 100.00 | 50.00 |
| ☐ C3-151 | 100.00 | 50.00 |
| ☐ C3-152 | 75.00 | 37.50 |
| ☐ C3-153 | 200.00 | 100.00 |
| ☐ C3-154 | 170.00 | 85.00 |
| ☐ C3-174 | 30.00 | 15.00 |
| ☐ C3-186 | 40.00 | 20.00 |
| ☐ C3-234 | 45.00 | 22.50 |
| ☐ C3-242 | 75.00 | 37.50 |
| ☐ C3-272 | 45.00 | 22.50 |
| ☐ C3-272Y | 45.00 | 22.50 |
| ☐ C3-293 | 75.00 | 37.50 |
| ☐ C3-708 | 40.00 | 20.00 |
| ☐ C3-708 | 40.00 | 20.00 |
| ☐ C3-742 | 80.00 | 40.00 |
| ☐ C3-745 | 60.00 | 45.00 |
| ☐ C3-746 | 75.00 | 37.50 |
| ☐ C3-750 | 100.00 | 50.00 |
| ☐ C3-766 | 30.00 | 15.00 |
| ☐ C3-744 | 55.00 | 27.50 |

## 220 / SCHRADE

| PATTERN NO. | MINT | VG |
|---|---|---|
| ☐ C3-787 | 75.00 | 37.50 |
| ☐ C3-808 | 25.00 | 12.50 |
| ☐ C3-808Y | 25.00 | 12.50 |
| ☐ 3C-810 | 45.00 | 22.50 |
| ☐ 3C-820 | 20.00 | 10.00 |
| ☐ 3C-822 | 65.00 | 32.50 |
| ☐ 3C-825 | 50.00 | 25.00 |
| ☐ 3C-834 | 35.00 | 17.50 |
| ☐ 3C-848 | 30.00 | 15.00 |
| ☐ 3C-861 | 80.00 | 40.00 |
| ☐ 3C-881 | 80.00 | 40.00 |
| ☐ C3-881Y | 80.00 | 40.00 |
| ☐ C3-890 | 50.00 | 25.00 |
| ☐ C3-900 | 60.00 | 30.00 |
| ☐ C3-906 | 60.00 | 30.00 |
| ☐ C3-951 | 45.00 | 22.50 |
| ☐ C3-967 | 45.00 | 22.50 |
| ☐ 3C-973 | 125.00 | 62.50 |
| ☐ C3-974 | 125.00 | 62.50 |
| ☐ C3-233S | 60.00 | 30.00 |
| ☐ 3C-233Y | 60.00 | 30.00 |
| ☐ C3-709SHA | 25.00 | 12.50 |
| ☐ C3-793SHA | 40.00 | 20.00 |
| ☐ 3C-809M | 22.00 | 11.00 |
| ☐ C3-863S | 65.00 | 32.50 |
| ☐ C3-863Y | 65.00 | 32.50 |
| ☐ C3-896K | 40.00 | 20.00 |
| ☐ C3-SS102 | 35.00 | 17.50 |
| ☐ C3-SS105 | 25.00 | 12.50 |
| ☐ C3-SS700 | 45.00 | 22.50 |
| ☐ 115S | 50.00 | 25.00 |
| ☐ 718 | 8.00 | 4.00 |
| ☐ 1091 | 60.00 | 30.00 |
| ☐ 2061 3/4 | 96.00 | 48.00 |
| ☐ 2062 3/4 | 75.00 | 37.50 |
| ☐ 2063 1/2 | 132.00 | 66.00 |
| ☐ 2063 3/4 | 110.00 | 55.00 |
| ☐ 2069BR | 96.00 | 48.00 |
| ☐ 2069 3/4BR | 96.00 | 48.00 |
| ☐ 2071 | 96.00 | 48.00 |
| ☐ 2071 3/4 | 96.00 | 48.00 |
| ☐ 2072 | 96.00 | 48.00 |
| ☐ 2072 3/4 | 96.00 | 48.00 |

| PATTERN NO. | MINT | VG |
|---|---|---|
| ☐ 2073 | 110.00 | 55.00 |
| ☐ 2073 3/4 | 120.00 | 60.00 |
| ☐ 2091 | 110.00 | 55.00 |
| ☐ 2093 | 144.00 | 72.00 |
| ☐ 2221 | 96.00 | 48.00 |
| ☐ 2222 | 96.00 | 48.00 |
| ☐ 2223 | 110.00 | 55.00 |
| ☐ 2224 AC | 80.00 | 40.00 |
| ☐ 2224GP | 80.00 | 40.00 |
| ☐ 226 | 162.00 | 81.00 |
| ☐ 2293 | 162.00 | 81.00 |
| ☐ 2363 | 132.00 | 66.00 |
| ☐ 2392 | 96.00 | 48.00 |
| ☐ 2392 | 45.00 | 22.50 |
| ☐ 2393 3/4 | 50.00 | 25.00 |
| ☐ 2813 | 156.00 | 78.00 |
| ☐ 2813 3/4 | 156.00 | 78.00 |
| ☐ 2814 3/4G | 140.00 | 70.00 |
| ☐ 2814 3/4P | 140.00 | 70.00 |
| ☐ 2814 3/4 AC | 140.00 | 70.00 |
| ☐ 7243B | 96.00 | 48.00 |
| ☐ 7243T | 120.00 | 60.00 |
| ☐ 7244HT | 90.00 | 45.00 |
| ☐ 7326 | 108.00 | 54.00 |
| ☐ 7812 | 190.00 | 95.00 |
| ☐ 7813 | 210.00 | 105.00 |
| ☐ 9113B | 192.00 | 96.00 |
| ☐ 116B | 264.00 | 132.00 |
| ☐ 8313B | 190.00 | 95.00 |
| ☐ 8313T | 180.00 | 90.00 |
| ☐ 8316B | 250.00 | 125.00 |
| ☐ 8323 | 180.00 | 90.00 |
| ☐ 8324S | 150.00 | 75.00 |
| ☐ 8443 | 192.00 | 96.00 |
| ☐ 8803 | 210.00 | 105.00 |
| ☐ 8813 | 210.00 | 105.00 |
| ☐ 9463 | 144.00 | 72.00 |
| ☐ 9803LB | 228.00 | 114.00 |
| ☐ 9466 | 240.00 | 120.00 |
| ☐ 9603 | 270.00 | 135.00 |
| ☐ 9806 | 225.00 | 112.50 |
| ☐ S2393 | 134.00 | 67.00 |
| ☐ S9463 | 144.00 | 72.00 |

## PUSH BUTTON

| PATTERN NO. | MINT | VG | PATTERN NO. | MINT | VG |
|---|---|---|---|---|---|
| ☐ 1514AC | 108.00 | 54.00 | ☐ 1553 | 180.00 | 90.00 |
| ☐ G1514J | 108.00 | 54.00 | ☐ 1553 3/4 | 180.00 | 90.00 |
| ☐ G1514K | 108.00 | 54.00 | ☐ 1613 3/4 | 330.00 | 165.00 |
| ☐ 1543 3/4 | 270.00 | 135.00 | ☐ 6489W | 150.00 | 75.00 |

## SCHRADE, GEORGE

| | | |
|---|---|---|
| ☐ 6489W | 150.00 | 75.00 |

## SHAPLEIGH

Shapleigh was a hardware company that has produced many collectable pocketknives, including Bridge Cutlery Company and Diamond Edge.

The hardware company was founded by A. F. Shapleigh in 1843, adopting the Diamond Edge logo in 1864. Made by Camillus and Schrade, the Diamond Edge was very popular. Shapleigh made over 600 patterns of pocketknives, including some Diamond Edge knives stamped Norvel Shapleigh (named for a Shapleigh Hardware company buyer, Sanders Norvel).

Shapleigh went out of business in 1960, making cutlery until that time.

The Diamond Edge trademark is currently used by Imperial Knife Associated Companies on one of their lines of cutlery and should not be confused with the older Diamond Edge knives.

| PATTERN NO. | MINT | VG | PATTERN NO. | MINT | VG |
|---|---|---|---|---|---|
| ☐ E101ST | 50.00 | 25.00 | ☐ E211ST | 60.00 | 30.00 |
| ☐ E102ST | 50.00 | 25.00 | ☐ E212C | 60.00 | 30.00 |
| ☐ E103ST | 50.00 | 25.00 | ☐ E217PC | 55.00 | 27.50 |
| ☐ E104C | 50.00 | 25.00 | ☐ E221PC | 45.00 | 22.50 |
| ☐ E105PC | 50.00 | 25.00 | ☐ E222PC | 45.00 | 22.50 |
| ☐ E201C | 50.00 | 25.00 | ☐ 1S440 3/4C | 160.00 | 80.00 |
| ☐ E202ST | 175.00 | 87.50 | ☐ 1S440 3/4CP | 150.00 | 75.00 |
| ☐ E205ST | 180.00 | 90.00 | ☐ 1S440 3/4S | 160.00 | 80.00 |
| ☐ E206C | 45.00 | 22.50 | ☐ 1S441 3/4C | 150.00 | 75.00 |
| ☐ E207ST | 90.00 | 45.00 | ☐ 1S442 3/4C | 90.00 | 45.00 |
| ☐ E208C | 90.00 | 45.00 | ☐ 1S442 3/4S | 90.00 | 45.00 |

## 222 / SHAPLEIGH

| PATTERN NO. | MINT | VG |
|---|---|---|
| ☐ 1S443 3/4S | 75.00 | 37.50 |
| ☐ 1S445 | 60.00 | 30.00 |
| ☐ 1S447 3/4C | 75.00 | 37.50 |
| ☐ 1S448 3/4C | 90.00 | 45.00 |
| ☐ 1S449 3/4C | 90.00 | 45.00 |
| ☐ 1S621 | 40.00 | 20.00 |
| ☐ 1S621 3/4 | 40.00 | 20.00 |
| ☐ 1S622ST | 70.00 | 35.00 |
| ☐ 1S662 3/4ST | 70.00 | 35.00 |
| ☐ 1S622 5/8ST | 70.00 | 35.00 |
| ☐ S14ST | 150.00 | 75.00 |
| ☐ S15ST | 150.00 | 75.00 |
| ☐ S101 | 60.00 | 30.00 |
| ☐ S104 | 60.00 | 30.00 |
| ☐ S103 3/4 | 165.00 | 82.50 |
| ☐ S104 3/4 | 165.00 | 82.50 |
| ☐ S105 | 130.00 | 65.00 |
| ☐ S106 3/4 | 130.00 | 65.00 |
| ☐ S209 | 50.00 | 25.00 |
| ☐ S210 | 45.00 | 22.50 |
| ☐ S211 | 110.00 | 55.00 |
| ☐ S212C | 100.00 | 50.00 |
| ☐ S217 3/4 | 60.00 | 30.00 |
| ☐ S218 3/4 | 55.00 | 27.50 |
| ☐ S231 | 50.00 | 25.00 |
| ☐ S232 | 45.00 | 22.50 |
| ☐ S233 | 50.00 | 25.00 |
| ☐ S234 | 45.00 | 22.50 |
| ☐ S235 | 55.00 | 27.50 |
| ☐ S236 | 45.00 | 22.50 |
| ☐ S248 | 50.00 | 25.00 |
| ☐ S249 | 50.00 | 25.00 |
| ☐ S301 1/4 | 100.00 | 50.00 |
| ☐ S302 3/4 | 100.00 | 50.00 |
| ☐ S303 3/4 | 90.00 | 45.00 |
| ☐ S304 1/4 | 80.00 | 40.00 |
| ☐ S305 1/4 | 65.00 | 32.50 |
| ☐ S306 3/4 | 90.00 | 45.00 |
| ☐ S307 3/4 | 90.00 | 45.00 |
| ☐ S308 1/4 | 125.00 | 62.50 |
| ☐ S309 1/4 | 100.00 | 50.00 |
| ☐ S310 1/4 | 80.00 | 40.00 |
| ☐ S311 1/4 | 65.00 | 32.50 |

| PATTERN NO. | MINT | VG |
|---|---|---|
| ☐ S405 1/4 | 75.00 | 37.50 |
| ☐ 2S272GS | 125.00 | 62.50 |
| ☐ 2S375C | 50.00 | 25.00 |
| ☐ 2S375S | 50.00 | 25.00 |
| ☐ 2S375CP | 35.00 | 17.50 |
| ☐ 2S376C | 50.00 | 25.00 |
| ☐ 2S276P | 60.00 | 30.00 |
| ☐ 2S376S | 55.00 | 27.50 |
| ☐ 2S377W | 550.00 | 275.00 |
| ☐ 2S380C | 50.00 | 25.00 |
| ☐ 2S380ST | 50.00 | 25.00 |
| ☐ 2S381 | 40.00 | 20.00 |
| ☐ 2½ S371 3/4ST | 50.00 | 25.00 |
| ☐ 2S305C | 50.00 | 25.00 |
| ☐ 2S305P | 60.00 | 30.00 |
| ☐ 2S311 3/4C | 60.00 | 30.00 |
| ☐ 2S311 3/4ST | 45.00 | 22.50 |
| ☐ 2S312P | 50.00 | 25.00 |
| ☐ 2S315P | 60.00 | 30.00 |
| ☐ 2S336 3/4C | 50.00 | 25.00 |
| ☐ 2S336 3/4S | 65.00 | 32.50 |
| ☐ 2S342C | 60.00 | 30.00 |
| ☐ 2S362P | 60.00 | 30.00 |
| ☐ 2S382 3/4C | 50.00 | 25.00 |
| ☐ 2S382 3/4ST | 50.00 | 25.00 |
| ☐ 2S383 3/4C | 40.00 | 20.00 |
| ☐ 2S383 3/4ST | 45.00 | 22.50 |
| ☐ 2S386C | 75.00 | 37.50 |
| ☐ 2S386ST | 75.00 | 37.50 |
| ☐ 2S404C | 100.00 | 50.00 |
| ☐ 2S404ST | 125.00 | 62.50 |
| ☐ S417P | 60.00 | 30.00 |
| ☐ 2S432C | 125.00 | 62.50 |
| ☐ 2S432ST | 150.00 | 75.00 |
| ☐ 2S443GS | 40.00 | 20.00 |
| ☐ 2S447C | 60.00 | 30.00 |
| ☐ 2S447 | 70.00 | 35.00 |
| ☐ 2S447 3/4C | 65.00 | 32.50 |
| ☐ 2S447 3/4ST | 70.00 | 35.00 |
| ☐ 2S450C | 90.00 | 45.00 |
| ☐ 2S450ST | 90.00 | 45.00 |
| ☐ 2S457C | 60.00 | 30.00 |
| ☐ 2S457ST | 100.00 | 50.00 |

*SHAPLEIGH / 223*

| PATTERN NO. | MINT | VG | PATTERN NO. | MINT | VG |
|---|---|---|---|---|---|
| ☐ 2S506C | 50.00 | 25.00 | ☐ 2S625ST | 175.00 | 87.50 |
| ☐ 2S506ST | 50.00 | 25.00 | ☐ 2S655 3/4ST | 175.00 | 87.50 |
| ☐ 2S514 1/2ST | 50.00 | 25.00 | ☐ 2S626 3/4C | 50.00 | 25.00 |
| ☐ 2S520ST | 55.00 | 27.50 | ☐ 2S626 3/4ST | 60.00 | 30.00 |
| ☐ 2S 526 3/4 ST | 140.00 | 70.00 | ☐ 2S627C | 50.00 | 25.00 |
| ☐ 2S527 3/4C | 170.00 | 85.00 | ☐ 3S20 5/8ST | 160.00 | 80.00 |
| ☐ 2S427 3/4ST | 170.00 | 85.00 | ☐ 3S67 1/4C | 60.00 | 30.00 |
| ☐ 2S528C | 40.00 | 20.00 | ☐ 3S67 1/4ST | 80.00 | 40.00 |
| ☐ 2S528CP | 45.00 | 22.50 | ☐ 3S67 3/4C | 80.00 | 40.00 |
| ☐ 2S534 3/4C | 40.00 | 20.00 | ☐ 3S67 3/4P | 150.00 | 75.00 |
| ☐ 2S535 3/4ST | 50.00 | 25.00 | ☐ 3S67 3/4ST | 110.00 | 55.00 |
| ☐ 2S538C | 50.00 | 25.00 | ☐ 3S76 3/4C | 70.00 | 35.00 |
| ☐ 2S539 3/4C | 50.00 | 25.00 | ☐ 3S76 3/4ST | 90.00 | 45.00 |
| ☐ 2S542C | 40.00 | 20.00 | ☐ 3S103CP | 100.00 | 50.00 |
| ☐ 2S542ST | 45.00 | 22.50 | ☐ 3S103ST | 125.00 | 62.50 |
| ☐ 2S555P | 60.00 | 30.00 | ☐ 3S105P | 100.00 | 50.00 |
| ☐ 2S546C | 50.00 | 25.00 | ☐ 3S105ST | 80.00 | 40.00 |
| ☐ 2S567C | 40.00 | 20.00 | ☐ 3S109 1/4C | 80.00 | 40.00 |
| ☐ 2S467CP | 40.00 | 20.00 | ☐ 3S109 1/4ST | 100.00 | 50.00 |
| ☐ 2S467ST | 45.00 | 22.50 | ☐ 3S109 3/4C | 110.00 | 55.00 |
| ☐ 2S580C | 50.00 | 25.00 | ☐ 3S109 3/4S | 130.00 | 65.00 |
| ☐ 2S580ST | 55.00 | 27.50 | ☐ 3S193C | 50.00 | 25.00 |
| ☐ 2S580CEO | 65.00 | 32.50 | ☐ 3S193P | 90.00 | 45.00 |
| ☐ 2S580SEO | 65.00 | 32.50 | ☐ 3S193ST | 65.00 | 32.50 |
| ☐ 2S580 3/4C | 50.00 | 25.00 | ☐ 3S209C | 90.00 | 45.00 |
| ☐ 2S580 3/4ST | 55.00 | 27.50 | ☐ 3S209P | 200.00 | 100.00 |
| ☐ 2S581C | 40.00 | 20.00 | ☐ 3S209ST | 125.00 | 62.50 |
| ☐ 2S581ST | 50.00 | 25.00 | ☐ 3S220C | 50.00 | 25.00 |
| ☐ 2S586 C | 50.00 | 25.00 | ☐ 3S220ST | 65.00 | 32.50 |
| ☐ 2S568 3/4ST | 60.00 | 30.00 | ☐ 3S253 1/4C | 75.00 | 37.50 |
| ☐ 2S587C | 45.00 | 22.50 | ☐ 3S253 1/4ST | 110.00 | 55.00 |
| ☐ 2S588 3/4C | 45.00 | 22.50 | ☐ 3S253 3/4C | 90.00 | 45.00 |
| ☐ 2S618C | 65.00 | 32.50 | ☐ 3S253 3/4P | 200.00 | 100.00 |
| ☐ 2S618S | 80.00 | 40.00 | ☐ 3S253 3/4ST | 125.00 | 62.50 |
| ☐ 2S623C | 50.00 | 25.00 | ☐ 3S261P | 50.00 | 25.00 |
| ☐ 2S623CP | 45.00 | 22.50 | ☐ 3S275C | 50.00 | 25.00 |
| ☐ 2S623ST | 55.00 | 27.50 | ☐ 3S275P | 90.00 | 45.00 |
| ☐ 2S623 3/4C | 50.00 | 25.00 | ☐ 3S275ST | 60.00 | 30.00 |
| ☐ 2S623 3/4CP | 60.00 | 30.00 | ☐ 3S311 1/4C | 100.00 | 50.00 |
| ☐ 2S623 3/4C | 60.00 | 30.00 | ☐ 3S311 1/4ST | 125.00 | 62.50 |
| ☐ 2S64 3/4C | 45.00 | 22.50 | ☐ 3S311 3/4C | 100.00 | 50.00 |
| ☐ 2S624 3/4ST | 60.00 | 30.00 | ☐ 3S311 3/4T | 125.00 | 62.50 |
| ☐ 2S625C | 100.00 | 50.00 | ☐ 3S354P | 50.00 | 25.00 |

# 224 / WINCHESTER

| PATTERN NO. | MINT | VG | PATTERN NO. | MINT | VG |
|---|---|---|---|---|---|
| ☐ 3S355P | 60.00 | 30.00 | ☐ 3S568 3/4ST | 90.00 | 45.00 |
| ☐ 3S362P | 75.00 | 37.50 | ☐ 3S568 5/8CP | 100.00 | 50.00 |
| ☐ 3S374P | 50.00 | 25.00 | ☐ 3S568 5/8S | 125.00 | 62.50 |
| ☐ 3S375C | 50.00 | 25.00 | ☐ 3S626 1/4S | 80.00 | 40.00 |
| ☐ 3S383 3/4C | 100.00 | 50.00 | ☐ 3S626 1/4ST | 95.00 | 47.50 |
| ☐ 3S447 1/4ST | 170.00 | 85.00 | ☐ 3S565 3/4C | 60.00 | 30.00 |
| ☐ 3S523 1/4C | 110.00 | 55.00 | ☐ 3S565 3/4S | 90.00 | 45.00 |
| ☐ 3S523 1/4ST | 140.00 | 70.00 | ☐ 4S20 1/4ST | 150.00 | 75.00 |
| ☐ 3S523 3/4C | 110.00 | 55.00 | ☐ 4S20 3/4ST | 150.00 | 75.00 |
| ☐ 3S523 3/4ST | 140.00 | 70.00 | ☐ 4S31P | 150.00 | 75.00 |
| ☐ 3S525C | 60.00 | 30.00 | ☐ 4S66 1/2ST | 200.00 | 100.00 |
| ☐ 3S525ST | 75.00 | 37.50 | ☐ 4S214 1/2ST | 150.00 | 75.00 |
| ☐ 3S525 1/4C | 70.00 | 35.00 | ☐ 4S215 1/2S | 200.00 | 100.00 |
| ☐ 3S525 1/4ST | 90.00 | 45.00 | ☐ 4S275ST | 85.00 | 42.50 |
| ☐ 3S529 3/4ST | 130.00 | 65.00 | ☐ 4S275 1/4ST | 125.00 | 62.50 |
| ☐ 3S565 1/4C | 100.00 | 50.00 | ☐ 4S374P | 125.00 | 62.50 |
| ☐ 3S565 1/4ST | 125.00 | 62.50 | ☐ 4S375P | 125.00 | 62.50 |
| ☐ 3S565 3/4C | 60.00 | 30.00 | ☐ 4S376P | 150.00 | 75.00 |
| ☐ 3S565 3/4S | 90.00 | 45.00 | ☐ 4S376ST | 80.00 | 40.00 |
| ☐ 3S568 1/4C | 100.00 | 50.00 | ☐ 4S517S | 75.00 | 37.50 |
| ☐ 3S568 1/4ST | 125.00 | 62.50 | ☐ 4S518S | 75.00 | 37.50 |
| ☐ 3S568 3/4C | 70.00 | 35.00 | ☐ 4S519CP | 65.00 | 32.50 |
|  |  |  | ☐ 4S519S | 70.00 | 35.00 |

# WINCHESTER

The pattern numbers used by Winchester are broken down as follows: first number, number of blades; second number, handle material; third number, variations of the knifemaking processes.

Winchester used almost every common pattern, handle material and bolster.

There were two distinct lines of Winchester knives. The higher quality knives tend to have a logo on every blade while the lesser quality line tends to have the logo on only one blade, but there are some exceptions to this.

| PATTERN NO. | MINT | VG | PATTERN NO. | MINT | VG |
|---|---|---|---|---|---|
| ☐ H1610P | 70.00 | 35.00 | ☐ 2H2009P | 100.00 | 50.00 |
| ☐ 2H1625P | 50.00 | 25.00 | ☐ 2H2049P | 80.00 | 40.00 |
| ☐ H1701P | 175.00 | 87.50 | ☐ 2H2123P | 50.00 | 25.00 |

## WINCHESTER / 225

| PATTERN NO. | MINT | VG | PATTERN NO. | MINT | VG |
|---|---|---|---|---|---|
| ☐ H2609 | 200.00 | 100.00 | ☐ 1937 | 150.00 | 75.00 |
| ☐ H2615 | 120.00 | 60.00 | ☐ 1938 | 125.00 | 62.50 |
| ☐ H2632P | 90.00 | 45.00 | ☐ 1950 | 1,200.00 | 600.00 |
| ☐ H2636P | 120.00 | 60.00 | ☐ 2028 | 150.00 | 75.00 |
| ☐ H2638P | 175.00 | 87.50 | ☐ 2037 | 90.00 | 45.00 |
| ☐ H2701P | 200.00 | 100.00 | ☐ 2038 | 150.00 | 75.00 |
| ☐ H2943P | 90.00 | 45.00 | ☐ 2039 | 90.00 | 45.00 |
| ☐ H2950P | 150.00 | 75.00 | ☐ 2051 | 145.00 | 72.50 |
| ☐ H2951P | 135.00 | 67.50 | ☐ 2052 | 80.00 | 40.00 |
| ☐ H2952P | 150.00 | 75.00 | ☐ 2053 | 120.00 | 60.00 |
| ☐ H2953P | 200.00 | 100.00 | ☐ 2054 | 80.00 | 40.00 |
| ☐ H2956P | 150.00 | 75.00 | ☐ 2055 | 80.00 | 40.00 |
| ☐ H2966P | 175.00 | 87.50 | ☐ 2057 | 120.00 | 60.00 |
| ☐ H3305P | 225.00 | 112.50 | ☐ 2058 | 90.00 | 45.00 |
| ☐ H3342P | 250.00 | 125.00 | ☐ 2059 | 90.00 | 45.00 |
| ☐ H3361P | 250.00 | 125.00 | ☐ 2067 | 110.00 | 55.00 |
| ☐ H3646P | 200.00 | 100.00 | ☐ 2068 | 175.00 | 87.50 |
| ☐ H3607P | 225.00 | 112.50 | ☐ 2069 | 150.00 | 75.00 |
| ☐ H3941P | 175.00 | 87.50 | ☐ 2070 | 150.00 | 75.00 |
| ☐ H3942P | 200.00 | 100.00 | ☐ 2078 | 110.00 | 55.00 |
| ☐ H3950P | 225.00 | 112.50 | ☐ 2079 | 100.00 | 50.00 |
| ☐ H3952P | 225.00 | 112.50 | ☐ 2082 | 110.00 | 55.00 |
| ☐ J3961P | 250.00 | 125.00 | ☐ 2083 | 150.00 | 75.00 |
| ☐ H4950P | 275.00 | 137.50 | ☐ 2084 | 175.00 | 87.50 |
| ☐ H4961P | 300.00 | 150.00 | ☐ 2085 | 125.00 | 62.50 |
| ☐ 1050 | 300.00 | 150.00 | ☐ 2086 | 125.00 | 62.50 |
| ☐ 1051 | 300.00 | 150.00 | ☐ 2087 | 125.00 | 62.50 |
| ☐ 1060 | 200.00 | 100.00 | ☐ 2088 | 110.00 | 55.00 |
| ☐ 1201 | 175.00 | 87.50 | ☐ 2089 | 100.00 | 50.00 |
| ☐ 1605 | 75.00 | 37.50 | ☐ 2090 | 120.00 | 60.00 |
| ☐ 1608 | 75.00 | 37.50 | ☐ 2094 | 200.00 | 100.00 |
| ☐ 1611 | 75.00 | 37.50 | ☐ 2098 | 175.00 | 87.50 |
| ☐ 1613 | 125.00 | 62.50 | ☐ 2099 | 200.00 | 100.00 |
| ☐ 1632 | 75.00 | 37.50 | ☐ 2106 | 150.00 | 75.00 |
| ☐ 1701 | 200.00 | 100.00 | ☐ 2107 | 125.00 | 62.50 |
| ☐ 1905 | 275.00 | 137.50 | ☐ 2109 | 80.00 | 40.00 |
| ☐ 1920 | 1,000.00 | 500.00 | ☐ 2110 | 150.00 | 75.00 |
| ☐ 1921 | 125.00 | 62.50 | ☐ 2111 | 150.00 | 75.00 |
| ☐ 1922 | 125.00 | 62.50 | ☐ 2112 | 150.00 | 75.00 |
| ☐ 1923 | 200.00 | 100.00 | ☐ 2115 | 150.00 | 75.00 |
| ☐ 1924 | 300.00 | 150.00 | ☐ 2117 | 125.00 | 62.50 |
| ☐ 1925 | 300.00 | 150.00 | ☐ 2201 | 60.00 | 30.00 |
| ☐ 1936 | 350.00 | 175.00 | ☐ 2202 | 75.00 | 37.50 |

## 226 / WINCHESTER

| PATTERN NO. | MINT | VG | PATTERN NO. | MINT | VG |
|---|---|---|---|---|---|
| ☐ 2204 | 70.00 | 35.00 | ☐ 2842 | 120.00 | 60.00 |
| ☐ 2205 | 75.00 | 37.50 | ☐ 2843 | 150.00 | 75.00 |
| ☐ 2215 | 75.00 | 37.50 | ☐ 2844 | 250.00 | 125.00 |
| ☐ 2306 | 90.00 | 45.00 | ☐ 2845 | 225.00 | 112.50 |
| ☐ 2309 | 120.00 | 60.00 | ☐ 2846 | 125.00 | 62.50 |
| ☐ 2316 | 140.00 | 70.00 | ☐ 2847 | 150.00 | 75.00 |
| ☐ 2338 | 150.00 | 75.00 | ☐ 2848 | 125.00 | 62.50 |
| ☐ 2352 | 175.00 | 87.50 | ☐ 2849 | 175.00 | 87.50 |
| ☐ 2361 | 110.00 | 55.00 | ☐ 2850 | 275.00 | 137.50 |
| ☐ 2369 | 90.00 | 45.00 | ☐ 2853 | 200.00 | 100.00 |
| ☐ 2375 | 90.00 | 45.00 | ☐ 2854 | 150.00 | 75.00 |
| ☐ 2376 | 120.00 | 60.00 | ☐ 2855 | 150.00 | 75.00 |
| ☐ 2377 | 150.00 | 75.00 | ☐ 2856 | 100.00 | 50.00 |
| ☐ 2380 | 300.00 | 150.00 | ☐ 2859 | 80.00 | 40.00 |
| ☐ 2603 | 150.00 | 75.00 | ☐ 2860 | 150.00 | 75.00 |
| ☐ 2604 | 150.00 | 75.00 | ☐ 2861 | 150.00 | 75.00 |
| ☐ 2605 | 200.00 | 100.00 | ☐ 2862 | 90.00 | 45.00 |
| ☐ 2606 | 150.00 | 75.00 | ☐ 2863 | 145.00 | 72.50 |
| ☐ 2608 | 125.00 | 62.50 | ☐ 2865 | 300.00 | 150.00 |
| ☐ 2610 | 150.00 | 75.00 | ☐ 2866 | 80.00 | 40.00 |
| ☐ 2611 | 125.00 | 62.50 | ☐ 2867 | 120.00 | 60.00 |
| ☐ 2612 | 200.00 | 100.00 | ☐ 2868 | 120.00 | 60.00 |
| ☐ 2613 | 200.00 | 100.00 | ☐ 2869 | 225.00 | 112.50 |
| ☐ 2614 | 200.00 | 100.00 | ☐ 2870 | 175.00 | 87.50 |
| ☐ 2627 | 125.00 | 62.50 | ☐ 2872 | 140.00 | 70.00 |
| ☐ 2629 | 175.00 | 87.50 | ☐ 2874 | 150.00 | 75.00 |
| ☐ 2630 | 175.00 | 87.50 | ☐ 2901 | 150.00 | 75.00 |
| ☐ 2631 | 90.00 | 45.00 | ☐ 2902 | 80.00 | 40.00 |
| ☐ 2633 | 110.00 | 55.00 | ☐ 2903 | 200.00 | 100.00 |
| ☐ 2635 | 150.00 | 75.00 | ☐ 2904 | 400.00 | 200.00 |
| ☐ 2636 | 200.00 | 100.00 | ☐ 2905 | 500.00 | 250.00 |
| ☐ 2638 | 150.00 | 75.00 | ☐ 2907 | 500.00 | 250.00 |
| ☐ 2649 | 150.00 | 75.00 | ☐ 2908 | 160.00 | 80.00 |
| ☐ 2660 | 150.00 | 75.00 | ☐ 2910 | 90.00 | 45.00 |
| ☐ 2661 | 150.00 | 75.00 | ☐ 2911 | 150.00 | 75.00 |
| ☐ 2662 | 150.00 | 75.00 | ☐ 2914 | 175.00 | 87.50 |
| ☐ 2665 | 175.00 | 87.50 | ☐ 2917 | 125.00 | 62.50 |
| ☐ 2665 | 175.00 | 87.50 | ☐ 2918 | 150.00 | 75.00 |
| ☐ 2702 | 250.00 | 125.00 | ☐ 2921 | 275.00 | 137.50 |
| ☐ 2703 | 250.00 | 125.00 | ☐ 2923 | 250.00 | 125.00 |
| ☐ 2830 | 70.00 | 35.00 | ☐ 2924 | 120.00 | 60.00 |
| ☐ 2840 | 90.00 | 45.00 | ☐ 2925 | 150.00 | 75.00 |
| ☐ 2841 | 90.00 | 45.00 | ☐ 2928 | 200.00 | 100.00 |

| PATTERN NO. | MINT | VG | PATTERN NO. | MINT | VG |
|---|---|---|---|---|---|
| ☐ 2930 | 200.00 | 100.00 | ☐ 3002 | 250.00 | 125.00 |
| ☐ 2932 | 145.00 | 72.50 | ☐ 3003 | 250.00 | 125.00 |
| ☐ 2933 | 140.00 | 70.00 | ☐ 3005 | 200.00 | 100.00 |
| ☐ 2934 | 90.00 | 45.00 | ☐ 3006 | 150.00 | 75.00 |
| ☐ 2938 | 140.00 | 70.00 | ☐ 3007 | 275.00 | 137.50 |
| ☐ 2940 | 200.00 | 100.00 | ☐ 3008 | 175.00 | 87.50 |
| ☐ 2943 | 120.00 | 60.00 | ☐ 3009 | 275.00 | 137.50 |
| ☐ 2945 | 90.00 | 45.00 | ☐ 3010 | 325.00 | 162.50 |
| ☐ 2948 | 110.00 | 55.00 | ☐ 3014 | 275.00 | 137.50 |
| ☐ 2949 | 150.00 | 75.00 | ☐ 3015 | 250.00 | 125.00 |
| ☐ 2950 | 150.00 | 75.00 | ☐ 3016 | 300.00 | 150.00 |
| ☐ 2951 | 150.00 | 75.00 | ☐ 3017 | 300.00 | 150.00 |
| ☐ 2952 | 200.00 | 100.00 | ☐ 3018 | 275.00 | 137.50 |
| ☐ 2954 | 200.00 | 100.00 | ☐ 3019 | 275.00 | 137.50 |
| ☐ 2956 | 150.00 | 75.00 | ☐ 3020 | 275.00 | 137.50 |
| ☐ 2958 | 150.00 | 75.00 | ☐ 3025 | 250.00 | 125.00 |
| ☐ 2959 | 200.00 | 100.00 | ☐ 3026 | 250.00 | 125.00 |
| ☐ 2961 | 150.00 | 75.00 | ☐ 3027 | 200.00 | 100.00 |
| ☐ 2962 | 100.00 | 50.00 | ☐ 3044 | 200.00 | 100.00 |
| ☐ 2963 | 120.00 | 60.00 | ☐ 3331 | 200.00 | 100.00 |
| ☐ 2964 | 150.00 | 75.00 | ☐ 3352 | 250.00 | 125.00 |
| ☐ 2966 | 275.00 | 137.50 | ☐ 3353 | 150.00 | 75.00 |
| ☐ 2967 | 325.00 | 162.50 | ☐ 3357 | 275.00 | 137.50 |
| ☐ 2969 | 300.00 | 150.00 | ☐ 3370 | 200.00 | 100.00 |
| ☐ 2973 | 175.00 | 87.50 | ☐ 3371 | 275.00 | 137.50 |
| ☐ 2974 | 150.00 | 75.00 | ☐ 3376 | 275.00 | 137.50 |
| ☐ 2976 | 200.00 | 100.00 | ☐ 3377 | 275.00 | 137.50 |
| ☐ 2978 | 300.00 | 150.00 | ☐ 3380 | 150.00 | 75.00 |
| ☐ 2980 | 175.00 | 87.50 | ☐ 3381 | 200.00 | 100.00 |
| ☐ 2981 | 90.00 | 45.00 | ☐ 3382 | 200.00 | 100.00 |
| ☐ 2982 | 300.00 | 150.00 | ☐ 3902 | 300.00 | 150.00 |
| ☐ 2983 | 125.00 | 62.50 | ☐ 3028 | 200.00 | 100.00 |
| ☐ 2988 | 300.00 | 150.00 | ☐ 3029 | 200.00 | 100.00 |
| ☐ 2990 | 125.00 | 62.50 | ☐ 3030 | 200.00 | 100.00 |
| ☐ 2991 | 300.00 | 150.00 | ☐ 3031 | 250.00 | 125.00 |
| ☐ 2993 | 350.00 | 175.00 | ☐ 3035 | 175.00 | 87.50 |
| ☐ 2994 | 150.00 | 75.00 | ☐ 3041 | 175.00 | 87.50 |
| ☐ 2995 | 200.00 | 100.00 | ☐ 3042 | 175.00 | 87.50 |
| ☐ 2996 | 175.00 | 87.50 | ☐ 3043 | 200.00 | 100.00 |
| ☐ 2997 | 160.00 | 80.00 | ☐ 3903 | 375.00 | 187.50 |
| ☐ 2998 | 150.00 | 75.00 | ☐ 3904 | 300.00 | 150.00 |
| ☐ 2999 | 200.00 | 100.00 | ☐ 3905 | 275.00 | 137.50 |
| ☐ 3001 | 275.00 | 137.50 | ☐ 3906 | 300.00 | 150.00 |

# For More Information...

*The Official Price Guide to Pocket Knives* was designed as a basic introduction course for the beginning collector and flea market shopper, as well as a handy, tote-along reference book for the more seasoned hobbyist.

This guide offers the beginner a general overview of collecting techniques, tips, and prices for the collectibles most commonly bought and sold on the market today. Sufficient information on how to start a collection and how to avoid costly blunders can aid the novice in "getting off on the right foot."

You can slip this price guide into a pocket or a purse and take along your own "official" expert on your next shopping excursion. By flipping to the sections on the items you're planning to buy, you can feel more confident about the type of articles you purchase and the prices you pay whether you're just learning or merely need to refresh your memory.

As your interest and your collection grows, you may want to start a reference library of your favorite areas. For the collector who needs a more extensive coverage of the collectibles market, The House of Collectibles publishes a complete line of comprehensive companion guides to the pocket-sized books. These larger price guides, which are itemized at the back of this book, contain full coverage on buying, selling, and caring of valuable articles, plus listings with thousands of prices for rare, unusual, and common antiques and collectibles.

The House of Collectibles recommends *The Official Price Guide to Collector Knives,* fifth edition as the companion to this pocket book.

## THE KNIFE COLLECTORS' BIBLE

- Over *13,000 current collector values*... the most comprehensive listing of collector pocket and sheath knives in print.
- **FEATURING ALL NEW, EXPANDED PRICING SECTIONS** — Buck, Cattaraugus, Fightin' Rooster, Ken Kutter, Kinfolks, Landers-Frary-and-Clark, New York, Parker, Remington, Robeson, Russell, Shapleigh, Schrade and Winchester.
- A complete price listing for *1,250 worldwide knife manufacturers.* Every known CASE pocket and sheath is listed and pictured according to pattern number, including all handle and blade variations. A complete pictorial price reference to KA-BAR KNIVES. Also includes special section on Ka-Bar Dogshead knives. **LIMITED EDITION KNIVES** are listed in a special section that includes photos and prices.
- **EXCLUSIVE IDENTIFICATION GUIDE**... pocket knife shields... knife nomenclature... blade and knife patterns... counterfeit guide and grading sections.
- Up-to-date list of KNIFE ORGANIZATIONS and TRADE PUBLICATIONS.
- **FULLY ILLUSTRATED.**

$9.95-5th Edition, 704 Pgs., Order #324-4
*Available from your local dealer or order direct from —
THE HOUSE OF COLLECTIBLES, see order blank*

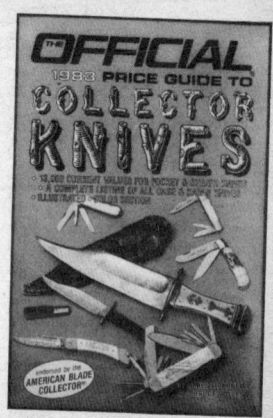

# There is only one...
# OFFICIAL® PRICE GUIDE

## THE MULTIPURPOSE REFERENCE GUIDE!!

THE OFFICIAL PRICE GUIDES SERIES has gained the reputation as the standard barometer of values on collectors' items. When you need to check the market price of a collectible, turn first to the OFFICIAL PRICE GUIDES ... for impartial, unbiased, current information that is presented in an easy-to-follow format.

- **CURRENT VALUES FOR BUYING AND SELLING.** ACTUAL SALES that have occurred in all parts of the country are CAREFULLY EVALUATED and COMPUTERIZED to arrive at the most ACCURATE PRICES AVAILABLE.

- **CONCISE REFERENCES.** Each OFFICIAL PRICE GUIDE is designed primarily as a *guide to current market values.* They also include a useful summary of the information most readers are seeking: a history of the item; how it's manufactured; how to begin and maintain a collection; how and where to sell; addresses of periodicals and clubs.

- **INDEXED FORMAT • FULLY ILLUSTRATED**

*Over 21 years of experience has made THE HOUSE OF COLLECTIBLES the most respected price guide authority!*

# PRICE GUIDE SERIES

## American Silver & Silver Plate
Today's silver market offers excellent opportunities *to gain big profits* — if you are well informed. *Over 15,000 current market values* are listed for 19th and 20th century American-made Sterling, Coin and Silverplated flatware and holloware. Special souvenir spoon section. *ILLUSTRATED.*
$9.95-2nd Edition, 576 pgs., 5⅜" x 8", paperback, Order #: 184-5

## Antique & Classic Still Cameras
More than *3,000 up-to-the-minute selling prices* for all types of popular collector cameras. An encyclopedia of American and foreign camera brands and models. Advice on buying and building a collection. *ILLUSTRATED.*
$9.95-1st Edition, 532 pgs., 5⅜" x 8", paperback, Order #: 383-X

## Antique Clocks
A pictorial price reference for all types of American made clocks. Over *10,000 detailed listings* insure positive identification. *Includes company histories. ILLUSTRATED.*
$9.95-1st Edition, 576 pgs., 5⅜" x 8", paperback, Order #: 364-3

## Antique & Modern Dolls
More than *6,000 current retail selling prices* for antique dolls in wax, carved wood, china and bisque; modern and semi-modern dolls in celluloid, chalk, plastic, composition, and cloth. Advice on where and how to buy, care and display, and selling dolls. *ILLUSTRATED.*
9.95-1st Edition, 544 pgs., 5⅜" x 8", paperback, Order #: 381-3

## Antique & Modern Firearms
This unique book is an encyclopedia of gun lore featuring over *20,500 listings with histories* of American and foreign manufacturers *plus a special section on collector cartridge values. ILLUSTRATED.*
$9.95-3rd Edition, 544 pgs., 5⅜" x 8", paperback, Order #: 363-5

## Antique Jewelry
Over *8,200 current collector values* for the most extensive listing of antique jewelry ever published. Georgian, Victorian, Art Nouveau, Art Deco. *Plus a special full color gem identification guide. ILLUSTRATED.*
$9.95-2nd Edition, 672 pgs., 5⅜" x 8", paperback, Order #: 354-6

## Antiques & Other Collectibles
Introduces TODAY'S world of antiques with over *100,000 current market values* for the most complete listing of antiques and collectibles IN PRINT! In this *new — 832 PAGE edition, many new categories have been added to keep fully up-to-date with the latest collecting trends. ILLUSTRATED.*
$9.95-4th Edition, 832 pgs., 5⅜" x 8", paperback, Order #: 374-0

## Bottles Old & New
Over *22,000 current buying and selling prices* of both common and rare collectible bottles . . . ale, soda, bitters, flasks, medicine, perfume, poison, milk and more. *Plus expanded sections on Avon and Jim Beam. ILLUSTRATED.*
$9.95-6th Edition, 672 pgs., 5⅜" x 8", paperback, Order #: 350-3

## Collectible Toys
Over *25,000 current values* for trains, windups, autos, soldiers, boats, banks, guns, musical toys, Disneyana, comic characters, Star Trek, Star Wars, and more. Valuable collecting tips. *ILLUSTRATED.*
$9.95-1st Edition, 540 pgs., 5⅜" x 8", paperback, Order #: 384-8

## Collector Cars
Over *37,000 actual current prices* for 4000 models of antique and classic automobiles — U.S. and foreign. Complete with engine specifications. *Special sections on auto memorabilia values and restoration techniques. ILLUSTRATED.*
$9.95-4th Edition, 544 pgs., 5⅜" x 8", paperback, Order #: 357-0

**For your convenience use the handy order form.**

# PRICE GUIDE SERIES

## Collector Handguns
Over **10,000 current values** for antique and modern handguns. Plus the most up-to-date listing of current production handguns. *ILLUSTRATED.*
$9.95-1st Edition, 544 pgs., 5⅜" x 8", paperback, Order #: 367-8

## Collector Knives
Over **13,000 buying and selling prices** on U.S. and foreign pocket and sheath knives. **Special sections on bicentennial, commemorative, limited edition, and handmade knives.** By J. Parker & B. Voyles. *ILLUSTRATED.*
$9.95-5th Edition, 704 pgs., 5⅜" x 8", paperback, Order #: 324-4

## Collector Plates
Destined to become the "PLATE COLLECTORS' BIBLE." This unique price guide offers the most comprehensive listing of collector plate values — *in Print!* Special information includes: *company histories; and helpful tips on buying, selling and storing a collection.* *ILLUSTRATED.*
$9.95-1st Edition, 672 pgs., 5⅜" x 8", paperback, Order #: 349-X

## Collector Prints
Over **14,750 detailed listings** representing over 400 of the most famous collector print artists from Audubon and Currier & Ives, to modern day artists. **Special feature includes gallery/artist reference chart.** *ILLUSTRATED.*
$9.95-4th Edition, 544 pgs., 5⅜" x 8", paperback, Order #: 189-6

## Comic & Science Fiction Books
Over **31,000 listing with current values** for comic and science fiction publications **from 1903-to-date.** Special sections on Tarzan, Big Little Books, Science Fiction publications and paperbacks. *ILLUSTRATED.*
$9.95-6th Edition, 544 pgs., 5⅜" x 8", paperback, Order #: 353-8

## Glassware
Over **60,000 listings** for all types of American-made glassware, pressed and pattern, depression, cut, carnival and more. *ILLUSTRATED.*
$9.95-1st Edition, 544 pgs., 5⅜" x 8", paperback, Order #: 125-X

## Hummel Figurines & Plates
The most complete guide ever published on every type of Hummel — including the most recent trademarks and size variations, with **6,100 up-to-date prices.** *Plus tips on buying, selling and investing.* *ILLUSTRATED.*
$9.95-3rd Edition, 448 pgs., 5⅜" x 8", paperback, Order #: 352-X

## Kitchen Collectibles
This beautiful pictorial guide has **hundreds of Illustrations** - truly a MASTERPIECE of reference. This first really complete *History of America in the Kitchen* describes hundreds of implements and lists **28,000 current market values.** *ILLUSTRATED.*
$9.95-1st Edition, 544 pgs., 5⅜" x 8", paperback, Order #: 371-6

## Military Collectibles
This detailed historical reference price guide covers the largest accumulation of military objects — 15th century-to-date — listing over **12,000 accurate prices.** Special expanded Samurai sword and headdress sections. *ILLUSTRATED.*
$9.95-2nd Edition, 576 pgs., 5⅜" x 8", paperback, Order #: 191-8

## Music Machines
Virtually every music-related collectible is included in this guide — over **11,000 current prices. 78 recordings, mechanical musical machines and instruments.** *ILLUSTRATED.*
$9.95-2nd Edition, 544 pgs., 5⅜" x 8", paperback, Order #: 187-X

**For your convenience use the handy order form.**

# PRICE GUIDE SERIES

## Old Books & Autographs
Descriptions of the finest literary collectibles available, with over **11,000 prices for all types of books:** Americana, bibles, medicine, cookbooks and more. *Plus an updated autograph section.* ILLUSTRATED.
$9.95-4th Edition, 512 pgs., 5⅜" x 8", paperback, Order #: 351-1

## Oriental Collectibles
Over **10,000 detailed listings and values** for all types of Chinese and Japanese collectibles, pottery, rugs, statues, porcelain, cloisonne, metalware. *ILLUSTRATED.*
$9.95-1st Edition, 544 pgs., 5⅜" x 8", paperback, Order #: 375-9

## Paper Collectibles
Old Checks, Invoices, Books, Magazines, Newspapers, Ticket Stubs and even Matchbooks — any paper items that reflect America's past — are gaining collector value. This book contains **over 26,000 current values** and descriptions for all types of paper collectibles. *ILLUSTRATED.*
$9.95-2nd Edition, 608 pgs., 5⅜" x 8", paperback, Order #: 186-1

## Pottery & Porcelain
Over **10,000 current prices and listings** of fine pottery and porcelain, plus an extensive Lenox china section. *Special sections on histories of manufacturers and identifying china trademarks.* ILLUSTRATED.
$9.95-2nd Edition, 576 pgs., 5⅜" x 8", paperback, Order #: 188-8

## Records
Over **31,000 current prices** of collectible singles, EPs, albums, plus 20,000 memorable song titles recorded by over 1100 artists. *Rare biographies and photos are provided for many well known artists.* ILLUSTRATED.
$9.95-4th Edition, 544 pgs., 5⅜" x 8", paperback, Order #: 356-2

## Royal Doulton
This authoritative guide to Royal Doulton porcelains contains over **5,500 detailed listings** on figurines, plates and Toby jugs. Includes tips on buying, selling and displaying. *Plus an exclusive numerical reference index.* ILLUSTRATED.
$9.95-2nd Edition, 544 pgs., 5⅜" x 8", paperback, Order #: 355-4

## Wicker
You could be sitting on a *fortune!* Decorators and collectors are driving wicker values to unbelievable highs! This pictorial price guide *positively identifies all types* of Victorian, Turn of the century and Art Deco wicker furniture. *A special illustrated section on wicker repair is included.* ILLUSTRATED.
$9.95-1st Edition, 416 pgs., 5⅜" x 8", paperback, Order #: 348-1

## Encyclopedia of Antiques
A total of more than **10,000 definitions**, explanations, concise factual summaries of names, dates, histories, confusing terminology . . . for every popular field of collecting. An exclusive appendix includes many trademark and pattern charts as well as a categorized list of museums and reference publications.
$9.95-1st Edition, 704 pgs., 5⅜" x 8", paperback, Order #: 365-1

## Buying & Selling Guide to Antiques
Covers every phase of collecting, from beginning a collection to its ultimate sale . . . examines in detail the collecting potential of **over 200 different categories of items in all price ranges.** *Special features include a dealer directory, a condition grading report, list of museums and reference publications*, plus a discussion of buying and selling techniques. *ILLUSTRATED.*
$9.95-1st Edition, 608 pgs., 5⅜" x 8", paperback, Order #: 369-4

---

**For your convenience use the handy order form.**

## MINI SERIES

### Antiques & Flea Markets
Discover the fun and profit of collecting antiques with this handy pocket reference to *over 15,000 types of collectibles.* Avoid counterfeits and learn the secrets to successful buying and selling. *ILLUSTRATED.*
$2.50-1st Edition, 240 pgs., 4" x 5½", paperback, Order #: 308-2

### Antique Jewelry
A handy-pocket sized update to the larger Official Price Guide to Antique Jewelry, lists *thousands of values* for bracelets, brooches, chains, earrings, necklaces and more. *Special sections on gold, silver and diamond identification.*
$2.95-1st Edition, 240 pgs., 4" x 5½", paperback, Order #: 373-2

### Baseball Cards
This guide lists *over 100,000 current market values* for baseball cards – Bowman, Burger King, Donruss, Fleer, O-Pee-Chee and Topps. *ILLUSTRATED.*
$2.95-3rd Edition, 332 pgs., 4" x 5½", paperback, Order #: 376-7

### Beer Cans
The first pocket-sized guide to list *thousands of values* for cone and flat top beer cans produced since the mid 1930's. Each listing is graphically detailed for positive identification. *ILLUSTRATED.*
$2.95-1st Edition, 240 pgs., 4" x 5½", paperback, Order #: 377-5

### Cars
Over *5,000 current auction and dealer prices* for all popular U.S. and foreign made antique, classic and collector cars. *Learn how to evaluate* the condition of a collector car the way the professionals do! *ILLUSTRATED.*
$2.95-1st Edition, 240 pgs., 4" x 5½", paperback, Order #: 391-0

### Comic Books
Young and Old are collecting old comic books for fun *and Profit!* This handy pocket-sized price guide lists current market values and detailed descriptions for the most sought-after collectible comic books. *Buying, selling and storing tips for the beginning collector. ILLUSTRATED.*
$2.50-1st Edition, 240 pgs., 4" x 5½", paperback, Order #: 345-7

### Dolls
Doll collecting is one of America's favorite hobbies and this guide lists *over 3,000 actual market values* for all the manufacturers! Kewpies, Howdy Doody, Shirley Temple, GI Joe plus comprehensive listings of Barbies. *ILLUSTRATED.*
$2.95-1st Edition, 240 pgs., 4" x 5½", paperback, Order #: 316-3

### *O.J. Simpson* Football Cards
The world famous O.J. Simpson highlights this comprehensive guide to football card values. *Over 21,000 current collector prices* are listed for: Topps, Bowman, Fleer, Philadelphia and O-Pee-Chee. *Includes a full color O.J. SIMPSON limited edition collector card. ILLUSTRATED.*
$2.50-2nd Edition, 256 pgs., 4" x 5½", paperback, Order #: 323-6

### Guns
Over *3,000 dealer prices* compiled from nationwide sales records for handguns, rifles, and shotguns. Covers American and foreign manufacturers. Information on the history of firearms, and collecting techniques! *ILLUSTRATED.*
$2.95-1st Edition, 240 pgs., 4" x 5½", paperback, Order #: 396-1

---

**For your convenience use the handy order form.**

## MINI SERIES

### Hummels
How much are your Hummels worth? You can become an expert on these lovely figurines with this guide, with a handy numerical index that puts *descriptions and 3,000 market prices* at your fingertips. Learn why the slightest variation could mean hundreds in value. *ILLUSTRATED.*
$2.95-1st Edition, 240 pgs., 4" x 5½", paperback, Order #: 318-X

### Military Collectibles
Over *4,000 current prices* for a wide assortment of military objects from all over the world — 19th century to World War II. Valuable collecting tips — How to build a collection, grading condition, and displaying your collection. *ILLUSTRATED.*
$2.95-1st Edition, 240 pgs., 4" x 5½", paperback, Order #: 378-3

### Paperbacks & Magazines
Old discarded paperbacks and magazines could be worth 50-100 times their original cover price. Learn how to identify them. *Thousands* of descriptions and prices show which issues are rare. *ILLUSTRATED.*
$2.50-1st Edition, 240 pgs., 4" x 5½", paperback, Order #: 315-5

### Pocket Knives
This mid-season update to the larger Official Price Guide to Collector Knives list *over 4,000 collector values* for Case, Kabar, Cattaragus, Remington, Winchester and more. *Special sections on buying and selling, plus a list of limited edition pocket knives.*
$2.95-1st Edition, 240 pgs., 4" x 5½", paperback, Order #: 372-4

### Records
Over *5,000 current market prices* for Rock and Country recordings. A chronological listing of discs from 1953 to date. How to begin a collection . . . how and where to buy and sell . . . and how to grade condition. *ILLUSTRATED.*
$2.95-1st Edition, 240 pgs., 4" x 5½", paperback, Order #: 400-3

### Scouting Collectibles
Discover the colorful history behind scouting, relive childhood memories and profit from those old family heirlooms. *Thousands of prices* are listed for all types of Boy and Girl Scout memorabilia. *ILLUSTRATED.*
$2.50-1st Edition, 240 pgs., 4" x 5½", paperback, Order #: 314-7

### Sports Collectibles
Over *12,000 current prices* for all the popular collectibles of baseball, football, basketball, hockey, boxing, hunting, fishing, horse racing and other top sports. Inside facts on buying from dealers and selling your sports collectibles. *ILLUSTRATED.*
$2.95-1st Edition, 240 pgs., 4" x 5½", paperback, Order #: 379-1

### Star Trek / Star Wars Collectibles
The most startling phenomena in decades! Star Trek and Star Wars fans have created a space age world of collectibles. *Thousands of current values* for books, posters, photos, costumes, models, jewelry and more . . . *Plus tips on buying, selling and trading.*
$2.95-1st Edition, 240 pgs., 4" x 5½", paperback, Order #: 319-8

### Toys
Kids from eight to eighty enjoy collecting toys and this comprehensive guide has them all! Trains, trucks, comic and movie character, space toys, boats and **MORE**. *Over 8,000 current market values* of toys, old and new, plus investment tips and histories. *ILLUSTRATED.*
$2.95-1st Edition, 240 pgs., 4" x 5½", paperback, Order #: 317-1

---

**For your convenience use the handy order form.**

## NUMISMATIC SERIES

**THE BLACKBOOKS** are more than just informative books, they are the most highly regarded authority on the nation's most popular hobbies.

### 1984 Blackbook Price Guide of United States Coins
A coin collector's guide to current market values for all U.S. coins from 1616 to date—over *16,500 prices*. **THE OFFICIAL BLACKBOOK OF COINS** has gained the reputation as the most reliable, up-to-date guide to U.S. Coin values. This new edition features an exclusive gold and silver identification guide. Learn how to test, weigh and calculate the value of any item made of gold or silver. Proven professional techniques revealed for the first time. Take advantage of the current 'BUYERS' MARKET'' in gold and silver. *ILLUSTRATED.*
**$2.95-22st Edition, 288 pgs., 4" x 5½", paperback, Order #: 385-6**

### 1984 Blackbook Price Guide of United States Paper Money
Over *9,000 buying and selling prices* covering U.S. currency from 1861 to date. Every note issued by the U.S. government is listed and priced, including many Confederate States notes. Error Notes are described and priced, and there are detailed articles on many phases of the hobby for beginners and advanced collectors alike. *ILLUSTRATED.*
**$2.95-16th Edition, 240 pgs., 4" x 5½", paperback, Order #: 387-2**

### 1984 Blackbook Price Guide of United States Postage Stamps
Featuring all U.S. stamps from 1847 to date pictured in full color. Over *19,000 current selling prices* You will find new listings for the most current commemorative and regular issue stamps, a feature not offered in any other price guide, at any price! There were numerous important developments in the fast moving stamp market during the past year and they are all included in this *NEW REVISED EDITION. ILLUSTRATED.*
**$2.95-6th Edition, 240 pgs., 4" x 5½", paperback, Order #: 386-4**

## INVESTORS SERIES

*The Official Investor's Guide Series* shows you, *step by step*, how to select the right items for your investment program, how to avoid the many pitfalls that can foil new investors, with full instructions on when to sell and *How And Where To Sell* in order to realize the *Highest Possible Profit.*

### Investors Guide to Gold, Silver, Diamonds
*All you need to know* about making money trading in the precious metals and diamond markets. This practical, easy-to-read investment guide is for everyone in all income brackets. *ILLUSTRATED.*
**$6.95-1st Edition, 208 pgs., 5⅜" x 8", paperback, Order #: 171-3**

### Investors Guide to Gold Coins
*The first complete book* on investing in gold coins. Exclusive price performance charts trace all U.S. gold coin values from *1955 to date. ILLUSTRATED.*
**$6.95-1st Edition, 288 pgs., 5⅜" x 8", paperback, Order #: 300-7**

### Investors Guide to Silver Coins
*The most extensive listing* of all U.S. silver coins. Detailed price performance charts trace actual sales figures from *1955 to date. ILLUSTRATED.*
**$6.95-1st Edition, 288 pgs., 5⅜" x 8", paperback, Order #: 301-5**

### Investors Guide to Silver Dollars
Regardless of your income, you can *become a successful silver dollar investor.* Actual sales figures for every U.S. silver dollar *1955 to date. ILLUSTRATED.*
**$6.95-1st Edition, 192 pgs., 5⅜" x 8", paperback, Order #: 302-3**

For your convenience use the handy order form.

## FOR IMMEDIATE DELIVERY

### VISA & MASTERCARD CUSTOMERS
# ORDER TOLL FREE!
# 1-800-327-1384

This number is for orders only, it is not tied into the customer service or business office. Customers not using charge cards must use mail for ordering since payment is required with the order — sorry no C.O.D.'s. Florida residents call (305) 857-9095 — ask for order department.

## OR  SEND ORDERS TO

**THE HOUSE OF COLLECTIBLES,** ORLANDO CENTRAL PARK
1900 PREMIER ROW, ORLANDO, FL 32809   PHONE (305) 857-9095

☐ *Please send me the following price guides—(don't forget to add postage & handling):*
☐ *I would like the most current edition of the books checked below.*

| | | | | |
|---|---|---|---|---|
| ☐ 184-5 @ 9.95 | ☐ 324-4 @ 9.95 | ☐ 186-1 @ 9.95 | ☐ 391-0 @ 2.95 | ☐ 379-1 @ 2.95 |
| ☐ 383-X @ 9.95 | ☐ 349-X @ 9.95 | ☐ 188-8 @ 9.95 | ☐ 345-7 @ 2.50 | ☐ 319-8 @ 2.95 |
| ☐ 364-3 @ 9.95 | ☐ 189-6 @ 9.95 | ☐ 356-2 @ 9.95 | ☐ 316-3 @ 2.95 | ☐ 317-1 @ 2.95 |
| ☐ 381-3 @ 9.95 | ☐ 353-8 @ 9.95 | ☐ 354-4 @ 9.95 | ☐ 323-6 @ 2.95 | ☐ 385-6 @ 2.95 |
| ☐ 363-5 @ 9.95 | ☐ 125-X @ 9.95 | ☐ 348-1 @ 9.95 | ☐ 396-1 @ 2.95 | ☐ 387-2 @ 2.95 |
| ☐ 374-0 @ 9.95 | ☐ 352-X @ 9.95 | ☐ 365-1 @ 9.95 | ☐ 318-X @ 2.95 | ☐ 386-4 @ 2.95 |
| ☐ 354-6 @ 9.95 | ☐ 371-6 @ 9.95 | ☐ 369-4 @ 9.95 | ☐ 378-3 @ 2.95 | ☐ 171-3 @ 6.95 |
| ☐ 350-3 @ 9.95 | ☐ 191-8 @ 9.95 | ☐ 308-2 @ 2.50 | ☐ 315-5 @ 2.95 | ☐ 300-7 @ 6.95 |
| ☐ 384-8 @ 9.95 | ☐ 187-X @ 9.95 | ☐ 373-2 @ 2.95 | ☐ 372-4 @ 2.95 | ☐ 301-5 @ 6.95 |
| ☐ 357-0 @ 9.95 | ☐ 351-1 @ 9.95 | ☐ 376-7 @ 2.95 | ☐ 400-3 @ 2.95 | ☐ 302-3 @ 6.95 |
| ☐ 367-8 @ 9.95 | ☐ 375-9 @ 9.95 | ☐ 377-5 @ 2.95 | ☐ 314-7 @ 2.50 | |

Add $1.00 postage and handling for the first book and 50¢ for each additional book.
Add $2.50 to each order for insurance and special handling. Florida residents add 5% sales tax.

☐ Check or money order enclosed $_____ (include postage and handling)
☐ Please charge $_____ to my: ☐ MASTERCARD  ☐ VISA

**Charge Card Customers Not Using Our Toll Free Number Please Fill Out The Information Below.**

Account No. (All Digits) _____ Expiration Date _____
Signature _____

NAME (please print) _____ PHONE _____
ADDRESS _____ APT. # _____
CITY _____ STATE _____ ZIP _____

(10)